ECLIPSE OF JUSTICE

Ethics, Economics, and the Lost Traditions
of American Catholicism

GEORGE E. McCARTHY AND ROYAL W. RHODES

ORBIS BOOKS

Maryknoll, New York 10545

The Catholic Foreign Mission Society of America (Maryknoll) recruits and trains people for overseas missionary service. Through Orbis Books, Maryknoll aims to foster the international dialogue that is essential to mission. The books published, however, reflect the opinions of their authors and are not meant to represent the official position of the society.

Copyright © 1992 by George E. McCarthy and Royal W. Rhodes
All rights reserved
Published by Orbis Books, Maryknoll, NY 10545
Manufactured in the United States of America

Library of Congress Cataloging-in-Publication Data

McCarthy, George E.
    Eclipse of justice : ethics, economics, and the lost traditions of
American Catholicism / George E. McCarthy and Royal W. Rhodes.
        p.   cm.
    Includes bibliographical references and index.
    ISBN 0-88344-806-8
    1. Catholic Church. National Conference of Catholic Bishops.
Economic justice for all.   2. Catholic Church—Doctrines.
3. Economics—Religious aspects—Catholic Church.   4. Sociology,
Christian (Catholic)   5. United States—Economic conditions—1981–
6. Liberation theology.   I. Rhodes, Royal W.   II. Title.
BX1795.E27M34   1991   91-34527
                                                                    CIP

INTRODUCTION

The issue is finally out in the open, and there is no longer any possibility of not discussing it in public: Is America a fair and just society? Does it permit the fullest development of our moral, spiritual, and intellectual autonomy? Liberal and conservative academicians have been discussing this for years in the works of Rawls, Nozick, Friedman, and Walzer. However, the question today has overflowed its academic boundaries with the publication by the American Catholic bishops of their 1986 letter *Economic Justice for All: Pastoral Letter on Catholic Social Teaching and the U.S. Economy*.[1] The letter focuses on a discussion of the poverty, inequality, and powerlessness in American society, on the nature of fairness in economic distribution, and on the institutions of political and economic democracy. It summarizes traditional Catholic social teachings and places them within the context of their philosophical and theological lineage in ancient Greek philosophy, Hebrew legal codes, medieval theology, and modern ethical thought. The bishops then proceed to judge America by these ethical standards of the church, and America is found morally wanting.

In this work we also wish to examine the classical concepts of social ethics and economic justice as they are applied by the bishops to an analysis of the social, political, and economic institutions of America. A study of the Bishops' Letter on social justice in America and the conservative and radical reactions to it provides us with an opportunity to look at the changing ethical values and perspectives of the hierarchy of the North American Catholic Church. In the process we are able to open up the full range of debate about the nature of social ethics, including political, ethical, and economic issues. Since the bishops borrow from such a broad range of intellectual traditions, including the Old and New Testaments, church doctrine and history, papal encyclicals, Aristotle, Kant, Rawls, and the U. N. Declaration of Human Rights, this letter also offers us an opportunity to rethink the nature of ethics and social justice in relation to current questions of political economy in American society.

This book is organized into three major parts: the moral dilemma created by the American Catholic bishops' critique of liberalism; the contemporary political and theological responses to it by the right and the left; and the issues of ethics and political economy as they are worked out in the Third World, that is, in the questions raised by liberation theology and dependency theory.

1

In 1984 the National Conference of Catholic Bishops released, after several years of preliminary study, the first draft of a controversial letter on economic justice in the United States; a year later a second, slightly shorter draft followed. By November 1986, when the final report, *Economic Justice for All*, was approved by the bishops, a long and intense process of public consultation had taken place. The original committee, including Archbishop Rembert Weakland (Milwaukee, WI), Archbishop Thomas A. Donnellan (Atlanta, GA), Bishop George Speltz (St. Cloud, MN), Bishop William Weigand (Salt Lake City, UT), and Auxiliary Bishop Peter Rosazza (Hartford, CT), incorporated in the text insights from economists, business and labor leaders, sociologists, theologians, and others, Catholic and non-Catholic alike. A similar pastoral, *The Challenge of Peace* (1983), critical of national policy on nuclear deterrence and an unbridled arms race under-cutting economic stability, had already prompted vocal criticism of the American bishops for their moral pronouncements on military spending and the dangerous stalemate of Cold War politics. The airing of critical views on the American economic system and nuclear brinkmanship by the bishops representing over 50 million U.S. Catholics was seen by critics and supporters alike as a powerful and influential factor in national debate, although the bishops took special steps to isolate these pronouncements from ties to party politics. Modern America was weighed in the balance and found wanting by the prelates, especially in its failure to address adequately the misery of the poor in our midst and abroad. The economic system of liberalism, whether in its politically conservative or liberal guise, was judged "a social and moral scandal."

This description of the moral dilemma for the materially prosperous Catholic Church in twentieth-century America drew from a long and complex historical experience and theological tradition in Catholicism, especially since the papal encyclical "On the Condition of Workers" (*Rerum Novarum*, 1891) by Leo XIII and subsequent letters on the social question by later popes. Archbishop Weakland, chairman of the five-member committee that drafted the economic pastoral, has referred directly to this distinctly Catholic body of social teaching that helped shape the bishops' thinking:

> I am grateful to all those popes and others who have worked on Catholic social teaching over the past hundred years or so. Without that body of reflection, we would be in a very difficult position today. When I deal with the non-Catholic community in dialogue of this sort, they can sense that their denominations did not evolve that same kind of a social teaching. They have the "Social Gospel" principles, but without the same body of reflection that we have in the Catholic tradition, coming from the end of the past century. Despite the fact that Catholic social teaching may have started as a response to par-

For my children
Alexa and Devin McCarthy

In memory of my mother and father
Rita L. and Royal H. Rhodes

CONTENTS

ACKNOWLEDGMENTS

Since we are indebted to such a large number of people, it would be impossible to mention everyone. The scholars who have aided us will see their ideas developed in our work. We can only hope that we did justice to them. Special mention, however, should be made of Father Frank Lane, of the Kenyon College chaplaincy and department of history, who read most of the manuscript. His comments, criticisms, and recommendations were a constant source of encouragement to us. We wish to thank the staff of Olin Library at Kenyon College and, in particular, Mr. Allan Bosch in general humanities research, Ms. Carol Singer in government documents, and Ms. Debra McCann in interlibrary loans. The staff at the Geschwister-Scholl-Institut für Politische Wissenschaft at the University of Munich was also very generous with its time and support. Though the metaphysics of modern economics and theology is at times difficult to fathom, it was Ms. Sharon Duchesne's help with the metaphysics of computer software that was, in the end, invaluable. The secretarial skills and patience of Ms. Pat Bosch are also gratefully acknowledged, along with the extraordinary graciousness with which she accomplished this demanding task.

We would like to thank Lynne Taddeo '93, Benjamin Arnold '92, and Marti Kunst '90 for their careful reading of this manuscript.

We must also record our special gratitude to those students over the last few years who have enrolled in our interdisciplinary course on ethics and social justice; their questions and enthusiasm have helped us sustain our own interest in and commitment to this challenging project.

ticular situations, I see it as a great boon for us today in dealing with situations in which we find ourselves.[2]

In the first part of this book we explore the principles and characteristics of the Catholic Bishops' Letter and the often hidden antecedents of diverse views: papal, episcopal, and lay, that have provided the ideas and vocabulary expressed by the bishops.

Two days before the publication of the first draft of the Bishops' Letter, a group of prominent, conservative Catholics, called the Lay Commission on Catholic Social Teaching and the U.S. Economy, issued *Toward the Future* (1984), a spirited defense of the American economic system which they alleged was under attack by the bishops who wanted to replace the free-market economy with some destructive brand of socialism, in a misguided attempt to alleviate poverty. William Simon, former Secretary of the Treasury and one of the organizers of the lay report, insisted that it was a clear fact of historic experience "that economics dedicated to freedom, individual opportunity, and non-inflationary economic growth do far more to alleviate poverty and suffering than all the schemes of the social engineers and commissars of history."[3] The 31 members of the lay commission, including such notable Catholics as former Secretary of State Alexander Haig, former Secretary of the Interior Walter J. Hickel, Clare Booth Luce, and J. Peter Grace, rejected the view they saw advocated by the bishops, in which the free-market system was depicted as the incarnation of greed and selfishness, inherently incompatible with Christian morality. Such positions, Simon insisted, are themselves unsupported by either the Bible or the traditional teachings of the church. Instead, they assert, the bishops have substituted the political agenda of the secular left, especially an enchantment with aggressive government intervention and redistribution programs. In Simon's view these meddlesome priests should stick to "canon law and Latin liturgies."[4]

This study also deals with the variety of criticisms of the Bishops' Letter from the right and left of the political spectrum. Chapters two and three analyze the redefinition of social justice in terms of the practical and theoretical views of conservative writers who have addressed the relationship of ethics to political economy. Michael Novak, coauthor of *Toward the Future*, and Robert Benne, a professor of church history, attempt to establish the ethical justification of democratic capitalism by grounding their theories in the liberal tradition. What is particularly fascinating is that Novak turns to John Locke and Robert Nozick, whereas Benne turns to the theory and method of John Rawls in their criticism of the welfare state, socialism, and liberation theology. But there is a major problem in these different variations on American conservativism: They have failed to understand the incompatibility between their political philosophy and their economic theory.

They have also failed to recognize the incompatibility of the different traditions within liberalism itself and thus unknowingly combine the categories of liberty and freedom, inequality and human dignity, consumerism and self-realization, and liberalism and democracy. The result is ambiguity and incoherence in their theories of liberalism. There is no attempt to resolve the contradictions between a social system founded on freedom within a community, human dignity, self-realization of human potentials, and democratic participation, on the one hand, and one founded on the principles of consumer choices, individual liberties, inequality and class, and market liberalism, on the other. Nor is the distinction between a liberalism of natural rights and a liberalism of technocratic elites seen as a problem in their combination of distinct traditions.

A second and related problem is that such hybrid theories make it unusually difficult to understand the history and structures of American political economy. In fact, it makes it unusually difficult to even develop a theory of political economy. The American bishops, to the extent that they uncritically accept such general views of liberalism, also fall into these dilemmas. They recognize neither the logical traps in liberal political philosophy nor the difficulties of developing a theory of political economy. Both the lay report and the Bishops' Letter fail to contain a developed historical and structural analysis of American political economy. In their desire and haste to move from moral principles to public policy recommendations, the bishops gloss over serious political and economic problems. The result is that their New American Experiment becomes entangled in a quagmire of unresolved conflicts within liberalism. The contemporary responses, left and right, to the Bishops' Letter can thus be read in the larger context of debates about economic structures in modern liberalism. Chapter four begins to resolve some of these difficulties by developing a more critical and radical view of American society and the existing interrelationships among labor, corporations, and the modern state.

In the final part of this work we examine the implications of the attempts by the U.S. bishops to relate Christian social doctrine to international political and economic issues. This means widening the area of discussion to include the Third World, since the bishops recognize in an increasingly clearer way what John Paul II has called, in his encyclical "On Social Concern" (*Sollicitudo Rei Socialis*, 1989), the "radical interdependence" that binds the First World to these desperately impoverished regions. As conservative theorists have been quick to map out in terms of geopolitical demands for national security, Nicaragua is closer to Texas than Texas is to Maine. One could easily say that the Third World is as close to Middle America as the nearest bankrupt savings and loan, as the most recently auctioned family farm, as a relocated factory leaving the Rust Belt, or as the fiscal effects of increasing economic instability brought about by the mushrooming national deficit. The Third World, rather than being a glimpse of America's preindustrial past, may be a glimpse of its postindustrial future.

While the biblical theology of justice and "preferential option for the poor" worked out on the local grass-roots level in the various theologies of liberation still seem more closely identified with the Third World, North American theology is also beginning to listen and speak in these words. Both First and Third Worlds have something to learn from each other regarding a more just distribution of goods and more open participation in economic democracy. Chapter seven examines how current liberal and conservative debates over economic development in the Third World, combining with the debates raging in liberation, biblical, and political theologies, define in new ways the nature and function of social ethics and shape the common social life of our citizens, religious and nonreligious alike. The ambiguous and tentative relationship between liberation theology and dependency theory is also examined in the writings of Latin American theologians.

Passages from both the Old and New Testament will be carefully studied in order to help clarify differences of interpretation of the political messages of the Bible. Our purpose here is to unravel the ways in which the American bishops have systematically stripped the Bible of its political content, resulting in a depoliticization of Scripture. A comparison of approaches will be made between the North American bishops and the more critical and revolutionary Latin American theologians. We are also concerned with asking the question: Why have the North American and European conservatives been so critical of both liberation theology and dependency theory? What are the assumptions and hidden values which underlie their different approaches—their theologies and metaphysics of economics?

Despite trenchant criticisms from various quarters, the Bishops' Letter remains an unparalleled achievement in articulating a moral vision applied to the contemporary crisis in American economic life. The insistence that ethical questions are central to economic and political decisions, not just a pious cog in the wheel of market forces, was not a widely welcome position in the early 1980s, euphoric over rapid payoffs in the business sector. As America faces the last decade of the millennium, the social and human costs of indiscriminant deregulation, junk-bond buy outs, backdoor lobbying, corruption in government agencies, and fraud (even from the suppliers of hardware for national defense) have made more citizens attentive to the issues raised by the bishops and subsequent declarations made by other religious groups. The icons of national greed and vulgar consumption have become a household litany: Boesky, Milken, Keating, Helmsley, and Trump. The bishops have done much to focus attention and provide an ethical vocabulary for the opening economic debate.

This is all the more remarkable because it has been done in the face of significant opposition within the ranks of the Catholic community, which is for the most part conspicuously enjoying the economic and political benefits of this free-market liberal democracy. The authority and prestige of the bishops as unquestioned religious guides have been placed at risk and their pastoral judgment has often been characterized as an ignorant or malevolent intrusion of an all-too-visible clerical hand into politics and the economy. The process of public consultation and debate, published and refined in succeeding drafts, was seen by some as an abdication of traditional authority, since earlier church proclamations had so often appeared as almost sacred oracles, above discussion and response. The bishops had drawn back the curtain and shown the delicate machinery by which some 300 bishops of diverse politics, training, and intelligence arrived by compromise at a delicate moral consensus tailored to the American scene. In itself, the process was a bold affirmation of the bishops' trust in the "new experiment" in democracy they advocated.

And yet for all the good achieved in this process, which stimulated a public debate on crucial issues, the letter remains a long, dry, and largely unread document, derived from a rich and subtle tradition of Catholic social thought which itself is hidden and seldom preached. The American Catholic bishops, as shepherds and teachers, have failed to teach their own followers the history and tradition of the church's social doctrine, which stretches back to biblical times. The bishops, while suggesting prudential proposals for addressing the crisis of poverty in American society, have consciously or unconsciously neglected to perform the needed structural analysis of American political economy necessary to make their recommended economic remedies and ethical prescriptions have any real effect for the common good. For this to occur there must first be an historical and hermeneutical recovery of those traditions which the bishops have recognized as foundations for the development of a theory of social ethics and justice. Though the Hebrew, Greek, medieval Christian, and modern church traditions are mentioned, there is little reflection on their relevance and applicability to the present situation in America. The real meaning and force of these documents are turned into reified rituals and consequently lost in a general moral amnesia. In our work there is an attempt to recover the lost meaning of some of these traditions by an archaeological rolling back of the layers of stale social science and biblical interpretation in order to uncover the theoretical potentials hidden beneath them.

These missed or rejected opportunities and traditions, which we explore more closely in the following work, are the reason that the Bishops' Letter on the economy, despite great expectations in these hard times, is more accurately seen as a chronicle of lost possibilities. The theoretical and structural possibilities of a new society are eclipsed when the traditions upon which they are based become pale reflections of the search for dignity and autonomy in the classical periods.

There has been much discussion in recent years about the rationalization of ethical language and the narrowing of moral discourse that has closed off reflective and critical discussion on a whole panoply of important social issues. The rich traditions of Western ethics from ancient to modern times have been reduced to issues of moral philosophy. This could be called the "social amnesia" of modernity. In this condition, moral language "works to preserve the status quo by presenting the human and social relationships of society as natural — and unchangeable — relations between things."[5] By limiting morality to issues of individual consciousness and concupiscence, we have produced a form of moral rationality and discourse that has been unable to see the connections among political, economic, and social issues and the moral questions of right and wrong. That is, ethics has lost its original theory of political economy. What had once been part of the classical traditions has been lost to Western society and moral rationality.

In the Anglo-American tradition of philosophy, the area of ethics has generally been interpreted to refer to "metamorality," that is, to an analysis of the logical aspects of moral choice. Ethics in this view deals with the logical clarification of the range of moral choices and options available to the individual, with whatever accompanying implications and ramifications. Thus it is an area for the philosophical articulation and clarification of the moral life itself. More recently the definition of ethics has been expanded with the renaissance in political theory, especially with the works of John Rawls and Robert Nozick, among others who reintroduce the political element back into ethics.

Though we applaud these efforts, we also recognize that even these important works in political philosophy have not included all those areas which were once part of the classical traditions of ancient Greece and Israel, and their conception of ethics: encompassing social traditions and customs, political philosophy, and economic theory.[6] In the later development of the classical traditions in nineteenth-century philosophy and theology, Hegel was the first modern thinker to bring together both political economy and philosophy as he moved from an ethics of morality to an ethics of politics. It was Hegel who rediscovered institutional ethics by integrating Aristotelian philosophy and Kantian morality. The moral autonomy and respect for human dignity of the modern individual was integrated with an examination of the culture, politics, and economy of the community. The religious tradition has also stressed the norms of human dignity and responsibility, based on a communitarian understanding of full participation by each individual in society. In Catholic social thought we see a consistent attempt to integrate a natural philosophy of community with one grounded in a "revealed" vision of faith.

Reading the works of Rawls and other social philosophers, one can see the traditional emphasis on moral philosophy and individual choice making begin to shift to a broader range of philosophical issues, which include questions of political freedoms, social justice, and the nature of the state. This advance, however, never fully captures the diversity and subtlety of issues contained in the classical traditions.[7] Ethics too often is still limited mainly to questions of economic distribution and issues surrounding the just distribution of public goods within the market. Analogies can be found, as critics have indicated, in modern Catholic pronouncements on social issues focusing almost exclusively on distributive justice, rather than on questions of the moral production of wealth or the dynamic nature of the modern economy. The ongoing debate has focused, instead, on the standard of measurement that would be used to better distribute the social wealth of the community, standards based on equality, needs, individual effort, contribution, or social agreement.[8] The more inclusive redefinition of ethics certainly was a positive step, since it moved morality away from its limiting features – the exclusive stress on individual rationality and freedom found in Kantian practical philosophy and religious doctrines focused solely on private moral culpability. Though ethics was now placed within the context of political institutions, it still had not encompassed the deep structures of political economy. A goal of our work, then, is to apply a developing theory of social ethics, which would include an analysis of personal moral values, as well as an analysis of economic, political, and social institutions that constitute the heart of American society to which the Catholic bishops have addressed their pastoral letter.[9]

Having said this, the first question which arises is: What is social justice when applied to an analysis of an advanced capitalist society such as the United States? Any definition of social justice must go beyond the traditional categories of *distributive justice*, possessive individualism, and political theory (income and wealth distribution). Going beyond justice does not entail a rejection of the notion, but a broadening of its range of theoretical and practical applicability. Since distributive justice is itself a function of deeper structural features of the economy, then the former must develop into a concern with *economic justice* and a critique of political economy (the analysis of corporate restructuring, reorganization of labor, and new functions of the state in an advanced industrial society). In turn it must also move beyond economics and the private sphere to include the area of *political justice* and the public realm, which deals with questions of the protection of human rights and individual freedoms, human capacities and potentialities, the social possibilities of self-realization and development, the social institutions for encouraging self-determination, and political and economic democracy. These three forms of justice – distributive, economic, and political – constitute what we call *social justice*. This form of structural and societal justice, when combined with an individualistic moral philosophy within a holistic framework, is then called *social ethics*. The possibilities of individual self-determination and self-realization depend on the establishment of basic moral and political principles, an historical and structural analysis of American political economy, and rational implementation through public policy of its social ideals.

An important question may be raised early. Why are these social arrangements necessary for a consideration of ethics? The answer is that, as in the case of the classical traditions, the primary philosophical question remains the examination of the nature of justice and the good life. That is, it requires a detailed study into those social institutions which make rational choice and self-determination possible. This, as Rawls has recognized, can only be adequately dealt with by an analysis of the basic structure of society.[10] But as the U.S. Catholic bishops themselves have seen, any analysis of society includes consideration of both political and economic arrangements, since only within the totality of social institutions can the questions of community, the common good, moral autonomy, and human dignity be adequately addressed. The specific questions which interest us in this book are those that center on the bishops' critique of American society and their understanding of the relationships between their moral values and their concrete policy recommendations for the implementation and realization of these values. Along with these central questions, there are others. Is the bishops' understanding of American social institutions and political economy adequate to realize the moral values they propose? What exactly is the relationship between social structures and moral norms, political economy and ethics? If their specific economic and political policy recommendations could not implement their underlying values, does this turn ethics into a political ideology? Can the moral vision the bishops articulate ever be realized within the structures of American social life, as they are now constituted?

In summary, the following are the major themes that form the central focus of this work:

1. Analysis of the ethical, religious, and economic components in the Bishops' Letter on social justice (chapter one)

2. Examination of the letter's ethical and religious foundations in the Old and New Testaments, Greek philosophy, church social teachings, social and political theories of Kant and Rawls, and the United Nations Universal Declaration of Human Rights (chapters one, two, and three)

3. Comparison of the letter to previous American Catholic bishops' statements on the U.S. economy since the early twentieth century and to papal encyclicals of the past one hundred years critical of the rise of liberalism and capitalism (chapters one and five)

4. Critique of the understatement or elimination in the letter of the critical ethical and religious traditions (chapters one and five)

5. Study of the conservative and radical responses to the letter (chapters two, three, and four)

6. Critique of the letter for not recognizing the contradictory nature of the concepts of equality and liberalism, liberty and freedom, democracy and capitalism in its political theory and for not developing a theory of political economy (chapters three and four)

7. Investigation of the economic and political structures of U.S. and Third World societies (chapters four and seven)

8. Development of a critical theory of political economy which includes an analysis of the restructuring in the American economy of the relations

among industry, government, and labor; examination of political economy as a form and sub-branch of ethics (chapters four and seven)

9. Study of the relationship between liberation theology and dependency theory (chapter seven)

10. Analysis of conservative and radical criticisms of liberation theology, its economic theory, and biblical interpretations (chapters six and seven).

1

SOCIAL JUSTICE AND
THE CATHOLIC BISHOPS' LETTER
ON THE U.S. ECONOMY

INTRODUCTION

The *Wall Street Journal* reported on November 14, 1986, that the National Conference of Catholic Bishops had approved a pastoral letter on the economy which called for increased government efforts to attack poverty and unemployment. Three days later, in an editorial titled "On Disagreeing With Bishops," the paper responded to a complaint lodged by Archbishop Rembert Weakland about the fairness of the *Journal's* coverage and interpretation of the letter, to which the editors again simply replied that the bishops had concocted "poor policy." The controversy, heated at times, which began when the pastoral letter's topic was first announced and continued through the lengthy public testimonies and afterwards, invariably centered on the prudence and practicality of bishops defining economic policy. For others the question of the government's role in regulating and restricting the market seemed the central issue.

What the disputants often overlooked, in thus defining the playing field of the controversy as bishops, budgets, and big government, were several features that made this letter unique in contemporary religious and economic debate. One new element was the long consultation process with experts across the political and ideological spectrum. Whatever one's stance on the positions reached, the bishops had arrived at their conclusions not by some mystifying process expressed as a sacred oracle, but as the result of public discussion, "consulting the faithful" and experts outside in the spirit of Vatican II. Another, and perhaps more powerful, element was the remarkable attempt in the letter to articulate and integrate diverse intellectual traditions on justice and apply these to the current crisis.

These traditions, at the heart of the Catholic understanding of the religious individual in relation to society, have often been hidden, ignored,

11

forgotten, or little discussed outside circles of theological experts. And yet they are powerfully present in the way questions of social justice are formulated and can be more adequately addressed. At one level, *Economic Justice for All* draws on a more immediately familiar intellectual reservoir: the natural-rights tradition of modern Western political and social thought. The autonomous individualism and personal liberties at the core of our nation's political, economic, and social life can be traced back to John Locke's linkage of "life, liberty, and private property," and then forward to neoclassical economics, Milton Friedman and the Chicago School, the conservative Catholic position paper *Toward the Future*, and the neo-Lockean philosophy of Robert Nozick. But even in the natural-rights tradition there are other elements the bishops are equally heir to: the anti-Federalist impulses of small farm communities and town meetings in America; the ideals of democratic participation defined by Franklin and Paine; and Thomas Jefferson's revolutionary adaptation of Locke to emphasize instead, "life, liberty, and the pursuit of happiness."

Less familiar, however, to modern American audiences is the much older and wider natural-law tradition that has over the millennia sought to describe the innate and universal moral order, superior and prior to any subsequent social contract, the basis of natural-rights theory. The bishops' pastoral letter synthesizes a number of major expressions of this natural-law tradition. First, it can be found at the core of Catholic social teaching, whether in the hundred-year modern sequence of papal encyclicals, the statements of conferences of bishops or individual theologians addressing specific problems, or social ethics at large. Tied closely to these statements, as both a basis of authority and as a challenge to current societal models, is the natural-law tradition as understood from the Bible. The Hebrew tradition in the Old Testament, combining both the Law (Genesis, Exodus, Leviticus, Numbers, and Deuteronomy) and the Prophets, is the source of the bishops' presentation of central themes of creation in God's image, human dignity, equality, and the vocation of labor. Because of increased interest in and awareness of the underlying social institutions and structures of ancient Israel brought about by a generation or two of interfaith dialogue and biblical study, the ancient concepts of community and covenant can now be seen in terms of practical and ongoing questions about the nature of social justice and political economy. The periodic redistribution of wealth, remission of debt, and liberation from bondage enforced by the practices of Jubilee and the sabbath year were clearly structural ways to insure economic justice for all in biblical society. These themes continue in the New Testament texts as the call to discipleship in community, establishing a communion of hope to reflect the divine justice issuing from creation and the new creation in Christ.

This natural-law position is drawn not only from the Hebraic and Christian biblical traditions, but also from the Hellenic and Greco-Roman world of statecraft and philosophy. It is Aristotle's *Nicomachean Ethics*, Book

Five, that provides the bishops with their tripartite definition of justice: commutative, distributive, and social. Filtered through the theology of Thomas Aquinas and the synthesis of other medieval schoolmen, the philosophies of Plato, Aristotle, and the Stoics, all reflecting natural-law theory, continue to inform the substance of Catholic moral and ethical thought. A similar line from outside the religious traditions explains the use the bishops made of the humanistic values found best expressed in the eighteenth-century philosophy of Immanuel Kant, who defined humanity in terms of the universal categories of moral autonomy and human dignity, and Jean-Jacques Rousseau, who stressed the essential role of social life and the general welfare of the community over against the possessive individualism of Hobbes and Locke. One document the bishops endorse specifically as an evocation of such values is the Universal Declaration of Human Rights issued by the United Nations in 1948.

Articles 1 to 21 in the U. N. declaration describe aspects of a natural-rights tradition which emphasizes the basic political freedoms of speech, assembly, trial, and religion. But articles 22 to 27 enunciate the far less customary guarantees of human rights: medical care, employment, housing, food, and leisure. It is undoubtedly because of these specific articulations of the natural-law tradition that the United States, alone of the major industrialized states, has refused to endorse this document. The cited examples of natural-law theory are important traditions to be noted in any discussion of society. Although largely unrecognized as part of their accomplishments, it is to the credit of the bishops that these traditions have been resurrected to add important voices to the current debate.

PRINCIPLES AND OUTLINE OF THE LETTER

By the time of the publication of the final version of the Bishops' Letter in November 1986, having been modified and revised in meetings with consultants and public hearings since November 1981, questions of the "recovery" in the economy were headline news: military spending and waste, a record-smashing deficit, precarious international loan repayments, small-farm foreclosures, the specter of the homeless, and whispering hints of problems with insider trading, leveraging, and savings-and-loan institutions.[1] Growing questions about whether this economy adequately protected and promoted human dignity and basic rights were the starting point, then, for what turned out to be a pastoral letter of 188 printed pages, the longest, most detailed and footnoted social statement in the history of the NCCB, and one which has generated continuing challenge and debate.[2] The letter can be broken down roughly into three parts. In the prologue, the bishops set out the reasons for the principal themes and issue a call to "conversion" as the basis for social action. It is here that they state their guiding beliefs in human dignity, the nature of societal bonds, and the deeper meaning of economic activity. In the second part, they set out to explore the relation of the Catholic church to the U.S. economy, describing a moral vision of America in the past, present, and future (chapter one) and grounding it in an extensive treatment of the biblical tradition and Catholic ethical norms (chapter two).[3] Like most of the bishops' letters since the 1940s, the use of the natural-law tradition has disappeared and been replaced by greater reliance on biblical citation and references to papal statements and Vatican II. In the third part, the bishops turn to selected economic policy issues: employment, poverty, food production and agriculture, and the role of the United States in the global economy, especially in relation to the developing countries (chapter three). They call for a "New American Experiment," based on cooperation of labor, management, and owners; partnership in developing national policies; and cooperative ventures at the international level (chapter four). They end by voicing a commitment to the idea of the Christian's vocation as a copartner with God in establishing a "kingdom of love and justice" (chapter five). A select bibliography of papal and Vatican documents, collections, and commentaries is also significantly provided. They acknowledge that the movement from principles to specific policies is complex and open to modification and criticism. Moral values, while essential in the formulation of social policies, "do not dictate specific solutions." The church as a moral teacher is not bound to any particular economic, political, or social system, but evaluates each according to the kinds of normative ethical principles presented in the first two sections of the pastoral letter. They do not claim for their prudential recommendations on public policy "the same kind of authority" they claim for their moral principles, but the latter must not be left at the level of generalities.

> We expect and welcome debate on our specific policy recommendations. Nevertheless, we want our statements on these matters to be given serious consideration by Catholics as they determine whether their own moral judgments are consistent with the Gospel and with Catholic social teaching. We believe that differences on complex economic questions should be expressed in a spirit of mutual respect and open dialogue.[4]

What was surprising was that critical responses questioned not only the policy proposals, but also the bishops' authoritative reading of the Bible and the tradition of Catholic teachings. The bishops found themselves unexpectedly attacked, from left and right, not only for their economics, but also for their theology. In a way it was a backhanded compliment to the bishops for the open dialogue they themselves had initiated in this process.

"Contextualism"—this new movement of national churches to define the content and application of Catholic social teaching in terms of their own social and economic contexts—was urged upon the world's bishops by Vatican II and Pope Paul VI's apostolic letter, *Octogesima Adveniens* (1971).[5]

The American Catholic bishops' pastoral letter, then, is their attempt to enunciate the "principles of reflection, norms of judgment and directives for action" advised by Paul VI and tailored to the American experience. Those principles and themes will be the focus of this section.

The underlying premise of the pastoral letter is that the bishops have a legitimate contribution to make in discussions of the U.S. economy, although they are not technical experts in political economy, and that moral criteria must be applied to economic systems and theories for the greater good of society. "Serious economic choices go beyond purely technical issues to fundamental questions of value and human purpose."[6] In these areas the bishops stake their claim to expertise. They reject a bifurcation in the modern world between "earthly activities" and religion, looked upon as "nothing more than the fulfillment of acts of worship and the observance of a few moral obligations."[7] Such a split causes "serious errors," a code phrase for a fundamental "heresy." Some conservative critics also reject such a separation but seek to reverse the process of moral discernment. Concepts such as "social justice" and "human rights" should be weighed, they say, in terms of the "truths" found in economic experience.

James Schall, for instance, sees in the productivity and innovation of modern capitalism moral criteria compatible with religious ethical teaching which until now has neglected these core contributions of the modern productive system that insure the good life. The previous pattern was to favor ideological theories about exploitation or deficiencies in distribution. In one remarkable statement he observes: *"Economics is a moral discipline insofar as it is also based on sound economic policy."* Efficiency, productivity, and technological advancement seem to be for him elements of a "moral" program; there is no morality unless needed goods are produced, and for that to happen, the norms—the "definitive laws" of economics—must be learned from history and experience, and are not "acquired from revelation."[8] Schall's argument, in reality, is with the whole tradition of Christian teaching about social justice and the criteria used to determine it. His aim apparently is to prevent utopian flights of fancy; its effect, however, could be to sanction any system, despite whatever else it does, that produces material goods in abundance. But such a basis does not guarantee human rights or a fair distribution of the abundance.

The bishops list six moral principles that govern their evaluation of United States economic life.

1. Human dignity is the benchmark for any moral evaluation of economic structures and decisions; this dignity is only "realized in community with others," as Pope John XXIII's encyclical *Mater et Magistra* (1961) insisted.[9] In a Kantian phrase, the letter declares that all human beings are "ends" to be served by institutions, not means for economic goals. Human dignity is both personal, fashioned from creation in the "image and likeness" of God (Genesis 1:26–27), and communal, based on divine covenant (which

differs from and extends beyond the social contract with which it is sometimes conflated by natural-rights theorists).

2. Human dignity can be realized and protected only in community. Human nature is essentially social. "What the Bible and Christian tradition teach, human wisdom confirms. Centuries before Christ, the Greeks and Romans spoke of the human person as a 'social animal' made for friendship, community, and public life. These insights show that human beings achieve self-realization not in isolation, but in interaction with others."[10] The language of self-realization through "friendship, community, and public life" echoes Aristotle's notion of ethical formation in the polis (community) presented in his *Nicomachean Ethics*, although the bishops want a society in which decisions are made by all members without the exclusion of certain groups (women, foreigners, artisans, slaves) that marked the Greek city-state. The bishops also describe this communitarian spirit, one that is dynamic, expressive, and creative, as "solidarity," a word that occurs as early as Augustine in Christian discussions of social theory. Against it they array the various "isms" that are anticommunitarian: class antagonism, egoism, racism, sexism, nationalism, or rugged individualism.

3. Basic justice demands that all people enjoy at least a minimum level of participation in the economy to meet material needs, develop their talents, and contribute to society.[11] Catholic social teaching distinguishes three related aspects of justice that are owed to all "in an imperfect world." *Commutative justice* is fundamental fairness in every agreement, contract, or exchange between individuals or private social groups, in particular workers and employers, who bear mutual responsibilities towards each other. *Distributive justice* is a fair allocation of income, wealth, and power in society. It can be judged in reference to those with basic material needs for whom, as Vatican II phrased it: ". . . we are obliged to come to the relief of the poor and to do so not merely out of our superfluous goods." *Social justice* (*"contributive justice"*) is a guarantee that all persons will have the opportunity to fulfill their own duty to be active and productive participants in society. Social justice also means that economic and social institutions should be constructed in such a way that human freedom and dignity are insured. This means that social structures for justice, not merely individual acts of charity, are necessary. Every citizen must work to secure justice and human rights through organized social means. "Charity will never be true charity unless it takes justice into account . . . Let no one attempt with small gifts of charity to exempt himself from the great duties imposed by justice."[12] The public policies that express a society's response to the poor are "the litmus test of its justice or injustice."[13]

4. Human rights are the minimum conditions for life in community, and these include economic, as well as civil and political rights. The bishops endorse, following papal precedent, the United Nations Universal Declaration of Human Rights, but recognize that some concerted effort on their part is needed to raise the issue and shape a wide-based national agree-

ment. "A first step in such an effort is the development of a new cultural consensus that the basic economic conditions of human welfare are essential to human dignity and are due persons by right. Second, the securing of these rights will make demands on *all* members of society, on all private sector institutions, and on government."[14] Implicitly they acknowledge the present absence of such a national consensus; they do not just state flatly, however, that the United States has never endorsed the U. N. declaration because of the document's insistence on economic rights. They do assert in the end of this section that economic rights and political democracy are mutually reinforcing. While disagreement is possible on *how* economic rights might be put into place, they do not allow any debate with the moral stand that these *should* be in place.

5. All members of the church and society have a specific obligation to the poor and vulnerable. This fundamental "option for the poor," which emerges from Vatican II, Paul VI's papal letters, and liberation theology, means that social and economic activity must not only serve the needs of the poor, but must be carried on "from the view point of the poor and the powerless," who have privileged claims, if social life and economics are to be truly biblical. These activities must be carried on *from* and *with* the poor, not just *to* and *for* them, if they are to have real power to make decisions and participate in every aspect of social life.

6. Society, acting through public and private institutions, has the moral responsibility to enhance human dignity, protect human rights, and secure basic justice. Government's lawful role is to guarantee the minimum conditions to insure the realization of the common good. Following the principle of "subsidiarity" (distribution of power at the most immediate level, as a safeguard against centralized bureaucracy), the letter states that government "should undertake only those initiatives which exceed the capacity of individuals or private groups acting independently."[15] This limit on government intervention, it says, does *not* endorse the concept that government "governs best that governs least." Government gives necessary assistance to direct, urge, restrain, and regulate the economy. The right of private ownership is upheld, but within limits, especially when some lack necessities. "The common good may sometimes demand that the right to own be limited by public involvement in the planning or ownership of certain sectors of the economy. Support of private ownership does not mean that anyone has the right to unlimited accumulation of wealth."[16]

In light of criticisms made that earlier drafts seemed to neglect the positive role of business and investments in securing the material base for economic justice, the final version of the letter included a quotation from Pope John Paul II to underscore the respect and freedom to be given to entrepreneurial, business, and financial forces. The pope says: "The degree of well-being which society today enjoys would be unthinkable without the dynamic figure of the business person, whose function consists of organizing human labor and the means of production so as to give rise to the goods and services necessary for the progress and prosperity of the community."[17]

The pastoral letter goes on to reassert that business is accountable to the common good and to norms of justice, especially since capital acts as trustee of natural and other resources. A broader vision of responsibility by owners, investors, and managers is needed, and capital itself should be owned by a wider sector of the population, lest overconcentration and subsequent abuse occur. Other central principles are also found throughout the letter: the doctrine of creation and, therefore, God's sovereign ownership of the earth; stewardship and the notion that all possessions are simply gifts from God; the biblical concepts of community and covenant; the insistence that the idea of sin, personal and social, is a valid safeguard against both unrealistic utopianism and omnicompetent institutions; and the meaning for dignity of life found in the New Testament doctrines of the Incarnation of the Word of God and the dawning of the new creation, God's kingdom on earth, symbols considered in a later chapter. The six principles outlined above, however, focus most of the bishops' argument with U.S. economic life. Like the letters issued during the Depression, the apparent failure of the system is the motivating force that galvanizes the bishops and the religious community as they lurch hesitantly toward rather moderate and muted criticisms. But the bishops, as they themselves say, cannot ignore that by the government's own figures, 33 million Americans, one in seven, are living in poverty, and this number is predominantly children. Using some of their most direct language, the bishops agree that these "failures" of the system are "massive and ugly": the poor and homeless who sleep in inadequate shelters; soup lines for the hungry; unemployment and underemployment for the young and middle-aged, many of whom once had jobs; the worry created as opportunities for jobs and communities wither; new economic pressures that drain families of social supports and hope; the loss of land and a valued way of life by small family farmers reduced to serflike conditions.[18] Whatever the signs of hope in economic life, and they acknowledge a number of them, there is still the crushing reality of economic burden at home and abroad, where 800 million live in absolute poverty and 450 million are malnourished. It is that massive crisis that prompted the bishops to ask these moral questions: "What does the economy do *for* people? What does it do *to* people? And how do people *participate* in it?"[19]

TRADITION OF THE U.S. BISHOPS ON ECONOMICS

Economic Justice for All describes itself as part of a tradition "rooted in the Bible and developed over the past century by the popes and the Second Vatican Council in response to modern economic tradition."[20] Its claim to authority, then, rests in the religious role of over 300 American bishops to interpret faithfully the biblical revelation and papal teachings in light of their own pastoral experience dealing with moral situations in contemporary American society. The papal and biblical traditions will be treated in later chapters. The bishops have also acknowledged their debt to the tradition developed by the U.S. hierarchy from the time of their 1919 Program of Social Reconstruction.[21] Among the other important statements made since then by the bishops, we will look at passages from the following: *Statement on Unemployment* (November 12, 1930); *The Present Crisis* (April 25, 1933); *Statement on Church and Social Order* (February 4, 1940); *The Economy: Human Dimensions* (November 20, 1975); and *Marxist Communism* (November 12, 1980). The bishops see themselves contributing to a living and growing legacy of Christian social thought, while reflecting back on the links to previous statements.[22]

In *The Economy: Human Dimensions* (1975), issued during a period of recession, "the worst since World War II," the bishops reflect on the social consequences of the troubled economy and its effects on the unemployed victims of the recession by recalling the earlier statements in 1930 and 1919. Going back to the 1919 Program of Social Reconstruction, the letter summarizes its contents and presents it as a framework for the resolution of the current economic ills. The program had called for: a minimum wage, unemployment insurance, health and old age benefits, child-labor laws, legal sanction of labor's right to organize, a national employment service, public housing, and a long-term program of wage increases. Regulation of public utilities, progressive taxes on inheritance, income, and excess profits, calls for labor's participation in management, wider ownership through cooperatives and stock options for workers, and control of monopolies, even by government competition, were also urged. The bishops wanted many of the emergency war measures kept in place to insure jobs for returning veterans, defuse growing labor strife, and provide a living wage for families. This was the minimum demanded by justice. They rejected as neither moderate nor reasonable the social reconstruction program of the British Labor Party designed by Fabian socialist Sidney Webb, and even the "more practical" reform proposals of the American Federation of Labor, since its land-tax plan could involve state confiscation and did not aspire to have the workers themselves become owners as well as users of capital.[23] They do, however, quote favorably from a statement by twenty British Quaker employers that talks about the spiritual transformation needed in labor relations, but they reject the principles and proposals advanced in the United States by the National Chamber of Commerce that contained "nothing of importance on the labor phase of reconstruction."[24] They conclude with their sense of a basic "Christian View," referring to the social encyclical of Pope Leo XIII, *Rerum Novarum* (1891), which had been enthusiastically read by some American bishops as papal justification not only for unionism, but even more specifically for social insurance and eight-hour-day legislation.[25] The 1919 program sets out a less euphoric basis for reconstruction in a "reform of the spirit of both labor and capital."

The laborer must come to realize that he owes his employer and society an honest day's work in return for a fair wage, and that conditions cannot be substantially improved until he roots out the desire to get a maximum of return for a minimum of service. The capitalist must likewise get a new viewpoint. He needs to learn the long-forgotten truth, that wealth is stewardship, that profit making is not the basic justification of business enterprise, and that there are such things as fair profits, fair interest, and fair prices ... The employer has a right to get a reasonable living out of his business, but he has no right to interest on his investment until his employees have obtained at least living wages. This is the human and Christian, in contrast to the purely commercial and pagan, ethics of industry.[26]

The program created a prolonged uproar, being defended and attacked from both inside and outside the Catholic church, which previously had been judged a profoundly conservative social institution. The president of the National Association of Manufacturers complained that it was "partisan, pro-labor union socialist propaganda," and non-Catholic liberal muckraker Upton Sinclair called it the "Catholic miracle."[27]

While calling for fundamental reforms, the 1919 program did not advocate abandoning the whole system for another. This nonradical, reformist perspective reflects the position of Monsignor John A. Ryan, later referred to as the "Right Reverend New Dealer," the chief draftsman of the 1919 program, who saw all the major proposals, except the call for labor's participation in management, adopted during the Roosevelt administration.[28]

The program does not argue on the basis of a visible theological agenda, and it explicitly declines "to formulate a comprehensive scheme of reconstruction," choosing instead to pursue reforms possible in "a reasonable time," with general principles for long-range goals. The bishops see no reason for the type of seismic social change rocking Europe, in particular because in the undisturbed postwar United States, "superior natural advantages and resources, the better industrial and social condition of our working classes still constitute an obstacle to anything like revolutionary changes."[29] Adopting the strong aversion of Leo XIII toward socialism, the bishops reject that model. Despite the present system's inefficiency and waste in the production and distribution of goods, insufficient income for wage earners, and wealth concentration within "a small minority of privileged capitalists," reform is still held possible. Utopia is not around the corner, only capitalism.

It seems clear that the present industrial system is destined to last for a long time in its main outlines. That is to say, private ownership of capital is not likely to be supplanted by a collectivist organization of industry at a date sufficiently near to justify any present action based on the hypothesis of its arrival. This forecast we recognize is not only extremely probable, but as highly desirable; for, other objections apart, Socialism would mean bureaucracy, political tyranny, the helplessness of the individual as a factor in the ordering of his own life, and in general social inefficiency and decadence.[30]

As commentators have pointed out, the only possible element requiring a revolutionized social structure is the call for copartnership.

The full possibilities of increased production will not be realized so long as the majority of the workers remain mere wage earners. The majority must somehow become owners, or at least in part, of the instruments of production. They can be enabled to reach this stage gradually through cooperative productive societies and copartnership arrangements.[31]

It is, in fact, partly the American dream of the worker achieving some degree of private ownership, and not remaining merely a wage slave. It is grounded in the premise of upward mobility by property ownership in a free and open society, especially attractive to immigrants and encouraging sentiments of social deference that deflect more radical and immediate demands for redistribution of wealth. The statement quickly goes on, however, to say that with an abolition of the wage system, no scheme of state ownership of the instruments of production is sanctioned; capital would still be owned by individuals "who are willing to work hard and faithfully."

The Catholic bishops did not for the next decade vigorously adhere to a reform agenda. Perhaps the most significant development was the permission granted the bishops by the Vatican to transform their National Catholic War Council into the permanent but voluntary National Catholic Welfare Council (later renamed the National Conference of Catholic Bishops — NCCB — along with its later public policy and information extension, the U.S. Catholic Conference — USCC). They also made John A. Ryan head of the Washington office of the NCWC Social Action Department, where he continued to be an important link between the Catholic community and liberal Progressivist groups, in which he used Catholic natural-law theory in new ways to demonstrate the case for social justice.[32] Basically, the administrative structure of the American Catholic bishops that served as the clearing house for later social policy statements, including *Economic Justice for All*, was established by the early 1920s and has continued to function since then.

It was only after the bubble broke in the Great Depression that many of the bishops began to ask whether the defects in the American system could be remedied by legislation alone; perhaps the whole system had gone sour, and national sentiment might be on the side of more basic changes. In 1939 Cardinal Edward Mooney of Detroit, Chairman of the Administrative Board of the NCWC, expressed those misgivings while writing about the 1919 program's failure to treat the topic of unemployment sufficiently. He asked whether pressure for major structural change was at hand.

> Important groups in America are now perfectly willing to jettison the whole system of private ownership out of which modern capitalism has developed. In fact, it is not too much to say that outside the sphere of Catholic thought, most intellectuals are advocating some kind of collectivism — either a moderate form of socialism or out and out communism. Our Catholic principles save us from being deceived by those destructive illusions, but, by the same token, they impose upon us the obligation of applying fundamental remedies to the glaring evils of the present time.[33]

Something new can be gauged in such statements. Besides the awareness of the bankruptcy of the liberal economic system brought on by the global depression and the growing threats of fascism and communism, more Catholic thinkers were responding to possible alternatives to existing structures posed by the yet undeveloped "corporativist" model in Pope Pius XI's encyclical *Quadragesimo Anno* (1931). It was a document whose fundamentals Cardinal Mooney saw as laying "the ax to the root of the evils in our capitalistic system."[34] In 1930 the administrative board of the NCWC issued a *Statement on Unemployment*, decrying "the tragedy of millions of men and women who need work" and rejecting only alms-giving, charity, as an adequate response: ". . . justice should be done." They go on to say, "this unemployment returning again to plague us after so many repetitions during the century past is a sign of deep failure in our country."[35] The economic system that tolerates or depends on such instability in the organization, distribution, and guarantee of work to provide an adequate living for families reveals a grave moral disorder not based in ignorance but in a lack of goodwill: "It is due to neglect of Christ."[36] In 1933 the statement on the *Present Crisis* picked up on other themes from Pius XI's *Quadragesimo Anno*, in particular the threat caused by anti-Christian ideologies: liberal capitalism and Leninist/Stalinist communism. A *Statement on Church and Social Order* (1940) uses the natural-law argument to defend ownership of property in language now reminiscent of *Rerum Novarum*; but in condemning the extreme concentration and control of wealth, they draw most directly from Pius XI. On the one side, the bishops in 1933 say that money has replaced the moral law and has defended:

> unrestrained individual economic freedom and the economic dictatorship that has succeeded it. That philosophy permits individuals, corporations, and nations to accumulate as much wealth as they can, according to the unfair methods of modern business, and to use such accumulated wealth as they see fit. It honors and proclaims as sov-

ereign rulers of economic empires, men who have succeeded in amassing unjustly these fabulous fortunes.[37]

These captains of industry have prevented the necessary formation of any protective organizations to ensure the production and distribution of wealth "in accordance with social justice and the interdependence of economic relations." Government is seriously hampered in its role to guard justice and the common good. Greed reigns. The "oneness and solidarity" of humanity are replaced by wealth, business, and the power bought by property as supreme ends in themselves. "Human rights must be sacrificed to those ends," under this materialist philosophy, and "humanity itself must become the mere instrument in the production of wealth." This system (liberal capitalism is not mentioned by name) "has literally taken God out of the world."[38] The themes of these passages—solidarity, human rights, the idolatry of wealth and power—could be quoted verbatim from the letters of the bishops and pope in the 1980s.

On the other hand, the letter says that the "extreme of individualism has led to the extreme of Communism." Fundamental truths about brotherhood, protests against injustice done the working classes, and the need to renounce exploitation and domination for a dedicated life of service, all language which is "distinctively Christian in origin and purport," only masks the insidious "social and religious tenets of Lenin and Stalin." This infection has a particular target in the United States: "Special efforts are being made to win the Negroes, who are the victim of injustice."[39] The basic objectives of communism remain destruction of religion, class warfare, and abolition of private property. It is significant that the bishops see liberalism as the momentum for this dialectical swing. In the final resort, liberalism and communism share a common philosophy that denies the supernatural and substitutes "a convention of man" for the "eternal law of God" as the basis of morality.

Besides the bishops, other groups of Catholic social thinkers and activists responded to this depression-era crisis. In 1935, shortly after the U.S. Supreme Court had invalidated the National Industrial Recovery Act, the social action department staff of the NCWC issued a pamphlet entitled *Organized Social Justice*, which was signed by 131 prominent Catholics and called for a constitutional amendment to empower Congress to pass emergency labor legislation.[40] They had seen in the "code authorities" of the NRA the basis for the professional/occupational group system suggested by *Quadragesimo Anno*; this, they thought, would guarantee wider participation and control of economic life while short-circuiting laissez-faire capitalism and obstructive governmental regulation. Such an occupational group system was the last viable safeguard against the social unrest which would usher in fascism or communism. They warned those who remained aloof or inactive: "To sit by with folded hands or to heed the selfish and misleading propaganda of the servitors of plutocracy, is to commit apostasy from Catholic social principles and treason against America."[41] And they saw this communitarian program as a system that would "again" become a vital component of American life and thought, because it was an expression of "fundamental democracy."

The language of this conclusion is more direct than prior or subsequent episcopal statements: "propaganda," "apostasy," and "treason" are powerful indictments. It is also interesting that the signators rhetorically emphasize the identity of this model of social reconstruction with the national ideal of democracy, and that its personalist and communitarian values are called upon "again" to characterize America. The ideas presented in Catholic social theory and expressed in the papal encyclicals are claimed to be deeply imbedded in the American national myth itself, and are not some foreign import.

The next step for some Catholics, and it was only a small step, was to argue for the legitimacy of democracy (and its economic face) within the Catholic religious tradition itself. In 1945 the latter-day adherents of the philosophy of Thomas Aquinas, Mortimer J. Adler and Walter Farrell, O.P., published "Democracy, the Best and Only Just Form of Government." This was a philosophical alternative to the customary utilitarian defense of democracy, this time from a neo-Scholastic position as the basis for further economic emancipation, democratic government, and the realization of a world community.[42] Catholicism began to be presented as not only compatible in theory with the pluralism of American social and intellectual life, but also as a valuable tool in supporting the "truth" of democracy as the only alternative to totalitarianism.

The aftermath of World War II brought prosperity to larger numbers of the working class and to the large mass of Catholics in particular. The Catholic bishops then widened their attention to urge increasingly affluent and politically powerful Catholics to reach out to the poor in American society experiencing the same kind of economic deprivation once suffered by the Catholic community. The statements of 1953 (*Statement on Man's Dignity*) and 1960 (*Statement on Personal Responsibility*) hail the "achievements of America" and align Catholicism with democratic capitalism as the best system to ensure the values of liberty (especially economic), justice, and personal responsibility.[43] The stress is on the inner, spiritual transformation that prepares and precipitates social reform. They even make the case for the connection between democracy and transcendent values by quoting from Karl Marx: "Democracy is based on the principle of the sovereign worth of the individual, which, in turn, is based on the dream of Christianity that man has an immortal soul."[44] It is only after the encyclicals and documents of Pope John XXIII, Vatican II, and Pope Paul VI that the American bishops begin to address the wider systemic poverty in the United States and the developing world, as well as the endemic problem of racism. The statements in 1966 (*Pastoral Statement on Race Relations and Poverty*) and 1970 (*Resolution on the Campaign for Human Development*) strike a new note for the bishops, moving beyond parochial concern for Catholic workers to questions about "sinful social structures": poverty and racism, and the ways the poor and minorities are kept dependent and powerless. The bishops ask how such poverty can exist amidst such great wealth and how racism can exist if there is truly equal opportunity and justice before the law. They begin, quite tentatively, to deconstruct some basic notions about the American myth.

It was in 1975 that the Catholic bishops issued *The Economy: Human Dimensions*, their most pointed moral condemnation of the "gross inequality in the distribution of material goods" since the Depression. They do not present themselves as experts in technical fiscal matters, economic theories, or political planning, but as moral judges concerned with the content and impact of economic policies. They are particularly distressed over the vast disparities of income and wealth distribution: "The top one-fifth of all families own more than three-fourths of all the privately held wealth in the United States, while over one-half of our families control less than seven percent of the wealth."[45] They summarize the social encyclicals, the documents of Vatican II, and the Synod of Bishops' statement *Justice in the World* (1971) to demonstrate the heritage of Catholic teaching that shows the interrelation of ethics and economics. This teaching, they assert, flows fundamentally from the church's commitment to human rights and human dignity. Seven principles for evaluating the economic situation and guiding policymakers and citizens are listed:

1. Economic activity must serve human needs, be governed by justice, and be enacted within the limits of morality

2. The right to share earthly goods sufficient for oneself and one's family is universal

3. A just distribution, not the sum total of goods available, is the standard of economic prosperity

4. The right to useful employment, just wages, and adequate support in case of real need is basic

5. Economic development at every level should be decided by as wide a number as possible, not just the few with economic power or the political community alone

6. There should be an equitable tax system assessed according to ability to pay

7. Government has a role to promote production of needed goods, to safeguard the rights of all citizens, and to help them find employment.

The document makes a shift back to perspectives in the 1919 Program of Social Reconstruction and the 1930 *Statement on Unemployment*. It recognizes that private self-help programs such as the newly instituted Campaign for Human Development are probably not sufficient, in the face of massive recession, to solve the problems of unemployment and underemployment, affecting even those who had achieved some level of economic prosperity.[46] Underlying the document is the uneasy question of whether the American system could really deliver on its promises.

This document, in ways not expressed until *Economic Justice for All*, articulates principles and policies that raised the ire of conservative Catholics. J. Brian Benestad has contrasted the statements of 1919 and 1975, seeing in the former an echo of the traditional teaching that society can be made just only by a return to Christian life and institutions. A personal change of heart, disciplined by training in Christian virtue, and not mere reliance on structural changes, is the only way to effect social reform. This stress on personal virtue was a central element in earlier approaches by the bishops to economic justice, but was abandoned, he notes, with the creation of the U.S. Catholic Conference in 1966.[47] Whereas the 1975 statement purported to speak on the moral, human, and social aspects of the economic crisis, it in fact endorsed partisan political programs, "such as improvement of the unemployment-compensation systems and the preservation of small family farms."[48] Such tactics leave the bishops open to charges of political interference or intrusion in affairs beyond their competence. It is the virtuous individual, shaped by the church's evangelization and education programs, who reforms society's institutions from within. The bishops, he asserts, have recently adopted, perhaps at the urging of a politically motivated staff, what has been called "a discredited liberal faith in the efficacy of policy statements," which compromises the distinctive Catholic outlook with a secular political agenda.[49] The bishops, in turn, assert that social consciousness is not a substitute, but a necessary context for the development of individual virtue, which all too often allows moral questions to be merely internalized, privatized, and then marginalized. They believe their prolife campaign shows a commitment to human dignity and values which have put them squarely in conflict with modern American culture; their consultative process belies the idea that their statements are a hodge-podge of leftist notions. The Catholic bishops are not liberal pawns.[50]

From another conservative perspective, the recent bishops' letters have evidenced a pronounced leaning toward "statism" and too little awareness of the value of private enterprise in creating jobs, wealth, demand, and abundance.[51] Schall, for example, cites the following passage from the 1975 statement to demonstrate the bishops' tendency to bypass the private-enterprise system entirely:

Fundamentally, our nation must provide jobs for those who can and should work and a decent income for those who cannot. An effective national commitment to full employment is needed to protect the basic human right to useful employment for all Americans. It ought to guarantee, through appropriate mechanisms, that no one seeking work would be denied an opportunity to earn a livelihood. Full employment is the foundation of a just economic policy.[52]

Although geared to the problems of a recession, the document fails, Schall judges, to deal with the complexities of full-employment theories, although he does not clarify why there may not be a moral basis in such a theoretical stance. On the other hand, the statement does call on both "the private and public sectors to join together to plan and provide better for our future," without merely accepting the unexamined presuppositions of the U.S. economic system. The social concerns mentioned — joblessness, housing, transportation, education, health care, and available recreation — are still issues around which hardships continue.

In many ways the most curious recent statement of the bishops has been their *Pastoral Letter on Marxist Communism* (1980), which they describe as neither a "polemical or political tract." They readily admit that this topic, the relationship of Christian faith and Marxism, "does not appear to have the urgency or interest in the United States that it has in other parts of the world."[53] They press on, they say, because of their office as pastors, to read the "signs of the times," because so many in the wider world are directly affected by Marxism and because it preoccupies "a sizable portion of the American intellectual community." Their last point seems particularly vague and overblown, considering the general ignorance and aversion within the American academy to serious Marxist studies.

One other point of their rationale is particularly intriguing. While acknowledging "the horrendous violations of human rights perpetrated in the name of communism," the letter says that Marxism "challenges the content and practice of our faith." Note that there is a distancing introduced between the intellectual, moral, and political content of Marxism and what is actually done "in the name of" communism. And the challenge to the "content and practice" of Christianity may be focused on just the social theory and activity of the Catholic community, or implicitly on the entire Western democratic, political, and economic system. The letter on communism, then, may be an indirect statement about capitalism. It also distinguishes between the typical features of crude communism — atheism, materialism, class warfare — and the more humanistic Marxist aspirations to justice and the elimination of social and economic exploitation. Enrico Berlinguer and George Marchais, the secretaries respectively of the Italian and the French Communist parties in the 1970s, Roger Garaudy, Ernst Bloch, Hannah Arendt, Leszek Kolakowski, and Eric Weil are all cited as thinkers who provide a more accurate picture of Marxian ideals to an American public accustomed to demonic stereotypes. Indeed, the political casting of one system or people as a permanent enemy seems to the bishops as inhumane as the theory of unmitigated class struggle to achieve social harmony. The letter, however, adopts a more realistic than expected appraisal of the nature and function of the notion of class struggle.

In refusing to accept class war as the only possible means for achieving social justice the Christian does not deny the all too real existence of those actual class antagonisms that result from both a blatantly unequal distribution of material possessions and a tenacious, often violent defense by the possessing classes of their privileged position. As the Roman pontiffs have repeatedly emphasized in their recent encyclicals, and as accepted Catholic morality has always taught, whenever a person or a group is deprived of their basic necessities, expropriation is justified. In such an extreme case the poor have not chosen social warfare: it is imposed upon them by the injustices of the possessors. Yet even then there is no sufficient ground to consider all those who belong to the ruling class as their irreconcilable enemies.[54]

While admitting limits to efforts by the oppressed to redress grievances, it is insisted that limits do not preclude Christians "from *effectively* participating in the struggle for social justice." This language of legitimate struggle and even social warfare is very recent and uncharacteristic of the U.S. bishops. One should also note that in this portion of the letter they are discussing Latin America. It is not clear if they might view their own regional situation as having come close to legitimating such class antagonism. At any rate, they reject the Marxian idea that no normative order exists beyond the one created through productive activity or revolutionary political action. The kingdom of God is the ideal that judges every earthly kingdom.

The U.S. bishops see the critical importance of East-West dialogue, especially in the areas of the nuclear arms race and the mutual responsibility of East and West to meet the dire needs of the poor in the southern hemisphere, issues raised by Paul VI in *Populorum Progressio* (1967) and later in John Paul II's *Sollicitudo Rei Socialis* (1987). In response to these twin responsibilities, North American Catholics are asked to explore solutions realistically in cooperative ventures with Marxist regimes, but with the following guidelines:

In engaging in practical and humanitarian dialogue two points require their serious attention. First, in judging social and political situations in other parts of the world they should avoid identifying the essential principles of the Christian doctrine of society with our own socioeconomic structures, and even more, with the theories of economic liberalism. In defending those structures or theories as the only acceptable ones to the Christian, they impose them in cases where they have, at best, a limited application and could, at worst, lead to grave social injustice. Indeed, Catholics should remain aware of the very severe judgment which the Roman pontiffs and various European hierarchies have passed on unrestricted economic liberalism.[55]

Indeed, it would have come as a surprise to most U.S. Catholics that the popes or bishops had done anything except "christen" capitalist economics, let alone pronounce a "severe judgment." It had not been a customary element in the catechisms of the American Catholic community. While praising historic acts of charity by North American Catholics toward the poor, the letter goes on to note the absence of a sense of "the deeper requirements of justice which touch the very political and economic structures through which the United States relates to the developing world."[56] The language of structures of justice was also relatively new to American Catholics, having been schooled in their ideas of individual acts of personal charity or personal sin. And the letter targets the obsessive consumerism, disproportionate claim on the earth's resources, and wasteful use of goods that seem to characterize the American life-style and undercut our national credibility in dealing with world poverty: "It is not merely envy but rightful indignation about our spending habits that accounts for the little friendship we generally receive from the poorer nations."[57] The story has been published that two French priests, classmates of Auxiliary Bishop Peter Rosazza of Hartford, mystified as to what prompted the American bishops to write on Marxism, asked him why there was no pastoral letter on capitalism.[58] Rosazza's subsequent proposal to the NCCB was approved in 1980, but the objective was shifted to a practical analysis of the current U.S. economy, not capitalism as a system. At no time have the American bishops explored the meaning of this major political, economic, and cultural force. The little they present is borrowed from the patchwork of papal pronouncements on capitalism and liberalism.

HIDDEN TRADITIONS AND LOST CRITICAL VOICES

Criticisms of the Bishops' Letter from the conservative side have argued that its descriptions of contemporary America and its public-policy recommendations are left-wing. Or they see the letter as little more than a manifesto of the "great society" at prayer. Michael Novak, the theological adviser to the conservative lay commission's report, *Toward the Future*, which criticized the bishops' politics, economics, and biblical theology, pointed, as confirmation of this, to the works cited in the pastoral letter's footnotes. He found that the ratio in the second draft was about nine-to-one in favor of the "Left and far Left."[59] This accusation is continued concerning the final draft, wherein only a handful of "moderate or conservative" writers are cited, for example: Milton Friedman, Charles Murray, Peter Berger, Martin Anderson, and Jack Meyer, whereas a host of liberal apologists are sampled: Gar Alperovitz, Charles Lindblom, Derek Shearer, Michael Harrington, Sheldon Danzinger, Peter Gottschalk, Robert Kuttner, Lester Thurow, Isabel Sawhill, and Arthur Okun, to name but a few.[60]

The pastoral letter was unusual in having included such extensive footnoting, leading some to ask whether the bishops had actually read the bulk of the material cited. On the other hand, one should look at the way Novak used language to describe the different categories of footnotes; he divides them between their minority of "moderate" or "conservative" writers and the mass of those on the "Left" or "far Left". Apparently the capitals indicate an ideological stance, whereas the lowercase moderates and conservatives voice an objective and realistic view of America. He does not include the designations of "far-Right" or "reactionary," with which some of the conservatives cited might be labeled.

Other conservative critics are not convinced that it is the bishops themselves who have coded this liberal conspiracy into the footnotes, which are, on the whole, definitely more progressive than the text itself. These critics are convinced that it was the liberal bias of the USCC staff, especially chief assistant Father J. Bryan Hehir, that "cooked" the research and expert resources used and that this "new class," governed by a leftist agenda and a "preferential option for the *State*" has damaged the authority and reception of the letter.[61]

What is not noted is how much the Bishops' Letter uses documentation from published government sources about poverty, unemployment, and the financial distress of different sectors in the American economy. If there is an unrealistic description given, then the conservatives need to show where the Congressional Budget Office, the U.S. Office of Management and Budget, the U.S. Congress Joint Economic Committee, and the Bureau of Labor Statistics are wrong and/or biased. Of course on political grounds, some conservatives are convinced of exactly that. (*See* chapter two for a more extensive development of the conservative criticisms of the Bishops' Letter.)

Perhaps the most radical reference in the footnotes is the one to E. F. Schumacher's counterculture book, the cult classic *Small Is Beautiful: Economics As If People Mattered*.[62] Using a comparison with "Buddhist economics," Schumacher gives a radical critique of the assumptions and values underlying capitalist culture and modern technology. The pastoral letter uses it only in a discussion of appropriate small-scale technologies in developing countries, but its application of simplicity of life-style, democratic planning, and ecological sensitivity, comprising a kind of civic asceticism or political spirituality, if implemented in the United States, would require fundamental restructuring. Schumacher's thought is linked to the utopian and communitarian experiments in the historic American experience that the pastoral letter passes over altogether; this serious omission can be seen as a further work of the deradicalized politics of the letter.

On the other hand, some recent readers have found in their interpretations of the language of the letter a theoretical push toward more extensive social action going beyond ameliorative reform. The bishops do, after all, base their call to conversion on the "radical command" of Jesus to love one's neighbor, which must transform every aspect of one's life, the personal and the public. There is such a disjunction, these critics find, between the description of poverty in America and the policies of reform suggested that the letter "deconstructs" itself.[63] The critical dissonance between the radical and prophetic rhetoric of the letter and the gradualist strategies is so great that it can be assumed the bishops realized their reformist policies were inadequate to the task.

> For instance, the Bishops speak of the need for a new political will and criticize both America's primitive attitude toward the poor and its excessive consumerism. The Bishops, no matter what their intentional strategy of the letter, talk not only in the language of mere correction, but also in the rhetoric of struggle, challenge, crisis, and conversion. Thus, language, facts, and the reading of tradition all introduce a far more critical meaning into the option for the poor — a position of critique and transformation of the values, consciousness, and social practices of our country.[64]

But whether the economy can expand infinitely to provide "meaningful" labor and whether modern bourgeois values can ever be converted to an option for the poor are questions that still leave grounds to criticize the bishops' rhetoric, as well as their strategies. Others see a more obvious call for social reconstruction, but fault the bishops for an "all or nothing" attitude which would either junk the whole capitalist system, successes as well as failures, or restrict action to charitable responses to problems, a "band-aid" approach that some have associated with the simple and personal charity of Mother Teresa of Calcutta, whose Missionaries of Charity also minister in the United States. Stuart Speiser, while arguing that the bishops have "no clear analysis" of the problems in American political economy, has observed that the calls for democratic participation and ownership of capital (including the model of universal stock options he has promoted) would certainly require reconstruction.[65] The bishops have seemed shy in talking about such radical change, and even avoided it in describing their vision of the "American Experiment" as one which must be built on "economic democracy," a concept used in testimony by Gar Alperovitz and contained in the footnoted material by Carnoy, Shearer, and Dahl. The term appeared in the first draft, but was excised in the final version, replaced by the circuitous phase, "a new experiment in bringing democratic ideals to economic life."[66] In a more recent evaluation, Arthur Jones has argued that most middle-class American Catholics do not recognize themselves as addressed by the letter. Instead, they are looking for the church to provide guidance on an economic spirituality of the laity, incorporating the importance of work, an emphasis on individual integrity and agency, and an appreciation of the spirit of self-reliance and entrepreneurial optimism.[67] American Catholics have prospered economically and from Jones's perspective are not interested in either a coded or direct call for social reconstruction, although remaining open to a possible reformist program that will face the complex moral issues present in wealth creation.

The bishops say that they build on the past work of their own bishops' conference, especially the 1919 program, papal teachings, and contributions from "the Catholic, Protestant, and Jewish communities, in academics, business or political life, and . . . different economic backgrounds."[68] While extensive use is made of papal documents, little is cited in a substantive way from the many previous letters by the bishops; they are largely silent about their own often critical tradition of social teaching. And there is no real engagement or dialogue with Protestant and Jewish positions in the text itself; the footnotes, however, are decidedly ecumenical.[69] Some have found it strange, then, that the letter does not even mention the lay commission's *Toward the Future*, issued as a preemptive first strike by conservative Catholics who were bellicose over an earlier pastoral letter decrying the nuclear-arms race and Cold War policy: *The Challenge of Peace: God's Promise and Our Response* (1983).[70]

The most striking omission is the absence of any mention of the long and noble tradition of more radical Catholic representatives. These figures and movements constitute some of the most original and theologically sophisticated contributions to the Catholic tradition. Their trenchant denunciations of abuses within the American system kept alive a distinctly religious moral vision, often at times when the episcopal leadership was silent or when the Catholic community was most carried away by popular nationalism. This liberal or radical Catholicism maintained the constructive dialectical relationship between being Catholic and being American.[71] Even more remarkably, many of these figures joined together conservative stands on doctrinal issues with progressive stands on social affairs. Monsignor Ligutti's Catholic Rural Life Conference, the Catholic Worker's "green revolution," and the forms of grangerism practiced by the Central Verein (a midwest German-Catholic movement) are some of these groups, along with numerous communitarian experiments: Grail Farm, Peter Maurin Farm, Mary Farm, Friendship House, Joe Hill House, Caritas House, Siloe House, Emmaus House, Il Poverello House, Fides House, and the Catholic Worker Houses of Hospitality which continue today.[72] The letter does not refer to a number of figures who actively sought to relate Catholic social teaching to the American ethos. Many of their concerns continue to be significant and are reflected in the issues treated in *Economic Justice for All*. The omission deprives contemporary American Catholics of a link to their past, to the developing insights of their faith community, and to their own historic identity. This radical Catholic tradition is a silent footnote in the pastoral letter.

CHARACTERISTICS: A NEW AMERICAN EXPERIMENT

Arthur Schlesinger, an adviser to President John F. Kennedy and a noted liberal historian, has remarked that "anti-Catholicism is the anti-semitism of American intellectuals." Prejudice against Catholics is a deep and recurrent phenomenon in U.S. society. Despite demographic shifts which have left the Catholic Church the largest single Christian denomination in America, economic advantages which have produced some of the highest per capita wealth of any religious group, and political openings since the 1960s which have meant elections or appointments of Catholics to the highest offices in the executive, legislative, and judicial branches of government, something of a second-class attitude still seems to pervade American Catholicism. Perhaps the immigrant and ethnic roots of this diverse community still shape this image, especially with the latest influx of Hispanics.

As late as the 1960s it was seriously asked whether a politician who was Catholic could in conscience defend the civil liberties guaranteed by the American Constitution. Ironically similar questions are now being asked of Catholic politicians by conservative elements of their own church, who oppose some of those liberties. Whatever the causes for the uneasy mindset about the relation of the American ethos to Catholicism, it is important to note the special care taken in the Bishops' Letter to claim that their principles and policies are in fundamental agreement with basic American ideals of "justice for all" in the social, political, and economic arenas. The question, however, is whether this understandable episcopal pledge of allegiance to "Americanism" in any way moderates or dilutes the prophetic challenge they give for the creation of a new "moral wisdom."

This Americanism can be seen either as a cultural or an intellectual form of nationalism.[73] Behind it lies another complex set of often-opposed traditions presenting different models for the American church. There was an attempt to translate Catholicism into the American idiom, the dream of the first bishop, John Carroll, representing that Old English element of the new American church that sought the evolution of vernacular Catholicism into something which in piety, practice, and political structure would draw from and reflect the American experience. This model dissolved as tidal waves of ethnic immigrants hit the shores of the United States and Rome continued to keep tight control, still regarding America as a mission land until well into the early twentieth century.

Then an attempt was made to homogenize Catholicism and Americanism, to wrap the church in the flag and declare that America filled a providential role in human history. This was a form of civic messianism, emphasizing America's religious role, whether in throwing off the "serpent" of racism, however belatedly, or later defending christendom against atheistic communism in the crusade preached by Cardinal Francis Spellman of New York and TV-priest Bishop Fulton J. Sheen. In the nineteenth century, solid Republican John Ireland, Archbishop of St. Paul, sanctioned this rhetoric in a passage employed by *Toward the Future* to underscore the religious legitimacy of the American dream.

We cannot but believe that a singular mission is assigned to America, glorious for itself and beneficent to the whole race, the mission of bringing about a new social and political order, based more than any other upon the common brotherhood of man, and more than any other securing to the multitude of the people social happiness and equality of rights. With our hopes are bound up the hopes of the millions of the earth.[74]

Ireland and the later lay report convey the sense that America constitutes a new Eden, where the sins of the Old World are cast off and the grace-filled element of creativity, the power to create new ideas, institutions, and social relationships, has untrammeled room to play. The lay report is far more generous than the Bishops' Letter with references to historic Catholic leaders and authors in America besides Ireland, such as John Lee Carroll of Maryland, Archbishop John Hughes of New York, Orestes Brownson, Bishop John Lancaster Spalding of Peoria, and the Catholic aristocrat Alexis de Tocqueville, who saw in the new republic hopeful signs and original solutions to the social and economic distress of the Old World. The position of the lay report is basically that these earlier Catholic commentators saw better the intrinsic identity of revealed doctrinal points and American economic and political habits which have been misunderstood and derided. Rather than rugged individualism, cut-throat competition, and socially destructive self-interest, the *real* American habits are supported by and identical with the morally centered values of free association, cooperation, and self-interest in terms of mutual responsibility; self-love is the gospel standard for love of the neighbor.[75] This school of thought is also reflected in those Catholic writers who identify the positions advocated in the papal encyclicals as having been fully realized in the American economy, or who see "John Ireland's vision" as the fundamental guide for renewal of both the church and the political order in the United States.[76]

Finally, a national pattern of Americanism can be seen in the attempt to demonstrate the compatibility of the natural-law tradition of the common good with the secular natural-rights position of political liberalism and the guarantee of individual rights. In the political arena, the work of Monsignor John Ryan can be viewed under this heading. Also, the social theory of John Courtney Murray, S.J., the American architect of Vatican II's declaration on religious freedom, has been cited by various factions as an important model in forging a public philosophy in a pluralistic culture.[77] Ryan and Murray both worked out plausible connections between the civic republican tradition and natural-law teaching without much reference to the biblical tradition. They did not, however, as later imitators have often done, merely lump the different traditions together. They did not think that an artificial hybrid, a univocal language and vision of the human good, was either true to the disparate traditions or productive in clarifying the rational, rather than emotive, elements of national debate on social issues. Murray himself distinguished between the common good of society—the material and spiritual dimensions that all individuals and communities are morally obligated to seek and over which government has no legitimate control—over against the narrower juridical notion of public order, which maintains justice, peace, decent public behavior, and prosperity, the factors that make up a free society and constitutional government. Economic resources are due to people by right as part of public order, not simply as a desired element of the common good, and limited government action in distributing economic necessities beyond the means of private groups is legitimate.[78] It is just such an understanding of Murray and Leo XIII that conservative Catholics such as Novak cannot see or accept.

The question not broached in any of these models of Americanism is whether something critically valuable is lost in the process. In constructing a "moral-vision," especially one which demands in an "option for the poor" that society be examined from their perspective, the element of being an "outsider," either not identified with or even antagonistic toward the perspective and power of the status quo, may function as a vital, dynamic element. To be "in the world, but not of the world" continues to define the moral stance in the Christian tradition; being an "alien in an alien land" may give a better, at least different, view of how the powerless and marginalized live. Catholicism's quest for its American identity might best be served not by White House prayer breakfasts but as a loyal opposition.

The pastoral letter utilizes a rhetorical line which appears to be drawn from the model that tends to identify Americanism and Catholicism in a one-to-one correspondence. In the section "Why We Write," the bishops say that they do not "seek . . . to make some political or ideological point but to lift up the human and ethical dimensions of economic life, aspects too often neglected in public discussion."[79] The resources for this task are the "dual heritage of Catholic social teaching and traditional American values." The twin components of this heritage seem to have equal weight, at least verbally. This passage is characteristic of the historical Americanism employed by the bishops. They distinguish, as moral teachers, between the "human and ethical dimensions" of the economy and the "political or ideological," as if principles could always be neatly separated from politics. They do not want to be seen as religious hierarchs voicing a particular political program. What they really should say is that they wish to avoid endorsement of a particular political party. The ethical program they offer is in itself already "political or ideological," because it urges action in the political (public) arena, based on ideological premises, its principles, such as the "option for the poor." At one level it falls into the same kind of dualism, separation of the worlds of matter (the political realm) and spirit (the religious realm), that it had previously condemned.

The letter goes on to describe the American values the bishops hold:

As *Americans*, we are grateful for the gift of freedom and committed to the dream of "liberty and justice for all." This nation, blessed with extraordinary resources, has provided an unprecedented standard of

living for millions of people. We are proud of the strength, productivity, and creativity of our economy, but we also remember those who
have been left behind in our progress. We believe that we honor our
history best by working for the day when all our sisters and brothers
share adequately in the American dream.[80]

It is hard to imagine that any other mainline Christian church in America
would feel compelled to reiterate that their leaders were writing a moral
statement "as *Americans*." This passage that affirms their patriotic identity
is an unmodified paean to American economic prosperity, derived from a
system that draws on resources and treats people in an unproblematic way.
At worst some "have been left behind in our progress," but the day is
possible when these too will "share adequately." It is only the next paragraph that admits that not all enjoy "the American dream." The bishops
flatly state that they have the experience to "manage institutions, balance
budgets, meet payrolls."[81] Their credentials as those who proclaim the gospel need further support to show they are practical money managers in the
real world of finance, not just fuzzy religionists. But the passage uses a
vocabulary that intensifies the sense of human crisis: hurts, pain, living on
the edge, hunger, injustice, suffering, despair. This is quickly balanced in
the next paragraph by a very different vocabulary: decency, generosity
(twice), vulnerability, a better future, faith, goodwill, hope. Whatever the
problems and moral prescriptions the bishops state, at least rhetorically
things are on the whole right with America; there is no verbal or conceptual
bridge between the languages of despair and hope, injustice and goodwill.
It is as if two dimensions of American life co-existed simultaneously, but
without contact or interconnection.

In the first chapter, the bishops go on to discuss the United States as
"among the most economically powerful nations on earth." In its brief
history it has provided an unprecedented standard of living, created productive jobs for millions of immigrants, allowed broadened freedoms for
them, improved the quality of life for their families; and in turn the nation
has been built up by their efforts. Giving the religious context for this, the
letter says: "Those who came to this country from other lands often understood their new lives in the light of biblical faith. They thought of themselves
as entering a promised land of political freedom and economic opportunity."[82]

The phrase "a promised land" is used straightforwardly, without irony.
The bishops have adopted here the biblical symbols that are part of the
American imaginative myth: the "errand into the wilderness" of the Pil-
grims and Puritans, a limited focus on America's English-speaking heritage,
and the venerable "city on a hill" image that has recurred in the political
propaganda of the 1980s. The letter does not recognize the cognitive dissonance of identifying America simultaneously as one of the "most . . .
powerful nations" and as the latter-day embodiment of the tribes of ancient

Israel in their desert exile, entering the struggle in Canaan, that paradoxical terrain of "milk and honey" and protracted warfare. It is one thing for the *Mayflower* settlers to identify with that myth, or boatloads of later immigrants to reinterpret it in their own experience; it is something else for the United States as a world power to think of itself in those embattled images as a "chosen people." It would be more accurate now to apply the images of Egypt, Assyria, and Rome, those world powers that the Bible also depicts.

The letter does recall this common history from another perspective, one that elicits "sober humility." It catalogs the injustices to Native Americans, the "blood of revolution" that produced national independence, slavery and civil war, women's suffrage, legal protection of workers, child-labor laws, the Great Depression, and the Civil Rights movement "of the 1960s." It says that they "all involved a sustained struggle to transform the political and economic institutions of the nation."[83] While using the vocabulary of conflict, violence, and suffering, there is no explanation of why that struggle was needed, what the factors were in political/economic life that required reform, or whether those conditions continue today. After describing the balance needed in the United States system between market freedom and fundamental human rights, the letter says that this "conviction has prompted positive steps to modify the operation of the market" and that unions help "resist exploitation" in this "creative struggle."[84] Somewhere in this passage lies hidden the difficult, often bloody history of American labor: the Knights of Labor, Molly Maguires, Wobblies, Pinkertons, sweatshops, massacres, and union-busting attempts that continue down to the 1980s. The rhetorical Americanism practiced by the bishops masks or denies any sense of actual confrontation of conflicting interests. For instance, while defending the right of workers to strike, they do not define how this relates to the idea of solidarity and love of neighbor. A motive could be their fear of social unrest and a disrupted civil order, since "great disparities lead to deep social divisions and conflict."[85] This can be read as either a liberal or conservative concern. Their expectation is that those "ostensibly privileged" will see the self-advantage of forming a coalition with the poor when more and more of the middle-class, those who once benefited from the system, recognize the "inner" impoverishment brought by the competitive economy and an actual lowering in the quality of life for them. The bishops do not seem to recognize the ingredient of actual conflict in American history that produced needed reforms and consolidated political and economic rights.[86]

Leonardo and Clodovis Boff and other Latin American liberation theologians have criticized the bishops for this ahistorical call to the moral reform of the political system. The Boff brothers also see it as unbiblical, since the scriptural notion of "option for the poor" is unavoidably adversarial. There is a real conflict of "powers," since the poor are both spiritually and politically oppressed and need liberation from those enslaving structures.[87] One cannot understand ancient Israel's myth of the Exodus without also discussing the bondage of building the Egyptian "treasure cities," Pharaoh, the ten plagues, and the deliverance from the chariots and riders.

As in *Toward the Future,* the bishops quote from Abraham Lincoln's Gettysburg Address as representative of moral reflection applied to society undergoing crisis. It is a reaffirmation symbolically of their identification with the martyred president who embodied a vision of national unity, government by and for the people, and the "unfinished work" to achieve freedom and justice for all, which the bishops adopt as their "unfinished business." Again, the letter seeks to create a noncontroversial vocabulary of words and images upon which to base a moral consensus about a form of community built on "dignity, solidarity, and justice." Lincoln is used as a public icon of those values. But again there is no connection made to the Civil War. And no mention is made of the constitutional definition of African-Americans in bondage that denied basic human rights and dignity; slavery is only mentioned once as having "stained the commercial life." They do not cite Lincoln's more darkly brooding theological reflection, his later sense of ambiguity in citing the Bible as the basis for specific political action, or his call, the last in American civic life, for a National Day of Prayer *and Humiliation* (italics added).

That War between the States also worked a powerful summons to follow Jesus as a political liberator, as Jaroslav Pelikan's classic study of images of Christ shows.[88] Julia Ward Howe's romantic and republican imagery of Jesus in "The Battle Hymn of the Republic" (1862) depicts how the "terrible, swift sword" has been unleashed to correct injustice and urge a national sacrifice, amending the past and transfiguring America: "As he died to make men holy, let us die to make men free,/While God is marching on."[89] While these lyrics are popular in contemporary liturgies in Catholic parishes, no link is made between the piety of hymnody and the ongoing militant action required for social reform. Instead, the bishops, in approving eucharistic prayers for civil holidays, affirm the undifferentiated identity between the American nation and the biblical "people of God."

> It happened to our fathers, who came to this land as if out of the desert into a place of promise and hope. It happens to us still, in our time, as you lead all men through your church to the blessed vision of peace.[90]

In the prayers for Thanksgiving and Independence Day, reference is made to a "task" and "promise" ahead, but fundamentally the message of Jesus already "took form in the vision of our fathers/as they fashioned a nation." The moral vision the bishops call for is apparently the American dream; in this they are much more like the conservative lay report than the latter realizes.

Recently there has been widespread interest in the possibility of reviving a more communitarian ethos for American society as a remedy to the rampant sense of fragmentation, atomism, and alienation, to move beyond individualism to humanitarian commitment.[91] It has been suggested that the possibility of genuine moral discourse in America depends on the will and ability to find a common moral vocabulary. Examples of successful constructs of moral discourse have referred to Walter Rauschenbusch and the "Social Gospel," Reinhold Niebuhr and "Christian Realism," and Martin Luther King, Jr., and the civil-rights movement as those who appealed to the nation and affected the political agenda "by combining biblical and republican themes in a way that included, but transformed, the culture of individualism."[92]

The authors of *Habits of the Heart* find themselves in sympathy with the purposes of *Economic Justice for All*, seeing social reconstruction possible only on the basis of changed "habits of the heart," and have included a portion of the Bishops' Letter in their companion anthology.[93] Real influence, some think, may still be exerted by drawing on the residue of moral language shaped by the repeated biblical texts that permeate our cultural imagination in art, music, and story. Using this material would fulfill the church's magisterial and prophetic role in the language of proclamation and denunciation and also provide the institutional structure for a new consciousness (creating a new moral imperative and mythic charter for change), the promotion of an empowered and participatory solidarity, and a model of relations and structures as alternatives to contemporary secular ones—ideas as old in U.S. history as the Plymouth Plantation, the Iroquois Confederacy, and the ideal of the "commonwealth."[94] In spite of this communitarian legacy, it is necessary to recall that the cultural narratives that have shaped America's internal and external images have not only been based on the Bible. Equally powerful are the images that prop up the American "gospel of success," the Horatio Alger tales of class deference and social mobility, the sovereignty of the individual where "Every man's a king," and the sense of the God-anointed global mission of America. These modern myths of industrial society are at the core of the legitimation of increased material production and use of resources, capitalist accumulation, and autonomous consumption for personal pleasure.[95] Coupled with this challenge is the one made to the bishops to get their own house in order first, in terms of economic fairness and democratic participation; the prophet's words are a judgment on the messenger as well as the community.[96] Whatever track this search for a moral language to express a vision for American economic life may take in the future, the bishops' statement that "no one may claim the name Christian and be comfortable in the face of the hunger, homelessness, insecurity, and injustice found in this country and the world" is already the framework for politically broad-based consensus, however much policies may vary.[97]

CONCLUSION

Economic Justice for All joins a long and distinguished tradition of statements on social issues by the American bishops. As with other documents from regional episcopal conferences, it reflects issues and principles previously set out in a series of modern papal encyclicals, several of the most challenging of which were penned by pre-Vatican II Italian pontiffs usually regarded as archconservatives. The twin tradition of episcopal and papal letters has developed in situations marked by social and economic crisis, often cited as providing the opportune moment for these moral pronouncements. If these writings can be called prophetic, they are prophecies voiced when the public order has been or may be disturbed, according to the clerical monitors. Overall the bishops' letters defend the role of the church in posing moral questions to political and economic situations, either articulating the more general defense of human dignity and social rights, or voicing specific recommendations for full employment, worker ownership of capital, and copartnership in economic planning. They consistently reject the idea of labor as a mere instrument of production. Like the papal pronouncements, they decry various, somewhat stereotyped ideologies — communism, socialism, fascism, or extreme liberal capitalism — but do not fully define the dangerous elements, beyond materialism, individualism, consumerism, and collectivism, that distort, they contend, the true Christian and human sense of personhood and community. They accept a limited but necessary role of the state. Under the banner of solidarity, a basic communitarian attitude, they renounce self-interested individualism for the common good, ruthless competition for reasonable state regulation, class conflict for copartnership, and monopoly/plutocracy/economic elites for democratic participation. They are nonconfrontational in their critiques of the prevailing system.

The 1986 letter is not as far-reaching as those of 1919 or the 1930s in calls for basic restructuring; war and depression seem to trigger the more radical perspective. In the 1950s and early 1960s, the letters stressed more the ideas of personal responsibility, sin, and virtue, whereas later documents, reflecting a shift in attitude after Vatican II, began to experiment with the language of social responsibility and structural sin. The five post-World War II letters omit the traditional natural-law position; inclusion of biblical material becomes more important. The selectivity and editorial cropping of those biblical citations seem to constitute a definite, if unconscious, principle of interpretation tailored to a modern American use of the Bible, as we shall examine in chapter six. They do not exploit the rhetorical possibilities of the passages cited. The biblical material seems to be more a chain of proof texts than part of a consistent scripturally based theology. Most of the letters, except for the one in 1933 and those in the 1980s, do not present a visible theological program at all.

The most recent letter is also remarkable for its silences. Apart from some spare references in two footnotes to the social teachings of the early church, there is no consistent presentation of the sayings of the church Fathers, crucial American Catholic theorists, both radical and conservative, the ongoing traditions in the Protestant, Jewish, and Muslim communities discussing social justice today, or even their own bishops' conference, going back to 1919. There seems to be a kind of amnesia about those earlier declarations, apart from passing references. While there are brief citations, there is no engagement in dialogue with the valuable episcopal pronouncements from Canada and Latin America. Perhaps on the occasion of the fifth centenary of the expedition of Columbus and the sobering reflection on the historical dual process of colonization and Christianization, there may be an opportunity, when CELAM meets at Santo Domingo for its next general conference, for the bishops of the Western hemisphere as a whole to gather and discuss the interdependent future of their region. At that time there may also be comments in response to the hundredth anniversary of papal teachings on social and economic issues. This influential papal legacy is the topic of discussion in chapter five.

2

CONSERVATIVE CRITIQUE OF THE BISHOPS' LETTER: ASSAULT ON THE WELFARE STATE

INTRODUCTION

Shortly before the release of the second draft of the American Catholic Bishops' Letter on social justice and the economy in November of 1984, a lay commission consisting of conservative social theorists, economists, and theologians issued its own separate response entitled *Toward the Future: Catholic Social Thought and the U.S. Economy*. Their purpose was to criticize those areas within the Bishops' Letter where they believed the bishops had inappropriately applied Catholic moral principles and social teachings to American political economy. They were specifically critical of certain impractical policy recommendations on the problems of poverty, unemployment, and lack of democratic participation in the economy. For the conservatives, the Bible represents a universal statement on Christian moral principles that transcends history and social relationships. It does not, therefore, offer guidance toward the restructuring of social institutions according to those principles.

It is this relationship between Scripture and church teachings, on the one hand, and concrete social policy, on the other, that is, between ethics and political economy, which the conservatives found most problematic in the Bishops' Letter. In an attempt to overcome real differences between the two economic statements, there is a clear effort on the part of the lay commission to detail the philosophical and theological continuity between the moral principles of the bishops and those of the conservative lay community. In spite of this, however, there does appear to be fundamental differences regarding their definitions of human dignity, creativity, freedom, participation, and human rights. Even within its analysis of political economy itself, the lay report emphasized the issues of production, invention, competition, and the creation of material wealth within the market, whereas the bishops stressed those of just distribution, inequality of income, wealth and power relations, and the common good of the whole community.

Although the lay commission attempted to ground the common foundations of the two documents and de-emphasize any fundamental differences between them, the conservatives defined the above categories within the framework of liberal market economies, while the bishops remained suspicious of the structures of American political economy. These real differences make a comparison of the two documents unusually instructive about the contradictory assumptions and values of the two statements and their two distinctive approaches to theological and political ideology. What makes it even more interesting is that the discussions between them cannot be broken down into a simple conservative-liberal dichotomy. In both perspectives, their moral ideals push against their views of history and society. They both theorize about American society in ways that reveal profound inconsistencies of thought: joining inconsistent theoretical positions, dissatisfactions with the present economic and political system, moral and political insights that push beyond the present set of institutions to incompatible new visions of the future, and ultimately incompatibilities between liberalism (market rationality) and democracy.

The lay commission report is divided into three parts, paralleling somewhat the Bishops' Letter. Part one deals with an analysis of the moral principles underlying their interpretation of Catholic social thought and the importance, for Catholicism, of the normative values of political economy in American society. The three key elements of its moral philosophy are found in Catholic social teachings, American views on social justice and the common good, and the new principles of American neoclassical economics.

Part two examines the normative principles of political economy and their relation to biblical and papal traditions, with special emphasis on a theology of economics that integrates creativity, liberty, and entrepreneurship. Here they connect the ideas of divine and human creativity from Genesis with the development of entrepreneurial skills, the implementation of profit incentives, the imaginative accumulation of private property, and the drive for business success in advanced industrial society.

Part three analyzes specific American social problems, which include: dysfunctions within the family, the existence of poverty and welfare, the need for an expanding economy and the creation of new jobs, the furtherance of free trade and global interdependence, and the examination of rationality and planning of social cooperation in the market. The real distinctions between these two statements on justice and the economy represent profound differences in their interpretations of both the moral principles of Catholicism and the relationship between ethics and political economy. As in the case of the bishops, the lay commission wishes to avoid the extremes of both individualism and collectivism, but unlike the bishops, there is no recognition of a conflict between their own moral principles and the structures of American society.

One reason for this is that the lay commission includes within its set of moral principles its views of the complementary relation of church ethics and the American economy; it is here that they emphasize creativity, invention, and productivity, along with the political liberties found in the ideals of the founding fathers and the Constitution. Thus any possible differences between moral principles and political economy are negated immediately by including the present values and structures of political economy into their perception of the Catholic legacy. This synthesis of Catholic social theory and the American experiment unconsciously integrates both ethics and programmatic solutions in an a priori fashion. This is the very thing they accused the bishops of doing in their letter: "Christian Scripture does not offer programmatic guidance for the concrete institutions of political economy."[1] By assuming a close connection between the rationality of the market and logic of moral principles, one can say that policy recommendations are actually included, if only unconsciously, in the very definition of their understanding of ethics. Thus this chapter will critically examine the conservative criticisms of the Bishops' Letter.

CONSERVATIVE REDEFINITION OF SOCIAL JUSTICE

The lay commission begins to attempt to establish a common ground with the Bishops' Letter by initially agreeing with the letter's three basic principles underlying Catholic social teaching: the dignity and uniqueness of each human person, the social nature of human life, and the principle of subsidiarity.[2] To further justify these common foundations, they quote from the papal encyclicals *Pacem in Terris, Mater et Magistra*, and *Quadragesimo Anno*. While the bishops spent their time examining the philosophical and theological foundations of these principles, along with their implications, the lay commission set itself the task of immediately incorporating them into the framework of their analysis of American political economy. Thus the ethical principles, for the bishops, were to be used as moral guidelines for the normative evaluation and critique of the American economy. Social ethics was to define moral values from within the ethical traditions of Western society and juxtapose them to the historical structures of political economy: "How we organize our society — directly affects human dignity and the capacity of individuals to grow in community."[3] For the lay commission, however, the consideration of moral values had a different purpose. Moral values were, from the very beginning of their report, to be used for the legitimation and rationalization of American capitalism.

As they interpret the nineteenth-century writings of Archbishop John Ireland and Bishop John Lancaster Spalding and the twentieth-century French theologian/philosopher Jacques Maritain, the lay commission makes the concept of human dignity synonymous with and reducible to individual rights, social justice reducible to political pluralism, and the principle of subsidiarity reducible to decentralized decisions within a market economy. This form of economic reductionism of moral principles to market rationality distorts both the traditional content of these principles and their applicability to the structures of American political economy.

The three fundamental principles of Catholic social thought — the dignity of the human person, the social nature of all human life, and the principle of subsidiarity — have correlatives in the fundamental American conception of the unalienable rights inhering in every single person, in the fundamental principle of "the consent of the governed," in the American conception of covenant and compact, in the American preference for decision making as close to the affected decision makers as possible, and in the principle of federalism.[4]

The real question, then, is whether definitions and clarifications of the basic moral principles given by both groups are compatible with each other or contradictory. Is there really a common moral ground between them, or are they simply using the same moral and political categories with entirely different normative assumptions, ethical ideals, and political implications? The lay commission asks: "How can Catholic social thought, formed in Europe under significantly different circumstances, be brought into fruitful contact with American institutions and American experience?"[5] It is clear that the intentions of the lay commission are entirely different from those of the bishops, for their central concern is focused on proving the compatibility of Catholic social thought with these American institutions. They then proceed to answer their own question by proclaiming that "we emphatically declare that there is no antagonism between them."[6]

Though at first there appears to be agreement between the two Catholic groups about the nature of these basic moral principles, there is, in fact, a wide disagreement over the meaning and interpretation of these categories.[7] In the first place, a major difference between the Bishops' Letter and the lay report lies in the logical organization and structure of their views on ethics. Both begin with the central moral imperative of realizing the worth and dignity of the individual. "The dignity of the human person, realized in community with others, is the criterion against which all aspects of economic life must be measured. All human beings, therefore, are ends to be served by the institutions that make up the economy, not means to be exploited for more narrowly defined goals."[8]

The Bishops' Letter clarifies the meaning of human dignity by examining the ancient traditions: the Hebrew ideas of creation, covenant, and community found in biblical texts and the classical Greek and medieval Christian views on social justice. The bishops then proceed to outline the social framework and preconditions that would encourage and aid the individual toward this integrated moral vision. The social aspects of the analysis are broken down into the following subsections of the letter:

1. Community, love, and social solidarity
2. Forms of social relations and basic justice: commutative, distributive, and social justice
3. Examination of the social preconditions of community in the common good and new economic rights
4. Social priorities of the community in the "option for the poor" and the principle of subsidiarity
5. The historical vision of the New American Experiment, public participation, and new forms of economic democracy
6. A social critique of those social relations that undermine and distort the formation of a just community examined in points one to five: unemployment, poverty, excessive inequality, racism, sexism, and so forth. This is then followed by an analysis of specific policy recommendations to overcome these problems.

What is obvious from the beginning is that the lay report does not ground its moral principles in Old or New Testament Scripture, but in its interpretations of the history of recent Catholic social teachings. Its discussion of human rights is taken from the American Constitution and Bill of Rights, not from John XXIII's *Pacem in Terris* or the United Nations Declaration of Human Rights. Its concept of creativity is taken from Adam Smith's analysis of the creation of wealth, rather than from John Paul II's idea of self-realization in the workplace in his *Laborem Exercens*. The changes in direction and meaning of their jointly held categories occur within the first few pages. What follows only compounds these initial differences in their approaches to social ethics and political economy. At every stage of analysis, the meaning and interpretation of such categories as human dignity, cooperation, freedom, the common good, and the community develop further apart in the two statements.

To take but two examples, which we will investigate in some detail in order to show these profound differences, we will examine the concepts of human dignity and social justice.[9] The lay commission report immediately defines human dignity as self-reliance and self-responsibility as the individual strives to attain its own well-being. This results from having unalienable human rights and liberty of conscience and is best expressed in the individual's drive for innovation, production, and private property in a competitive market economy. In a separate article, Michael Novak, the cochairman of *Toward the Future*, states that dignity is not something that can be imposed upon a passive people, but must be generated from within "the spiritual depths of individuals." He also implies in the same essay that poverty is, in fact, the social result of this lack of spiritual awareness.[10] "The lay group sees that dignity has its roots in the self—in the acquiring of self-esteem, attitudes, habits, and skills which make one an independent participant in all aspects of life, including the economic. 'Participation' is not conferred; it comes from acts which spring from within the self."[11]

On the other hand, the bishops define human dignity as the full expression of individual potential within a community of friends having civil, political, and economic rights. The concepts of possessive individualism, production, private property, and competition neither hold a central place in their theory nor are they viewed without some skepticism and suspicion. Catholic social thought has always critically viewed the articulation of human dignity solely within the natural-rights tradition as being a too narrow and limited understanding of human nature and individual rights.[12] As we have already seen, Catholicism has been uncomfortable with the anthropological assumptions of liberalism for some time. Certainly the view of basic justice announced by the bishops transcends, while still incorporating, the positive components of the natural-rights tradition. The lay commission does recognize this aspect of church teaching and attempts to supplement their views on natural rights and human dignity with a concern for the common good of the community. But there is a suspicion, even within the conservative community, that the notions of individualism and common good, from the natural-rights and natural-law traditions respectively, are incompatible in a pluralist society.[13]

> A distribution of income according to one's contribution to the society—to the "common good"—requires that this society have a powerful consensus as to what the "common good" is, and that it also have institutions with the authority to give specific meaning and application to this consensus on all occasions. Now, when you have such a consensus, and such authoritative institutions, you do not have—cannot have—a liberal society as we understand it.[14]

The theories of possessive individualism of Hobbes and Locke and the common good of Rousseau represent two entirely different and opposed philosophical traditions, and their integration into a single theory in the commission report remains unreflective, arbitrary, and uncritical.

The concept of social justice as defined in the Bishops' Letter is only one of three forms of justice. Catholic social teaching has emphasized three forms of basic justice: *distributive, social,* and *commutative justice.* In the lay report, the only form of justice mentioned and developed is that of social justice. Why is the breadth of traditional understanding of justice reduced to this one simple category? What are the implications for the conservative perspective of the loss of the other two meanings of justice? The three categories of justice, for the bishops, have their philosophical origin in the three forms of particular justice found in book five of Aristotle's *Nicomachean Ethics.* Here the concept of justice was broadly directed at the just distribution of public honor and social wealth; legal justice in civil and criminal cases; and fairness in economic exchange relations, which are crucial for the survival and vitality of complex political communities. The Catholic tradition has incorporated Aristotelian ethics into its teachings, which has had profound implications for the manner in which it responds to liberalism. In the process there has been an alteration of the meaning and distinctions of some of these categories in order to emphasize the church's concern for socially dispossessed and marginal groups within a market society.

For the bishops, *social justice* means that "persons have an obligation to be active and productive participants in the life of society." The lay commission defines this concept simply as a form of legal justice in which everyone has a basic equality of natural rights. The concept also contains, for the latter group, a directive to develop free associations in a pluralistic society in order to "redress grievances and to improve the daily workings of institutions" for the purposes of realizing the common good.[15] There is an implicit redefinition of the concept of common good here also. Social justice is concerned mainly with those public goods which cannot be provided efficiently to society by the private sector or achieved by individual initiative. It generally includes military, education, and ecological priorities. The traditional use of the concept of common good, with its emphasis on egalitarianism, participation, education, and self-development of individual potential, is missing. Next, the issue of fairness is raised by the lay commission, but in the context of the "fair routines" of these public institutions. In comparison to the expanded bishops' characterization of social justice as extended political and economic rights, social participation, and economic democracy, the lay commission reduces the concept to the protection of legal and individual rights for the purposes of the public good. Within this conservative perspective, social justice becomes the institutional support of individual liberty as well as a political legitimation of market rationality.

The radical thrust of the bishops' view is deflected, as is their call for new forms of economic and social relationships. The history of ethics, from the ancients to the moderns, has been reduced to a defense of Enlightenment political philosophy. Left out entirely are the other two definitions of justice found in the Bishops' Letter: *commutative justice*, which "calls for fundamental fairness in all agreements and exchanges between individuals and private social groups," and *distributive justice*, which "requires that the allocation of income, wealth, and power in society be evaluated in light of its effects on persons whose basic material needs are unmet."[16] The bishops' focus on distributive justice emphasized the issue of the "preferential option for the poor." The concern here is with the distribution of society's material goods and the community's obligation to help those in dire physical need. Social justice contains the moral imperative for individuals to actively participate in the social, political, and economic life of the community; it represents the bishops' radicalizing of participatory democracy. But this view of democracy is itself radically at odds with traditional conservative views of liberalism.[17]

The bishops are here drawing upon a view of justice whose roots run from Aristotle and the Greeks to Kant, Hegel, and Marx. They do not seem to be aware of this, and thus fail to develop the possibilities that lie dormant within these traditions. The bishops' goal is to create the social conditions for the general welfare of individuals and the community as a whole. Finally, commutative justice calls for "fundamental fairness" in all market interactions, while maintaining equal respect and dignity for the individual. Individuals are not to be treated as mere fetishes or instrumental means for the accumulation of wealth and property.[18] While the bishops emphasized the common good and fairness in contracts in their definition of commutative justice, the lay commission stressed the issues of equality and market liberties. The notion of economic fairness disappears in the latter's political theory. The bishops' view of human dignity is thus tied together with their theory of basic human needs and self-expression and the institutional support (basic justice) for those needs. Another way of expressing these differences between the two statements on the American economy is that the lay commission's theory rests on the liberalism of a natural-rights theory, whereas the bishops' view is tied to a theory of needs whose foundations lie in the natural-law tradition of the ancient Hebrews, Greeks, and medieval Christians.

From the description of these three forms of justice, it is clear that Aristotle's original categories have been integrated into Christian and Kantian moral philosophy. The result is an emphasis on both the common good within the community and the dignity of the individual within market economies and industrial societies. By ignoring the ethical principles of each of these three forms of basic justice and by reducing justice to a market category of individual choice and liberties, the lay commission has avoided discussion of the central issues of the Bishops' Letter. The former's economic reductionism has resulted in an emptying of their substantive moral values and the disembodiment of ethics. They have also avoided the need to question any American institution that does not meet the moral standards implicit in their redefinitions of the principles of social ethics. In the process they have also reduced the critical analysis of liberalism to a very technocratic model of market rationality.[19] The consequences of this "technocratic liberalism" will be developed in chapter three.

The conservatives do not have to deal with the issues generated by the bishops' call for basic justice: the call for economic fairness in market and contract relations, the moral imperative to fulfill basic material and spiritual needs, and the demand for true political and economic rights and democracy. By redefining these categories, they have redefined the need to respond to the bishops. They do not have to deal with the issue of the minimum social standards by which human dignity can and should be measured. They do not call into question the existing rationality and fairness of market relations between employees and managers, the excessive concentration of political and economic power in the hands of a small minority of individuals, and the need for creativity in the workplace characterized by structures of nondemocratic authority and control.

Finally, the notion of distributive justice and the fairness of the general social allocation of income, wealth, and power in American society found in the Bishops' Letter is missing from the lay commission report. Although it is stated throughout the commission's work that a concern for the poor is important for their perspective, the concept of distributive justice is not worked into their overall definition of universal justice. We can thus see that when the lay commission calls for liberty and justice, they are resting their ideas on political and philosophical traditions that are quite different from those of the bishops, who call for human dignity and social justice. It is this difference in their basic principles of social justice (used in the sense we developed in the Introduction) that will help explain their different understandings of society, political economy, and specific policy recommendations. It is also these differences which will help clarify their specific disagreements with the Bishops' Letter. To appreciate more fully their disagreements and the different traditions upon which they are based requires that we further clarify the meaning of the lay commission's use of terms such as liberty, justice, and the common good within a modern industrial society.

Novak criticizes the concept of distributive justice found in the first draft of the Bishops' Letter. There the bishops listed five criteria of distributive justice: equality, needs, effort, talent, and the common good, which they had borrowed from John Ryan's *Distributive Justice*.[20] Novak's response was that the criteria were limited and should include others, such as incentives for creativity and invention, social mobility, a welfare safety net, economic dynamism, encouragement for savings, investment, and capital accumulation, and finally, the maintenance of a positive climate for business. It is questionable whether these additions could be part of a theory of distributive justice. Although we wish to integrate ethics and economics, we also recognize that there are important distinctions between them which must not be confused. Novak is confusing political theory with economics as he slips neoclassical economics into his moral theory of just distribution. That is, the principles of distributive justice are being too finely and systematically integrated into existing economic institutions, which does not permit the distance and objectivity necessary for critical reflection. The result is an a priori defense of the status quo.

For Novak, economics functions not only as the material basis for society and justice, but is incorporated into its very definition. But in doing so, ethics becomes synonymous with economics and there is no critical distance between evaluative norms and the society one is judging. The quest for justice becomes indistinguishable from a rationalization and defense of democratic capitalism. After considering the different standards of distributive justice mentioned by Ryan, Novak concludes this part of his analysis by saying that "the crucial point is to try to imagine a system which, in a rough but routine and regular way, fulfills more of these criteria than any other."[21] There is no distinction between the categories of equality, need, effort, talent, and the common good; no recognition that they may have different philosophical traditions; and thus no recognition that they may be incompatible.[22]

A system based upon productive contribution and a class structure with a high degree of social stratification and division of labor would certainly be incompatible with an egalitarian society based on individual need and broad social participation. This attempt at synthesizing incompatible and contradictory traditions weakens Novak's critique of the bishops, but also undermines his own attempts at an integrated and coherent ethical theory. He does recognize that political economy is crucial for the development of ethics, but in the process he seems to have reduced the latter to the former. Novak has moved from the justification of democratic capitalism based solely on moral principles to a justification based on its structures of political economy. In the end, ethics is lost, along with the possibility of developing an adequate and comprehensive theory of social justice.

The bishops have called into question the basic presuppositions of democratic capitalism, American pluralism, and material consumerism. They have done so in a way that ties the foundations and justifications of their moral principles to the Bible, Christian teachings, and contemporary social and political theory. In a separate statement on this issue, William Simon, the other co-chairman of the lay commission, says, "I especially regret the thrust of the Bishops' Letter that strongly implies that a free economic system cannot be compatible with Christian doctrine."[23] Further comparisons of these two Catholic documents could be continued for the rest of this chapter, but the basic differences have been examined. The reader can now continue this line of argument throughout both works. Novak and Simon recognize the real differences and distance between their report and that of the bishops, especially when dealing with its normative foundations. Robert Benne, a conservative Protestant theologian, has also argued against the policy recommendations issued in the Bishops' Letter because, as he states, there can be legitimate disagreements only of the implementation of the generally agreed values of democratic capitalism.[24] Benne has failed to appreciate or recognize the actual distance between the two works, and his analysis is itself symptomatic of a more serious problem.

TWO VIEWS ON DEMOCRACY AND CAPITALISM

Besides the differences between the moral and political categories used in the two statements, along with their political and economic implications, their social theories and theologies of economics are also different. As we have already seen, there are always political and economic assumptions attached to ethical principles. The conservative approach incorporates the assumptions of democratic capitalism into the framework of Catholic social teachings in a way that undermines its ability to reflect critically upon both their values and their hidden assumptions. With almost no analysis of the moral principles themselves, the lay commission recognizes that morality without institutional support is empty. They therefore begin to analyze the institutional arrangements guaranteed by liberal democracy and a market economy. Democratic capitalism is characterized by three distinct social spheres: a market economy, democratic political system, and a pluralist moral and cultural system. This tripartite division of society into distinct divisions with their own imperatives and priorities is linked by the report to the belief in the Trinity: "all three systems are incarnated into one."

This is an important point, since the argument we have been developing is that though the lay commission develops its basic principles of ethics and social justice, they are ultimately tied to the value system of liberalism, which overrides the originally stated positions. The moral system of the conservatives is, in fact, the moral system of advanced industrial society. All choices, deliberation, and decisions about morality are ultimately tied to the ethics and logic of capitalism, and these values are the ones that eventually override and dictate the direction of both religious and social development.

> The most obvious difference [between the two reports] is that the lay letter is very anxious to endorse one kind of economic system loosely called capitalism and its key components, which include profit, self-interest rightly defined, to borrow the phrase from Tocqueville, enterprise, the market and the corporation, including the multinational corporation.[25]

Thus the initial concern and critique of tyranny and poverty as the "ancient enemies of the human race" are framed within the context of neither ethics nor religion, but within the logic of market possibilities. Since the Bishops' Letter does not begin with this set of social and economic assumptions underlying its moral principles, the content and application of ethics is different for both groups. The conservatives view ethics as a form of technical knowledge for the purpose of properly organizing social life, while the bishops appeal to ethics as the means for a broader public deliberation within the political and religious communities about the nature of society itself. Nowhere is this integration of moral principles and social institutions more clearly seen than in the following statement by the lay commission:

> One of the clearest limitations on the state is the principle of private property. Catholic social thought holds that the right to private property is a natural right, guaranteeing to conscience the means of self-

expression, and holding the state in check. (This right, which the Church also exercises, also anchors the liberty of the Church.) The right to private property is further justified in light of the common good. For private property makes possible the right ordering of the use of goods, providing incentives for good stewardship, and imposing upon all responsibilities to respect the rights and property of others.[26]

Private property is such a crucial phrase in this document, since it anchors and supports the conservative moral demands for human creativity and dignity, individual responsibility to the community and common good, man's relation to God and nature, and man's relationship to the development of individual potentialities. If private property or the use of private property in advanced societies is at all questionable, so too, then, is the whole foundation of the lay commission's argument. It seems equally clear that the conservatives have reduced morality to political economy, as occurs in the natural-rights tradition, rather than having political economy serve the needs of morality, as is the case in the natural-law tradition. To justify private property, the commission returns to both the Augustinian and the Lockean traditions of sin and possessive individualism respectively.

Though the commission emphasizes the rights and dignity of the individual, they are, however, cognizant of some of the problems associated with the radical individualism of the doctrine of natural rights. In a justification of their position, they defend the "principle of self-interest rightly understood," which also takes into consideration the practice of free association and the habit of cooperation. These are "the three American habits." They then quote twice from Tocqueville's *Democracy in America* for added emphasis. A difficulty which emerges is whether Tocqueville is being used to lay the foundations for the commission's political philosophy or to justify an argument in defense of the existing social relationships in America. As we have been saying throughout this chapter, the confusion between values and institutions, normative principles and social reality is never really clarified in this document.

The use of Tocqueville to legitimate one's values and place them within a philosophical tradition is one thing, but to use Tocqueville's arguments from the nineteenth century as a means to explain late-twentieth-century American society is problematic. The commission continues to stress its opposition to the concepts of blind individualism by further analyzing the idea of the law of cooperation. Cooperation is viewed as the heart of private and public institutions and is used to counterbalance the negative and most deleterious features of a Darwinian view of market competition. Tocqueville is again quoted to supply the requisite validation.

While giving passing mention to Joseph Schumpeter's principle of "creative destruction" in the marketplace, the commission turns to investigate the organization of production. The internal organization of market institutions is structured around a different set of principles than individualism or competition: "The system works best by incentives, by the flowering of natural virtues, by candor and open communication, by a sense of dignity and belonging. Good managers and good workers are characteristically team players, caring individuals."[27] This is the institutional framework for the ideal of individual productivity, with its anthropological implications about human creativity and its economic implications about technical efficiency and material production. The commission stresses the mutual cooperation and human satisfaction that are both its final end and its underlying organizational imperative. Rather than quoting exclusively from Tocqueville, it would have been better for the commission's argument to get into the literature examining American labor history and political economy. Doing so would have detailed the evolution of the social organization of private industry in order to determine its structural development, institutional organization, and the nature and quality of its social relationships. In the end, the lay commission finds the means for a synthesis of competition and cooperation, individual self-interest and the common good, thereby updating Adam Smith's integration of the private and public spheres.

One of the more interesting sections of the lay commission report is the one in which there is a direct confrontation with Pope John Paul II's encyclical *Laborem Exercens* over the issue of work and creativity. As Gregory Baum writes in the Introduction to *The Priority of Labor*, the Pope is drawing upon a rich intellectual tradition that has its roots in the nineteenth-century German social theories of Hegel and Marx and not in that of Aristotle and Aquinas. Though this point can be debated, what is clear is that neither tradition is used by the lay commission in the development of its theory. Here again the reliance on different intellectual traditions when dealing with similar issues demarcates the fundamental differences between the two Catholic documents.

> It is not only good in the sense that it is useful or something to enjoy; it is also good as being something worthy, that is to say, something that corresponds to man's dignity, that expresses this dignity and increases it. If one wishes to define more clearly the ethical meaning of work, it is this truth that one must particularly keep in mind. Work is a good thing for man — a good thing for humanity — because through work man not only transforms nature, adapting it to his own needs, but he also achieves fulfillment as a human being and indeed in a sense becomes "more a human being."[28]

Work is not only a defining characteristic of being human, but is a central means by which our humanity and individuality are expressed in the real world. Through our individual effort and our social organizations, we create the values, institutions, and objects of our perception. The world becomes human to the extent that our work is human and an expression of our innate creativity and dignity. Through the "externalization" and "objecti-fication" of ourselves in the work process, we create our world and our-selves. Without this ability to create, or with work confined to distorted social and economic relationships (alienation), human worth and dignity are undermined. For Hegel, the truth of objectivity is subjectivity; the truth of all forms of objective experience, whether in the form of perception, science, culture, or social institutions, is that they are manifestations of human consciousness, work, and creativity.

Kant's emphasis on moral action and human dignity is given a social setting by Hegel and Marx within which self-worth and dignity find histor-ical expression. In a society characterized by the errors of economism and materialism, the creativity of work becomes impossible, since the individual is subsumed under the technological demands of a market economy for greater productivity and efficiency at the expense of human dignity. By relying on this tradition, Pope John Paul II called into question the whole social organization of production within capitalist societies and the con-comitant economic exploitation of workers in the workplace. This, of course, does not fit the lay commission's view of capitalism, and the second part of its report starts with an understated critique of this papal encyclical. Rather than being an impediment to creative growth, capitalism is pre-sented as the only means for its assurance.

> Only a market system allows economic agents regular, reliable, ordi-nary liberties. Only a market system respects the free creativity of every human person, and *for this reason* respects private property incentives (rather than coercion), freedom of choice, and the other institutions of a free market. A market system obliges its participants to be other-regarding, that is, to observe the freely expressed needs and desires of others, in order to serve them.[29]

According to conservative social theory, the market mechanism is the only form of economic relationship that permits and encourages individual liberty, creativity and entrepreneurship, personal freedom and consumer choices, and community cooperation and mutual respect. Thus according to its view, by focusing upon worker and manager creativity in the market, the lay commission is directly responding to the papal encyclical's inter-pretation of work, creativity, and freedom. In the process the lay commis-sion redefines Pope John Paul II's ethical and political categories to suit its ideological needs. There is less of a direct confrontation than an incor-poration of the latter's ideas into its own. Referring to the works of Adam Smith, Abraham Lincoln, Irving Kristol, Herbert Vorgrimler, and John Courtney Murray, S.J., the conservative theorists leave behind any critical remnants of nineteenth-century German social philosophy. The values of Kant, Hegel, and Marx are ignored and rejected in favor of the market biases of these other authors. This can only lead to a very distorted interpretation of the papal encyclical.

Creativity is made synonymous with the inventiveness and risk-taking of the modern enterprise. They become the moral virtues of modernity. According to the lay report, the Bishops' Letter neither takes into account economic productivity in its discussion of social justice, nor does it consider the moral characteristics of an inventive and creative personality. Again these categories are always understood within the logic of market economies and capital accumulation. "Catholic social thought has not yet put sufficient emphasis upon the creative instrument through which new ideas and inventions are brought into service to human beings: the practical insight of the entrepreneur."[30] This inventiveness, let loose by the market, permits the development of cooperative associations, material wealth undreamed of before modern times, individual creativity of expression, and the public manifestation of individual talents and abilities. It unlocks the material secrets of nature to the collective advantage of the community by creating new wealth, while permitting the full flowering of individual potential and imagination. The market supplies the institutional framework within which this abstract potential can be manifested and realized. "A free economy allows for the fullest possible range of motivation." But again we are back to the dilemma first stated at the beginning of the chapter: moral, anthropological, and religious categories are being reduced, without serious reflection, to the logic and priorities of the market economy.

> Strictly speaking, then, profit is the regard for risk taking and invention. In this sense, it is the chief incentive for creative growth. Without such profit, an economy is simply spinning its wheels in stagnation or in decline. Without profit, there is little creative development. ...
> Philosophically, though, in free societies profit is a social device which expresses a society's esteem for personal liberty and creativity.[31]

The joining together of individual creativity and market productivity, with deeply unconscious philosophical and historical biases and assumptions, is the very thing that should form the central focus of this discussion and debate. In conservative philosophy and theology, however, it takes on the form of a social given. Are there individual potentialities, human possibilities, forms of self-expression, and types of motivation which cannot be met by the rationality of the market? Is the human imagination simply a subset of possibilities found in the market?

THE LAY COMMISSION REPORT ON ECONOMICS AND THE WELFARE STATE

Though the lay commission relies very heavily on conservative political philosophy and economic theory, it contends that its analysis of American political economy and the welfare state is not reducible to these conservative theorists. In spite of this disclaimer, however, it is from these authors that it draws its data, ideas, and insights. To them we must now turn in order to understand better the foundations upon which the commission builds its critique of the bishops and develops its own variation on conservative themes.

Conservative political economy has had a resurgence since Reaganomics became a real force in American politics. We will outline the conservative theory of the history and structure of the welfare state in order to understand its view of the proper role and function of the modern state and its relation to advanced industrial society. Since the state is seen as a necessary corrective to the weaknesses and inadequacies of the market mechanism, the analysis of the state is important to any understanding of the nature of the economy. Thus, a theory of the state will show the worst side of any theory of the economy. The next chapter will do the same for the radical critique of political economy.

Part three of the lay report analyzes the concrete policy recommendations it draws on as the basis of its own interpretations of moral principles and theory of the economy. Unlike the Bishops' Letter, however, it extends its list of recommendations to include issues concerning the family, the failure of the welfare system, the priority of economic expansion and need for new avenues of job creation, the furtherance of free trade and global interdependence, and the new emphasis on social cooperation found in the market. The report does recognize the importance of poverty as a moral consideration and social standard by which the whole of society is judged; it is the social criterion by which the common good of society is measured. Since productivity and the creation of social wealth are also essential elements in the defense of capitalism, a large group of poor and unemployed represent a glaring critique of the social system and admission that there is something wrong with both the production and distribution of its products.

As the report turns to the issue of poverty in America, the authors also return to the same statistical evidence relied upon by the bishops in their analysis of the problem: Greg Duncan, et al., *Years of Poverty, Years of Plenty*. This book represents a summary of a ten-year study of poverty undertaken at the University of Michigan from 1969 to 1978. Though the lay commission concedes that poverty is an important moral and social issue, it is also suspicious of reports on the nature and extent of poverty, the political ideology underlying its definition and measurement, and the present role of the state in its alleviation. For its alternative analysis, it relies on published government documents from the Department of Commerce and the Bureau of the Census, as well as on the writings of John Palmer, Isabel Sawhill, Charles Murray, Roger Freeman, Martin Anderson, Thomas Sowell, and Peter Drucker.

The Bishops' Letter went into some detail on the nature of poverty by describing the different characteristics, situations, and needs of children, women, and racial minorities living in poverty, along with consideration of other issues such as wealth and income distribution, minimum and just wage, and the benefits of the poverty program and public assistance (AFDC: Aid to Families with Dependent Children). The commission begins at a different point with a statement about the rising affluence and standard of living in American society, which is a result of the country's transition to an advanced capitalist economy. The commission then recites the Parable of the Wise and Foolish Virgins from the New Testament (Matthew 25:1– 13). The creative use of the productive resources of a society is a moral imperative, since a misuse of society's resources results in a waste of its productive capacity, increases the power of a centralized state bureaucracy, and undermines the resourcefulness and creativity of its citizens. The goal is to help the poor "without generating an incapacitating dependency."[32]

The commission next proceeds to mention some statistical evidence about poverty by drawing upon the Michigan study during the 1970s. Though one out of four Americans experienced poverty in that ten-year period, only 2.6 percent of them were "persistently poor" for eight years or more. The majority of poor were either disabled, elderly, or in female-headed households. According to the commission, in 1982 the total cash income necessary to bring those who had fallen below the official poverty line above it amounted to only $45 billion. But the amount spent on federal poverty programs amounted to over $100 billion, more than enough to bring every poor person in American above that line. This is a theme that runs consistently throughout most conservative examinations of the issue. Thus, the state's poverty program has been grossly inefficient in its main purpose of alleviating poverty and has further intensified this social problem by encouraging the breakup of the nuclear family. Though highly critical of the cash programs to the poor, the commission recognizes the importance and impact of noncash benefits in the form of Medicare, Medicaid, Social Security, food stamps, housing allowances, and so forth.

What draws the ire of the commission is the high rate of "illegitimacy" among the poor, especially among the Black population. In an interesting logical shift away from those who argued that poverty and illegitimacy are structural problems associated with American political economy, the commission contends that the liberals themselves are guilty of a "blaming the victim" argument. That is, it is they who have not given full credit to the moral autonomy and responsibility of the individual in solving his or her own social and personal problems. By reducing these problems to structural issues, they have taken direct human control and accountability away from individuals and have treated them as mere "victims" of the social system.

The lay commission argues that there is no statistical evidence for the belief in a large underclass of permanently poor individuals. Between 1969 and 1978, one out of four Americans experienced at least one year of poverty, but there is no evidence to indicate that a large group of Americans is continually faced with poverty over a long period of time and living in a "culture of poverty." The poverty population is fluid and changes rapidly. Over half the poor in 1983 were either children, elderly, or disabled and therefore could not be considered part of the labor market. The conservatives seem to indicate that the application of Social Security, retirement and disability benefits will adequately deal with the elderly and disabled, while demographic changes will automatically eliminate poverty among children: They will get older and be integrated into the economic system by finding proper employment.

The real problem in dealing with poverty, according to the lay commission, rests with that group which represents nearly 50 percent of the poor. This is the female-headed household with dependent children. According to the lay commission, the welfare system is responsible for causing the high rates of illegitimacy among Black households. Thus, the real cause for lingering poverty and the continuing burden on social services in America lies in the encouragement of this arrangement by the welfare state itself. The moral and political goal of society must be to help these women achieve a sense of self-esteem and provide them with the proper counseling and education necessary to acquire the incentives and personal drive requisite for finding successful employment and self-reliance.

Given these reservations about the welfare state, the commission argues that the real problems are neither structural nor monetary, but, in reality, are human and spiritual problems. The state's true goal should be to help the poor "acquire the human skills of productive economic independence."[33] The welfare system must redirect its energies in order to encourage self-reliance and personal dignity. Those poor and capable of working must be helped through an increased activity of private voluntary associations (i.e., the principle of cooperation and voluntarism) in order to restore a consideration of the human and cultural aspects of the spirit of democratic capitalism. "Poverty is not primarily a problem of the state. It is a *personal* and a *community* problem which each of us and all our appropriate associations, not only the state, ought to address. Government programs are important, but they are not sufficient."[34]

When it comes to concrete policy recommendations for the poor, the commission does not offer anything specific beyond the belief in policy pluralism. Though critical of key aspects of the welfare state and its poverty programs, the commission is incapable or unwilling to offer any concrete alternatives other than the idea that "we value a pluralism of approaches." The one specific recommendation that is mentioned in the next section of their report is the need to deal with unemployment and the creation of new jobs by economic expansion. Their specific statements notwithstanding, their understanding of poverty still refers back to the culture of poverty idea of the 1960s and its implications of "blaming the victim" and the avoidance of any critique of structural changes. There is, thus, a good deal of symmetry and logical consistency between their basic moral principles and economic policy recommendations. Both emphasize the centrality of production and creativity.

The point is stressed that what is not required is a structural change in American political economy. The last paragraph in this section begins with the sentence, "One of the best ways to help the poor, and especially to help family life among the poor, is to generate new jobs." Though this paragraph was designed to be the lead-in to the next section on employment generation in the economy, the reference to unemployment is more of an afterthought than a serious cause of poverty. The emphases throughout this section have been on a revitalization of the creative spirit and the critique of the breakdown of the Black family.

The title of part three is "Improving the U.S. Economy," which gives the reader a strong indication of the perceptions of the commission regarding social problems and their policy proposals. While it praises the economic growth and job creation from 1970 to mid 1984, in spite of the recessions and economic stagnation during this period, they are aware of the enormous need for the economy to produce more jobs in the 1990s. During this same period the most dynamic aspect of the economy has been in the private business sector. The commission contends that employment in the large corporations and in the government has been relatively static during this time and more effort must be made to clear away government interference and bureaucratic stumbling blocks to the renewal of the entrepreneurial spirit. Examples of these stumbling blocks include the economic benefits given to workers in European social democracies: job security, higher benefits, strict regulation, and restrictive labor markets. Entry into particular areas of the economy are further restricted by government licensing delays and high employee social costs offered by these mixed economies.

To complicate matters even further and to bridle the economy with more difficulties, the demographic changes in America have added to our economic problems. The economy has been forced to absorb both the "baby boomers" and the dramatic influx of women into the market. All this adds to further strains on the economic system. The commission recognizes that the state can and must aid in the process of continued economic growth and prosperity, but it must pay closer attention to the supply side of the economic ledger. More emphasis must be placed on macroeconomic policy for creating more investment capital and opportunities, rather than stressing the need for a demand-side economy, that is, economic redistribution within the welfare system. Dealing with issues of joblessness, community problems, and social disruption caused by a dynamic market economy is the proper domain of the state. But too much stress must not be placed on this role, since this only undermines our commitment to market rationality.

Aside from the swift, objective, and indispensable information they give about real choices by real people, what is most valuable about markets is that they are open. Those concerned about stewardship, unmet needs, new necessities and future requirements are able to enter markets and do new things. Markets, in short, allow for self-correction. They encourage habits of foresight and anticipation. They are a social device permitting the virtues of human providence to set to work with them.[35]

The workings of the market are likened to the providence of God, who permits the development of the arbitrariness and contingency in a changing world but still orders things according to his essence. Behind the appearance of the anarchy of production, there is rational social planning based on a myriad of pluralistic and utilitarian choices. This expresses a freedom of choice as well as a structuring of the world in a rational fashion. The free market is an example of human providence and stewardship over nature, because it is the social device which ultimately encourages human creativity, imaginative anticipation, and foresight.

The questions that we must ask of the commission's policy recommendations and its underlying theory of the economy is whether its understanding of the market mechanism, the nature of corporations and business enterprise, the organization and structure of these corporations, the role of the contemporary state, and the social and economic problems related to them is adequate to understanding the complexities of late-twentieth-century society. The lay report is too short to help us, since it only involves a snapshot picture of our economy from a limited perspective. Since it contains elements traditionally associated with both conservative and liberal traditions within democratic capitalism, the next section of this chapter will analyze two social theorists whose works were relied upon by the lay commission.

CONSERVATIVE POLITICAL ECONOMY: ANDERSON AND MURRAY

The lay commission relied on a variety of experts to help it form its economic opinions. It also has left us with an extensive list of endnotes, which provide further help in following its arguments and supplementing its research. This section will begin to analyze some of the more important literature in conservative economic and political theory, in order to aid us in expanding our knowledge about its views concerning the underlying structure and history of American society. This in turn will help us better understand the rationale and implications of its policy recommendations. We are aware that *Toward the Future*, like the Bishops' Letter, represents compromise positions within the commission itself. Therefore, to analyze only one or just a few social theorists or theologians would not fully represent the complexity of the commission's membership. We do feel, however, that through examining the secondary literature used in the report, we will provide a deeper understanding of and more profound insight into the mind of the commission and the assumptions implicit in its arguments.

It was certainly easier to follow the trail of the commission's moral and theological beliefs than to follow its political economy and policy recommendations. Though the commission is more open to the importance of the welfare state and the interests of the common good than many of its conservative allies, there are close similarities in their common criticisms and understanding of the internal dynamics of the American economy. The commission's report does advance a broader picture of the role of the state in both social and industrial policy. Macroeconomic and microeconomic policies of the state are important for the continued well-being of the economy; they also reject the narrow night-watchman approach (call for minimalist government) of Robert Nozick and Milton Friedman. Given this, however, they remain highly critical of the welfare state and its continued interference into the market, which they blame for a sluggish economy in the 1970s. Changes in the nature of the American family are also blamed for much of the new poverty. The underlying causes of economic crises, poverty, and unemployment are never seen as structural problems of the political economy itself. They are always peripheral to the central workings of the economic system.

Certainly an important work within the conservative tradition is Charles Murray's *Losing Ground*. Murray attempts to explain an interesting historical phenomenon that occurred throughout the 1970s. In 1980, 13 percent of the American population was considered in poverty, which was the same number by the end of President Johnson's War on Poverty in 1968. He seeks to show that the common explanations for this, such as economic stagnation, demographic changes, racism, the Vietnam War, energy crisis, and the political corruption of Watergate were not adequate to explain the constant rate of poverty in 1968 and 1980.[36] What was happening in American society to explain this phenomenon? Was the poverty program ineffective? He concluded that it was the welfare system itself that had caused this increase in the number of recipients over time. People below or near the poverty level were simply responding to their own rational, material self-interest in seeking income from the state rather than seeking work in the private sphere. Throughout the 1970s and 1980s, there had been a paradigm shift in the designation of poverty to the view that poverty was the result of structural elements in society. The key problem for Murray was not the existence of poverty, which was undeniably real, but its characterization as a structural feature of American society. This perspective led to unintended consequences, which resulted in an increase in state bureaucracy and centralized power, lessened market incentives, and made the welfare system a permanent part of the American landscape.

Martin Anderson's *Welfare: The Political Economy of Welfare Reform in the United States* is another work relied upon by the lay commissioners in their economic report. He, too, was concerned with the dramatic rise in government spending and public programs and the limited success at eliminating poverty. Anderson states that, while government spending on social welfare programs increased from $77 billion in 1965 to $215 billion in 1973, the percentage of Americans living in poverty had decreased by less than a third. Using the Census Bureau's figures there were, in fact, 500,000 more poor in 1975 than in 1968. What could explain this massive redistribution of society's wealth from the middle and upper groups to the lowest groups without any major appreciable effects? Relying on the works of Edgar Browning, Edward Banfield, John Palmer, Joseph Minarik, Roger Freeman, and Morton Paglin, Anderson concluded that part of the problem was the underreporting of family income to the Census Bureau, as well as the Census Bureau's own accounting procedures.[37] In their official definition of poverty, they have consistently failed to consider the enormous transfer of social wealth to the poor by means other than income transfers. These in-kind transfers included food stamps, school lunches, unemployment benefits, housing allowances, and the medical benefits of Medicare and Medicaid. The result is a gross underreporting of social benefits and over-reporting of poverty in America.

With the creation of a new format for the estimation of poverty by the Congressional Budget Office in 1977, new figures were arrived at which included transfer income from public assistance, AFDC, Social Security, and in-kind benefits. Morton Paglin's calculations indicated that, when all forms of public assistance were calculated, the percentage of poverty in America was only 3 percent, indicating that the poverty program was working. There was a real difference between the official definition of poverty at 12.3 percent in 1975 as opposed to this revised definition at 3 percent. The definition of poverty became a political football that could be adjusted for any ideological reason. According to Anderson, there was a conservative consensus forming, based on the revised statistical evidence, that by the mid-seventies poverty in America had been eliminated.

Both Anderson and Murray have different perspectives on the issue of poverty, with one emphasizing the increasing poverty rates and the other the official overstating of poverty numbers. They both agree, however, that the percentage of poverty was grossly exaggerated and the welfare state in one way or another was to blame. Murray traces the historical evolution of the welfare system from the Kennedy and Johnson years to the Carter presidency and is concerned with two historical facts. The first is that there was a dramatic increase in spending on public assistance during the Nixon years — an almost threefold increase over the previous five years. However, though poverty fell from 18 percent in 1964 to 13 percent in 1968, by 1980 the number of persons living in poverty was at the highest level since 1967. It was this apparent discrepancy between the rise in welfare spending during the 1970s and the continued increase in poverty that is the focus of Murray's analysis. Why had poverty rates continued to increase while the amount of spending also increased? Why did the fight against poverty begin to falter after 1968, sputter in the early 1970s, and then fall apart in the 1980s, when the number of people living in poverty began to rise in 1979?

Though the War on Poverty began in the mid 1960s, the real spending increases began during the Republican administrations in the 1970s, and with them also the rise in poverty itself.

Murray then proceeds to examine a variety of historical and structural interpretations in order to explain these features of poverty. To accomplish this he compares the growth rates of the American economy during the 1950s and 1970s. He states that the annual growth rate from 1953 to 1959 was 2.7 percent, while for the period between 1970–1979 it was 3.2 percent. The 1970s growth rates were "as high as those of the palmy days of the 1960s," even after the rates were adjusted for inflation and population changes. After an examination of various theses proposed to explain these occurrences, including the existence of a stagnating economy, demographic changes and an increasing elderly population, and increasing Black poverty in a segmented labor market, Murray concludes that none of these things could explain the rise in poverty along with the corresponding rise in government spending. The one set of figures that he viewed as important were those that dealt with "latent poverty." Latent poverty is the pretransfer poverty caused by the working of the marketplace; it is calculated on the basis of the number of poor prior to a calculation of the effects of government transfer programs such as Social Security, public assistance, unemployment insurance, and so forth.[38] Latent poverty was on the decline throughout the 1950s and early 1960s, until it started to rise in the late 1960s and early 1970s and continued to rise throughout the 1970s. It reached 22 percent in 1980. What was really happening to cause the reversal of the gains on poverty during the 1960s?

To explain these historical changes, Murray reverts to a metaphysics of psychologism. The increase in net poverty is explained (away) by a return to a brand of psychology that characterizes individuals as inherently shiftless and amoral beings who are brought to work only by material incentives and disincentives. This crude psychologism was meant to explain the whole structural transformation of American society and the growth of poverty in the 1970s. As he says: "Sticks and carrots work."

> Specifically, I will suggest that changes in incentives that occurred between 1960 and 1970 may be used to explain many of the trends we have been discussing. It is not necessary to invoke the *Zeitgeist* of the 1960s, or changes in the work ethics, or racial differences, or the complexities of the post-industrial economies, in order to explain increasing unemployment among the young, increased dropout from the labor force, or high rates of illegitimacy and welfare dependence. All were results that could have been predicted (indeed, in some instances were predicted) from the changes that social policy made in the rewards and penalties, carrots and sticks, that govern human behavior. All were rational changes to the rules of the game of surviving and getting ahead.[39]

By examining the effects of the Seattle and Denver negative income tax experiments and by creating the "Phyllis and Harold thought experiments," Murray hoped to show how the welfare system itself was responsible for creating the social conditions conducive to continued poverty.[40] That is, it was government public assistance that encouraged people to remain unmarried, stay out of the labor market, and accept welfare assistance. Welfare programs offered rational incentives to remain unemployed and on welfare, while at the same time offering equally rational disincentives to work.

The state had developed a public assistance program which, when coupled with the rational calculus of choice making, led to an increase in the number of poor and thus directly to the costs for social welfare. It is more rational for a person to accept welfare than work at a low-paying, tedious, dead-end job. Decisions made by the Supreme Court and the Department of Health, Education, and Welfare that liberalized eligibility requirements and access to benefits had the unintended consequence of opening the floodgates to many people who were not deserving poor but could play the system for all it was worth. The system provided the wrong psychological incentives and actually encouraged a net increase in poverty.

One example of Murray's use of the "thought experiment" to prove his policy positions was that of the program designed to help individuals quit smoking. According to this experiment, a reward of $10,000 would be offered to any individual who had been smoking at least one pack of cigarettes a day for five years or more and who could quit smoking for one full year. Murray argued that on the face of it, it appeared a serious attempt to encourage people to quit smoking. However, in reality, this experiment could actually result in encouraging people who normally smoke less than a pack a day to increase their consumption. It also had the danger of encouraging those who might have quit on their own to continue smoking until they reached the five-year period, so they could qualify for the reward. This same type of "thought experiment" is used in a similar way to explain the behavior of welfare recipients. As in the case of the smokers, it remained in the immediate self-interest of both the smokers and welfare recipients to continue smoking or remain on welfare in order to qualify for benefits.

Murray's solution to the welfare and poverty problems was to dismantle most of the welfare system; the poor would then have to be absorbed by the job market, families, or private charities. The federal monies formerly used for the welfare system would now fuel capital investment and supply better social services for the truly needy. Whatever role remained for government services would be better served by local and state communities. This is the conservative variant of the principle of freedom and subsidiarity.

George Gilder, in his work *Wealth and Poverty*, argues in a similar fashion. He claims that poverty and unemployment are not causal agents of family breakdown but are rather the results of the disintegration of family life. The welfare system undermines the psychological factors necessary for the maintenance of a stable personality and produces individuals whose time horizons shift to immediate gratification, violence, promiscuity, and escapism. "The man has the gradual sinking feeling that his role as provider, the definitive male activity from the primal days of the hunt through the industrial revolution and on into modern life, has been seized from him."[41]

By connecting public assistance to female-headed households, the state encourages the deterioration and breakup of American family life and with it the foundations of a stable economy. Along with this occurs the fraud and illegitimacy associated with welfare mothers: "welfare, by far the largest economic influence in the ghetto, exerts a constant, seductive, erosive pressure on the marriages and work habits of the poor and over the years, in poor communities, it fosters a durable 'welfare culture'."[42] To further complicate the matter, the actual benefits to the poor are well above the wages of "common labor" and only exacerbate the situation. Public assistance must be made less attractive by letting inflation cut into its benefits package and by giving less in the form of cash transfers; in-kind benefits should be stressed more. It is unclear from Gilder's own analysis whether the scenario he presents is indirectly more an indictment of the welfare system or an indictment of the low level of wages for American labor.

CRITIQUE OF THE BISHOPS' NEW AMERICAN EXPERIMENT IN ECONOMIC DEMOCRACY

Based on their reading of the historic papal encyclicals, Catholic social teachings, and the United Nations Declaration of Human Rights, the American bishops called for an extension of fundamental natural rights to include not only civil and political liberties, but also new economic rights. These new rights would be: the right to life, food, clothing, shelter, employment, security, rest, medical care, and basic education.[43] Without this extension of human rights into areas of health, education, and welfare, the basic social foundations of human dignity would be denied. This necessitates transforming the programs of the American welfare system from a social safety net into a program insuring basic human rights for the whole population. "These fundamental personal rights—civil and political as well as social and economic—state the minimum conditions for social institutions that respect human dignity, social solidarity, and justice. They are all essential to human dignity and to the integral development of both individuals and society, and are thus moral issues."[44]

To protect and secure these new rights, a set of social institutions would have to be constructed radicalizing and expanding the traditional view of political participation. New forms of the social and economic life of the community would have to be created. In chapter four of their Letter, the bishops entitled this program a New American Experiment in economic democracy. Only this would fulfill their principle of subsidiarity and forge a closer connection between individual rights and freedoms and expressions of the common good.[45] It would also recreate "the virtues of citizenship," expand the freedoms and choices available to the community, increase public participation in its own decision-making process, and provide for greater social accountability in both public and private institutions.

Some of the bishops' recommendations in this field included: profit sharing, employee stockholder options, direct worker democracy, and worker cooperatives. The goal of the bishops was to break down class barriers to real cooperation and joint participation in the workplace by both workers and managers in order to extend freedom and power to all. Drawing upon *Quadragesimo Anno* and *Laborem Exercens*, they argued for the extension of economic rights and social justice through the institutionalization of real social democracy.[46]

There are a variety of opinions critical of the proposal for extending the range of democratic institutions to include economic or workplace democracy. There is disagreement over whether this theory of participation is an expression of the church's view of justice, whether it is "a new ideology in Catholic social thought"[47] or a scheme of "social engineers and commissars of history."[48] In all the conservative criticisms of this idea, a central theme revolves around a concern for the effect that these policy recommendations, if implemented, would have on the functioning of a free market and the proper psychological motivations for competition and entrepreneurship. How would these new economic rights and democratic institutions affect innovation, creativity, and productivity? Would they not undermine the rationality and planning of the market system and introduce new forms of political totalitarianism with the extension of the bureaucracy of a centralized government?[49] The liberties and freedoms guaranteed by the numerous individual market decisions that protect everyone's natural rights would be in jeopardy. In the end it would result in the loss of individual rights and liberties, political freedoms, individual incentive and creativity, and finally, the loss of crucial capital investment and industrial expansion.

As in the case with all the other important ethical and economic categories, the differences between the Bishops' Letter and the lay commission report over the nature of "participation" also involves conflicting assumptions and policy recommendations. Some have argued that the American system already involves economic democracy; others say that the bishops' form of democracy would result in a crude equalization of wealth and undermine standards of excellence and the basis of economic motivation. This in turn would lead to undermining the spiritual foundations of democratic capitalism, its ability to generate new wealth, and finally, lead to the "immizeration of the populace."[50] Thus the call for new economic rights and public participation would act counter to true liberalism and undercut the productive apparatus of modern society. This call for economic equality is a misplaced and crude leveling process designed to artificially make everyone equal; it results in undermining the very principle that makes us different, free, and creative. Democracy, according to this view, presupposes liberalism: a healthy, expanding economy that in turn presupposes the proper motivation to encourage those with ability, drive, and promise to apply themselves in their occupations.[51] "The great achievement of capitalism has not been the accumulation of property, it has been the opportunities it has offered to men and women to extend and develop and improve their capacities."[52]

The lay commission, as we have already seen, has defined social justice as improving the daily routines of the social institutions. Though the term is undeveloped in their report and its actual content remains ambiguous, it appears that social justice refers to the structural protection of the daily routines of the market economy. That is, justice is concerned with making the market more efficient and productive, because it is the ultimate arbiter of the just distribution of social wealth. This would explain why the lay commission does not use the term *distributive justice* or respond to the bishops' use of it. The lay commission does reply to the bishops' concept of social justice in their criticism of the latter's use of the term *participation*. For the conservatives, distributive justice is already included in their concept of social justice, since market rationality encourages individual achievement, efficiency, and productivity, and results in a fair distribution of the scarce resources of the community. If the final disposition of society's wealth is determined by individual effort, then the wealth of society is fairly distributed. Morality is justified on the basis of possessive individualism. This is the position taken by Irving Kristol in his work *Two Cheers for Capitalism*.

> It is the basic premise of a liberal-capitalist society that a "fair" distribution of income is determined by the productive input—"productive" as determined by the market—of individuals into the economy. Such productivity is determined by specific talents, general traits of character, and just plain luck (being at the right place at the right time). This market-based distribution of income will create economic incentives and thereby encourage economic growth. As a result of such economic growth, everyone will be better off (though not necessarily equally better off).[53]

By tampering with the behavioral and motivational underpinnings of democratic capitalism, the rationality of the competitive market system is called into question. Democracy, as defined by the conservatives, rests on the liberty of choice offered by a consumer society. Participation, in this sense, is increased by the increased choices permitted by expanding industry and opening up the consumer market to a wider range of previously excluded peoples. This industrial expansion will also permit more individuals to "participate" directly in finding new job opportunities and involving themselves more in the American dream of democratic capitalism.[54] To repeat, production is the foundation for their ethical views, while production itself is interpreted by the technical standards of efficiency and productivity. Economic democracy would only interfere with this process and result in an increasingly centralized and bureaucratized state. The integration in *Toward the Future* of technical productivity, political pluralism, and a narrow definition of natural rights leads to a misunderstanding and misrepresentation of the bishops' proposals. The integration of contradictory ethical and political traditions in this form of technocratic liberalism leads to an even more profound danger. Thomas Spragens has indicated the implications of this type of thinking.

> Finally, the constitutive goals of justice and the common good also lose their meaning and force under the aegis of positivist pluralism. One of the reasons why interest group liberalism "cannot achieve justice" is that it cannot conceive of justice. Just as right is reduced to intense preference, so "justice" is reduced to balance-of-power and the outcome of bargains based on it . . . The impact of positivist pluralism substantially erodes and transforms the constitutive ideals of liberal democracy. Liberty turns conceptually into license; equality means denial of merit; common good is reduced to a collection of individual ends; right is measured by mere subjective intensity; justice is dismissed as a not genuinely meaningful end of government.[55]

Robert Benne, in "Two Cheers for the Bishops," admits that economics has a moral dimension, but argues that the former is fundamentally concerned with technical "factors of production" and should be kept separate from ethics. The bishops, who have failed to understand the nature of efficiency and production in a competitive economy, have also failed to recognize the conflict between equality and efficiency. By reducing economics to a political and moral category, they have obscured the nonmoral technical and instrumental nature of production. There is a danger that the bishops' specific policy proposals will, if enacted, "proliferate the moral and political impingements on economic life in such a way that the goose which lays the golden egg could indeed be throttled."[56] The logically prior issues of technological efficiency stressed by conservatives require a different social and economic system than that offered by the bishops with their New American Experiment based on an alternative understanding of economic democracy. Without the scientific and technological solutions to the problems of the domination of nature, democracy becomes a fanciful ideal. The bishops' proposal for economic democracy is a technological regression that could seriously damage the prospects for the further creation of material wealth.

Novak criticizes the ambiguity of the concept of "economic participation" in the first draft and asks if it refers to effective equality of opportunity, effective employment opportunities, or access to credit.[57] He also reduces the bishops' notion of economic rights to equal opportunity within the market. The idea of participation in the decision-making process in the public and private spheres is not considered. Also not discussed are the different anthropological assumptions distinguishing between human beings who compete in the market for scarce material goods and those who create their own institutions and lives in an expanded political process. The relationships between liberalism and the market, on one hand, and democracy, on the other, are being constantly confused. Conservatives have always accepted a privileged relationship between the two categories, which has never been proven beyond its own a priori assumptions.[58] Novak seems unwilling to deal with the bishops' call for a New American Experiment on their own terms and reduces the issues of economic rights and democratic participation to further economic liberties and market choices.

The very designation of the term *economic rights* beyond the traditional ideas of natural-rights theory is a cause for serious concern. Some have argued that there is a real ontological difference between the political rights of free speech, assembly, conscience, and private property and the rights to adequate nutrition, housing, education, and so forth. The former are universal negative rights, which require that others not interfere in our activities, but they impose no obligations to act in a certain way. The positive economic rights proposed by the bishops are historically contingent on the economic base of society. They demand a moral imperative to supply the disadvantaged with the material goods necessary to satisfy the new economic rights under discussion.

> The designation of a "right" to food, housing, adequate nutrition and the like to be on a par with the rights of free speech, religion and assembly reflects a collectivist moral vision, a vision that is wholly inconsistent with designating "the dignity of the human person, realized in community with others" as "the criterion against which all aspects of economic life must be measured."[59]

There is a serious misunderstanding about the nature of property among some of the conservative theorists. The bishops have dealt with the issues of cooperation and sharing in the economic decisions at the point of production. By proposing an experiment in economic democracy, they are attempting to limit the unrestrained accumulation and the nonaccountability of private property, that is, to limit public power disguised as private right. This should not be confused with consumer property, as occurs in Novak's analysis.

> True economic democracy would mean, for example, that Mr. Jones could not alone determine the usage of his own automobile, home, or even his own shoes and socks. Rather, all of us, "we the people," would have a share in such decision-making. But were such a proce-

dure to actually take place, it would mean the end to all private property as we have known it.[60]

This misunderstanding of the nature of private property and its confusion with consumer goods has also deflected attention in conservative social theory away from issues of power and democratic control in the economy. They fail to recognize the concentration and centralization of economic and political power that arise out of the normal workings of the market in their exclusive emphasis on the dangers of the centralized state. Thus the distinction between positive freedoms "toward something" and negative freedoms "from something" is built on an inadequate understanding of the nature of the market as value free and neutral in deciding economic issues. Negative freedoms have always presupposed a certain ontological teleology about man and the good of society as expressed in consumerism and the market. Freedom "from" is always a freedom "toward the market." More will be said on this issue in the next chapter.

3

THE CREED OF CONSERVATIVE ETHICS: CAPITALIST THEOLOGY AND THE METAPHYSICS OF ECONOMICS

INTRODUCTION

In this chapter we will develop a further examination of the foundations for the conservative critique of the Bishops' Letter. The real distance between that letter and the lay commission report lies in an analysis of the underlying basis of conservative social theory and its metaphysics and theology of economics. This analysis is to be accomplished by a detailed exegesis of the works of Michael Novak and Robert Benne. They establish the full range of the conservative spectrum by turning to the political theories of Robert Nozick and John Rawls, respectively. Though they borrow from different ideological and methodological forms of liberalism from the right and the left, they both conclude with a conservative analysis of the American welfare state and critique of the Bishops' Letter. Benne stresses the importance of equality within a society which is structured to benefit its least-advantaged citizens, while Novak stresses the liberty of choice and action in a market economy.

Methodologically, Benne begins with the contract model of Rawls's "original position" and "veil of ignorance," while Novak starts with an a priori assumption of justice as free exchange. While beginning with different models and normative assumptions, they have much in common. They both base their social theories on the separate functions of a market economy, political pluralism, and cultural diversity; they both turn democracy into a technical method based on free elections and the circulation of elites; and they both rely on the rationality of the market and private sphere to make the most important decisions within society. They represent, however, two distinct dimensions within the conservative tradition. Benne claims that Rawls's principles of "liberal equality," "the difference principle," and "fair equality of opportunity" are already present in the actual economic features of the American social system. Novak, on the other hand, defends the competitiveness, inventiveness, and creativity manifested in the U.S. market economy.

Both men are concerned with justifying the moral foundations of democratic capitalism. Being more eclectic than Benne and thus having a broader range of moral and political categories, Novak appeals to the traditional values and perspectives of American society with his emphasis on self-realization, individualism, liberty, pluralism, and the rationality of the marketplace. Novak, like Benne, believes that the political and moral values that ground capitalist society have not been clearly articulated or accurately presented. In the same manner as Benne, he attempts to integrate moral philosophy and political economy, but without the former's recognition of the need for methodological clarity. Benne is more interested than Novak in metatheoretical issues, as he attempts to ground his normative assumptions in a clear methodological framework, which takes into consideration current debates within the philosophy of the social sciences. For Novak the distinguishing characteristics of the American social system are not found in a one-sided materialism and economism, but in the possibilities of its own political and economic idealism. That is, they are to be found in its values of fraternity, teamwork, republican spirit, nonideological pragmatism, equality of rights and opportunity, and political diversity and liberty.[1]

MORAL FOUNDATIONS OF NOVAK'S DEMOCRATIC CAPITALISM

After summarizing the general indictments and criticisms of capitalism by European social theorists, Novak begins his *Spirit of Democratic Capitalism* with a general definition of democratic capitalism. He relies on Daniel Bell's tripartite separation of the economic, political, and cultural elements that constitute the essential components of capitalism's social structure.[2] It is a market economy based on political rights and freedoms and grounded in the cultural ideals of universal liberty and justice. According to Novak, the classical sociological criticisms of liberalism and modernity are based on theories of alienation (loss of power), rationalization (loss of meaning), and anomie (isolation and normlessness). They thus have their reference points in traditional societies and thereby judge democratic capitalism by standards not appropriate to it. The search for individual difference and variety are the hallmarks of this new form of society, not the adherence to traditional values and social cohesion. This freedom of intellectual inquiry is even capable of questioning its own moral and social foundations. It is this freedom that can lead to anomie and alienation; it is also this freedom upon which the liberties and values of modern pluralist society rest.

What are the intellectual traditions that form the basis for a cultural legitimation of democratic capitalism? What is the foundation for Novak's critique of sociology and modern political economy? He begins his analysis with a critique of both utilitarian and Rawlsian political philosophy, since both traditions begin with the ontological primacy of the individual over society. Kant, Bentham, Mill, and now Rawls did not see the danger of the radical individualism inherent in their social theories, since they eliminated the "transcendental" order of reality and its concern for the moral good of mankind. Novak is suspicious of the universal moral claims of traditional political philosophy, because, for him, there is no correct moral ordering of the social world. Rather there is a plurality of competing intellectual and moral perspectives, none of which is totally correct and none of which transcends the limits of personal interests.[3] Neither reality nor rationality itself conforms to the universal claims made by individuals calling for some social good. Political pluralism is the necessary result of a more fundamental problem of epistemological pluralism. That is, there is no universally correct set of political principles which can guide human activity. This necessitates that the economic and political market be the arbiter of social consensus and ethical truths.

Throughout this work, it is clear that Novak bases his ethical and political perspectives on what has been called the "theory of democratic elitism."[4] The major assumptions of this political philosophy are:

1. Traditional moral and political claims to universalism cannot be justified philosophically or scientifically.
2. Knowledge of morality must be expressed in realist categories and not in terms of idealism or utopianism of the common good.
3. Democratic pluralism must be defined in terms of democratic methods and the circulation of elites.

This tradition of epistemological pluralism has its roots in classical liberalism in the works of John Stuart Mill (1806–1873). Novak integrates these ideas with those of twentieth-century theorists Isaiah Berlin and Joseph Schumpeter. Novak's epistemological pluralism is the result of his skepticism regarding traditional political philosophies and their inability to deal with the issue of the common good. Authoritarian oppression has resulted from people believing they had a privileged claim to truth. This inability to establish rationally the priority of one ethical position over another pushes Novak to the conclusion that only in a society built around interest-group pluralism will there be a true search for the substantive good. He completes this analysis by recognizing that he is not advocating a moral relativism. In the end there can be a single truth established by this process of "humble conflicts." Truth is thus the result of practical interaction, dialogue, conflict, and resolution, and not the product of prior philosophical reasoning.[5] Novak is also developing the political implications of Karl Popper's liberal philosophy of science.

Novak does not take over this philosophical skepticism from the intellectual traditions without first responding to some of the criticisms leveled against a theory of political pluralism, especially by political scientist Theodore Lowi. Lowi's criticism of this theory is that there is no specification of the relationship between means and ends. Everything is reduced to the process of conflict as the means of resolving political differences. In the end there is no ethical substance or universal ethical criterion for determining the social good.

Novak argues that, on the contrary, it "is a mistake to imagine that they do so through ignoring substantive goods in the name of procedural goods."[6] For Novak, there is a substantive good in the moral or social truth of the development of the human spirit and the integrity of its person, as well as in maintaining the social structure within which the common life of society is made possible. The issue, put simply, is Novak's defense of the substantive good of democratic society adequate to meet the criticisms made against it? The substantive values of traditional political philosophies, with their a priori metaphysical and political assumptions, are rejected, but Novak does not go to the opposite extreme of political relativism. Despite his criticisms of traditional ethical objectivity, he holds to the view that democratic capitalism does have specific objective moral values at the heart of its system. He wants to develop this insight into a theory of ethical values midway between the traditional metaphysical perspectives and their modern critics who move in the direction of relativism.[7]

MORAL SELF-DEVELOPMENT AND ECONOMIC INEQUALITY IN LIBERALISM

Throughout Novak's work there is a constant criticism of the assumed moral superiority of socialism. His purpose in writing is to replace socialism with democratic capitalism as the moral foundation for individual development and social cohesion. He stresses that the social system contains expressions of both private and public power, which liberalism finds so dangerous; it is just this fear which pushes the capitalist system to pluralism and economic dynamism. Responding to the moral criticisms of capitalism by socialist theorists, Novak contends that economic inequalities are not evil or immoral, but rather expressions of different physical, psychological, and mental capabilities; that is, the economic hierarchies and inequalities of capitalism are the product of natural inequalities of talents, abilities, and accomplishments.

Any political economy which wishes to be as creative as possible must try to invent a system which permits persons of talent in all fields to discover their talents, to develop them, and to find the social positions in which their exercise bears maximal social fruit. Necessarily, such a system must encourage self-discovery and self-improvement. Such a system must promote considerable fluidity and mobility. It must reward performance and learn to seek out talent wherever it may be found.[8]

This passage points to one of the profound difficulties of a comparative analysis of intellectual traditions. Connections between categories in this one paragraph are so complex that it takes a great deal of hermeneutical effort to unravel the interrelationships among moral, political, and economic categories. For example, what Novak has said could be accepted by a socialist theorist. However, the difference would lie in a more detailed understanding of the relationship between moral ideals and social goals. Does Novak confuse and mix different social issues to make his point? Other questions must be answered before Novak's ideas can be accepted. What are the issues of self-development and personal improvement, and what would they entail? What are the moral and structural issues involved when dealing with the question of getting the best people into the most important social positions? Are there two distinct issues of social stability and progress, on the one hand, and personal self-realization, on the other?

Joshua Cohen and Joel Rogers, in their work entitled *On Democracy*, have argued that the question of *material incentives* for the good of society is a separate issue from that of *moral incentives* for self-development. If the two questions are joined together, as in Novak's analysis, then moral self-development becomes an appendage to social stability, development, and economic efficiency. For Cohen and Rogers, the separation of the two issues results in a recognition that inequality has a structural rationale only if it enhances the material wealth of society; it cannot be a reward for better skill or talent. The rationale for inequality lies not in personal development, but in its ability to create wealth and provide for the material good of society as a whole. This is a straightforward utilitarian argument. If this is the case, then "it must be shown that the material inequalities they generate contribute to the material well-being of the least well-off."[9] In turn, it must be asked if there is any direct moral connection between self-development and economic inequality. It seems that the issues of moral self-development and the material good of society are related, but not in the crude way that Novak would like us to believe. One could even argue, as we will later, that to make a direct connection between the two results in economic inefficiency and distorted self-development. It reduces self-development to the materialism and violence of market competition.

In our worship of the survival of the fit under free natural selection we are sometimes in danger of forgetting that the conditions of the struggle fix the kind of fitness that shall come of it: that survival in the prize ring means fitness for pugilism, not for bricklaying nor philanthropy; that survival in predatory competition is likely to mean something else than fitness for good and efficient production; and that only from strife with the right kind of rules can the right kind of fitness emerge.[10]

In the end, this type of thinking by Novak simply rationalizes the economic inequalities of a class society.

A more sophisticated understanding of individual self-development, from different psychological, ethical, and sociological perspectives, is required. This would necessitate developing a theory of needs. However, Novak assumes the connection between inequality and self-development as given, along with a connection between self-development and the market. That which is to be proven and justified is assumed from the start of the argument. A more comprehensive comparison of the Bishops' Letter and the lay commission report requires that we investigate the implication of these types of assumptions. The major one is whether the chief motivation of individual behavior is the need for material success and security; a position which goes back to the seventeenth century and the theory of possessive individualism of Hobbes and Locke.

The real question is, why is inequality necessary?[11] Novak states, consistent with the realism of his initial methodological assertions, that while the socialist would like to create the new virtuous man, he begins with the sinner, "Humans as they are." But the analysis of what human beings are is itself a reflection of the material priorities of the acquisitive society. Certainly the anthropological and psychological assumptions that underlie the development of liberalism from its classical to its modern form assume a concept of man compatible with the institutions and structures of modern democratic capitalism.[12]

Novak next analyzes the second institutional element in his definition of democratic capitalism: the market economy. For him, the major advancement in the economic sphere is the continued creation of material wealth and economic variety. It is the law of supply and demand resulting from a free consensual agreement that becomes the integrating moment in society; it binds us together without restraining our activity or will. The market has created new modern technology and inventions, urban centers, higher industrial production, and more consumer goods from which to choose. The excitement generated by the dynamism of these new economic and social forces provides Novak with the insight that our liberty is enhanced by the technological and social forces which have developed out of this new social system.

Novak is aware, however, that there are other social theorists more skeptical and suspicious of the advances of this new system. He mentions four criticisms by socialists:

1. Markets solve problems on the basis of economic might
2. Advertising distorts rational decision making in the market

3. Large corporations have eclipsed the rationality of the market mechanism

4. The economy continues to create class antagonism between rich and poor.

He is willing to concede that the market does not always act according to the logic of textbooks, but despite reservations, he concludes "that [the market] is economically the most productive, intellectually the most inventive and dynamic, and politically the only system compatible with liberty."[13] The above problems are only the "price" we must pay for these benefits. For a justifiable grounding of the moral foundation of capitalism, these criticisms cannot be dismissed by Novak as simply the price we must pay. For his theoretical and theological defense of democratic capitalism to be successful, it is absolutely necessary that he adequately respond to these critics, whom he recognizes as having some validity. This is crucial, since their criticisms go to the heart of the ethical and political validity of liberalism itself. The critics recognize that society is founded upon class inequality and antagonism and that the ability to rationally deliberate and choose is hindered by the creation of false consciousness and needs through advertising. Large national and multinational corporations have been able to transcend the workings and logic of the local market mechanism, thereby undermining the social institutions upon which liberty, choice, and self-development of the individual rest.

Finally, if the social system continues to create class antagonisms, then the concepts of social mobility, economic dynamism, and inequality based on natural characteristics have a false ring and undermine the legitimacy of democratic capitalism. The adequacy of Novak's response is important for his justification of the ethical foundations of democratic capitalism, since they provide the best comparative test for his theory. If his analysis cannot decisively respond to these criticisms using his own theoretical and historical facts, then there is something problematic in his theory.

Novak responds by emphasizing the market and consumer side of the economy and the expanded purchasing power of the general mass of people. He says that as of 1978 there were 103 million automobiles in use in the United States by 57 million families. The question is: Does the expansion of consumer goods in the private sphere (leaving aside the issue of the deterioration of the public means of transportation) adequately respond to the socialist critique that "the market resolves problems according to the purchasing power of those with money."[14] This is a structural issue within political economy and goes to the heart of the decision-making process in a class society. There are two implications buried beneath this main point. The first is that the wealthy have the ability to make a broader range of consumer choices and thereby enjoy a happier material life. The second implication is that the private sphere, based on class inequality and a market economy, makes crucial decisions that could and should be made within the public realm. Political problems are solved by market decisions independent of the wishes of the people in society.

Some, like Milton Friedman, defend this form of economic democracy, since, according to him, this is the only form of true democracy. However, the danger is twofold. On the one hand, it is extremely doubtful that the market works according to the simple neoclassical logic of supply and demand as presented by Friedman in *Capitalism and Freedom*.[15] This theory omits from consideration the internal constraints of choices within the market created by structural barriers to information gathering, decision making, social mobility (racism, sexism, and class barriers), and access to power. Second, it is also very problematic that crucial political and public decisions that affect the everyday lives of people can be determined simply by the workings of a market, independent of serious reflection, public deliberation, dialogue, and compromise. The market reduces all choices to economic criteria and eliminates all other values as irrelevant.[16]

The second criticism of advertisement in democratic capitalism is not examined. There is no analysis of advertising, its effects on consumer habits, or the consumer's ability to make free and rational choices. Novak does admit, however, that if the objections are correct, then "the idea of democracy is in great jeopardy."[17] If this is as serious as Novak admits, then one would have expected a more detailed response; there is none. This is surprising, given the admitted importance of the issue to the whole question of democracy within capitalist society. In fact, the little time he does devote to the question, he spends asserting that advertisements are not that effective; that there is competition within industry; and that ultimately most consumers in the marketplace have a blending of both intelligence and ignorance. Finally, Novak concludes that this is really not as serious a problem as state propaganda, anyway.

The third objection is a very complex issue. Novak asserts that since the majority of economists and corporate executives do not accept the theory of administered prices in monopoly industries, there must be nothing to it. Again the emphasis on the status quo and the structures of the immediately given override any critique that might jeopardize the generally accepted theories. There is unfortunately no analysis of the data used to support the contention of the increasing concentration of economic and political power of large corporations; nor is there an analysis of corporate power and its ability to eclipse the workings of the market. There is no attempt to give serious consideration to the issues at hand and discuss their strengths and weaknesses. They are dismissed as simply beyond the realm of the generally accepted position in economic theory. But of course this would always be the case when social theorists, moralists, and theologians critique the generally accepted values and traditions in society. These issues will be further discussed in chapter four.

Finally, Novak responds to the argument that there is increasing class antagonism between the rich and the poor and growing disparity and distance between them. "Under market economies, the historical record shows gains in the real incomes for the poor."[18] The real problem for Novak is not the market, but rather not enough of the market. People are poor to the extent that they have not been integrated into the market economy. As compared with life in traditional societies, the spiritual and material well-being produced by market economies is superior.

In this sense, a defense of the free market is, first a defense of efficiency, productivity, inventiveness, and prosperity. It is also a defense of the free conscience—free not only in the realm of the spirit, and not only in politics, but also in the economic decisions of everyday life. It is, thirdly, a defense of the pluralist order of democratic capitalism against the unitary and commanded order of socialism.[19]

SOCIAL IDEALS AND MARKET RATIONALITY

When Novak talks about the market economy, his metaphors and hyperboles abound in praise of a system which excites individuals to imagination, creativity, and progress. It frees the individual from servitude to past traditions and opens up the future as an emergent possibility. Throughout his analysis of the ideals of democratic capitalism, Novak stressed the notion of the self-realization of the individual. Aspirations were limited only by abilities and talents. Society was so structured as to encourage these aspirations, whose goals were the self-improvement and self-realization of the individual.

It is in commerce and industry that the framework for the satisfaction of one's creative energies and the possibilities for self-fulfillment are realized. However, this position is not unproblematic. For example, it is on this very point that the eclectic method of Novak's political philosophy becomes a liability. There are a variety of traditions in Western political thought that have stressed the idea of initiative and creativity. However, as C. B. MacPherson in his *Life and Times of Liberal Democracy* has noted, these traditions are sometimes in total opposition to each other in terms of the meaning and implications of their ideas. The emphasis by Novak on self-development and creativity within the market economy was viewed with skepticism by the classical liberal theorist John Stuart Mill in his analysis of these same ideals. MacPherson has said:

Men as shaped by the existing competitive market economy were not good enough to make themselves better. Mill deplored the effects of the existing market society on the human character, which made everybody an aggressive scrambler for his own material benefit. He deplored even more strongly the existing relation between capital and labour, which debased both capitalist and labourer. He believed that there could not be a decently human society until that relation was transformed. He put his hopes on an enormous spreading of producers' co-operatives, whereby workmen would become their own capitalists and work for themselves jointly.[20]

Mill questioned the assumptions of a social system in which work and creativity were to be defined in terms of consumption and passivity. He saw it as problematic that the worker had no opportunity to determine the workplace decisions that were made or the ultimate meaning of the work itself. Novak does not understand that there is a fundamental contradiction in his analysis of the capitalist system between the ideals of individual self-development and social relations of the marketplace. That is, the ideals of self-realization are constrained, if not repressed, by the structures of the marketplace. There is a contradiction between a life spent on accumulation of wealth and property and one spent in the spiritual, cultural, and social quest for self-realization. Money can neither be the goal nor the measure of success in this latter venture. In capitalist economies, individuals are not seen as creators of their own lives or as creators of the institutions that affect them most immediately in the workplace. They are viewed more as passive consumers of the material goods and logic of the market.

Though Novak never really informs us as to the nature of self-realization, it is clear that it can occur only within the structures of capitalist society. And these structures are bounded by alienating work, hierarchical power structures, materialism, passive consumption, and social ideals turned into cosmic stereotypes by the media. Self-realization for Novak occurs only when the individual has become successful within the market. He contends, in his book *Will It Liberate?*, that J. S. Mill in his *Principles of Political Economy* defended the political economy of democratic capitalism as resting on cooperation and respect for human dignity. Novak has misread Mill. In his later writings, Mill recognized that self-realization was possible only outside the traditional institutions of competition. Because of this insight, he called for new forms of work relations, limitations on wealth, high taxes on inheritance, equality of opportunity, and socialism.

> The form of association, however, which if mankind continue to improve, must be expected in the end to predominate, is not that which can exist between a capitalist as chief, and the work-people without a voice in the management, but the association of the labourers themselves on terms of equality, collectively owning the capital with which they carry on their operations, and working under managers elected and removable by themselves.[21]

It was Mill who saw the contradictions between cooperation and competition, respect for human dignity and class conflict, and equality of opportunity and wealth inequality. He believed that the form of work organization, competition, and class conflict undermined the very possibility of human dignity and cooperation. Mill, Novak, and the American Catholic bishops view creativity as a process. Where Novak differs from the others is in his fundamental understanding of the concept. Mill and the bishops view creativity as an intellectual, spiritual, and political category with an emphasis on the value of participatory democracy. Novak defines creativity as wealth creation through the development of entrepreneurial skills. When creativity and imagination are bound by the economy, the limits of self-transcendence are set by the rationality of the marketplace. The only form of creativity to develop out of the market is the creativity to make money, not the creativity to expand one's values and freedom. By not articulating the content of that liberty, by abstractly and obtusely setting no limits beyond the rationality and capacity of the individual, and by reducing liberty to market choices, the substantive content of Novak's political philosophy lies in alienation, rationalization, and anomie. The theories developed by nineteenth- and twentieth-century sociologists, pointing out these developments, provide us with a clearer insight into the real possibilities and limits of capitalist society.

Another serious weakness of Novak's theory lies in his negative concept of freedom and his corresponding underdeveloped theory of social psychology and political economy. The individual is social and enmeshed in the complex web of interactions and social structures. A more developed social psychology would imply the need to expand the concept of liberty to include not only public institutions, but private ones also. It is a question of the nature and form of coercion that is the real issue. Novak, like most neoconservatives, views coercion as the limitation of individual freedom resulting from a command economy or absolutist state; what is overlooked to the detriment of his theory is the coercion implicit in all forms of institutional relations, especially at the microeconomic and macroeconomic levels. The nature of the workplace, the worker's relations to employers and fellow workers, and the social forms of technology and production are overlooked in a theory which sees the economy as based on free and uncoerced agreements between individuals. The control over the nature of work—its rhythm, organization, and purpose—and the control over the macro-decisions in the market by large corporations, government expenditures, taxation, and monetary and budgetary priorities, are in the hands of a very small group of corporate and political elites.

FETISHISM OF HUMAN RIGHTS: REDUCTION OF RIGHTS TO MARKET LIBERTIES

Novak does not provide a systematic presentation of his understanding of the organization of American political economy. His structural analysis is mixed with his analysis of the values and norms that ground democratic capitalism. This makes it more difficult to properly analyze Novak's defense of the institutions of advanced capitalist society. However, given these limitations, there is still enough information supplied by Novak to give us a picture of his structural orientation.

Whereas Benne stresses the manner in which the structural components of American political economy manifest and realize the moral principles of John Rawls's theory of social justice, Novak stresses the manner in which capitalism protects and buttresses moral autonomy and self-development of the individual, liberty, and market rationality. Both authors represent different sides of the conservative debate over the moral foundations of modern capitalism. Novak, like Robert Nozick, has a concept of individualism that includes a strong spiritual and communal component, while at the same time emphasizing the market forms of liberty and rationality.

Scattered throughout his writings are his thoughts on the structural nature of political, economic, and social institutions and how they are interrelated with one another. Novak deals with the market, its structural configuration, its importance for social order, voluntary relations, and rational social organization. An important presupposition in Novak's thinking is that the economic realm is independent of both the political and social realms. This is crucial, since it is this very independence of the market which results in personal freedom and a liberal society. He accepts the notion of the invisible hand of the market structure, whereby the pursuit of self-interest leads to the general social good. The logic of the market incorporates the intentions of each individual as well as the unintended consequences of the competitive quest for improvement and efficiency.

The rationality and liberty of the marketplace is far superior to the totalitarianism of imposed social control from centralized planning. "The reason the hand is 'invisible' is that the rationality of the market is not commanded."[22] The greater freedom of action and rational decision making based on individual self-interest expands individual liberties. Novak admits that it is the order created by individual decisions, that protects the possibility of liberty and democracy itself. The central point in his analysis is that the market does not coerce, dominate, or distort the wishes of the individual; in fact, the market is neutral. Decisions and the results of those decisions in a free market are voluntary and lead to the continued protection of individual liberties and rights.

Novak's analysis represents a continuous theme in liberal thought from Locke to the present: The individual must be protected from all forms of "absolute, arbitrary power."[23] However, the concept of arbitrary power is itself never fully clarified, as well as its major assumption that the state is always capable and likely to exercise absolute and arbitrary power. Excluded from consideration is a broader and more sophisticated understanding of the nature of political power that includes all forms of social constraint upon rationality and freedom, all forms of constraint upon the free exercise of individual talents and abilities. Included in this definition of power would be the economic sphere. Novak views this sphere as that part of the social system where voluntary associations and free contracts protect individual liberties. However, he, along with most conservatives, fails to see that the market is not a neutral social entity that facilitates the flow of information, products, prices, and exchanges. Rather it structures, however unconsciously, the manner in which options, choices, and decisions are made; it affects the formation of the individual's personality and consciousness; and finally, it structurally limits the range of decisions that are possible. The market is that social mechanism which puts into play the relationships among corporations, labor, and the state. Under the guise of market exchange as the free exchange between particular individuals, the market is a complex set of social arrangements in which the form, range, and orientation of various issues, problems, and exchanges are preselected and prestructured behind the backs of the individual participants. The invisible hand becomes an ideological sleight-of-hand.

The market influences the types of decisions which can be made and, in the process, the very nature of rationality itself. The rationality that results from the market, even assuming adequate information and awareness of the circumstances surrounding exchange, is limited to a calculable, instrumental rationality based on immediate self-interests of those involved.[24] A broader economic rationality of ethical and political decisions, as they affect the social whole and the common good, is not possible using this form of reason. An example of the dilemma inherent in liberal rationality is the problem known as the "logic of the commons."[25] This principle argues that, when decisions are based on rational self-interest, the broader interests of society are structurally and conceptually excluded. An example sometimes used is that of the dangers of overgrazing on common pasture by individual herders. In the "logic of the commons," decisions regarding the size of a herd of animals permitted to graze on a common pasture are left to the self-interests of each of the owners. Since the common field is limited, the growth of the herds will eventually result in the deterioration of the pasture and undermining of the foundation of economic productivity and efficiency. But the rationality of the market indicates that each herder decides on the basis of self-interest and not the common interest of the general welfare. The personal gain from adding more animals to the field more than outweighs the potential damage to it caused by the overgrazing of the pasture by a single individual.

According to William Ophuls, "competitive overexploitation of the commons is the inevitable result."[26] Given the market economy, the rationality of self-interest, the internal dynamics of competition, and the drive for ever-increasing profits, the result is a social system in which issues of the common good cannot be clearly articulated or represented. Individuals do not have full knowledge of both the individual and the collective implications of their particular actions. The free exchange of the market does not result in optimal transactions, nor are the private decisions of individual consumers without glaring broader effects. The decision to buy a bottle of beer, an automobile, or leaded gasoline all have implications which affect the amount of litter, decline in natural resources, pollution, quality of life, and governmental responsibilities toward refuse removal. Another theorist argues that the very logic of individual decisions is different from those of collective decisions.

Using the "Sen's Isolation Paradox," David Schweickart says that the decision to buy a disposable six-pack of beer, when viewed from the perspective of the buyer, is influenced by the convenience of not having to return the bottles to the store. However, in the public realm the political decision could be made, not inconsistent with the first, that the disutility caused by litter and pollution outweighs the convenience of not having to return the bottles to the place of purchase. Schweickart argues that there is no consistency between the two forms of logic, for they are entirely different: logic of convenience and self-interest and the logic of a clean environment. There is thus a contradiction between the logic of private interest and public good, upon which depends the rationality and legitimation of the market mechanism.

> It follows that a society of quite rational people, all of whom prefer a litter-free environment to the convenience of disposable bottles, might well find themselves inundated anyway—if they allow the market to effect the decision. Such an outcome is clearly not optimal, not even in terms of the individual's own preferences ... What we get is not necessarily what we want, nor what we would have chosen had the alternative been differently posed. Macroscopic outcomes do not reveal the preferences of even quite rational consumers.[27]

Left to itself, the market produces results which are neither optimal nor rational. Novak's praise for the rationality and order of the market is premature and requires further consideration. Though conservatives have considered the implications of externalities produced by the market, they have viewed them as extraneous to the heart of the system; they are externalities. Ophuls, when analyzing the issue of automobile pollution, argues that the logic of the market results in decisions such as "it will always be rational for me to pollute if I can get away with it."[28] The costs to the individual of controlling emissions is greater than the proportionate share of the damage to the environment. Thus, all forms of common property such as land, riverways, the biosphere, and genetic development—all of our ecological subsystems—will be damaged using this form of distorted rationality. When the market is left to itself, "the eventual result is bound to be common environmental ruin."[29]

RATIONALIZATION OF INDIVIDUAL RIGHTS

Marx had recognized the effects of permitting the market to make the key decisions in people's lives. It reduces all social relations between individuals to relations between things. It reduces the moral community to an instrumental relationship in which the other is treated both as a means to an end and as the personification of a particular economic activity and interest. The other person becomes a commodity, and all social relationships become fetishized. This too affects the way in which the framework within which rational decisions are made structures future decisions. It also affects our consciousness about the way goods and services are perceived. R. M. Titmuss studied the form of blood donations in England in his work *The Gift Relationship*. His examination revealed that there were two systems of blood distribution in England, one based on the right to sell blood (a market concept) and the other based on the right to donate blood (a personal gift).[30]

What interested Titmuss was the effect of one form of distribution on the articulation of personal rights and freedoms and how the rights and freedoms of one type of social activity were influenced and affected by another. Which form of blood distribution, that based on market values of self-interest or that based on moral values of the community, best expresses the rights of the individual? In his analysis of this dilemma, Peter Singer stresses two main points. Only the system based on the free giving of blood supports the right of recipience: right to life and free access to the appropriate medical care to sustain that life. The commercialization of blood donation inevitably alters the perceptions and exercise of this right. Also, the market may violate some rights that are not reducible to the narrow individualism defined by traditional natural-rights theory. Freedom, as defined exclusively by the market, is the right to sell commodities without infringing on the rights of others to sell their goods. Any interference in this process of free exchange is an infringement on the rights of the person. Singer and Titmuss argued that the existence of the market changes the way in which goods and services are perceived by the community and thereby changes the circumstances of voluntary exchange.

In his empirical study, Titmuss found that the existence of the market and the commercialization of blood giving discourages voluntary donations. The meaning of the gift changes in a commercial setting, and the communal bonding that resulted from it is lost. Both the right to give blood and the right to sell blood are incompatible, since they require two different types of distribution systems, two different types of communities, with their corresponding different types of expectations, perceptions of what is important, and social interaction systems. The existence of one form of right excludes the other form. A major implication of this discovery is that markets are not neutral in their protection of individual rights; they in fact protect a certain form of rights based on property ownership, market exchange, and self-interest: the right of possessive individualism. The debate over rights is a debate over human nature, the form of community, and the goals of society, which the authors represent in their writings.

Titmuss's study also reveals some more subtle ways in which the market may violate rights, including rights which are not rights of recipience. It does this in two ways. First, it provides an example of how individual actions which appear harmless can contribute to the restriction of the freedom of others. Second, it shows that one cannot assume without a great deal of argument about the nature of rights, that the state acts neutrally when it allows people to trade without restriction.[31]

With the acceptance of the doctrine of natural rights, one is also assuming a certain type of political economy and social structure which would institutionally support and protect these rights. The institutional buttresses can and do have psychological and sociological implications, in that they help form the type of personality appropriate for social interaction in these settings. This form of the commodification of individual development and social relationships, including the social relations of production, distribution, and exchange, undermines the ability of the individual to be conscious of the social forces affecting his or her decisions and thereby undermines the ability to control such forces. The market has a strong potential to be antidemocratic. Certain types of social decisions are structurally precluded from consideration within a market economy. The market can undermine the information, rationality, and consciousness formation necessary for a truly free and democratic society. The right of self-interest, as voiced in capitalist exchange, restricts the right to self-determination and the real moral autonomy which results from rational, conscious control over the decisions that affect our daily lives.

Self-determination becomes impossible within an unrestrained market. The market prestructures the mind, community, and the forms of rights in ways compatible with the underlying imperatives of self-interest, competition, private property, and capitalist social relations. Alternative forms of rights, freedoms, consciousness, and social interaction are precluded by these imperatives and institutions.[32] The view that the market is neutral, rational, and voluntary requires a very narrow understanding of these categories.

There can be no doubt, however, about the main thrust of Smith's argument: that markets as free as possible from governmental and religious command best serve the common good. Such a system frees the intelligence, imagination, and enterprise of individuals to explore the possibilities inherent in world process, which he conceived of — to employ the language of this chapter — as a universe of emergent possibilities.[33]

BENNE'S USE OF RAWLS'S PRINCIPLES OF JUSTICE

Robert Benne in his work *The Ethic of Democratic Capitalism* presents another discussion of the moral grounds upon which democracy and capitalism rest. This book is important because it offers the reader an alternative conservative defense of capitalism by relying on the liberal political theory of John Rawls. As in the case of the bishops, Benne begins his theory of justice with the neo-Kantian principles of human dignity and moral autonomy. Though the bishops apply these political and moral values differently, both they and Benne fail to see their inner connection to the structures of political economy; they both begin with a critical morality and end in conservative politics. An analysis of his thought throws more light on both the conservative and liberal applications of Kantian practical philosophy.

In Benne's analysis, morality is transformed into a question of the normative foundation of capitalism, dealing especially with the issues of social justice, fairness, and equality. He is critical of what he calls the mainstream theological condemnation of democratic capitalism and the leftward movement of academia toward democratic socialism. Using the philosophy of ethics of Rawls and the theological perspectives of Reinhold Niebuhr, Benne attempts to reconstruct the moral foundations upon which rest the justification of democratic capitalism.

Benne's method of analysis is intriguing, since he outlines the methodological and theoretical essence of Rawls's *Theory of Justice* as the basis for his own ethical theory. He then compares the results to a political economic analysis of American society. His conclusion is that only within the present institutions will one see the realization of the values and ethics of Rawls's position. That is, American society, with its democratic capitalism, is the only type of social system capable of realizing the ethical ideals of a just society. Benne begins his analysis of Rawls with a restatement of the latter's method of an ideal contract situation. Rawls articulates his theory of justice as fairness in his famous two principles of justice and grounds the whole discussion in his theory of the "original position" and "veil of ignorance." Benne painstakingly analyzes the crucial points of Rawls's complex philosophical arguments. One can assume also that with the exception of the specific critiques by Benne, the latter will accept most of Rawls's theory.

Rawls wants to establish unequivocally and transcendentally the universal validity of his ethical theory of social justice. Benne begins by outlining Rawls's dissatisfaction with traditional ethics and political philosophy. Criticizing the intuitionist and the utilitarian perspectives, Rawls argues that both theories begin with unproven and often unacceptable assumptions about what is ethically important. For him, there is no privileged access to moral truth and thus no foundation of the principles of social justice through a priori reasoning, empirical evidence, or religious tradition. There are no innate natural rights, rational moral imperatives, or proper metaphysics that can provide us with the universal and necessary insights into political truths.

> I do not claim for the principles of justice proposed that they are necessary truths or derivable from necessary truths. A conception of

justice cannot be deduced from self-evident premises or conditions on principles; instead, its justification is a matter of the mutual support of many considerations, of everything fitting together into one coherent view.[34]

To overcome these limitations, Rawls turns to a very interesting mechanism — a modern consensus theory of truth based on an updated social contract theory. The theory of justice is not to be imposed a priori, as with the intuitionists and utilitarians, but rather will result from the rational articulation of moral premises, goals, and values. No idea or principle will be accepted as true, according to Rawls and Benne, except what would be assented to by a rational individual in a free and open discussion. It is not philosophical reflection, but public discourse in the "original position" which will produce the desired results. The search for a universally and rationally accepted set of moral principles of social justice, agreed upon in an ideal setting, results in the following set of principles of justice: "First: each person is to have an equal right to the most extensive basic liberty compatible with a similar liberty for others. Second: social and economic inequalities are to be arranged so that they are both (a) reasonably expected to be to everyone's advantage and (b) attached to positions and offices open to all."[35]

In the course of his analysis, Rawls amends and develops the implications of these two principles because of their ambiguous nature. In particular, the phrases "to everyone's advantage" and "open to all" provide Rawls with some concern. Individuals are free when their values and obligations are made concrete in specific social institutions. That is, freedom is not an abstract philosophical category, but rather a concept that must be made real in history; it must be given structure and support by the institutions of society. The two key principles underlying these institutions are found in the political and civil liberties of the first principle and inequalities resulting from the distribution of the primary goods of society (income, wealth, and social positions) in the second principle.

The "principle of equal liberty" refers to the political liberties of equal citizenship, which include the right to vote, to hold public office, freedom of speech and public assembly. It also refers to the civil liberties of the right to liberty of conscience, freedom of thought, right to own personal property, and the general freedoms defined by the rule of law.

The second principle, known as the "difference principle," deals with the fair distribution of political, economic, and social power within society. Rawls begins his analysis with a hypothetical social arrangement within which all social primary goods (public and private liberties, economic and political powers) are distributed equally. In this starting position, all changes within and between principles can be measured and closely examined. "This state of affairs provides the benchmark for judging improvements. If certain inequalities of wealth and organization would make everyone better off than in this hypothetical starting situation, then they accord with the general conception."[36]

The actual form these inequalities may take are limited only by the difference principle or the idea that social inequality must be to everyone's advantage. Though Rawls states that extensive accumulation of wealth should not be allowed, there is no indication of where to draw the line and how much inequality is too much. This reference to limitation is then lost in his attempt to justify inequality through the mechanism of economic efficiency and productivity and the distinction between liberty and worth of liberty.[37]

The two principles are arranged serially so that no appreciable increase in material goods would warrant a decrease in political liberties. The first principle can never be sacrificed to the second. Economic development will never compensate for the loss of political liberties, and one can never be exchanged for the other. However, with the second principle itself, economic inequalities may occur if, and only if, they result in the improvement of the least advantaged's position in society. Just at the point where his political theory calls for consistency of argument, Rawls falls back upon neoclassical economics and the priority of material production.

> Supposedly, given the rider in the second principle concerning open positions, and the principle of liberty generally, the greater expectations allowed to entrepreneurs encourages them to do things which raise the longterm prospects of the laboring class. Their better prospects act as incentives so that economic process is more efficient, innovation proceeds at a faster pace, and so on. Eventually the resulting material benefits spread throughout the system to the least advantaged.[38]

This one paragraph attempts to justify the inequalities of the market based on stratification and economic productivity. There are a variety of very serious and unarticulated assumptions here. The first is that the market is the most efficient and productive form of economic system. There is no attempt at defining productivity or efficiency. The second is that inequality produces hard work, entrepreneurial creativity, and material satisfaction. The third is that economic growth compensates for the resulting social inequality and does not affect political and civil liberties. And finally, there is an assumption as to whom the concept of "least advantaged" refers and as to what "improvement" and "better off" refer.

A crucial methodological consideration here is the justification for the distinction between the first and second principles. The separation of political and economic principles, creating a hierarchy of importance between them and permitting the political equality of the first principle to be unaffected by the social and economic inequality of the second principle, remains unjustified. Norman Daniels believes that this dichotomy between equal political freedoms and economic inequality is a deleterious part of traditional liberalism. "Liberal theorists uniformly assumed that political equality is compatible with significant social and economic inequalities."[39] In the context of Rawls's social theory, the inequality permitted by the second principle undermines the equality of the first. This is the Achilles heal of liberalism, since economic inequality may destroy the very possibility of political freedom, solidarity, and community.[40] Concerning this issue, Carole Pateman critically adds the following: "The liberal view of 'democracy' holds that social inequalities are irrelevant to political life."[41]

The nature of the concept of inequality must be further discussed. There are various forms of material inequality, especially concerning the distribution of personal private property and public property. Some forms of economic equality within a socialist perspective would be permissible using the Rawlsian criteria, and others would not. For example, does it make a difference in Rawls's examination of the distribution of economic inequality if he is discussing inequality of personal property (non-income-producing property), such as the possession of a house, automobile, clothing, jewelry, and so forth? Would the serial ordering of the principles be affected if the inequality was the result of the distribution of private property (income-producing property) such as rental property, land, stocks, bonds, or bank accounts? There is certainly an important distinction between the two that would have enormous implications for the further development of a democratic theory of justice and for a further development of the forms of institutional arrangements most compatible with a Rawlsian approach to ethics.

While one principle of inequality refers to consumer inequality, the other becomes the basis for class inequality, economic exploitation, and the maintenance of a hierarchical system of power relations and dependency. Both Rawls and Benne are concerned with the further clarification of the two components of the second principle: the principle of democratic equality ("everyone's advantage") and the liberal principle of fair equality of opportunity ("equally open"). Rawls accomplishes this through a comparative analysis of the conservative and liberal interpretations of meritocracy and the social good. It is by means of this comparison within contemporary political philosophy that Rawls and Benne clarify their position on the classical tradition.

In a critique of a theory similar to that held by Novak, with its emphasis on natural talents and personal abilities within the marketplace, Rawls rejects the designation of a social system as just when founded only on the principle of natural liberty. Throughout his analysis of the various possibilities of meaning to "equally open" and "everyone's advantage," Rawls assumes that the first principle of equal liberty is satisfied even when the economy is a free market system. The fair allocation of income and wealth, authority and responsibility in a market economy is the normative underlying principle of his theory. A social system based on this principle of justice assumes the validity of the Pareto principle, whereby a system is efficient when there is no alternative redistribution pattern of social goods that would improve the position of any individual and at the same time not harm the position of another. Rawls's critique of the conservative theory of natural liberty, with its focus on meritocracy, market liberty, and formal equality of opportunity, is based on the fact that the initial distribution of personal assets and the social distribution of income and wealth is "strongly influenced by natural and social contingencies." Natural abilities, as they have been left undeveloped by personal contingencies or because of social and familial reasons, cannot be the basis for the moral justification of economic inequalities. In either case, chance cannot be the basis for a system of social justice. Benne develops this argument further.

> It also means further enabling those who have been hindered by social contingencies to compete better for those open positions. If equality of opportunity means that everyone should be able to run the same race for the open positions without unjust discrimination, fair equality of opportunity means that those encumbered by social disadvantage so badly that they are not even near the same starting line as the others are moved closer to that starting line by compensatory treatment.[42]

In fact, there is a strong element of injustice in such a system where morally arbitrary categories assume so much importance for the ethical grounding of a social system. The "liberal tradition" is more aware of this issue and attempts to counteract the negative effects of an open market based on competition, maximization of self-interest, and talent utilization. Liberals, on the other hand, combine an acceptance of a free labor market with the principle of fair equality of opportunity. Not only should all positions of authority in society be open to fair competition, but all should have a fair chance to get them. This means that not only personal ability but social standing have a place in the allocation of social positions. Thus the "liberal position," according to Rawls, wishes to impose structural constraints on the market allocation of social positions in order to correct for any unfair advantage due to social class. There must not only be a formal equality of opportunity, there must also be a fair equality of opportunity; this necessitates some form of state intervention into the economy.

The two main structural requirements and imperatives of the state in this view of liberal equality are the maintenance of equal opportunity of universal education and the prevention of extensive accumulation of property and wealth. Rawls feels that this perspective is morally and philosophically superior to that of natural liberty; it does accept a class structure and unequal market allocation for the distribution of income and wealth. The "liberal position" is concerned with mitigating the effects of this type of system, but not eliminating them. However, it does so not by restructuring the system to correspond to its moral ideals. Rawls returns to a more classical definition of social justice by combining the liberal principle of fair equality of opportunity with his difference principle. He states it as a position whereby "the social order is not to establish and secure the more attractive prospects of those better off unless doing so is to the advantage of those less fortunate."[43] Inequality is to be permitted when the result is a more efficient, innovative, and productive economic system that raises the material standards and quality of life of all, but especially the least well off in society: the working class. Benne also favors this difference principle and believes that it would be the principle of justice chosen in the original position.

> The difference principle would be chosen by those in the original position because it would provide a way in which all could share in the benefits of the distribution of natural talents and abilities. The inequality conditioned by the natural distribution of talents would work out to the advantage of the most unfortunate representative individuals. In fact, the inequality is permissible because eliminating it would make the least advantaged even worse off than before. Thus, a just system will distribute the primary social goods—liberty and opportunity, income and wealth, and the bases of self-respect—in such a way as to maximize the long term prospects of the least fortunate.[44]

There are two crucial assumptions being accepted here by Benne. The first is that a major motivating factor in the determination of economic activity is personal inequality and self-interest. Second, the resulting economic inequality would not in any way negatively affect the political and civil liberties of the individual. In fact, the way in which both Rawls and Benne define freedom, social justice, and individual liberty tends to maintain the continued liberal distance between economic and political categories. That is, economic inequality and political liberties are compatible, since the nature of political power and individual freedom have been defined so narrowly; there is no discussion of the effects of a class system on self-determination and democratic participation. A discussion of the political process in terms of market categories such as competition, pluralism, and rational choice theory results in the further rationalization and weakening of democracy. Though Novak too is aware of these possible implications and dangers in his writings and is thus critical of Weber's and Schumpeter's theory of plebiscitary democracy (also called democratic elitism), he unwittingly falls into the same problems by developing an economic theory based on similar ideas of the circulation of elites, leadership, and market pluralism. Novak, too, moves into a form of technocratic liberalism.

RATIONALIZATION OF DEMOCRACY: TECHNOCRATIC LIBERALISM FROM WEBER TO BENNE

Benne's description of America's political economy is based on his reading of Milton Friedman and Joseph Schumpeter. What Benne fails to recognize is that the economic theories of these two authors undermine his initial defense of Rawls's theory of justice and ethical principles, since the philosophical traditions of all three individuals are in contradiction to one another. The result is that Benne's conservative political economy undermines his liberal ethics and political theory. He has obviously not noticed the contradictions between his acceptance of Rawls's liberalism — with its defense of moral individualism, equal liberty, political participation, and self-respect — and the normative assumptions of his own economic theory. It is this contradiction between Benne's ethics and his social theory that weakens his argument that American society has realized the moral goals of Rawlsian political philosophy.

Relying on Paul Samuelson's analysis of the free market economy, Benne describes capitalism as having the following characteristics: a free market economy where economic decisions are made through economic competition and free choice, private ownership of the means of production, and a legal order that protects the boundary conditions of the market economy. Benne then turns to Schumpeter for guidance in his definition of democracy: "The democratic method is that institutional arrangement for arriving at political decisions in which individuals acquire the power to decide by means of a competitive struggle for the peoples' votes."[45]

This passage, quoted from *The Ethic of Democratic Capitalism*, is an abridgment of the definition found in an earlier part of Schumpeter's work, *Capitalism, Socialism and Democracy*. Following the initial definition of democracy as an institutional method for arriving at political decisions, Schumpeter writes that democracy is "incapable of being an end in itself, irrespective of what decisions it will produce under given historical conditions."[46] He examines the distinction between the classical definition of democracy (represented by Rousseau) and his reworking of it to fit the historical circumstances of an advanced industrial society. As recognized by many authors in political philosophy, the differences between the classical and modern views have startling implications for the manner in which one interprets democratic values and institutional arrangements. Benne seems unaware that, by viewing American society in terms of Schumpeter's definition, he has developed an analysis of American political institutions that undermines his original position on equal liberty and moral autonomy. He combines incompatible traditions. This is the disease of conservativism.

The classical definition of democracy stressed that decisions were to be made for the common good and that the people themselves were to decide the issues that affected their lives. Elected officials were to be the executors of this general will of the people and were not to replace the latter as sovereign. The political process was the means by which citizens decided the ends and goals by which the society as a whole was to be organized; it was a process in which the individual matures, is educated, and develops those characteristics necessary for social virtue. It was a creative and dynamic sense of democracy, in which the possibilities for the political future of a country rest with its citizens. There was no static view of human nature, since individuals create themselves in this process of political development. The goal of democracy was to be the cultivation and development of the highest potentials of human creativity in the public realm.

With the rationalization of democracy, however, the moral content of the classical perspective was drained. Democracy is reduced to a technical method of formal procedures from which the normative content of the classical ideals has been eliminated. The aim of the election process is to choose the country's leadership and produce an efficient government from among the competing elites, while the collective consciousness of the electoral mass is formed by the management techniques of the party (theory of competitive leadership). This represents a strictly instrumentalist view of politics in which the moral element of individual development and improvement has been eclipsed. There are, in fact, no goals to be realized in this social system, other than the technical efficiency of the political process.

Schumpeter argues that the people in an advanced industrial society are incapable of formulating serious opinions about political issues. Therefore it is necessary that the popular will be "manufactured" in the same manner as consumer opinion is artificially constructed by means of advertisements and the creation of new consumer needs through the manipulation of the subconscious.[47] Images that affect peoples' fears, anxieties, frustrations, and hopes are constructed in order to further material consumption; advertising is successful to the extent that it circumvents and avoids rational deliberation about private and public choices. On the other hand, the hallmarks of the classical perspective were rational discussion, debate, compromise, and clearly articulated thinking. These are the very things dangerous to a modern society, since control of the political process by elites requires the replacement of politics by technology and apathy; the public sphere must be incorporated into the market.[48]

Schumpeter had realized "that in reality they [citizens] neither raise nor decide issues but that the issues that shape their fate are normally raised and decided for them" through the circulation of elites.[49] Individuals control those in leadership positions by their power of voting, but they no longer decide the issues which determine their fate. The sloganeering, party banners, speeches, and apparent absurdities of the election process are part of the psycho-techniques of party management by which opinion is shaped. In the electoral process, the citizens are only capable of stampede. Pluralism is the mechanism by which differences among the elites are worked out and decided in the electoral process. But democracy becomes unworkable, if not dangerous, when carried out according to the imperatives of the classical model. "The principle of democracy then merely means that the reins of government should be handed to those who command more support than do any of the competing individuals or teams."[50] This political model assumes the validity of the market mechanism, since it is upon this institution that the new definition of democracy rests. Individuals are consumers of political opinion and through competition in the political market make democratic choices regarding their leaders. It is this synthesis of pluralism (political competition) and elitism (circulation of leadership) that has attracted so much critical review. The inherently undemocratic implications of this process go unrecognized by Benne and Novak.[51]

Peter Bachrach has written that the reduction of democracy to a political technique or tool results in the loss of questions that have been at the heart of traditional political philosophy: those concerning the nature of man and the good society, and moral dignity and worth of the individual. With the elimination of normative goals from the definition of democracy, the stage was set for the synthesis of elitism and democracy, two seemingly contradictory concepts. With no overriding ideals or goals, the critical edge of the traditional perspective is lost, along with its ability to judge, evaluate, and to ethically critique liberalism.

> The fundamental disadvantage of this criterion (political method) is that it gives the theorist no basis for judging whether the system is becoming more democratic or more elitist in nature.[52]

> Since there are no objective criteria of good and bad, the assumption runs, there are also no such things as better and worse. There are only *different* actions, choices, desires, and accomplishments, all of which possess equal worth.[53]

With the modern concept of democracy developed by Schumpeter and expanded by later political theorists, the moral content of the theory had been emptied.[54] Without a moral grounding in a theory of the good society and with this systematic denuding of all moral content, there was no longer a basis upon which contemporary social theory could evaluate the democratic progression or totalitarian regression of formally democratic institutions. The validity of democracy rests on a formal set of institutional procedures that, if technically applied and properly carried out, confirm its validity. However, there are no transcending normative criteria by which to evaluate the direction of modern political institutions. There is no ethic, which is capable of confirming or denying the self-development of human potential or political freedoms in the modern state. The realm of moral discourse disappears, and language itself is rationalized. The ultimate ends of this system are the maintenance and justification of the current political method. Positivism and technocracy have become the epistemological and political ideologies of liberalism. Any normative goal of popular participation, realizing the general good, individual self-development, or fulfillment of the general will are omitted by definition from philosophical consideration. This is known as the scientization of politics. The logic and priorities of Schumpeter are expanded decades later by the Trilateral Commission. Some of the most famous neoliberal businessmen, politicians, and theorists, including former President Jimmy Carter, participated in the work of redefining the nature of democracy in advanced industrial societies.

The traditional ideals were viewed as part of a metaphysical system within classical political philosophy that could no longer support itself through an objective epistemology. Science and empiricism (positivism) became the focal points for the analysis of democratic institutions, the latter being defined not in terms of an ultimate teleology, but rather in terms of the criteria of science: the analysis of that which "is" and not that which "ought" to be. This is certainly part of a broader intellectual movement in America known as the "end of ideology." According to this theory, if the ideological and political conflicts of class struggle and liberalism in the nineteenth century no longer exist, then politics is really concerned with the administrative and technical questions of efficiency, crisis avoidance, and stability maintenance; it is concerned with the equilibrium and balance of the system. Traditional politics and public disagreements over the nature of the allocation of political benefits, along with the ultimate and underlying questions of the nature of the good society, are no longer an issue. As Jürgen Habermas has said:

> The substitute program prevailing today, in contrast, is aimed exclusively at the functioning of a manipulative system. It eliminates practical questions and therewith precludes discussion about the adoption of standards; the latter could emerge only from a democratic decision-making process. The solution of technical problems is not dependent on public discussion. Rather, public discussion could render problematic the framework within which the tasks of government action present themselves as technical ones. Therefore, the new politics of state intervention requires a depoliticization of the mass of the population. To the extent that practical questions are eliminated, the public realm also loses its political function.[55]

This is a theme which runs throughout a variety of works, including those of Arendt, Wolin, Weber, Marcuse, and Offe. Benne, after relying on Schumpeter, uncritically continues this theme of reducing the range of the public sphere and the arena of democratic participation by developing the thought of Milton Friedman. Democracy is to be achieved by the further extension of market rationality into areas which formerly were reserved for public participation and discussion; this is a clear process of what Habermas called "structural depoliticization." For Friedman and Benne, this process transfers from the public to the private sphere the mechanism for decision making in a modern democracy; it is designed to enhance economic democracy and the individual autonomy of the consumer. It limits the number of issues to be discussed in the political process and cuts down on the possibilities of political instability that result from the creation of internal political divisions and conflicts within a country.

Schumpeter, Friedman, and Benne view the restrictions of the public arena as a positive good in a complex industrial society where public discussion of issues has the potential to organize opposition to state programs and undercut the technical efficiency of its crisis-avoidance and stability-maintenance policies. "Democratic distemper" and the "revolt of the young" are Samuel Huntington's euphemisms for the 1960s' protests against racism, the war in Southeast Asia, and calls for equality and political and civil liberties. The young have caused a rise in ideological passions which overloaded the political system and which, in turn, must be curtailed in the future.[56] Franz Hinkelammert has said that this "new democracy is not the legitimate heir of liberal democracy: it is an illegitimate offspring. It is the legitimate heir of fascism."[57] His point is that this "new democracy" rejects natural rights and the basic values of traditional liberalism in its attempt to maintain capital accumulation.

One of the real political fears of conservatives has traditionally been the political centralization of power in the hands of the state and the limitation of individual liberties. In reality, the function of the modern state has been to aid in the creation of centralized economic and political power in the private sphere. In the process, the education, self-development, and maturation of the citizens in the public sphere are reduced to the point where individuals do stampede in the political process. Quite possibly Schumpeter, Benne, and Huntington are correct in their realistic evaluation and description of the way in which American democracy works today. The question, however, is: Is this the cause of depoliticization or its result? We would argue that a more sophisticated understanding of the process of socialization would reveal that the political consciousness of individuals is formed within this very distorted institutional arrangement to the point where they become incapable of making intelligent decisions about their future. They have not been educated in the political process, as Rousseau and Mill had hoped, since the meaning of politics is reduced for them to a simple technical form of voting. For Habermas, there is a real danger in this process.

> But the technocratic consciousness is not based in the same way on the causality of dissociated symbols and unconscious motives, which generates both false consciousness and the power of reflection to which the critique of ideology is indebted. It is less vulnerable to reflection, because it is no longer only ideology. For it does not, in the manner of ideology, express a projection of the "good life" . . . Of

course the new ideology, like the old, serves to impede making the foundations of society the object of thought and reflection.[58]

The ideology assumes the validity of basic structures; no longer do normative goals have to be fulfilled, which could be used later to criticize the social organization of production and distribution and form a theory of social justice; nor is there a public sphere in which consciousness could be developed and sustained to consider the crucial issues facing society.[59] Benne does not consider that, in a class society where both income and wealth are so unevenly divided, where the market concentrates economic and political power and controls the form and structure within which public and private decisions are made, it may be impossible for this society to be organized for the benefit of those who are the least advantaged.

Benne argues that there are important economic gains to be had from this process of limiting access to the democratic process in the name of economic and political stability. Competition and innovation are increased, while consumer sovereignty is further protected. The political and philosophical justification for this view of economic democracy in a depoliticized universe has been clearly laid out by Schumpeter's critique of the classical tradition and by basing democracy on the foundation of positivism and science. Claus Offe and Jürgen Habermas have recognized that this reduction of the government to the administration of technically solvable problems eliminates from public review the issues of the ethical and political implications of governmental decisions.[60] This rationalization of the political results in further class control over the decision-making apparatus of modern society as democracy is turned into a political technology (method) for the rationalization and justification of class-based decisions. Chapter four will develop this theme when we examine the nature of the contemporary state within American political economy.

CONTRADICTIONS BETWEEN ETHICS AND POLITICAL ECONOMY

As we have seen, Rawls, Benne, Novak, and the lay commission report rest their theories on the primacy of human dignity. For Benne this fundamental principle is best understood as an expression of Rawls's category of "equal liberty." This is articulated in the section of *A Theory of Justice* entitled "On the Kantian Interpretation of the Original Position." The real meaning of equal liberty lies in the critical insights of Kant's view of the autonomy and freedom of the moral subject. It is this Kantian vision of moral philosophy and practical reason which informs the political theory of Rawls to such an extent that equal liberty was the necessary first moral principle. This principle is grounded in the desire to develop and maintain a moral character with a rational plan of life within a "community of rational agents who find their highest good and their most complete fulfillment in the rational discourse and collective deliberation by which they manage their collective affairs." The goal of this communal interaction is the development of individual autonomy and rationality through the formation of the self-legislation of the moral will. Individuals, as they develop their moral reasoning, realize their potential as real human beings. "To realize our nature we have no alternative but to plan to preserve our sense of justice as governing our other aims."[61] The primary goods of rights, liberty, authority, status, income, and wealth are of value, since they may help the individual as a rational chooser of ends (not as a chooser of consumer goods). Liberties, opportunities, and wealth ensure a sufficient social scope in order to pursue rationality and self-consciousness in a meaningful manner. The restriction of opportunities, unprotected liberties, and unavailable resources undermine both rational criticism and choice of ends.

Does the theoretical and institutional analysis of Benne, based on the moral principles of Rawls, support this view of moral autonomy of the individual? (Does the economic and political theory of the other conservative thinkers support this moral principle?) Returning to Schumpeter and Friedman, we see that the moral content has been eliminated from their theories, the political virtues of citizenship, education, and participation have disappeared, and the notion of individual self-development is gone. In the section of Benne's work entitled "The Virtues of Democratic Capitalism," he attempts to synthesize his ethics and political economy by joining Rawls's two principles of justice with his analysis of American political economy. He examines the historical and structural conditions that support these very principles and help realize their intentions. While recognizing that liberty includes public and private freedoms, Benne never once deals with an institutional analysis of equal liberty either through an examination of the intentions behind the concept or the structural supports necessary for its survival.

There is no recognition by Benne that he understands or is concerned with this principle. He directs his full attention to an analysis of the welfare state as the realization of the difference principle and the principle of fair equality of opportunity. At first this is very surprising, even though he did not consider the concept in the section devoted to Rawls's theory. A possible reason for this is that Benne interprets the first principle, which is the foundation of civil and political liberties, as representing economic rights and market liberties. In the process of transforming the concept of equal liberty from a political to an economic category, Benne has undermined Rawls's intention of protecting the moral subject. In effect, what Benne has done is to interpret the first principle in light of the political economy of Schumpeter and Friedman, while dropping the strong Kantian element at this point; he has fused (or depoliticized) the political and economic categories into one principle.

This can be clearly seen when Benne does mention the first principle in this section.

There is a certain sense in which the economic liberty encouraged by the American economic arrangement constitutes freedom itself. In the market economies such as ours, individuals are free to enter the market when and where they please. We can sell our goods or services to whomever we wish. In other words, we can choose our vocation. Of course, our freedom is limited by our own abilities and initiative as well as by what the market wants at a particular time.[62]

Half of this chapter represents a praising of the virtues of economic productivity and efficiency of democratic capitalism. Only once does Benne come close to perceiving the moral implications of the first principle, when he says that the self-transcending view of freedom is crucial in preserving the dignity of the individual. This is said, however, in the context of preparing the basis for a defense of the difference principle and the welfare state. There is no further discussion of the first principle nor any consideration of what the "self-transcending freedom of the human spirit" could mean outside the rationality of the marketplace. Benne reduces the Kantian moral heart of Rawls's analysis to the dictates and rationality of neoclassical economics. Any tension within Rawls over this issue has disappeared. The autonomy of the moral self is sacrificed on the altar of the normative order of the market economy. Choice and freedom are restricted and condensed to mean economic choices in the consumer economy. The self-transcending notion behind the Rawlsian category is lost and replaced by a materialistic principle of individual self-interest. Market freedom and self-development are in constant tension, since the latter requires the development of the moral freedom and rationality of the individual and not the maximization of the principle of pleasure and utility.

However, it is Benne who reduces political liberty to economic efficiency and growth. It appears that his reliance upon an intellectual tradition that has reduced rationality to an instrumental and means-oriented category and, thereby, has reduced moral autonomy and subjectivity to consumer freedom and market choice, has denuded the Rawlsian perspective of its critical practical rationality. In the process it has lost the normative and evaluative component of his political philosophy. Benne is unaware of the deeper norms and distorting effects that Schumpeter and Friedman have had on his moral philosophy. That they have directly affected his political thought, his analysis of the structures of political economy, and his attempt at the moral justification of democratic capitalism is very clear.

Benne has argued that the pluralism and diversity of the market, countervailing private power, a nonpoliticized economy, voluntary exchange, economic opportunity and social mobility, consumer sovereignty, and the natural justice of the marketplace have resulted in an efficient, free, and productive economic system. Economic growth has been steadier than in the past, with the economic benefits of the system more widely dispersed. Most of Benne's attention is directed at the growth of the capitalist market and the ever-increasing material pie that it produces. He commits the same mistake as Rawls by not examining the social relationships or basic structures that underlie the productive process he so highly admires. It is here that much of the traditional criticisms of capitalism have been directed, especially at the alienating and exploitative social relationships. A real emphasis on the subjective freedom and moral autonomy of the individual could not possibly fail to consider these social circumstances that so directly affect the very possibility of a moral will, rational consciousness, and public participation in the democratic process.

His focus on distribution and the difference principle as opposed to production and power relations and the social prerequisites for self-development greatly hinders his ability to deal with the structures of society and in the end limits his notion of self-respect and individual liberty to very narrow ranges of the distribution of social goods. Rawls analyzes the basic structure of the society in order to avoid the deficiencies of modern theories of justice. But Rawls in turn fails to examine the underlying social institutions and their relationships to the different moral imperatives of economic distribution based on status, need, contribution, effort, equality, and work. In the end he fails to consider the key institutional arrangement upon which the distributive features are ultimately based. Nor does he question the centrality of the distributive issue.

Does the redistributive function of the state in any way affect the inequality of power relations that underlie the productive process in advanced capitalist society? According to Rawls, the distributive function ameliorates some of the more obvious forms of inequalities and injustices. But on the other hand, as we will see in chapter four, through its transfer, stabilization, and distribution functions, the state maintains, supports, and expands the systems of control that create class, economic, and political inequality. Again there is a contradiction between ethical principles and social reality. "Consequently, inequality is construed in narrow pecuniary terms that neglect the psychological and political roots of exploitation in relationships conditioned by domination and submission, depersonalization and alienation, or socialization and public opinion. Rawls's formulation simply immunizes him to sociological modes of understanding."[63]

The Bishops' Letter had been criticized for its Rawlsian approach. It, too, stressed the priority of individual human dignity and self-respect. But the bishops were more aware than Benne of the contradictions between their moral principles and American social structures. Rawls and Benne had reduced social justice to issues of economic distribution, while the lay commission report reduced social justice to the efficiency and rationality of the market. But to the extent to which the bishops accept the principles of liberalism without careful scrutiny, they too fall into serious difficulties. For at its foundations, as we have seen in this chapter, liberalism is fundamentally an incoherent social philosophy. This is a result of the internal contradictions between its theory and social reality, political philosophy and political economy, political equality and economic inequality, and its explicit political ideals and implicit social assumptions about the market.[64] To the extent that the bishops simply graft on to liberalism a more humane political ideology, a critique of the unrestrained market, and a support for the welfare state, their theory of economic justice for all remains incoherent. Benne has been important in this critique of conservatism, since he more than the others explicitly defines his methodology and moral categories in relation to the broader social structures. There is a fundamental inconsistency in a liberalism which attempts to integrate the principles of human dignity and moral autonomy with the irrationality of a market economy and technocratic society. All the conservative theorists discussed in this chapter participate in this contradiction of liberalism. To the extent that the bishops in their letter draw upon Kant and Rawls and do not integrate ethics and political economy, they too participate in this incoherence of liberalism.

4

TOWARD A CRITICAL THEORY
OF POLITICAL ECONOMY

INTRODUCTION

As we have already seen, some have criticized the Bishops' Letter as just another form of New Deal democratic social theory proposing the same old, failed policy recommendations. Others have complained that the underlying economic assumptions of its proposals assume a healthy, growing economy as existed in the 1960s during the first War on Poverty.[1] But today's economic world, they say, is characterized by problems of productivity, economic growth, and very high deficit spending. In this type of world, the bishops' proposals—with their emphasis on the "option for the poor," *distributive*, *commutative*, and *social justice*, and new economic planning—fall on deaf ears.

For the conservatives, the major economic priorities are increased productivity, capital investment, and cutting the capital gains tax to encourage investments. Increased social spending is not part of this list. In fact, it is the latter, they argue, which has inhibited the possibility of economic expansion by absorbing scarce surplus which should have been used to rejuvenate the economy, certainly not for ethical experiments. In fact, they say, social justice will only come about as a result of economic growth, when more people have access to the material benefits of an ever-expanding economic pie. The uncontrolled growth of the welfare state, with its excessive government regulation of the workplace (Occupational Safety and Health Administration) and environmental protection (Environmental Protection Agency), along with excessive social spending on the undeserving poor, has lead to the problems we face today. Though we have been critical of this conservative perspective already, there is an element of truth in their critique of the welfare state which must be considered further. A closer look at the actual economic conditions is important, not simply to determine whether the policy recommendations of the bishops are realistic and appropriate, but also because more serious work must be done in the area of an analysis of political economy itself.

This requires that we begin with an examination of the historical structures of American political economy. The conservatives have avoided this by focusing on the symptomatic appearances of American social problems and attributing to them causal properties that they do not have. Yes, economic growth and productivity are important issues, but an analysis of the underlying structural deficiencies of the system is deflected to issues of spiritual growth, development of self-esteem, shoring up the traditional American family and its values, and increasing the incentives for the wealthy to invest in industry. This is an agenda designed to rationalize and justify the redistribution of income from the bottom to the top portions of American society and to avoid public discussion of this policy. There is something fundamental missing from this conservative approach.

CRITIQUE OF THE BISHOPS' LETTER FROM THE LEFT: THE DOMESTICATION OF SOCIAL ETHICS

Two critical social theorists have said that the Bishops' Letter is "probably the most radical document on political economy to have come out of a mainstream American institution in living memory."[2] Though they do not offer a blueprint for social change, according to Cockburn and Pollin, they do offer a sound philosophical foundation for their ideas, which call for full employment at decent wages, economic democracy, substantial reduction in military spending, and a partial socialization of investment and public planning. However, in spite of this praise for the letter, there is still something lacking in the bishops' approach. They make an important contribution to the contemporary debate by moving beyond a possessive and individualistic moral philosophy to a social ethics. Though they reincorporate economic and political categories back into ethical thought and apply moral standards drawn from rich philosophical and religious traditions, they have left out an important component in their analysis: a critical theory of political economy. According to the bishops themselves: "The pastoral letter is not a blueprint for the American economy. It does not embrace any particular theory of how the economy works, nor does it attempt to resolve the disputes between different schools of economic thought. Instead, our letter turns to Scripture and to the social teachings of the Church."[3]

Larry Rasmussen has said that "the bishops' account does not include a presentation of the institutional dynamics that generate the very results they lament. What command the bishops' attention are *outcomes* rather than *structural causes*."[4] This is a result of the inadequacy of the bishops' methodology, and Rasmussen traces it back to a serious flaw in liberalism itself, with its inability to understand the relationship between concentrated economic power and democratic political institutions. It is this unconscious reliance on the values and structures of liberalism that causes the bishops one of their most serious problems.[5] Liberalism influences the bishops' method and their policy recommendations in ways they are not fully aware of. A disparity exists at two distinct levels, which results in serious flaws in their work. There is the conflict in the bishops' method between their concentration on economic and social outcomes at the expense of an analysis of their underlying structural causes. And there is a disparity within their social theory between their communal moral principles of democratic solidarity and economic democracy, on the one hand, and the unarticulated values of liberalism based on self-interest, inequality, and undemocratic power relations, on the other. The latter values severely restrict the possibility of realizing the former, since there is a fundamental contradiction between the two. Their communal and moral ideals and policy recommendations become utopian when measured against the reality of the existing liberal values and institutions.

Liberalism will frustrate and undermine those aspects of their social theory that are democratic and socialistic.[6] The two problem areas are connected. If the bishops were more aware of the institutional and structural relationships of capitalism, they probably would have constructed a more radical social critique of American society and at the same time would have been more skeptical and cautious about the real possibilities of the evolution of socialism from liberalism. Sharp criticism also comes from the Third World, as from Clodovis and Leonardo Boff, who saw the "ideological inversions" contained within the Bishops' Letter. They call it a variant of bourgeois moralism that leaves unquestioned the basic logic and structure of capitalist economic development in both the First and Third Worlds.

> What seems to be most lacking in the vision presented in the pastoral letter is a clearer consciousness regarding the structural dimensions of morality. Perhaps we can speak of this as a case of moralism. Certainly, it is not seen how evil is incarnated in social laws, mechanisms, structures and institutions, nor is the existence of "structural sin" or the "structures of sin" taken into account. For this reason there is never a call for the suppression of these structures, but rather for their "moralization." ... In this sense we can say that the letter does not evidence strong "ethical/structural thinking." Its morality is more a morality of "acts" rather than of "structures." Because of this the letter is highly "individual" and not very "political."[7]

The Boff brothers examine the ideological assumptions hidden beneath the economic and social model used by the bishops: functionalism, pragmatism, reformism, and an abstract moralizing of the market. The result is an inability on the part of the bishops to examine and criticize the logic and structures of the capitalist mode of production.

The Bishops' Letter is divided into four parts, as we have already seen in chapter one. There are sections on their collective moral vision, the social problems in America, a description of these problems, and finally, specific policy recommendations for the future. What is seriously lacking is a developed historical and structural examination of political economy, with an analysis of the power and class relations in advanced capitalist society. This would have provided the missing link between the bishops' initial ethical views and later policy recommendations.[8] Both conservative and radical critics have argued that their policy proposals have been developed within an historical vacuum.

A radical critique of both the lay commission report and the Bishops' Letter thus would focus on their general lack of a structural analysis of American political economy. In order to have an integration of ethics and political economy, there must be three crucial components: moral principles, a critique of political economy, and specific policy recommendations. The central category is missing from both the liberal and conservative perspectives because this would force a serious questioning of the rationality of the market economy, the real reasons for the maldistribution of income and wealth in the United States, the dangers of concentrated economic power, and the theoretical inadequacies of classical and modern liberalism.

The Boffs also stress this point when, referring to the letter, they say that "what is basically missing in the letter is an analysis and critical understanding of what Capitalism really represents."[9] This is what they call a socio-analytic mediation. They also contend that the bishops criticize the American economy on the basis of moral demands (moralizing capitalism), but with little or no understanding of its underlying historical structures or real possibilities for social change. The bishops hope to restrain and improve the system through the use of moral imperatives without calling into question the system itself.

Andrew Greeley takes another approach in his analysis of the Bishops' Letter by stressing the historical process of the rationalization of the Catholic bureaucracy.

> Perhaps the pastoral does not challenge the power of vast corporate bureaucracies because it is itself a product of one such bureaucracy. If, for example, one asks how American steel and automotive industries deteriorated from greatness to rustiness in the space of a decade or a decade-and-a-half (at the most), one is forced to respond that both industries had become overcentralized, bogged down in internal corporate struggles, shortsighted, unimaginative and incapable of competition with foreign industries, precisely because they were bloated, muscle-bound, sluggish, oversized monopolies that for many years did not have to worry about price competition. Why modernize when you seem to control your own universe?[10]

Greeley, working within a more Weberian tradition, argues that the poverty examined in the Bishops' Letter is caused by structural deficiencies within the economy that lead to unemployment. And unemployment itself is the result of even deeper structural disturbances caused by the growth of large conglomerate business institutions, with their increasing concentration of economic and political power and their growing technical inefficiency. Economies of scale do not work effectively under these types of corporate structures. To seek a structural analysis would require questioning much that the lay commission and Bishops' Letter take for granted. The question of why the bishops failed to develop such a theory is more difficult to answer. Since they apply moral standards from outside the capitalist tradition, there is no unconscious attempt at an integration of principles and structures as occurs in the conservative perspective. Thus there is no need to avoid a theory of political economy, because it will not affect their stated ethical principles.

The danger could be more political than methodological. To develop a structural analysis of American society would be to confront directly its contradictions and the incompatibility between the bishops' ethics and American society. To avoid this unnecessary conflict, and anticipating strong pressures and disagreements within both the Catholic and non-Catholic communities over their policy recommendations, they simply decided to avoid another potentially disruptive debate. Their central focus is certainly on a clarification of the moral traditions upon which their ethical principles rest. They are also concerned with responding to the question of how to become an ethical Christian in modern society. The impact of the contradictions between ethics and social life would be exacerbated, if a long analysis of political economy were undertaken. Also there would be a danger that a theory of political economy would turn into a stronger condemnation of American capitalism, which in turn would demand a more radical change in society than the bishops were willing to undertake.

Thomas Schindler contends that there are three areas in which the second draft of the Bishops' Letter subtly differs from the first. The centrality of the "preferential option for the poor" is replaced by a more neutral position, which deals neither with political economy nor with changes within the welfare system from the perspective of the poor themselves. Also, the first draft called for a new social experiment based on the common good, which would be a break with the present system. He also charges that by the second draft, the continuity between the original American experiment two hundred years ago and the present system is stressed, thereby downplaying the need for an alternative socialist system. The third point mentioned by Schindler is that, whereas the bishops' moral criteria of solidarity, participation, and economic rights and their critique of inequality, poverty, and unemployment are radical, their overall critique of American political economy is grossly inadequate. That is, their political and economic theory is inadequate to their more radical moral values.

The bishops' pragmatic approach, however, domesticates their potentially explosive moral criteria. The bishops simply accept the overall structures of the U.S. economy and seek to work within them. They do not consider more basic questions of whether it is even possible within the U.S. economic framework to respond to poverty or unemployment or the farm or international problems with a commitment of solidarity, participation, and economic rights.[11]

The way in which the Bishops' Letter is organized places a renewed emphasis on the compatibility of Catholic social values and Catholic social life. What kind of life does an individual build, if he or she professes to be Christian? The clear dynamic here is between Catholicism and modernity. There is disagreement enough about the meaning of Catholic moral values, but a debate about the American political economy might unnecessarily make the issue too complex and obscure the central issue of social ethics. The bishops are calling for a New American Experiment not because of a need for a new political economy, but because of their interest in revitalizing the Christian message of the Good News.

However, the danger in using this approach is that it avoids a very complex area of economic and political questions and in the process distorts the adequacy and applicability of policy recommendations. If the critics are correct and the bishops have unreflectively retreated back into the past decades for their concrete insights, then their recommendations are suspect and their ethics will wither away, having no institutional support. There is a real possibility that without a critical theory of political economy, ethics will become an abstract, reified set of moral dogmas that "have now become obsolete verbal rubbish" and "ideological nonsense."[12] For moral principles to be made real and relevant, there must be an appropriate institutional framework which maintains, nurtures, and protects these values. Without it, the moral principles merely become part of a complex set of ideological rationalizations for an unjust social system. Therefore, between the moral vision and the policy recommendations for a new social experiment, a developed theory of political economy must be placed: a political economy that deals with the vast array of structural transformations of the American economy since the turn of the twentieth century. Only then will we be in a position to adequately understand and judge the bishops' proposals.

There is another danger in not developing a structural and historical theory of political economy. The bishops can never be sure if their moral and economic proposals could be accommodated by the present set of social institutions. Norman Birnbaum asks if, under the present conditions of a capitalist iron cage, moral autonomy is possible. Is self-conscious reflection, rationality, and human dignity even possible in a society characterized by rationalized social relationships, materialism, class system, and self-interest? When happiness and liberty are defined as material pleasure and consumer choice, are the ethical foundations of society threatened? By not developing a more historically concrete analysis of American institutions, "Have the bishops in their own thought reproduced that separation of ethics from economics and politics they so rightly deplore?"[13] In the process have they returned, however unconsciously, to an individualistic moral philosophy? As we move toward a theory of political economy, we will consider the development of the American economic system, its multinational corporate structure, and its present economic and social crises through an analysis of the following:

1. Income and wealth distribution and the inequality of power: the role of the welfare state

2. The development of economic crises (economic stagnation: stagflation of the 1960s, declining productivity and capital investment of the 1970s, and high deficits of the 1980s)

3. Declining research and development, capital investment, and social productivity, and the resulting deindustrialization of America

4. Wasteful military spending

5. The historical formation of corporate monopolies and the merger movements since the turn of the twentieth century: corporate restructuring through horizontal, vertical, and diagonal integration and the new phenomenon of leveraged buy outs

6. The social reorganization of labor and the workplace through Taylorism, scientific management, and the creation of a dual labor market (monopoly and competitive sectors of the economy)

7. Political economy of the state: role of state as encouraging capital accumulation and political legitimation.

Only when we outline these structures will we be in a better position to understand the nature of poverty, inequality, unemployment, and the other social problems mentioned in the Bishops' Letter. Problems associated with contemporary income-wealth distribution and social classes are the results of corporate restructuring and the reordering of the power relationships among the corporations, labor, and the state. The development of a theory of political economy also necessitates a rethinking of social ethics, since the latter is so closely tied to the former. We therefore go beyond traditional distributive justice and political theory (income and wealth distribution), since this is itself a function of broader issues found in economic justice and the critique of political economy (corporate restructuring, reorganization of labor, and new roles for the state). Political justice deals with questions of the protection of human rights and individual freedoms, human capacities and potentialities, the social possibilities of self-realization and development, the social institutions for self-determination, and political and economic democracy. The three forms of distributive, economic, and political justice constitute social justice. And when combined with moral philosophy in a holistic framework, we call it *social ethics*. The possibilities for self-determination and self-realization depend on the establishment of basic moral and political principles, an historical and structural analysis of

American political economy, and rational implementation of these social ideals. We cannot cover all the issues of social ethics in this book. But by playing off liberal and conservative ethics and social theory, we can begin to see an outline of what such a theory might look like. For the development of a theory of political economy we will start not with an analysis of the economic structure directly, but with that social mechanism that holds the whole system together: the contemporary welfare state.[14]

THE POLITICS OF POVERTY AND INEQUALITY IN THE WELFARE STATE

Conservative authors have admitted that poverty is real, but dispute its extent, causes, and implications for government policy. In the process they also carefully avoid imputing any causality to the economic system as a whole, while continuing to draw the distinction between the deserving and undeserving poor. They attempt to shift the locus of emphasis to the female-headed family, demographics, the political nature of the Census Bureau's official definition of poverty, and the welfare system itself. If the government would only include the in-kind government services (food stamps, housing allowances, Medicare, Medicaid, etc.) along with the cash assistance programs, then the level of poverty would be statistically reduced.[15] In the case of Charles Murray's argument in *Losing Ground*, poverty would be reduced dramatically if the public assistance programs were also eliminated or curtailed.

A more careful consideration of these issues, however, reveals a different set of conclusions, which require a more comprehensive analysis of political economy.[16] The 1980s have experienced serious economic transformations for the poor, which have resulted in dramatic reductions in public assistance programs, increasing before- and after-tax inequality between the lowest and richest quintiles in America, lower median incomes in the 1980s than in the 1970s, a growing poverty gap (those living below the poverty line), continued high poverty and unemployment rates, decreasing effectiveness of the antipoverty impact of government public assistance and social insurance programs, and faster rising poverty rates. These outcomes should be viewed as connected with deeper macro and structural changes in the economy: the transformations within the workplace (management-labor relations), the increasing number of low-wage service jobs, deindustrialization, declining productivity, declining real growth in the Gross National Product (GNP), declining corporate profit rates, declining wages and standard of living for the average American, declining rates of capital investments, rising military spending, rising domestic and international debts, rising government deficits, and increasing paper investment, paper profits, and conglomerate mergers. There appears to be no "white knight" on the horizon under the standards of Reaganomics. The first group of social problems is directly related to the structural changes in the second group.

There has been a sharp increase in poverty since the late 1970s, resulting from the Reagan fiscal, budget, and taxation policies. In fact, the average poverty rate during the Carter, Nixon, and Ford administrations was 11.9 percent, while during the supposed economic recovery of the Reagan administration, it increased to 14.2 percent. When we recognize that there is nearly another 20 percent more American families living just above the politically set poverty level, the actual extent of poverty is critically higher than normally thought.[17] The increase in poverty has affected all types of families, not just those headed by females, as Murray has argued. In fact, the percentage of female-headed families has dropped slightly, from 38 percent in 1978 to 37 percent in 1987. Only about one-quarter of female-headed families receive public assistance.[18] Robert Greenstein wrote in 1985 that even when female-headed households were on the increase, there was no correlation between that increase and increasing welfare enrollments or benefits.[19] The poverty level in 1987 was higher than in any year in the 1970s, with the Black and Hispanic minorities being the hardest-hit groups in the population. In a further response to Murray, David Ellwood, in his work *Poor Support*, writes that AFDC and single parenthood could not have been the cause of rising poverty rates and welfare usage, since fewer children were actually receiving public assistance benefits after 1972. In fact, the benefits from AFDC were about the same in 1988 as they were in 1960.[20] The image of the enormous feeding of the undeserving poor at the public expense is a difficult myth to dispel.

Not only did the poverty rates increase, but the nature of poverty below the poverty line changed. The gap between the rich and poor families grew to the widest point in the past 40 years, as the income of the average poor family continued to fall further below the official poverty line. In 1987 it was $4,165 below the poverty line, and in 1988 it was $4,851. This is the largest poverty gap since 1960.[21] Neither of the two most prestigious poverty research groups in the United States, the Center on Budget and Policy Priorities in Washington, D.C., and the Institute for Research on Poverty at the University of Wisconsin, see the transformation or breakdown of the family as the crucial element in explaining this rising poverty. They do see a connection between the rising poverty rates and the doubling of the unemployment rate since the late 1960s. The implication drawn from their statistical analyses is that structurally deeper economic forces are at work, causing a rise in poverty rates.

According to another important research group, the Urban Institute, the rise of poverty during the 1980s could not have been the result of more generous federal outlays, as stated by Murray, since real spending on Aid to Families with Dependent Children (AFDC) had declined by 30 percent between 1970 and 1980; it is this program that constitutes the heart of public assistance programs.[22] Spending on poverty programs increased during the 1960s and early 1970s, but stalled in the late 1970s and fell in the 1980s. By 1980, fewer persons were receiving AFDC than in 1976, because of eligibility restrictions, even though the number of poor was increasing.

It should be mentioned that the level of public assistance benefits was never high. For example, up to the end of the Reagan administration, the maximum cash benefits in 32 states to a family of three receiving AFDC was below 50 percent of the poverty line, and in only one state did the combined benefits of AFDC and food stamps lift a family without other income above the poverty line.

In 1987 the cash public assistance benefits for a family of three ranged from a low of $118 a month in Alabama to almost $500 in New York and over $600 in California.[23] This money was expected to pay for everything from rent, utilities, telephone, household and personal goods, to school, transportation, clothing, and entertainment. According to the poverty schedule of the Census Bureau, the poverty threshold in 1987 was $11,611 for a nonfarm family of four. This amounted to about $2.65, or 88¢ per meal, per person, per day. The benefits of AFDC in 1987 in 32 states reached only half this amount, while the combined benefits of both AFDC and food stamps still never reached even this low amount, except in Alaska. The benefits of the poverty program only result in more poverty and are themselves the clearest expressions of the "poverty" of the welfare system in America.

According to the Urban Institute, the Institute for Research on Poverty, and the Center on Budget and Policy Priorities, the two main reasons for the rise in poverty in the United States have been the reduction in federal benefits since the late 1970s and the general performance of the economy. As we have already seen, the lay commission had argued that more money is actually spent on the poor than is really necessary to eliminate poverty. For the commission, this represented *"prima facie* evidence of faulty design in poverty programs."[24] However, they equated social welfare with public assistance, and in the process confused income redistribution with social insurance; that is, they obscured the distinction between social security for the middle class and public assistance for the poor. Of the total social welfare spending, only a small portion is actually directed at the poor. In fact, as Christopher Jencks has recognized, "social welfare spending is not mostly for the poor."[25] It includes a wide variety of programs that are chiefly directed at the middle class, such as Social Security, unemployment compensation, Medicare, veterans' benefits, and so forth.

A theme running throughout the presentations of those at the December 1984 Williamsburg, Virginia, conference on poverty, called by the Institute for Research on Poverty and the U.S. Department of Health and Human Services, was that most of the social welfare programs found in social insurance and the in-kind public assistance programs were not designed to alleviate income poverty. Social Security "was really designed to protect middle-class income," that is, the income of those who were employed, but because of outside causes, which the individual was incapable of controlling, resulted in an inability to work.[26] This represents a redistribution of income, but within the middle class, and a temporal redistribution from a time of employment and high income to a time of nonemployment and low income.

A number of authors have attempted to explain why poverty has declined so little when transfers have risen so much. As suggested above, the goal of the most expensive transfer programs is not primarily to reduce income poverty. Social insurance programs protect family incomes when wages have been lost because of unemployment, retirement, death, or disability. In-kind assistance programs are designed to ensure the provision of certain merit goods — food, housing, and medicare care.[27]

This theme will be developed further later in this chapter when we discuss the role of the state and the political purposes of redistribution.

At the same time that poverty was rising during the Reagan administration, the government was cutting the cash benefits of AFDC by tightening the eligibility requirements and eliminating programs. Though Social Security and the Supplemental Security Income (SSI) benefits are automatically adjusted for inflation, those of AFDC are not. AFDC benefits have been cut back 33 percent in real terms during the 1970s as a result of their failure to keep pace with inflation.[28] As Greenstein has indicated, there is no mention by Murray in his book of either the reduction in public assistance benefits to the poor or of the declining economy in the 1970s. At the very time when pretransfer poverty (poverty measured prior to the intervention of government programs) was moving upwards in the 1980s to over 24 percent and the official poverty rate to over 14 percent (with a high of 15.2 in 1983), the transfer payments were being reduced by the government. Public assistance payments removed 6.3 percent of pretransfer poor from poverty in 1972, but only 3.4 percent in 1983. By 1983 only 33.7 percent of the poor were removed from poverty by social insurance, while in 1976 it was 37.6.[29]

Actually Murray paints a rather glowing picture of the economy during this period and certainly does not consider the possibility that rising poverty could be caused by falling AFDC benefits, rising unemployment, the widening of the poverty gap, growing income inequality, and a faltering economy. According to him, "economic growth during the 1970s was actually *greater* than during the peacetime 1950s, memories of Eisenhower prosperity notwithstanding."[30] This unwillingness to deal with the reality of the market and the economic stagnation of the 1970s expresses a serious defect in conservative economic theory. Since the justification for their theories lies in the logic and structure of the market, in its efficiency, productivity, and rationality, a recognition of economic stagnation would also force a recognition of the stagnation of their own theories.

The Center's analysis of the data revealed that in 1979 the cash benefits from AFDC, SSI, and unemployment compensation lifted 9.6 percent of families with children out of poverty. These same programs in 1985 lifted out only 4.7 percent. Social Security lifted 10.3 percent out of poverty in 1979, while only 7.0 percent in 1985. Finally, food and housing benefits lifted 20.1 percent of families with children out of poverty in 1979 and only 13.1 percent in 1985.[31] The report continued that the group especially hard hit by the budget cuts during the Reagan years had been the female-headed families. Throughout his administration, the attempts to control the rising deficits fell disproportionately on the public assistance programs, which in a trillion-dollar economy constituted less than 10 percent of the federal budget.

The Reagan administration attempted in the early 1980s to cut many of the public assistance programs directed at the very poor. In 1985 the proposed federal budget, if enacted, would have cut food stamps and child nutrition programs by nearly 50 percent, AFDC by 28.6 percent, Medicaid by 15.7 percent, the Special Supplemental Food Program for Women, Infants and Children (WIC) by 63.6 percent, and eliminated entirely public service employment, work incentive programs, and community service block grants. Social Security was to be cut 10.4 percent and Unemployment Insurance by 19.1 percent. In the proposed budget of 1988, one-third of the budget cuts would have come from the public assistance programs to the poor.[32] The actual reductions enacted by Congress were less, but any cuts in its meager budget would affect the ability of the welfare system to reach the poor.

To counter the mounting statistical evidence of these social problems, conservative theoreticians have been contending that the official statistics are problematic, since they do not include all the benefits received by the poor from the federal government. Since 1979 the Census Bureau has been collecting data under four other alternative measures of poverty that do include in-kind benefits. However, at a December 1985 conference sponsored by the Census Bureau, it was found that there were many technical errors and distortions which arose from using these new measurement techniques. The result is that "such a high value is given to Medicare and Medicaid coverage that in the average state, *all elderly couples enrolled in both these programs are automatically considered to be above the poverty line*, regardless of whether they have any other money at all on which to live."[33]

It has been estimated that if the cash benefits programs (Social Security, unemployment insurance, and public assistance) had the same antipoverty impact in 1985 as they had in 1979, then 458,000 fewer families with children would have been poor. Even using the broader criteria of noncash benefits, the effectiveness of these government programs continued to decline, and poverty rates increased.[34] Along with the effects on poverty, the impact of the cuts in government spending on unemployment resulted in only 32.7 percent of the unemployed receiving unemployment benefits in 1986. This is the lowest amount ever recorded.

Another important element in determining the social and economic well-being of the country is the gap in the income between the richest 20 percent and the rest of the nation. This disproportion of income distribution levels between rich and poor is one of the issues that originally led the bishops to write their letter on the economy. Income inequality is an important measure of the impact of the war on poverty.[35] It is also a crucial indicator of the level of potential economic and political participation within society. In 1985, during the heart of the Reagan revolution, the poorest fifth of the population received 4.6 percent of all after-tax income, while the richest fifth received 42.3 percent. This is the largest gap between the top fifth and bottom fifth of the nation since the Census Bureau has been keeping these records. In fact, according to the Center, since 1980 all households have been losing income, except for the wealthiest fifth. In 1985 households earning less than $8,925, or $2,000 below the poverty line, suffered a $6 billion loss because of this redistribution. On top of this, the lowest groups are being required to carry an increasingly heavy regressive tax burden with the rise in state, local, and Social Security taxes in the mid 1980s. "The Census data show that from *1980 to 1985, the typical (or median) family in the poorest 40 percent of the population saw its income decline by $236, after adjusting for inflation. During the same five-year period, the typical family in the top 40 percent of the population saw its income rise $2,915, while the typical family in the richest 10 percent saw its income increase by $7,130."*[36]

In his new work *The Politics of Rich and Poor*, Kevin Phillips, relying on the Federal Reserve Board's income distribution series, which included the effects of adding capital gains to its calculations, also pointed to these same trends toward uneven economic distribution and income concentration. It was becoming more alarming across political ideologies. According to the Congressional Budget Office, from 1977 to 1987, the average after-tax family income of the lowest 10 percent fell from $3,528 to $3,157, while the top 10 percent experienced a 24.4 percent increase.[37]

A different model developed by Joseph Pechman at the Brookings Institution includes a more comprehensive concept of both income and taxation than the Census Bureau's own calculations.[38] It is based on an "adjusted family income" concept and refers to all income earned in the market, which includes wages, salary, dividends, interest, rents, government transfer payments, accrued capital gains, and imputed rent. The after-tax calculation is based on any burden that would decrease money income. This includes not only federal income tax, but state and local taxes, as well as business taxes passed on to the consumers. Thus the scope of Pechman's analysis of income distribution and taxation includes a wider range of both income and taxes and therefore offers a better insight into the nature of distribution in America.

A redistributive policy based on a progressive income tax and welfare policy has had no real effect on the overall distribution of income over the last two decades. According to Pechman, the poorest fifth in America received just under 4 percent of the total income in 1966 and just over 4 percent in 1985, while the richest fifth received 45.7 percent in 1966 and over 47 percent in 1985. Thus in 1985 the richest fifth of American families received ten times more income as the bottom fifth. This latter group has also received a smaller share of the economic pie since the 1960s, which is probably due to the stagnating economy and regressive taxation, especially Social Security, state, and local taxes. There is even a noticeable fall in the redistribution of after-tax income to the poorest Americans, which is probably the result of the cuts in the social welfare programs and the increasing tax breaks to the wealthy since Reagan's tax giveaways to the rich with the Economic Recovery Tax Act of 1981. There is also a noticeable redistribution to the wealthiest fifth of the population, which has come mainly at the expense of middle-income groups.

Despite the apparent stability of the figures from the 1960s to the 1980s, the latest figures for the decade of the 1980s indicate a return to the distribution patterns that existed prior to the infusion of government transfer programs at the time of the War on Poverty in the mid 1960s. In an address he had written before he died in August 1989, Pechman argued, using data from the Internal Revenue Service, that income inequality is greatly understated. The top 1 percent of Americans received between 8 and 9 percent of the total income reported on tax returns between 1952 and 1981. But after that, things began to change rapidly. The lower-income classes began to receive a noticeably smaller share of the total income, while the upper 1 percent received 14.7 percent in 1986. A very dramatic increase, indeed. In 1988 the highest fifth received over 44 percent of the aggregate division, which is the highest they have ever recorded. Pechman explained the declining share by the bottom groups was a result of economic and demographic changes, but the highest fifth's increase was due to changes in the tax codes. Between 1966 and 1985, the effective tax rates for the top 5 percent decreased by one-fifth and the rates for the top 1 percent plummeted by more than a third. These changes resulted from the reduction of the top federal income tax rates, the declining share of corporate income tax contributions to the federal pie, and the increase in various forms of tax shelters. In 1988 the top 5 percent paid only 27.7 percent in federal, state, and local taxes, while in 1966 they paid 32.7 percent; the top 1 percent paid only 26.8 percent in taxes, while in 1966 they paid almost 40 percent.[39] This means that the growing bills for all forms of increasingly costly transfer payments were and continue to be paid for by low- and middle-income groups.

The model used by the Census Bureau in its *Current Population Reports*, because it does not include capital gains and the regressive taxes, shows less disparity between the income groups. In 1968 the poorest fifth, according to its latest figures, received 5.7 percent, while the richest fifth received 40.5 percent of the before-tax family income. In 1980 the poorest fifth received 5.2 percent and the richest fifth 41.5 percent, while in

1989 the poorest fifth received just 4.6 percent and the richest fifth 44.6 percent.[40]

The Urban Institute reports that over the past few years, "Families at the top of the income distribution have gained substantially; those in the bottom two quintiles have actually lost all the ground they had gained over the preceding decades. The share of total family income received by the bottom quintile fell by 0.7 percentage points."[41] But between 1980 and 1984, the families at the top of the income groups gained $25 billion at the expense of the other groups, which translates into $2,000 per family for this richest group. Those families at the bottom lost their economic gains from the 1960s and 1970s. The real disposable income of the lowest fifth fell nearly 8 percent, while that of the richest fifth increased nearly 9 percent. In real terms, this means that in the mid 1980s over 33 million Americans lived in poverty, with double this number living precariously close to the line. While one-third of Blacks were poor, the majority of the poor were white. The poverty rate for children was double that of adults, with almost one-quarter of all children under six years of age living in poverty.[42] To determine the range and extent of poverty in America, Greg Duncan calculated, as we have already seen, that during the time period between 1969 and 1978, one-quarter of all Americans lived in poverty for a least one year.[43]

The latest figures released by the Census Bureau show that for the income distribution of American families in 1988, the poorest 20 percent (those receiving $16,003 or less) received its lowest share since 1954; the second poorest fifth ($28,000) received its lowest share ever recorded by the Census Bureau (since 1947); the middle fifth ($40,800) its lowest ever recorded; the next richest fifth ($59,550) received the lowest since 1969; while the richest fifth received its highest share ever recorded.[44] These figures are adjusted for the effects of inflation. The recently released report of the Congressional Budget Office on the before- and after-tax distribution of income during the 1980s, entitled *Overview of Entitlement Programs,* has caused a further flurry of excitement.[45] There is a wealth of continued information detailing the growing class and income gap between rich and poor in America that has not narrowed even after seven years of "uninterrupted economic recovery."

The CBO's Green Book reported that the average before-tax income of the richest one-fifth of American households rose $24,168, or 30 percent per household, between 1980 and 1990. The richest 5 percent increased by $64,000, or 45 percent, and the richest 1 percent increased by a whopping $236,000, or 75 percent, during this same period. For household income of the middle group, there was little change during the decade of Reaganomics, while the poorest one-fifth of the population lost $306, for a minus 4 percent per household. The poorest of the poor ended the decade with $439 less than they began with, for a decrease of 9 percent.

Changes in Average Before-Tax Household Incomes, 1980–1990
by Various Income Groups[46]

National Income Category	1980	1990 (projected)	Change: 1980–90 ($)	($) (%)
Poorest Fifth	$ 8,031	$ 7,725	$ -306	-3.8%
Next Poorest Fifth	19,088	19,348	260	1.4
Middle Fifth	30,047	30,964	917	3.1
Next Richest Fifth	41,640	44,908	3,268	7.8
Richest Fifth	81,041	105,209	24,168	29.8
Richest 5 Percent	142,306	206,162	63,856	44.9
Richest 1 Percent	313,206	548,969	235,763	75.3

Changes in Average After-Tax Household Incomes, 1980–1990
by Various Income Groups

National Income Category	1980	1990 (projected)	Change: 1980–90 ($)	($) (%)
Poorest Fifth	$ 7,357	$ 6,973	$ -384	-5.2%
Next Poorest Fifth	16,088	16,124	36	0.2
Middle Fifth	24,031	24,691	660	2.7
Next Richest Fifth	32,075	34,824	2,749	8.6
Richest Fifth	58,886	78,032	19,146	32.5
Richest 5 Percent	100,331	151,132	50,801	50.6
Richest 1 Percent	213,675	399,697	186,022	87.1

The 1980s was a decade of mass theft, from those least able to pay to the richest Americans. A look at the average after-tax income indicates that during this 10-year period, the income of the poorest one-fifth of Americans fell by over 5 percent; the poorest tenth fell by 10 percent. The richest fifth's income increased by an average of 33 percent. The richest 5 percent will have increased by 50 percent, and the richest 1 percent will have an after-tax bonus of 87 percent. According to the Center's analysis of this data, the increase of the richest 1 percent of American households during this period will equal the total after-tax income received by the poorest one-fifth of Americans this year. This means that because of Reagan's tax giveaways to the wealthy, the after-tax income of the richest 2.5 million Americans from 1980 to 1990 will equal the total income of the poorest 100 million in 1990. "The top one percent of the population [in 1990] will have nearly as much after-tax income as the bottom 40 percent. Stated another way, the combined incomes of the richest 2.5 million Americans now nearly equals the combined incomes of the 100 million Americans with the lowest incomes."[47]

Another perspective is offered by the recently published information of the Census Bureau. Relying on the statistical changes in family incomes between 1979 and 1989, their data reveals that the average before-tax income of the poorest fifth of American families fell during this time. Reagan's taxation policies helped the wealthiest 5 percent of families increase their average income by 23.4 percent. This represents an aspect of a deeper and more structural form of poverty, since the poverty rate during the prosperity of 1989 exceeds the poverty rate during the worst recession years of the 1970s. Finally, when income distribution is examined by studying the average before-tax income gains and losses by family quintiles between 1979 and 1989, the poorest fifth lost 6 percent, the second poorest gained 0 percent, the middle fifth gained only 3 percent, the second richest fifth gained 7 percent, while the richest fifth of American families gained 17 percent. What this means is that during the decade of the Reagan recovery, the average middle-income American family gained about $90 per year.[48]

What these figures indicate is that the economic recovery of the past few years under Reagan has been unequally shared, with only the richest fifth receiving a higher percentage in 1989 than in 1980. This means that there has been a redistribution of billions of dollars to the richest group in America.[49] There really is a welfare state, but the question is: For whom? The latest budget proposal that passed the Congress on October 27, 1990, does attempt to roll back some of these abuses in the tax system. While the taxes of the richest 1 percent of households will increase by 6 percent next year, this will only partly make up for the Reagan tax breaks of over 14 percent to this group in the past decade.[50]

We have seen how the cutting of the federal programs, budget priorities, and taxation policies have negatively affected those below the poverty line. Among the majority of households above the poverty line, things have not gotten any better, either. This is quite clearly reflected in the income and wealth distribution figures, the unemployment rates, and the stagnant real hourly wages. If income distribution is highly concentrated, the most recent analysis of the distribution of wealth in America undertaken at the request of the Joint Economic Committee of Congress with special emphasis on the rich (90th to 99th percentile of families), the very rich (lower half of the top 0.5 percent), and the super rich (top 0.5 percent of American families) indicates that wealth distribution is even more so. (See table on page 121.)

When the value of home ownership is deducted from the gross assets, we see that economic concentration is even more pronounced, with the top 10 percent of American families owning nearly 81 percent of America, including 90 percent of the corporate stocks, bonds, trusts, and business assets, about half of the real estate, checking accounts, and life insurance. These figures and the conclusions reached in this committee report about the extent of wealth concentration in the United States are rather startling, especially when viewed within the context of a democratic and pluralistic society. They also indicate, at an economic level, the split in American society between the values of liberalism—with its shades of Lockean rights, individualism, inequality, and competition (Nozick, Friedman, and Rawls)—and the values of civic republicanism, community, and neo-Aristotelian philosophy (John Harrington, Sandel, Walzer, Bellah, and MacIntyre).[51] The Joint Economic Committee concluded:

> The most striking result from the survey data is the extraordinary amount of national wealth held by the top half of 1 percent of families. These super rich households accounted for more than 35 percent of net wealth and 32 percent of gross wealth. If equity in personal residences from net wealth is excluded, the top half of 1 percent of households owned more than 45 percent of the privately held wealth of this country. . . . When the assets of the rich were combined with those of the very rich and super rich, 71.8 percent of the net wealth of American families was owned by this top 10 percent of families. This included almost 94 percent of unincorporated business assets and nearly 90 percent of all personally held stock.[52]

Michael Novak has argued that these figures are deceptive because they fail to consider the real assets of American households, which consist of

Top Wealth Holders by Amount and Type of Wealth, 1983[53]

Assets	Value of gross assets held by (in billions of dollars)			Percentage held by		
	Top 0.5%	Top 1%	Top 10%	Top 0.5%	Top 1%	Top 10%
Real estate	821.8	1048.4	2632.6	15.3	19.5	49.0
Corporate stock	456.6	688.8	976.5	46.5	60.0	89.3
Bonds	143.6	168.2	297.7	43.6	51.1	90.4
Checking accounts	12.0	20.3	52.3	10.4	17.6	45.2
Savings accounts	4.0	4.7	11.8	2.1	2.5	6.3
Money market & call accounts	46.5	65.8	163.5	17.5	24.8	61.6
IRAs and Keogh	21.1	31.6	95.9	14.8	22.2	67.3
Life insurance	16.9	26.0	80.2	6.5	10.0	46.8
Trusts	378.4	402.9	467.8	77.0	82.0	95.2
Business assets (net)	1904.9	2168.1	3065.7	58.2	66.2	93.6
Miscellaneous	25.9	43.7	84.2	16.4	27.7	53.3
Gross assets	3867.9	4630.6	8078.7	32.1	38.4	67.0
Debt	153.8	202.2	481.1	10.4	13.7	32.6
Net worth	3714.1	4428.4	7597.6	35.1	41.8	71.7
Gross assets minus home value	3678.8	4329.8	6827.6	43.4	51.1	80.6

home equity, cars, property, and so forth. But he has failed to understand the nature of wealth and class power and thus make a distinction between private property (production) and personal property (consumption). Also, for those people in the bottom two quintiles, their net worth is many times offset by their debts. Financial wealth is more of an indicator of both concentrated economic wealth and economic power. The Federal Reserve Board, in its 1983 "Survey of Consumer Finance," found that 2 percent of the American families owned 54 percent of the total net financial assets in the United States; 10 percent owned 86 percent; and 55 percent had zero or negative net worth. In fact, in 1983, 48 percent of American families had less than $2,000 in total financial assets, and 40 percent had less than $1,000 in liquid assets; 50 percent had less than $2,000 in liquid assets.[54]

INEQUALITY, ETHICS, AND HUMAN POTENTIAL

These figures call into question the very possibility of an economic democracy and New American Experiment without first considering a structural transformation of the U.S. economy. Once the issue of political and economic participation is raised, then too must that of equality and income and wealth distribution be raised. With the development of orthodox democratic theory by Joseph Schumpeter and others after World War II based on theories of political pluralism and the circulation of elites, the classical theory of democracy (Rousseau and Jefferson) was left behind. The classical model, with its emphasis on public participation and the common good, still retained a handful of adherents, but for the most part only on the fringes of the left. Thanks to the Bishops' Letter, a discussion of these issues is now returning, and with it, questions about the maldistribution of income and wealth and a rethinking of the nature of democracy and freedom. The lay commission report places great emphasis on self-esteem and self-reliance as the means by which individuals can move out of the poverty cycle; they emphasize the freedom of choice within a market economy, as well as the equality of opportunity and the inequality of results that lie at the foundation of American social justice.

In all these cases, however, they fail to consider how the maldistribution of income and wealth distorts market choices, undermines an equality of opportunity, and turns self-reliance into self-abasement. Under these conditions, their call for social justice is simply an ideological call for domestication, passivity, and defense of the status quo. Freedom does not require a political and economic leveling to some predetermined social standard, nor does it require that individuality, talent, and creativity be sacrificed for the common good. But social justice certainly calls into question the class inequality that we have chronicled above and the resulting economic poverty and social dislocation that place a large number of people outside the range of real possibilities for individual autonomy and self-expression.[55]

Defense of market rationality is only a formula that will undermine the very ideals which Novak and the lay commission wish to develop. Liberal institutions are incapable of realizing liberal values, for they are contradictory; self-realization within a community cannot be accomplished amid market competition, self-interest, and a materialist culture. Bellah, Lasch, Jacoby, Slater, and Habermas have traced the debris of social psychology left in the wake of capitalism, that is, "the dead end of radical individualism" and the inability to move from the emptiness and loneliness of selves in a market economy to a concern for the common good within the community.[56]

For Novak, inequality is necessary to provide the hierarchy of incentives, that is, for the motivation and rewards, for the stability of our competitive social system and the preservation of the common good; inequality is part of natural law.

> Nature itself generates inequality of looks, stature, intellect, and heart. Should a good society repress inequalities, or should it respect them, while teaching cooperation and respect? Democratic capitalism is loathe to repress natural human energies which manifest obvious inequalities. Such energies are perennial, universal, and irrepressible; the attempt to repress them breeds yet more dangerous evils.[57]

Material and economic inequality does not and cannot enhance spiritual, intellectual, or any kind of truly human self-development. It simply reduces the latter to the former; it reduces human potentiality to material categories defined within the limits of market rationality. As Max Weber has said, it is a rationality characterized by a substantive irrationality within an iron cage of formal and technological reason. It is only in the distorted logic of this instrumental and technical rationality that economic inequality, poverty, and human deprivation can be seen as the basis for the development of human potentiality. Self-realization is then defined in terms of these technological categories; it is measured and evaluated in terms of the criteria of the "economic man" in the market which places primary emphasis on self-interest, competition, and monetary success.

Desires, values, and ideals that are incompatible with the market (and by definition with freedom and social justice) cannot be realized or even articulated.[58] This is what makes the discussion between the bishops and the lay commission so difficult and interesting. The conservative perspective forces a redefinition of the ancient Hebrew, Greek, and medieval Christian traditions in order to make their concepts and ideals compatible with "market rationality." It requires that the bishops' use of categories such as the community, covenant, social justice, and creativity be redefined according to market criteria. The key question, of course, is whether the market and its definition of self-realization defines out of existence those very aspects of individual development which make us truly human (and these ancient traditions still relevant). By failing to see that economics provides the material foundations for the possibility of the community and the development of personality, the lay commission has turned into an ultimate goal that which is only a necessary social precondition. They have reversed the proper relationship between means and ends.

The bishops were certainly aware of these dramatic poverty and income statistics, which we have updated from other sources. In the first draft of their letter, but left out of the final statement, they said:

> Catholic social teaching does not suggest that absolute equality in the distribution of income and wealth is required. Some degree of inequality is not only acceptable, but may be desirable for economic and social reasons. However, gross inequalities are morally unjustifiable, particularly when millions lack even the basic necessities of life. In our judgment, the distribution of income and wealth in the United States is so inequitable that it violates this minimum standard of distributive justice.[59]

Paul Heyne has responded to the bishops by arguing that they neither analyze the just criteria of distribution nor state how much inequality would be acceptable in a free society.[60] As with many conservative theorists, the real issue is reduced to the stabilization and legitimation of the social system. This requires that the motivational system upon which capitalism rests not be interfered with by an egalitarian set of priorities. This is certainly Murray's central critique of the welfare system. We think that it is Novak who unknowingly best responds to this type of objection when he states, "Democratic capitalism not only permits individuals to experience alienation, anomie, loneliness, and nothingness. Democratic capitalism is also constantly renewed by such radical experiences of human liberty."[61] In a society structured around these experiences which so characterized nineteenth- and early twentieth-century European social theory, inequality acts as a monetary incentive within a repressive society. The conservatives themselves implicitly admit that without this incentive arrangement, the system could not motivate people. Thus all the talk about invention, productivity, and creativity becomes simply an ideological facade behind which hides the real truth of this social system: greed, self-interest, and class power.

In order to make sense of the statistics from the welfare state—income and wealth distribution, increasing poverty and poverty gap, growing inequality and homelessness, and continuing spending cuts in the welfare programs for the poor—it will be necessary to examine the changing structural dynamics among corporate industry, labor, and the state. Changes in one area will affect the institutional arrangements in other areas. Together they make up an organic whole with interdependent yet autonomous parts. This requires that we follow the changing forms of economic crises and corporate policy and their effects on the budgetary and fiscal decisions of the state and the relations between labor and corporate management. Government fiscal, taxation, and monetary policies, in turn, will affect relations with both the economy and labor. As we move beyond the statistics of income and wealth considerations to their underlying structural causes, we also move beyond issues of distributive justice to those of economic and political justice. This is a direction the bishops do not overtly stress in their letter. The politics of statistics is manifested both in the way "poverty" and "unemployment" are defined by the government and in the way that they are the result of the government's industrial and public policy. The state participates in the creation of economic hardships, then attempts to define them out of existence or at least ameliorate their worst excesses. It is only in a theory of political economy that the existence of poverty and the poverty of its statistics is explained. According to the Boffs, it is only within the structures of political economy, which include the categories of inequality, exploitation, and domination, that the existence of poverty begins to make sense.[62] A theory which fails to be radical—a theory which fails to examine the roots of these problems, as is the case in the Bishops' Letter—will fail to make adequate proposals for their alleviation and for social change.

ECONOMIC CRISES AND CORPORATE RESTRUCTURING

Because they never get to the root structural reasons of these problems, the bishops therefore are never able to offer cogent and concrete policy recommendations that reflect the historical and institutional reality and real possibilities of American political economy. That is to say, their ethics, analysis of social problems, and their policy recommendations are not connected by any systematic theory of the way society works. The result is a disjointed relationship among these key factors. As we have already seen, the statistical changes in the distribution of inequality and poverty in America have deeper structural causes than demographic changes and the nature of the family, as the conservatives would have us believe. They reflect changes in welfare policy, deepening recessions, high unemployment, a stagnating economy, corporate restructuring, and falling rates of corporate profit.

The Institute for Research on Poverty reported that "the performance of the economy is a dominant determinant of the economic condition of the poor."[63] Each decade in the last thirty years has been characterized by a certain distinguishable form of economic crisis. During the 1960s the economic crisis manifested itself as stagflation; in the 1970s it was the declining productivity within the workplace; and in the 1980s it has been the high deficit spending. We will see that each of these phenomena is characteristic of transformations within the macroeconomy and each reflects problems within the social organization of production.

There have been a variety of attempts to explain economic stagnation, falling productivity, and declining profit rates, along with their concomitant social problems, over the past twenty years. Some of the major reasons given for these structural and historical developments are:

1. Rising class conflict and the breakdown of social accords agreed upon at the end of World War II (*See* Gordon, Bowles, Weisskopf)

2. Poor management and management priorities (Thurow and Reich)

3. Deindustrialization of America and corporate restructuring (Bluestone and Harrison)

4. Further economic concentration, merger movements in the 1960s and 1980s, and the growth of paper entrepreneurialism (Blumberg, Edwards, Rhoades, and Magaziner and Reich)

5. Continued high military spending and the depletion of funds for capital investment (Melman, Lens, Blumberg)

6. The transformation of the economy from the industrial production of manufactured goods to service industries (Reich, and Bluestone and Harrison)

7. Stagflation (Blumberg, and Best and Connolly)

8. High deficits and increasing domestic and foreign debt (Center for Popular Economics)

9. The fiscal crisis of the state (O'Connor, and Best and Connolly)

10. The failure in the workplace of the mechanisms of social control through scientific and technological management (Braverman and Edwards)

11. Conflicting cultural ideologies and outmoded organizations of work in the United States (Reich)

12. Underconsumption crisis caused by monopoly industry (Baran and Sweezy, Magdoff and Sweezy, Foster, Nell, and Perlo)

13. Capitalist mode of production and intensified mechanization of production—the organic composition of capital school (Mandel, Laibman, Shaikh, and Castells)

14. Intensified international competition (Cohen and Rogers).[64]

Though they may stress a particular aspect in their analyses, most of the above-mentioned authors will include more than one major cause in their study. There is no common theoretical consensus about the immediate underlying structural causes, but there appears to be general agreement that these causes have their origins in the historical transformations of the corporate economy as it adjusts to its changing physical and human environment. That is, these historical problems are associated with the attempts by the large corporations to gain access to and control over their various "factors of production." They have attempted to control the market in a variety of ways:

1. By eliminating or controlling competition through corporate concentration, mergers, interlocking directorates, diversification, multinationalism,

administered pricing, and government loans and tax subsidies

2. By controlling labor through scientific management, labor stratification, market fragmentation, and the creation of a dual labor market

3. By controlling access to raw materials through science and technology, vertical integration, and economic and military imperialism.

Though the above-mentioned authors place weight on different aspects of this system, we view these causes within an interconnected, holistic framework. The differences in their theories are less reflections of distinct economic and social elements than analytic and theoretical clarifications of complex historical changes. At certain points in time, however, specific aspects and structural problems will have a dominant position, but when viewed historically, they are all interconnected in an advanced capitalist society geared to capital accumulation and private profits.

From the mid 1960s, unemployment and inflation have gone up, while economic growth as measured in real spendable earnings and increased working hours per capita started to decline. The average annual rise in productivity between 1948–1955 was a respectful 3.4 percent; between 1965–1980 it was only 2.0 percent as against 5.2 percent for West Germany and 8.1 percent for Japan.[65] Between 1973 and 1977, it was just 1 percent. Profit rates were also down. "After the recession of 1969–1970, the after-tax profit-rate peak in 1972 was one-third lower than it had been in 1965. After the recession of 1974–75, once again, the after-tax profit-rate peak in 1977 had fallen below its 1972 peak."[66] The rate of manufacturing profit has declined from 13.7 percent in 1966 to 7.6 percent in 1979. Since the mid 1960s, the combined effect of high unemployment and inflation, declining productivity and profit rates, a lower worker standard of living, and static government social spending has given us a sobering picture of the American economy. This has been neglected by the conservative authors we have already examined. Even the seven years of economic growth of the 1980s rests on questionable economic foundations of spiraling stagflation and increasing domination over the work force.[67]

Sagging Economic Performance of U.S. Economy[68]

	Unemployment Rate	Real GNP Growth	Changes in Real Wages	Productivity Growth	Inflation Rate
1949–53	4.1	5.0	4.0	3.7	2.2
1954–56	4.7	2.5	3.5	2.2	.5
1957–59	5.5	2.5	2.7	3.0	2.4
1960–69	4.8	4.2	2.8	2.9	2.3
1970–73	5.3	3.7	2.1	2.6	4.9
1974–79	6.8	2.8	.3	.8	8.6
1980–85	8.1	2.1	-.005	1.3	6.7

The place to start in this examination of the modern corporation is with an analysis of the structural transformations of corporate America. Moving beyond the ideology of free and open competition, we see that one of the first imperatives of the corporation is to control its immediate environment within the market and the related dangers of competition. Since the turn of the century, there have been four major merger movements, each having different goals and being different responses to historically specific economic problems. The horizontal merger movement occurred during the period of 1897–1904; the vertical movement from 1925–1930; the diagonal or diversification movement from 1967–1969; and the megamergers, leveraged buy outs, and unfriendly takeovers characterizing the Reagan administration during the 1980s.[69] Edwards states that the major reasons for these mergers were twofold:

> Centralization has altered the core firm's situation in two specific ways: it has increased the average profitability of the firm's investments and it has decreased the risks associated with those investments. Market power and size contribute to increasing the average profit and to reducing the risk. Multinationalism further enhances the profit rate and vertical integration and diversification tend further to reduce risk.[70]

Horizontal integration within the same industry is a direct attempt to eliminate competition through the creation of monopolies and market dominance. These mergers were concentrated in heavy industry, metals, food, transportation equipment, nonelectrical machinery, tobacco products, fabricated metal products, and chemicals. During this first wave of mergers, many of America's largest corporations were formed, including U.S. Steel, Ford Motor Company, Standard Oil, General Electric, AT&T, Alcoa, General Motors, Swift and Armour, and American Tobacco. According to John Brooks, 15 percent of the nation's assets were involved, and this merger movement resulted in the creation of more than seventy near monopolies.[71]

Vertical integration refers to the acquisition of key firms involved in extracting raw materials, production, transportation, and distribution in an attempt to control access to all the key elements in the chain of production. The second merger movement involved only about 10 percent of the nation's assets in 1,200 firms and was concentrated in the areas of banking, public utilities, and heavy industry.

The third form of merger characteristic of the last three decades has been that of diversification or the purchase of companies outside the area of the parent company. In 1969 alone, it involved more than 6,000 acquisitions, with 25,000 firms lost during the frenzied feeding.

The fourth type is the megamerger, which is a form of diversification and monopolization marked by the merger of the largest corporations. Within a three and one-half year period starting in 1980, there were 37 mergers of over $1 billion each, and by 1986, there were 4,323 mergers and acquisitions valued at over $200 billion. These acquisitions were characterized by an aggressiveness, speed, and hostility not seen before, by their debt structure of payment (leveraged buy outs), and by the dismantling of the subsidiaries to pay for the merger. New terms proliferated to describe this new phenomenon, such as junk bonds, hostile takeovers, white knights, golden parachute, greenmail, poison pill, PAC-Man defense, shark repellents, and many others. A dramatic example of this form of takeover was the purchase in 1985 of Beatrice Foods by the nine-year-old investment banking house of Kohlberg, Kravis, and Roberts for $6.2 billion. This occurred one year after this same leverage buy out specialist failed in its bid of $15.6 billion for Gulf Oil; three years later it purchased RJR Nabisco for $25 billion. Walter Adams and James Brock called this form of profit making without production "cowboy capitalism."[72]

Theories attempting to explain this new phenomenon are as abundant and complex as the mergers themselves. During the 1980s, the Chicago School and the Reagan White House defended these mergers, using the logic of a free market. Their position was that the new mergers were the result of economic competition, market rationality, and the intelligent reallocation of scarce resources from less efficient to more efficient firms. Economic Darwinism increased national wealth and improved technological and managerial efficiency through greater integration and synergy, as well as the effective use of economies of scale (efficiency theory).[73] Some theorists saw the changing nature of the corporation, with its diversified portfolio, resulting from changing public policy and the loosening of government regulation against horizontal (monopolies) and vertical (oligopolies) mergers. With the Reagan administration, the traditional hindrances to the creation of monopolies were removed.[74] Others have made the argument that these megamergers resulted from takeovers precipitated by management's desire for more power and privilege, the acquired firm's poor use of productive capacity ("failure to pursue value-maximization policies"), the undervaluation of targeted firms, and a desire for increased efficiency through corporate pruning (empire-building theory).[75]

Others saw the problem resulting from high inflation and economic stagnation, low stock prices in relation to the costs of building new plants and equipment (the Q Ratio), and to the book value and assets of companies (undervalued-assets and bargain theory).[76] Some contended that mergers resulted in the acquisition of new investment capital and significant tax reductions (internal capital market theory), were encouraged by the enormous profits of investment bankers, or were created for the purpose of maintaining monopoly power (monopoly theory).[77] To make these discussions even more difficult to follow, others held the thesis that the firms taken over during the 1960s, 1970s, and 1980s were well managed and above average in profitability, and that the mergers resulted in a decline in both efficiency and profitability.[78] Still others theorized that these historical examples of corporate restructuring were the result of corporate responses to the declining profit opportunities in the market.[79] While the truth lies somewhere in between these theories, corporate restructuring of the 1970s and 1980s was largely a response to the serious macroeconomic problems faced by the economy: stagflation, declining rates of corporate profit, and the need for more control over the various factors of production (raw materials, capital, and labor).

A question that comes immediately to mind is: How concentrated is American industry? During the 1970s, less than 1 percent of the manufacturing firms owned 88 percent of the assets and 87 percent of the profits. The largest corporations with assets over $1 billion held almost half of all corporate manufacturing assets.[80] The largest two hundred firms accounted for over two-thirds of the assets of large firms acquired during mergers since 1948. This has resulted in these large corporations attaining a higher percentage of the market share in manufacturing. They also received 54 percent of the total market profits in 1973, as opposed to only 40 percent in 1960. In 1960, the 100 largest manufacturing firms controlled more productive assets than the largest 200 firms in 1950.[81] The assets controlled by the 200 largest firms increased from 45 percent in 1947 to nearly two-thirds in the 1970s. In 1966 there were 199 industries in which 4 or fewer firms controlled more than half of production; by 1974 oligopolies controlled nearly two-thirds of all manufacturing.[82] Over 20,000 firms were acquired by manufacturing and mining interests between 1955–1973, with most of this activity occurring between 1965–1970. One hundred and ten of *Fortune 500*'s largest industrial firms were acquired between 1962 and 1968.[83] The largest 200 firms acquired 315 other large firms (assets over $10 million) during this period of the late 1960s, and 25 of these firms accounted for the majority of mergers. On top of this, the 49 largest banks have a controlling interest in the 500 largest corporations.[84]

This was only the beginning, since by the 1980s the government had shifted its concern away from regulation to efficiency, a "free market," and the relaxing of antitrust enforcement. The result was that during Reagan's administration, mergers skyrocketed. In 1980 the value of conglomerate mergers was $44.3 billion, but by 1986 it was $190 billion. It was during this time that Dupont acquired Conoco for $7 billion, Gulf Oil purchased SOCAL for $13.2 billion, Texaco paid $10.1 billion for Getty Oil, Mobil purchased Superior Oil for $5.7 billion, and U.S. Steel purchased Marathon Oil for $6.2 billion.[85] Industries were becoming more centralized and concentrated in the hands of the largest corporations, which dominated substantial portions of the American economy.[86]

What effect does this level of increased economic concentration and control over industrial assets have on the market, the law of supply and demand, efficiency, productivity, fair resource and income allocation, and the ideals of political equality and democracy? How adequate is the conservative view of the economy based upon market rationality and a competitive model, or of the bishops' hopes for a New American Experiment, given this economic reality?

According to Bluestone and Harrison, two out of every three new manufacturing plants among the *Fortune 500* during the 1970s were not newly constructed, but acquired through mergers.[87] More money was being spent in the 1980s on mergers than on research and development, while plant expansion in this group was almost nonexistent. At this time, U.S. Steel was investing 46 cents on every dollar in the purchasing of chemical companies and shopping malls. Economic concentration brought with it a rise in both prices and profits that no longer reflected consumer sovereignty. Prices and profits went up because of the oligopolistic control of the market. The profits which these large corporations receive are about 30 percent higher than in nonconcentrated industries, which provide the cushion for stability and growth during hard times. Because of their market power and administrative pricing, the risks of economic failure and bankruptcy are much lower among these corporations.[88]

The effects of this increasing economic concentration of American industry have been detrimental to the economy, efficiency, productivity, and to labor.[89] First, it distorts an accurate picture of the economy, since the increase in merger activity gives the appearance of high economic growth and an expanding GNP, when in fact it is only frenzy feeding by large corporations. "The tremendous growth was, in general, attributable to intensive acquisition activity rather than to major breakthroughs in product development and technology."[90] The initial profits from the mergers were on paper, and by the end of the 1960s, stock prices began to decline. The emphasis on short-term growth and profit margins have more negative long-term effects. Investment that should have been going into rebuilding the infrastructure of the company with new buildings, machinery, up-to-date technology, research and development, competitive strategies, labor training, and so forth was being spent on acquisitions.

Along with these misallocations of investment funds, these megamergers also resulted in a loss of efficiency and innovation. This was due to corporate growth well above what was necessary for the creation of economies of scale (and efficient productivity) and the resulting creation of inefficient bureaucracies.[91] The Federal Trade Commission examined the performance of nine conglomerates that acquired 348 firms during the sample period. Half the firms studied had a decline in their profit rate from 1960 to 1969. Louis Lowenstein and Edward Herman, in their study of mergers, concluded that "in short, after the takeover, the bidders [newly acquired companies] performed well below the level of either the bidders or their targets during the years before the bid." Another study by Ravenscraft and Scherer concluded that postmarket profits of companies in the mid to late 1970s were below premarket profits for the same groups.[92]

Others have argued that one result of the formation of a concentrated economy was that these large corporations were no longer required to adhere to the laws of supply and demand. Prices were determined by administrative decision of the corporation and not by market demand, as

John Kenneth Galbraith had noticed years ago.[93] Estimates of the over-pricing of commodities and its effect on inflation vary. During the 1970s some have estimated that it ranged from $50 to $100 billion per year. In those very concentrated industries, prices may be 10 to 15 percent higher than normal.[94]

Summarizing the studies on these topics, Samuel Reid said: "All these studies indicate that while mergers add *size* dimensions to individual firms, it does not necessarily follow that profitability and efficiency are realized."[95] Thus there is an enormous amount of waste built into the system in terms of military spending, overpricing, underutilization of labor and productive facilities, misallocation of resources and wealth, and so on. It has been estimated that in 1970, $60 billion was wasted in this fashion and lost from the GNP, while in 1980 it amounted to over $1 trillion of the GNP.[96] The effects on the political process and possibilities for democratic participation are not any brighter.[97]

PRODUCTIVITY, SCIENTIFIC MANAGEMENT, AND THE DUAL LABOR MARKET

The lay commission stressed that the organization of the workplace in capitalist societies was to be built around cooperation, creativity, and self-expression. As we have already seen from our analysis in chapter two, the three fundamental principles of social organization from their perspective are: the practice of free association, the habit of cooperation, and the principle of self-interest rightly understood. By implementing these principles, the capitalist system expresses not only self-interest, but permits the manifestation of individual talents and "natural virtues": competition, but also cooperation and communication; individual merit, but also human dignity and self-expression. It is the most rational form of work organization because both the individual and social components are integrated into a harmonious whole.

> The task of lay persons in the economic order, whether investors, workers, managers, or entrepreneurs, is to build cooperative associations respectful of each other's humanity. Such enterprises should be as far as feasible participative and creative, in order to bring out from creation the productive possibilities and the human resources that the Creator, in his bounty, has hidden within. Economic activism is a direct participation in the work of the Creator Himself.[98]

Creativity and self-development require the liberty of choice found only in market economies, which respect human freedom and private property. It is in this type of society, says the lay commission, that inventiveness, risk taking, and creativity develop. The lay commission has integrated creativity and democratic capitalism in a way that would be problematic to John Paul

II in his encyclical *Laborem Exercens*. By so integrating them in this fashion, they have negated the internal antagonisms and conflicts between them and have avoided the necessity to consider both the organization of the workplace and its historical evolution. They have failed to recognize that democracy and capitalism (economic liberalism) are incompatible and contradictory concepts.

By dealing with labor and labor conditions in the abstract, the lay commission avoids having to consider the substance of John Paul II's writings as well as the numerous historians who have examined the development of the labor market in the context of Taylorism and scientific management. As in the case of the attempts made by large corporations to limit competition structurally and the exigencies of the external market, scientific management was and is used to create and control an internal labor market and pliant labor force in the quest for both market control and profits. Creativity, self-expression, and individual development have been ideals expressed for the workplace in which human labor creates its own world of interaction and meaning. Only the lay commission sees these ideals already existing in the social relations of corporate production. However, the category of worker alienation is still as relevant today as it was in 1844, when Karl Marx wrote his *Economic and Philosophical Manuscripts*. In the twentieth century, the loss of creativity and self-expression, the alienation of the worker from the process and products of production, and the distorted development and degradation of the self in an unfriendly and dangerous work environment have been clearly documented by Harry Braverman and Richard Edwards. The techniques of social control have become more sophisticated in the twentieth century, but the effects are as damaging.

To alienation, division of labor, and a class society must be added the synthesis of private property and scientific and technological management. The workplace is now organized according to the imperatives of technical and administrative control, justified on the basis of modern scientific methods and procedures. This system of work is characterized by: the separation of intellectual from manual labor, the reduction of physical activity to the criteria of efficiency and productivity, the elimination of all craft skills and their replacement by managerial initiatives, and the depoliticization of the process through the claims of scientific objectivity and neutrality. This is what Weber meant by the process of rationalization within the iron cage.[99] The social and physical sciences now become part of the disenchantment of the social world and the degradation of the workers as control over the meaning, purpose, goals, and implementation of work are more firmly placed in the hands of capital. "All of life seems full of 'futility, meaninglessness, and purposelessness,' since it is not, in fact, being directly experienced. The real self is completely blocked, barred from any spontaneous expressions or real freedom of action, and totally sterile."[100]

Power is transferred from direct social control through owners and managers to control by technique, scientific rationality, and bureaucratic organization. This eliminates the problem of direct class confrontation and thereby "depoliticizes" the situation, since it is more difficult for workers to oppose rational rules, technical procedures, and formal organizations. Through social engineering, the worker becomes just another "factor of production," a tool for the creation of profits. The mode of the scientific organization of work is reduced to the priorities of capital accumulation, whose goal is not the spiritual, intellectual, or physical development of labor; profit becomes the criterion for social organization, not creativity.[101] Braverman has summarized the mechanism of this process in his important work *Labor and Monopoly Capital*.

> This attempt to conceive of the worker as a general-purpose machine operated by management is one of many paths taken toward the same goal: the displacement of labor as the subjective element of the labor process and its transformation into an object. Here the entire work operations, down to its smallest motion, is conceptualized by the management and engineering staffs, laid out, measured, fitted with training and performance standards — all entirely in advance. The human instruments are adapted to the machinery of production according to specifications that resemble nothing so much as machine-capacity specifications.[102]

Edwards has argued that even these technical controls were not completely effective, as labor continued to resist. As labor was internally divided through the segmentation of work activities, seniority system, and bureaucratic controls, the external situation underwent a similar form of segmentation. The marketplace was structured in a fragmented manner, so as to created a dual labor market as another effective weapon of labor control.[103] This segmented labor market divided labor and the market into a system of highly paid, well-organized, skilled and semiskilled unionized labor in the monopoly sectors of the economy. In the smaller competitive sectors or secondary labor market, workers are poorly organized and protected, if at all, have low pay scales, and are subject to immediate firings and the arbitrary control of management. This split in the work force has become an effective means for social control, since it divides labor against itself in the monopoly and competitive industries. The interests of labor in both markets are different and generally at odds with each other, thereby undermining any possibility of a consciousness of common class interests. Usually women and minorities are concentrated in the secondary labor market, which is then used to rationalize their lower pay and job security. "Thus, in probing the causes of segmented labor markets, we seek in part to understand how racial discrimination and sexual discrimination have become incorporated in the instituted processes of labor markets."[104] The social mechanism which has legislatively institutionalized and judicially justified industry's control over labor (Wagner Act, Taft-Hartley Act, and Landrum-Griffin Act) and over its own mode of organization (Sherman Anti-Trust Act, Clayton Act, and Celler-Kefauver Amendments) is the state.[105]

CLASS FUNCTIONS OF THE WELFARE STATE:
ECONOMIC ACCUMULATION AND POLITICAL LEGITIMATION

There has been a good deal of conservative criticism of the American welfare state, as we have already seen. Much of it occurs because of the continuing frustrations with the government's inability to solve persistent social problems and eliminate poverty in the midst of relative affluence. These social problems force us to continually reconsider our pluralistic forms of social arrangements in ways that are sometimes unpleasant. The conservative approach attempts to avoid the difficult questions and resorts to variations on the theme of "blaming the victim." The liberal perspective, however, also attempts to avoid the real issues by overstressing their humanistic impulses, failing to evaluate critically the slowness of the accomplishments of the welfare state, and by avoiding almost entirely the structural reasons why poverty has not been eliminated under the present system.

In response to the conservatives, it must be noted that important gains have been made by the welfare state in temporarily helping those at the very bottom of the economic system. In response to the liberals, it can be declared that the welfare state is that social institution which continues to maintain high levels of social inequality, poverty, and unemployment. There seems to be an unwillingness by both political ideologies to investigate the role of the modern state and its political and economic functions: preserving the political legitimation and economic growth of advanced capitalist society through its welfare and industrial policies. Thus its goal is to maintain high levels of capital investment and satisfy consumer wants, but in an economic form that results in a maldistribution of income and wealth, in the formation of social classes, in a narrow definition of the common good based on self-interest, and finally, in a society which gravitates toward economic crises and intransigent social problems. Increased welfare spending will not solve these problems, because the welfare state is itself part of the problem. Its purpose is to maintain the very system that generates these economic and social crises through its fiscal, monetary, and taxation policies. The welfare system is the price that must be paid for increased economic expansion and corporate restructuring. This represents the crisis and bankruptcy of liberalism.[106]

This section will examine the federal budget in order to determine the functions, priorities, and beneficiaries of government spending—who gets the money. Ralph Nader's Congress Watch estimated that government subsidies of corporations (corporate welfare) was about $80 to $100 billion in the early 1980s, while the Congressional Budget Office estimate for 1984 was $90 billion.[107] For a more accurate, but still underestimated account, these figures must be supplemented with the amounts spent by the government to subsidize corporate growth and economic expansion. These are listed by functions and subfunctions in the description of the federal budget and include: money spent on military appropriations, international affairs, space explorations, as well as on direct aid to private businesses through government loans and loan guarantees and indirectly through tax breaks and incentives to private corporations. Though these figures remain only an estimate, this will offer us a more comprehensive picture of the growth of corporate welfarism and the poverty of social welfarism in the United States.

Federal Expenditures by Function 1970-1989 [108]
(outlay in billions of dollars)

	1980	1981	1982	1983	1984	1985	1986	1987	1988	1989
TOTAL OUTLAYS	590.9	678.2	745.7	808.3	851.8	946.3	990.3	1003.8	1064.0	1143.6
National Defense	134.0	157.5	185.3	209.9	227.4	252.7	273.4	282.0	290.4	303.6
Internat. Affairs	12.7	13.1	12.3	11.8	15.9	16.2	14.2	11.6	10.5	9.6
Income Security	86.5	99.7	107.7	122.6	112.7	128.2	119.8	123.3	129.3	136.0
Health	23.2	26.9	27.4	28.6	30.4	33.5	35.9	40.0	44.5	48.4
Social Security & Medicare	150.6	178.7	202.5	223.3	235.8	254.4	268.9	282.5	298.2	318.0
Veterans Benefits	21.2	23.0	24.0	24.8	25.6	26.3	26.4	26.8	29.4	30.0
Education	31.8	33.7	27.0	26.6	27.8	29.3	30.6	29.7	31.9	36.7
Commerce & Housing Credit	9.4	8.2	6.3	6.7	6.9	4.2	4.9	6.2	18.8	27.7
Transportation	21.3	23.4	20.6	21.3	23.7	25.8	28.1	26.2	27.3	27.6
Nat. Resources & Environment	13.9	13.6	13.0	12.7	12.6	13.4	13.6	13.4	14.6	16.1
Energy	10.2	15.2	13.5	9.4	7.1	5.7	4.7	4.1	2.3	3.7
Community & Regional Development	11.3	10.6	8.3	7.6	7.7	7.7	7.2	5.1	5.3	5.4
Agriculture	8.8	11.3	15.9	22.9	13.6	25.6	31.4	26.6	17.2	16.9
Net Interest	52.5	68.7	85.0	89.8	111.1	129.4	136.0	151.7	165.7	169.0
Science, Space, & Technology	5.8	6.5	7.2	7.9	8.3	8.6	9.0	9.2	10.8	12.8
General Government	13.0	11.4	10.9	11.2	11.8	11.6	12.5	7.6	9.5	9.1
Admin. of Justice	4.6	4.8	4.7	5.1	5.7	6.3	6.6	7.5	9.2	9.4

The expenditures of the federal budget must then be integrated with the previous analysis of the nature of the American economy. This will provide us with the basis for a judgment about the role and function of the modern state in maintaining industrial growth, economic prosperity, and social harmony. We will also see that its function of providing for economic expansion and capital accumulation is antithetical to its other structural role of maintaining social welfare and political legitimation. The debates between the two major parties in American politics—between the Republicans, with their emphasis on economic expansion, and the Democrats, with their emphasis on entitlement programs—are simply the unrecognized political and cultural manifestations of these prior structural contradictions. The result is a displaced economic crisis in the form of a political crisis of the state.

The information provided by the Executive Office of Management and Budget is broken down into functions and subfunctions. These headings are defined by that office, but their descriptions hide more than they actually reveal. By investigating the various functions of the federal budget and the priorities of federal spending, it will be easier to determine the structure and role of the state and its relation to the economy.[109] This is a more effective way of measuring the involvement of the federal government in the formation and execution of an industrial economic policy than is generally found in theories of political philosophy. The central issue is: What are the real *class functions* of the federal budget? What are the structural functions of budget spending, who really benefits from these spending programs, and what is the implicit industrial policy of the federal government buried beneath its publicly stated ideology of spending priorities?

We must first rearrange the federal budget according to the criteria of its economic accumulation and class functions in order to determine the percentage of government spending actually going to the military and the defense of the international economic system; to determine how much is appropriated for encouraging industrial investment and economic expansion of the large corporations; to determine how much goes to the middle class in the form of Social Security, unemployment benefits, medical, education, and housing benefits; and finally, to determine how much goes to the poor through public assistance programs such as Aid to Families with Dependent Children (AFDC) and Supplemental Security Income (SSI).

James O'Connor has given us some valuable theoretical help in this area with his theory of the state. For him, the state fulfills two essential roles in a capitalist society: capital accumulation and political legitimation. To accomplish these ends, state expenditures may be broken down into two groups: *social capital*, which includes both social investment and social consumption, and *social expenses*.[110] O'Connor states that *social investment* is government spending that directly increases productivity and the rate of profit (state subsidies for the economic infrastructure). It includes money spent on transportation facilities, industrial development projects, urban renewal, agricultural subsidies, industrial research and development, and education and human investment. The budget expenses for *social consumption* lower the costs of labor and, in turn, increase the rate of productivity (social insurance). These programs include funding for suburban development, urban renewal, child care, hospital and medical facilities, and the Social Security programs.

Social expenses are those expenditures which legitimate the social system in the eyes of its citizens (welfare system) and protect it from domestic and foreign disturbances (military system).[111] The goal of social expenses is not to affect industrial growth, but to maintain social harmony and thus provide necessary social and cultural preconditions for economic expansion. Unlike the conservative theorists who argue that the growth of the modern state undermines economic activity, O'Connor's thesis is that the state is a necessary precondition for economic development. Through its spending priorities, the state socializes the costs of production and capital accumulation at one end, while at the other end insuring "mass loyalties" and quieting social discontent caused by its first function. In a similar fashion, Edward Greenberg has stated that the role of the state and its relations to the economy may be categorized in the following five ways[112]:

1. The provision of some minimal benefits to those at the bottom of the social order as a preventive to radical discontent and turmoil
2. The maintenance of the system of inequality and class stratification
3. The regulation of the economy to create an environment of stability, predictability, profitability, and growth of corporate enterprise
4. The protection of the social, economic, and political order from radical internal threats
5. The protection of the worldwide interests of giant corporations through the machinery of American foreign policy.

It is to this issue of the state's maintenance and stabilization of a class society that we now turn.

SPENDING PRIORITIES OF THE STATE: SOCIALIZATION OF THE PRIVATE COSTS OF PRODUCTION

The amount of federal money spent on the subsidization of corporations and their economic expansion and capital accumulation is significantly more than that spent on public assistance and welfare programs. In its now-famous report of 1984 entitled *Federal Support of U.S. Business*, the Congressional Budget Office detailed government spending and budgetary priorities that have been used for the purposes of both "industrial support" and "economic stabilization" policies. "The federal government extends financial aid to business as part of its constitutional duty to promote industry and commerce."[113] It accomplishes this aid for industrial, agricultural, and commercial development though its *Direct Expenditure Programs*, *Credit Programs*, and *Tax Expenditure Programs*. The CBO was very clear about the purpose of these three government programs. They were created to further international competition, encourage investments, support industrial expansion, stabilize the economy during the business cycle, subsidize specific industries with loans and credits, and directly influence the allocation of resources and spending within the economy. To accomplish these goals, they aim at reducing capital costs and increasing productivity, stimulating exports, and reducing imports.[114] The following chart from their report outlines these industrial support and stabilization programs in more detail.

The Categories of Industrial Support Programs 1984-1988
(in billions of current dollars)[115]

	1984	1988 (Projected)
I. Direct Spending Programs		
Direct Expenditures	13.7	17.3
Credit Expenditures	8.8	7.4
II. Credit Programs		
Direct Loan Obligations	20.9	23.4
Loan Guarantee Commitments	17.7	18.6
III. Tax Expenditures		
Accelerated Cost Recovery System	18.3	15.8
Preferential Treatment of Capital Gains	16.4	21.5
Investment Tax Credit	15.7	27.5
Reduced Rates on the First $100,000 of Corporate Income	6.5	9.1
Exclusion of Interest on State and Local Gov. Industrial Development Bonds	3.5	5.9
Research and Development Expend.	2.5	2.7
Excess of % Depletion Over Cost Depletion: Fuels	2.1	2.6
Safe Harbor Leasing	1.9	0.5
Exclusion of Interest on State and Local Pollution Control Bonds	1.5	2.3
Deferral of Income of Domestic Internt. Sales Corporations	1.2	1.1
Expensing of Exploration and Development Costs: Fuels	1.2	1.9
Sub Total	**131.9**	**157.6**
IV. Other Government Programs		n.a.
Department of Defense Spending	140.0	
Medical and Housing Subsidies to Business	110.0	
Further Research and Development Programs	35.0	
Sub Total	**285.0**	
V. Collateral Industrial Programs		n.a.
Tax Deduction on Interest for Home Mortgage	27.9	
Exclusion of Employer Contribution to Med. Insur. Premiums and Medical Care	21.3	
Deductibility of Medical Expenses	2.6	
Deferral of Capital Gains on Home Sale	4.9	
Sub Total	**56.7**	
Total Government Spending for Industrial Development	**473.6**	n.a.

The first program specifically designed to promote industry and commerce is the *Direct Expenditures Program.* It includes:

1. Government money spent on research and development projects in agriculture, aeronautics, and energy to promote production and commerce
2. Direct subsidies to businesses that are at a competitive disadvantage or maintain unprofitable routes for construction and operating costs (shipping and airline industries)
3. Supplying statistical and technical information to businesses in agriculture, aeronautics, water transportation, and mining
4. Providing of agricultural price support, income stabilization programs, and guaranteed markets (Credit Commodity Corporation)
5. Improving energy technologies
6. The implementing of economic development projects such as housing rehabilitation and public works and private projects in order to create new jobs in low-income neighborhoods.

Funds for these economic development projects have gone to such businesses as the Hyatt Corporation, General Motors, and Sherwin-Williams, along with other corporations who have built 262 hotels nationwide in poor neighborhoods.[116]

The second type of government program is *Credit Programs*, which includes "non-recourse loans," income maintenance and price support policy for agriculture, offering loans and loan guarantees at below-market rates, providing loans to businesses who cannot get them elsewhere (Credit Commodity Corporation, Farmers Home Loan Association, Small Business Administration, Rural Electrification Administration, loans to large corporations who are in danger of defaulting—Chrysler Corporation, Lockheed, etc.), and providing loans and loan guarantees to foreign purchasers of United States goods (Export-Import Bank and the Agricultural Credit Insurance Fund). The direct spending and loan programs were developed to support economic stabilization and industrial development.

The third program, *Tax Expenditures*, was designed to encourage development through investment support and represents the most important method for government subsidization of the economy.[117] This form of government help is calculated on the basis of the anticipated loss of federal revenues resulting from selective tax relief and preferential treatment to certain groups of taxpayers. The methods used in determining "tax preferences" included tax exemptions and exclusion, preferential tax rates, credit deductions, and tax deferrals. There are two basic types of tax expenditures. The first type is multisector tax expenditures: tax deductions for accelerated depreciations (deferred taxation), preferential treatment of capital gains, a 10 percent investment tax credit, the exclusion of certain forms of corporate income from taxation (industrial development bonds: IDBs), preferential rates for certain types of corporate income, finance leasing of tax credits (safe harbor leasing), and tax credits for research and development. The second type is the sector-specific tax expenditures: accelerated cost depletion allowances, high percentage depletion provisions, and expensing (deduction) of exploration and development costs for the fuel industry and deduction of capital expenses in agriculture.

In past years, agriculture has received the most direct aid through the direct expenditures, along with the second highest amount of credit funds, while utilities received the most help through the credit programs. Manufacturing received the most overall help in multisector tax benefits. Corporate tax expenditures have grown from $7 billion in 1970 to over $83 billion in 1986.[118] Besides these three specific programs, government spending in other areas has a direct and indirect effect on industrial development. The CBO provided the anticipated expenditures for 1984 and the projected federal government expenditures for the following years to 1988 and concluded that in 1984 the government would spend $473.6 billion on capital accumulation.[119] While O'Connor dealt with direct government spending, the CBO's report also included indirect government spending in the form of tax breaks, which would also directly affect economic development.

The Direct Spending Programs, the Credit Programs, and the Tax Expenditure Programs were designed to build and maintain the physical infrastructure of the U.S. economy: highways, public transit systems, wastewater treatment facilities, water resources, air traffic control, airports, and municipal water supply. They promote the research and development of energy sources, search for old and new forms of energy, and clean up the problems and waste created by them (Nuclear Waste Disposal Fund). They were also intended to provide incentives for capital investment and industrial growth, mainly through the industrial policy behind the application of the Accelerated Cost Recovery System (ACRS), Capital Gains Deductions, and the Investment Tax Credit (ITC), loans to small businesses, and by the secured large profits and cost overruns in the military industries. A similar policy is in effect for agriculture (Credit Commodity Corporation).[120] In relation to the goal of economic stabilization, these programs differ in their effect on the business cycle. The agricultural credit programs are countercyclical and help farmers maintain income during periods of economic recessions, while the other programs are mainly procyclical, used during periods of economic expansion. Finally, all three programs directly or indirectly support the competitiveness of U.S. firms internationally.

Not only does it subsidize the production of commodities, the government also helps with the sale of these products by price support guarantees, international security assistance, and by promoting the international sale of American products through loan guarantees through the Export-Import Bank and the Domestic International Sales Corporation. In 1984 the direct loan obligation for the Export-Import Bank was $2.5 billion and the loan guarantee program was at $9.6 billion; both encouraged U.S. exports of aircraft and electrical power plants and equipment by providing below-market loans or by guaranteeing risky loans.[121] From the building of the economic infrastructure, research and development, investment, production, transportation, and promotion of the sale of agricultural and industrial goods to enforcing limits on foreign competition, the government does have an industrial policy, even if only weakly articulated. Every part of the production chain, from the beginning of the process to the end, from production to consumption, is subsidized through the use of public funds for the advancement of private industry.[122]

Many of the programs have been altered in the past few years due to the economic problems of the country, high federal deficits, privatization, government sale of land and loans, and rationalization of tax policies. Of the major tax expenditure programs designed to directly increase investment, the investment tax credit and accelerated depreciation allowances were either repealed or modified by the Tax Reform Act of 1986.[123] Before the passage of the new tax codes, their projected total benefit to corporations and individuals for 1991 was an anticipated $75.4 billion. With its passage, these business savings were either eliminated or scaled back; the capital gains deduction was also repealed.[124] However, the Tax Reform Act did lower the marginal tax rates for both individuals and corporations and broaden the tax base toward the goal of increasing the availability of investment capital. The act reduced the top individual marginal rates from 50 percent in 1986 to 28 percent in 1988, while the maximum corporation tax rate was reduced from 46 percent to 34 percent by 1988.[125] But these advantages were offset by continuing high government spending, public debt, and high interest rates.

The federal government guaranteed loans worth $450 billion and had $252 billion in its own direct loans through the Federal Credit Programs at the end of 1986. Through this federal credit program, the government was directing the allocation of over $1 trillion in loans. The beneficiaries of these loans have been mainly farmers, homeowners, small businesses, exporters, shipbuilders, and state, local, and foreign governments. These loans are 26 percent larger than the loan assets of the two largest U.S. commercial banks.[126] Investment outlays for 1988 are estimated to be $218.8 billion, down from $230 billion in 1986 and $220 billion in 1987. This includes monies spent by the federal government for acquisition, construction, and rehabilitation of physical assets in military and nonmilitary areas, research and development, and education grants to state and local governments.

There are various public research institutions which attempt to oversee this growing corporate welfare system. The Public Citizen's Congress Watch specializes in examining tax expenditures, direct subsidies, and credit subsidies, and an analysis of the corporate welfare bureaucracy, that is, those government agencies which subsidize corporations by restricting competition or limiting liability.[127] This would include the Interstate Commerce Commission, the Maritime Administration, the Federal Maritime Commission, the International Trade Commission, and agencies within the Department of Commerce. They also include those laws which further subsidize business by exempting firms from antitrust legislation, creating tariffs and quotas against foreign competition, providing limitations on nuclear disaster liabilities, and restricting purchases by the government through the "Buy American" laws. The result of all this government activity is to restrict and regulate competition, encourage price-fixing, create antitrust exemptions for exporters, insurance companies, and farmers, and subsidize the accumulation of private profits with public funds.

More money was spent on investment tax credit in 1986 ($38 billion) than on food stamps, welfare, student loans, and V.A. medical care combined. The Accelerated Cost Recovery System (ACRS) tax benefits have resulted in many corporations paying no income taxes at all. From 1983–1985, General Electric paid no federal income taxes on $6.5 billion in profits, while still claiming $238 million in tax refunds. The story is similar for other large corporations. Dow Chemical, with profits of $776 million, received $233 million in tax refunds; Union Carbide, with $613 million in profits, received $70 million; and W. R. Grace, with $684 million in profits, received $12.5 million in refunds.[128] After analyzing these tax benefits to major corporations, Congress Watch concluded:

> First enacted in 1962, it [ACRS] has proved useless for combatting recessions; it has created severe economic distortions by reallocating capital from structures to equipment; and has failed to create jobs . . . it may even have the effect of eliminating jobs. . . . Because it subsidizes capital and labor, it also provides most of its benefits to capital intensive big business—most of which would have made investment anyway.[129]

By combining a theory of the state and its fiscal and budget priorities developed by O'Connor with a description of the various budget functions of the federal government provided by the Office of Management and Budget and the Congressional Budget Office, we can see more clearly the real *class functions* of these programs and their costs, which are geared to social investment, social consumption, and social expenses. In turn, by organizing the federal budget around budget functions, industrial support programs, tax expenditures, and its class functions, we can develop a more comprehensive theory of the role of the modern state in maintaining industrial expansion. These functions serve the purpose of maintaining international hegemony of American capitalism, the institutions of a class system, and the social and economic inequality of a market economy. "The evidence is overwhelming, even discounting that proportion of the budget devoted to military purposes, that the *net impact of public sector spending in the United States is to maintain the system of class inequality.*"[130]

Social Investment	*Social Consumption*	*Social Expenses*
1. Military	1. Education	1. National defense
2. Agriculture	2. Social Security and	2. International
3. Community & regional	Medicare	affairs
development	3. Health	3. Space research
4. Transportation		4. Veterans benefits
5. Commerce and		5. Interest on debt
housing credit		6. Income security
6. Energy		7. General government
7. Natural resources		8. Administration of
and environment		justice
8. General science		

The total amount spent by the Bush administration on national defense and the military in 1989, which included the following budget items: national defense, international affairs, space research and technology, veterans benefits and services, and interest on the national debt, was about $523 billion or 46 percent of the total federal budget. This is in marked contrast to the priorities given to public assistance programs for the poor, such as food stamps and child nutrition ($21 billion), SSI ($12.6 billion), and AFDC ($11 billion). These latter programs, equaling about $44.6 billion, constituted slightly less than 4 percent of the total federal budget. The social insurance programs for the middle class included funds spent on Old Age Survivors and Dependent Insurance ($233 billion), unemployment compensation ($16 billion), and Medicare ($85 billion), or $334 billion. This is only 29 percent of the federal budget and represents a marked decline from its 32 percent mark in the early 1980s.[131]

From what has already been said, the inclusions under social investment and social expenses are obvious. However, the concept of social consumption needs to be clarified in its role of managing the system's stability.

> Although social security contributes to social and political stability by conservatizing unemployed and retired workers, the primary purpose of the system is to create a sense of economic security with the ranks of employed workers (especially workers in the monopoly sector) and thereby raise morale and reenforce discipline. This contributes to harmonious management-labor relations which are indispensable to capital accumulation and the growth of production. Thus the fundamental intent and effect of social security is to expand productivity, production, and profits. *Seen in this way, social insurance is not primarily insurance for workers, but a kind of insurance for capitalists and corporations.*[132]

Health benefits and education work as forms of social consumption in the same manner. O'Connor argues that the government imperative to foster capital accumulation at the same time as it furthers political legitimation leads to contradictory management priorities and ultimately to a fiscal crisis of the state. Claus Offe holds a similar position when he argues that it is the contradiction within the state between its goal of the socialization of the costs of production and the privatization of investment, profits, and distribution which leads to political crises. For both theorists, the state's main purpose is to encourage the creation of wealth and the acquisition of private property by using public resources to further the private ends of capital accumulation. But this leads to a conflict of priorities within the system. Jürgen Habermas describes these conflicts using systems theory language of systems integration and social integration. He too speaks of the irrational social system which is torn between the Scylla of administrative rationalization of the economy and the Charybdis of the necessity to maintain mass loyalty and social welfare through the cultural system. These contradictory demands on the social system result in a rationality crisis (inability to politically steer the economy) and a legitimation crisis (undermining of the political values of society).[133]

Federal money spent on legitimizing the social system through social welfare undermines the ability of the state to further capital investment and industrial growth. Industrial policy in its present form only furthers inequality, poverty, and class antagonisms, while creating the need for increased social welfare spending. The pull by these two opposing functions of the state leads to a drain on the state treasury and a widening gap between expenditures and taxation. By viewing the role of the state from a variety of perspectives, we can see that elimination of poverty and inequality is not an important priority. Any attempt to revitalize the welfare state in order to eliminate poverty, inequality, and social injustice, as is the case in the Bishops' Letter, expresses only a misdirected humanism that unfortunately has not carefully considered the issues of political economy and the historical role of the state in liberal society.

The top priority of the state is to expand industrial and commercial development through providing direct financial aid, maintenance of the economic infrastructure, relevant and marketable information, tax benefits, and military protection to corporations. It also underwrites the wage costs by subsidizing education, health care, disability, and retirement benefits, thereby insuring for the market a healthy, educated, and pliant work force. O'Connor put it most succinctly when he stated that we should view the state budget as another source of corporate profits, since the state socializes the various costs of production, research and development, investments, loans, competitive risks, guarantees a ready market, and internationally protects these same investments and markets. The state also cleans up environmental as well as domestic and international social problems created by this system of private accumulation of socially produced wealth.[134] O'Connor refers to the federal budget as "systems maintenance expenditures," whereas Offe, using similar systems theory terminology, refers to the process as the "crisis management" function of the state; both see this as leading to budgetary confusion and a fiscal crisis. Economic contradictions in contemporary society are manifested as political conflicts over government spending priorities.

THE REAGAN LEGACY: LEVERAGING OF A DEINDUSTRIALIZED AMERICA

How these crisis management functions of the state work in reality can be seen by examining the Reagan state during the 1980s. As the state responded in the 1970s and 1980s to high inflation, economic stagnation, rising unemployment, growing poverty and inequality, environmental decay, and rising international debt, it was responding to a variety of complex changes in the corporate structure, in the labor market, and in the international economy, as well as changes within its own organization. These, in turn, were either symptoms of serious economic problems of a declining economy—declining productivity and rates of profit—or symptoms produced by the new role of the state in fighting stagflation. As Harrison and Bluestone said in their new work *The Great U-Turn*, the state reversed the Keynesian prescription for fighting inflation by means of dampening the economy and created instead an economic depression in 1980–1981.

Throughout the Reagan years, the power of the state was used to assist in the corporate restructuring of the American economy through a variety of mechanisms:

1. The use of the cold bath of planned recessions, tight money, high interest rates, and high unemployment to control inflation and labor costs

2. Tax cuts for the wealthy, for the purpose of increasing industrial investment

3. Economic deregulation of communications, banking, stock-market transactions, airlines, etc. in order to encourage competition

4. Privatization of business, or the sale of government businesses and assets to private corporations, such as the sale of Consolidated Rail Corporation (Conrail)

5. Social deregulation, or the cutting of the federal budgets to government agencies which restrict corporate profits, including such organizations as the Environmental Protection Agency, Occupational Safety and Health Administration, Consumer Product Safety Commission, Equal Employment Opportunity Commission, and many others

6. Rationalization of labor by the government, or the use of more contingent or part-time labor in the public and private spheres, thereby cutting labor costs, fringe benefits, and medical costs for workers

7. Urban revitalization, or the subsidization of urban real estate and commercial development for large corporations

8. Direct assaults on labor unions, beginning with the firing of the air-traffic controller union members (PATCO)

9. Use of government fiscal and tax policy to encourage the development of a "casino economy," stock market booms, mergers, and diversification, instead of industrial investment, expansion, and increasing productivity

10. Government's creation of the illusion of economic growth, a healthy private economy, and sustained higher profits through the use of the dual mirrors of increasing military expenditures and high public and private debt.[135]

These programs resulted in the megamergers of the 1980s, the deindustrialization of America, the shift from manufacturing to service industries, the deterioration of the average worker's standard of living, declining and stagnant productivity, growing inequality, poverty, and unemployment, and a polarization of the work force and increasing numbers of low-wage jobs.

Concern for the issues of poverty and care for the disenfranchised are important only to the extent that they affect the primary function of the state. This is certainly clear from the amount of money spent by the federal government on the poor. The historical development of the state and the use of its taxation, budgetary, and fiscal policies have resulted in no real redistribution of income and wealth, no concern for the abstract issues of social justice and economic redistribution, and certainly no attempt to restructure the economy in order to confront the underlying causes of these social problems. Concern for these issues of justice represents the myths of liberalism, which are perpetuated by humanistic liberals in order to justify the welfare state or by conservatives to be used as criticisms of public assistance. In both cases, the political ideology deflects us from a critical reflection on the structural failures of American political economy. Best and Connolly have called this "the poverty of liberalism." The state advances the economy, while it perpetuates inequality and poverty.

> When the production of profit requires extensive inequality and alienating work, the state will refuse to tamper with these institutions . . . But the poverty of liberalism assumes other dimensions as well. By making public promises in the name of the welfare state, liberals encourage unemployed workers, victims of inflation, paralyzed urban residents, and welfare recipients to support policies that will not securely provide their needs over the long run.[136]

Thus the bishops' policy recommendations for improving the welfare state only exacerbate the social problems. By failing to develop their own analysis of American political economy, the bishops have taken a neoclassical liberal position, whose implicit and explicit moral values and social goals contradict their stated policy recommendations. From our analysis above, it becomes obvious that the focus of concern on the amounts of money spent for public assistance are trifling in comparison to the enormous sums of money spent on direct expenditures, loans, tax expenditures, capital and human investment, information, and so forth by the federal government. If the actual amount of money spent on services to the poor is so small and trivial, then what has been the historical role of the government toward the poor? Piven and Cloward have argued in *Regulating the Poor* that the role of social welfare programs is to preserve civil order, retain economic inequalities, stabilize the market during periods of high unemployment, enforce low-wage work for the marginal labor population, and maintain the ideology and legitimation of the market; it is "a surrogate system of social control."[137] The welfare state developed as a response to the great social and political disorder in the 1930s and 1960s.

> To buttress weak market controls and ensure the availability of marginal labor, an outcast class—the dependent poor—is created by the relief system. This class, whose members are of no productive use, is not treated with indifference, but with contempt. Its degradation at the hands of relief officials serves to celebrate the virtue of all work, and deters actual or potential workers from seeking aid.[138]

The poverty programs, then, are a sophisticated social mechanism for the control of those individuals displaced by the corporate welfare system and the market. The poor are maintained with below poverty wages in order to insure a readily available supply of low-wage workers during periods of cyclical change in the economy; to act as a negative reinforcement and disciplinary force on those workers who do have jobs, in order to keep their demands and wages down; to justify the economic inequality in society by creating the appearances of merit based on market productivity; and to act as a safety valve for the venting of social frustrations of public discontent with the whole economic system.

Michael Novak, Milton Friedman, and Daniel Patrick Moynihan have recommended the elimination of many of the inefficient welfare programs and their replacement by direct cash payments. This might eliminate some of the more obvious repressive aspects of government bureaucracy and its contradictory messages and incentives.[139] But by defining the issue as that of poverty, rather than that of inequality and social injustice, the solutions and policy recommendations are defined in terms of money and not substantive structural changes of society.[140] This occurs at the same time that billions of public dollars are used to subsidize major corporations in the procurement and maintenance of military hardware—what Richard Barnet has called "the economy of death."

Certainly the permanent war economy in America has been one of the leading causes of misplaced public funds, distorted economic priorities and development, decline in civilian research and development, a critical brain drain from civilian to military industry, declining investment and productivity in key civilian industries, and growing economic inequality of the country.[141] The government, through the military industry, has also provided large corporations with a form of public welfare in which industry is assured of enormous profits outside of traditional market mechanisms. The official military budget for fiscal year 1990 was just over $300 billion, while funds earmarked specifically for the poor continue to pale by significance. Recent political and economic developments in Eastern Europe, the disappearance of the Warsaw Pact, the dismantling of the Soviet Union, and the reunification of Germany have all resulted in calls for drastic cuts in the military budget. But the much-talked-about and anticipated "peace dividend" is unlikely to take place, given the priorities of the American state and declining economy. Any benefits from reduced tensions and a thawing of the Cold War will more than likely be spent on dealing with the legalized leveraging of the American economy during the Reagan-Bush administration: a federal budget deficit approaching $3 trillion, a banking crisis, and a savings and loan industry fiasco that requires a bailout scheme currently calculated to cost between $500 billion and $1.4 trillion. All is to be paid for by the American taxpayer; the profits have been privatized, while the costs are being socialized. It is estimated that in the next fiscal year alone, there will be a $160 billion federal budget deficit, along with a savings and loan bailout requirement of over $40 billion.[142] Cowboy capitalism in the banking and savings and loan industry has given rise to what Robert Sherrill has called the "looting decade."[143] Comparing the bankruptcy and breakdown of East European Communism to the "fraudulent system of capitalism," Sherrill writes that "our system is just as bogus and corrupt and irrelevant and defeated in its own way, offering neither the risks of true capitalism nor the safeguards of true democracy. Our system is a hoax."[144] On top of all this lie the expenses for the maintenance of the international economic system, e.g., the Iraq War.

The economic prosperity of the eighties during the Reagan administration was made possible because of the tax giveaways to the wealthy, high federal budget deficits and private debt, exorbitant military spending, cuts in the social welfare programs, rampant fraud in the government (Department of Housing and Urban Development) and savings and loan industry, increasing poverty and class antagonisms, the deindustrialization and leveraging of America, restructuring of the relations among the state, business, and labor to the detriment of the last, and the mortgaging of America's future and the next generation's expectation of a better life. It was not built on the foundations of rebuilding the economic infrastructure, reemphasizing science and technology, research and development, increasing economic productivity, opening up and democratizing the workplace, or of producing a more free, just, and egalitarian society.

The overemphasis by economic theologians analyzing the nature of the modern state on the allocation of poverty funds in the welfare programs is itself a clear example of a distorted sense of what the historical role and function of the state has been. The bishops call for a critical examination of these expenditures,[145] but do not call for a rearrangement of the military-industrial focus of the state in that document. The bishops have also consistently failed to appreciate the nature of the welfare system as that mechanism designed to contain the social wastes of an irrational economic and political ecology. A policy directed at simply improving the delivery of social and economic services to the least advantaged only further rationalizes and legitimates such a system of incoherent liberalism.

The bishops have also failed to understand the inherent contradictions between liberalism and democracy, between a culture of egoism and self-interest fostered by the market and a culture of civic virtue and concern for the common good required by republicanism. There is no recognition of the conflicting pulls from these different philosophical traditions, nor do they seem to notice the contradictions between their theory of political philosophy and the historical reality of American political economy. To attempt to graft onto liberalism institutions of political and economic democracy without fundamentally altering the nature of capitalism can only result in more rational management and social engineering of liberalism, but not the constitution of a society in which economic decisions and social relationships ensure the dignity of the human person. The failure to see mainstream economics as a theology can only result in more gilded forms of the "iron cage." The failure of theology to develop a critical theory of political economy can only result in the increased idolatry of conservative economic metaphysics—even by its most ardent liberal critics. We do not offer alternative policy recommendations here. That would be the topic of another work. But what we do observe is that, if the underlying ideological norms and structural foundations of liberalism are not adequately understood and examined, there is no real possibility of escaping the exile of critical reason and eclipse of social justice.

5

NINETEENTH- AND TWENTIETH-CENTURY CATHOLIC SOCIAL CRITIQUE: THE POPES SPEAK

INTRODUCTION

When the American Catholic bishops constructed their pastoral letter on the U.S. economy, they drew not only from their own earlier pronouncements, but perhaps more importantly from the century-old ongoing tradition of papal encyclicals and Vatican statements about the social question. By quoting these documents of the Holy See and aligning the principles they used to address the American social situation, the U.S. bishops were making implicit claims about their continuity with the highest religious authority of their church. Rome had spoken, and the American hierarchy was the choir that resonated that unified voice.

The historic papal encyclicals themselves, perhaps too little known even to Roman Catholics, constitute a self-conscious tradition of concepts, references, and vocabulary, used especially by Leo XIII (1878–1903) and his successors to address immediate and more theoretical issues of social concern.[1] While often prompted by specific political and economic situations, the claim is made by the popes themselves that their statements are grounded in the eternally valid scriptures and later church writings, from apostolic times to the present, echoing and restating a common inheritance of basic values and religious teachings.

In fact the Church's teaching finds its source in Sacred Scripture, beginning with the Book of Genesis and especially in the Gospels and writings of the apostles. From the beginning it was part of the Church's teaching, her concept of man and life in society, and especially the social morality which she worked out according to the needs of the different ages. This traditional patrimony was then inherited and developed by the teaching of the popes on the modern "social question," beginning with the encyclical *Rerum Novarum*. In this context, study of the question of work, as we have seen, has continually been brought up to date while maintaining that Christian basis of truth which can be called ageless.[2]

The various letters are seen as historically linked, providing timely readjustments in the interpretation of a "Catholic Social Doctrine." This pattern of papal "social teaching" and action is viewed as undergoing an organic development of ideas, highlighted by different emphases, rather than as novel additions or corrections to the earlier authoritative writings. Popes do not contradict their predecessors; they stress instead the evolving but consistent nature of the insights contained in previous statements. Thus, John Paul II, reflecting back on a century of teaching by the supreme Magisterium (the papal teaching role), alludes to a refocusing of the church's attempt to solve the "labor question" as only an expansion of the issue from one of "class" within particular nations, the more Eurocentric approach of Leo XIII and Pius XI, to one that shifts to the "world" discussion of questions of injustice and inequality begun by John XXIII and carried on by the Second Vatican Council.[3] Nothing has changed, only the arena for proclaiming the church's message. The popes speak with one voice, but with a changing vocabulary.

Rerum Novarum (1891) by Pope Leo XIII commenced this tradition of official, authoritative documents on social issues. Besides that initial text, the present work will consider some of the most important of these numerous statements: Pius XI, *Quadragesimo Anno* (1931) and *Divini Redemptoris* (1937); different speeches by Pius XII; John XXIII, *Mater et Magistra* (1961) and *Pacem in Terris* (1963); the Pastoral Constitution of the Church in the Modern World of the Second Vatican Council, *Gaudium et Spes* (1965); Paul VI, *Populorum Progressio* (1967) and *Octogesima Adveniens* (1971); the document of the World Synod of Bishops, *Justice in the World* (1971); and John Paul II, *Redemptor Hominis* (1979), *Laborem Exercens* (1981), *Sollicitudo Rei Socialis* (1987), and *Centesimus Annus* (1991).

The question of whether the papal teaching does contain differing and even contradictory material is an often ignored but ongoing one.[4] There are a number of points usually stressed by commentators to show that the papal authors have drawn from the same underlying doctrinal content in their encyclicals, and thus there is substantial continuity in their teachings. The following are an amalgam of central issues treated by the various encyclicals, but not all present in any one:

1. The church is committed to a deep concern for the poor and powerless which only later is articulated as a "preferential option for the poor."

2. A central stress is placed on the dignity of the person and the rights of the person for full development in society. These rights — political, economic, and social — become defined in more specific and expansive terms in later papal writings.

3. An affirmation is maintained for the right of private property as a natural safeguard of personal dignity and freedom, but always subordinate to the preeminent common good which insures the right of all people to use the goods of the earth (Pius XII).

4. A categorical assertion of the church's appropriate role in applying social morality to social, political, and economic affairs. The essential inter-relation of economics and ethics is stressed, but any radical solutions to problems are rejected by the papal authors.

5. Labor is viewed in terms of useful employment, a just wage, decent working conditions, and the right of organization and association. While condemning planned unemployment and the maldistribution of resources, the popes give changing directives about the usefulness of the strike and other adversarial strategies to achieve justice, but finally call for labor's share in decision making, setting production goals, and even ownership. With John Paul II, the nature of labor itself is interpreted as part of a Christian biblical vision, linking the meaning of work to the essence of human dignity.

6. Capital is viewed in different ways in agrarian and industrial contexts, but always in terms of moral guidelines for the creation and use of wealth which bears a "social mortgage." From Leo XIII, but more explicitly and conclusively stated by John Paul II, the popes insist that labor creates capital, the wealth of nations, and has priority.

7. One controversial note consistently struck is the right and obligation of the state to intervene for the common good, even to the point of expro-priation of property, albeit only in cases of dire national emergency. To allay the specter of "statism," or as some conservative critics phrase it, "economic Constantinianism," the papal letters stress the limits on the exercise of state power and control. In a startling reversal of historical stereotypes, the Catholic Church is now often depicted as the most visible and effective opposition to a number of oppressive governments.

8. The popes challenge and denounce various social ideologies, most particularly Marxism, socialism, and liberal capitalism, at least in their more classic nineteenth-century forms, as separate but similar expressions of phil-osophical liberalism (see below). Social models constructed around collec-tivism or individualism are analyzed and rejected in favor of models deemed more compatible with Catholic principles, models that are variously soli-darist, communitarian, corporatist, personalist, or social democratic. The effects of the long-term ideological battles in multiplying human misery have also been weighed.

9. From the 1950s on, there has been an internationalization of the papal overview, especially touching the Third World. Shifts can be seen from primary concern about private property to a focus on poverty, from concern for political stability as the foundation of order to development as the new word for peace (Paul VI). The most recent participant in this papal tra-dition, John Paul II, has reiterated the claim that successive contributions

of the Magisterium, in fundamental accord with human reason and scientific insight, have updated a doctrinal core to help believers pursue "their vocation as responsible builders of earthly society."[5] He reaffirms that the continuity of this social doctrine, as well as its constant renewal, is the basis of its perennial value:

> This twofold dimension is typical of her teaching in the social sphere. On the one hand it is *constant*, for it remains identical in its fundamental inspiration, in its "principles of reflection," in its "criteria of judgment," in its basic "directives for action," and above all in its vital link with the Gospel of the Lord. On the other hand, it is ever *new*, because it is subject to the necessary and opportune adaptations suggested by the changes in historical conditions and by the unceasing flow of the events which are the setting of the life of people and society.[6]

The reader needs to ask, however, whether the views and resources in the chain of encyclicals are entirely continuous. Is there a fundamental change in attitude in the displacement of private property as the focal point, substituting a concern for poverty, the scandalous disparity of resources, and an "option for the poor"? Later encyclicals have abandoned the notions of a guild apparatus for workers' associations, the corporatist model of the modern state, and the prohibition on strikes. Some later papal letters barely make a reverential nod to Leo XIII's *Rerum Novarum* and do not utilize or develop the positions taken in it. Instead, we can see the later papal authors recreate the earlier material in their own likenesses to address radically different socioeconomic and political conditions. The real continuity is, instead, the insistence on papal access to a bully-pulpit by which to uphold a social morality in the face of a social, political, and economic order alien or antagonistic to religious values. Rather than forms of "Constantinianism," the church's subservience to the established order of society, these papal pronouncements, whether viewed as progressive or atavistic, recall the religious challenge to the state symbolized in the Bible by the prophet Nathan's judgment on the sin of King David (2 Samuel 12). In short, popes speak on the basis of claims of ancient authority to challenge prophetically the modern, antireligious philosophy of liberalism and the variety of often-opposed forms of political economy evolved by the modern state.

The Catholic Church's opposition to liberalism is best epitomized in the writings of Pius IX (1846–1878), who was initially regarded as a "liberal" reform pope, but later as a reactionary under whom liberal Catholicism was crushed by the ultramontane party and the definition of papal infallibility at the First Vatican Council (1869–1870). Lurking behind the high-sounding liberal ideals of liberty, equality, and fraternity the popes did not see a divinely inspired revolution of the people, but only anarchy and a godless mob bringing a Reign of Terror. For "Pio Nono" the church stood as a fortress bulwark against the tide of modern liberalism whose several politically aggressive and philosophical guises were all virulently anti-Catholic: naturalism, absolute rationalism, scientific materialism, radical individualism, communism, socialism, and collectivism. In his "Syllabus of Errors," appended to the encyclical *Quanta Cura* (December 8, 1864), the pontiff imposed a solemn anathema on the eighty "principal errors" of his time. He ended by damning any who held or taught the notion that the "Roman Pontiff can, and ought to, reconcile himself, and come to terms with progress, liberalism, and modern civilization."[7]

More recently some authors have argued that while the church has rejected the ideology of bourgeois liberalism, it has come to accept the consonance of its moral teachings with liberal institutions, for example, in human rights, democracy, and a free-market economy.[8] As a moral doctrine, the popes viewed liberalism as opposed to religious authority, leading to "indifferentism" in the name of tolerance and moral relativism. It was, in short, a pagan philosophy. Its individualistic dimension undermined the preeminence of the common good and the unity of the family. As a political theory, it fostered republican forms of government, political rights for individuals, democracy with majority rule, equality, economic liberty, and unchecked competition. But these were also politically the seeds of the omnicompetent, totalitarian state. Viewed from the negative side, these same "natural rights" guaranteed by liberal regimes were grounded in a philosophy of human nature radically opposed to the religious view. In economic liberalism, property rights pushed aside the natural-law understanding of the common good; egotism and self-interest replaced community-based values. Nonhuman, deterministic, scientific market forces replaced the human face of compassion and the fair exchange of goods. This view of the modern Western economic system as generator of inequality, poverty, and exploitation, especially in the Third World, still pervades many traditionally Catholic cultures. This pejorative sense is enshrined in the slogan: *Liberalismo es pecado* (liberalism is sin).[9] Conservative critics, while applauding the church's condemnation of the various types of socialism, view this early and mutual rejection of liberalism and Catholicism as unfortunate but correctable:

> This was a tragedy both for Catholicism and for liberalism. Liberalism needed the Catholic sense of community, of transcendence, of realism, of irony, of tragedy, of evil. And Catholicism needed the institutions of liberalism for the incarnation in society of its own vision of the dignity of the human person, of the indispensable role of free associations, and of the limited state respectful of the rights of conscience.[10]

While the church since Vatican Council II (1962–65) has embraced more characteristically liberal institutions, there is still a rejection of the underlying principles of liberalism, hence the recent papal critiques of the hedon-istic aspects of contemporary liberal democracy. Whether liberals or conservatives, the upholders of current Western political economy are seen as inheritors of unquestioning belief in narcissistic individualism, materi-alism, commercialism, and consumerism.

It is strange that many conservative critics of liberation theology deny that one can separate what they see as the negative Marxist ideology of its social analysis and the morally positive economic and political concerns and remedies suggested by these Third World theorists. Yet that is what they themselves ask for with regard to liberal bourgeois democracy and a free-market economy, both of which are presumed compatible in principle with traditional Catholicism. The system built on "natural rights" drawn from Thomas Hobbes, John Locke, and Adam Smith is made indistinguishable from the "natural law" of Augustine, Aquinas, and the papal encyclicals. Yet Pius IX's "Syllabus" and its condemnation of the idea that the modern state (*Reipublicae status*), "being the origin and source of all rights, is endowed with a certain right not circumscribed by any limits,"[11] is a fun-damental rejection of the basis for the "natural-rights" argument. Despite what appear to be consonances on the surface with the "natural-law" posi-tion on private property assumed by Leo XIII, one can perhaps see the reintroduction of Thomas Aquinas and a scholastic theology of "natural law" as an antidote to liberal "natural-rights" theory. The popes have never accepted the "state of nature" argument of seventeenth-century "possessive individualism" to replace the Eden of Genesis or the "natural law" implanted by God before the formation of any "social contract." Whatever openings the church has made to the modern world, there remain basic differences between its traditional principles and those of modern liberal-ism.

LEO XIII (1878–1903): NATURAL LAW OVER NATURAL RIGHTS

"During this trip through Belgium, my sojourn in Aachen and the tour up the Rhine river I have come to the conviction that we have to combat the clerics vigorously, especially in the Catholic areas. . . . The scoundrels are flirting with the workers' question whenever it seems appropriate" (Karl Marx to Friedrich Engels, 25 September 1869).[12]

In 1891 the English novelist Thomas Hardy published *Tess of the d'Ur-bervilles*, a realistic depiction of the personal tragedies stemming from the conflict in a changing rural society brought on by the "dark, Satanic mills" of industrialization. The same year, artist and social theorist William Morris completed *News from Nowhere*, an imaginative utopian forecast of an Eng-lish socialist society. The "workers' question," raised in polemical form by Marx and Engels in the *Communist Manifesto* (1848), had generated endless discussion and response in political, economic, and even literary circles for over forty years before Leo XIII's official pronouncement on the situation of the working class.

The timing of this encyclical, belated by comparison to the response of socialists and others, has been used to decry the church's lack of interest or shortsightedness in addressing the need for structural reform and workers' rights, beyond just pleas for charity. But it represents, from another perspective, a capstone to a long and complex process of political debates and social movements within Catholicism itself in the nineteenth century.[13] As so often in the past, the pronouncement from Rome came only after protracted local discussions; but when it did come, it won Leo XIII the title of the Workers' Pope within Catholic circles (although disgruntled traditionalists preferred to use the epithet "the Freemason Pope"), and his encyclical was later hailed by Pius XI as the "Magna Carta" of workers' rights, even if at the time it had little real impact on labor's struggle.[14]

It was Baron von Ketteler (1811–1877), later Bishop of Mainz, who began in 1848 to take the challenge of the *Manifesto* seriously and shaped a position of Christian social reform to alleviate the misery and degradation of the workers in Germany and Europe.[15] It was through his speeches and writings that German clergy and laity were motivated to undertake the reform of social conditions in significant ways, such that more radical attempts to galvanize workers' unrest were deflected, as Marx observed in the letter to Engels quoted above. A number of politically active aristocrats and Romantics rallied to this work: Baron Karl von Vogelsang, Prince Johann von Liechtenstein, Prince Charles von Löwenstein, Count von Küfstein, and in France the Marquis René de la Tour du Pin and Count Albert de Mun, among others, who despite their aristocratic backgrounds favored a more radical stance against industrial capitalism and the often anticlerical bourgeois captains of industry in place of the legislative reform favored by Ketteler.[16] In turn the aristocratic Cardinal Pecci, later Leo XIII, was influenced by these noble critics of the "cash nexus" of laissez-faire economics and the "atomism" of political liberalism.

Leo XIII's encyclical *Rerum Novarum* (May 15, 1891) came as a declaration that the papacy itself would play a role in the working-class question. Overall, it sided with:

1. The social thinking of Ketteler, although remaining more ambiguous on the right to strike and the need for structural changes
2. The "interventionist" policy of the "Liege School," promoted after 1890 against the more traditionalist groups opposed to any state intervention, especially by modern liberal governments
3. The social program associated with Cardinal Gaspard Mermillod and the Fribourg Union.[17]

It is in this last program that the direction of subsequent Catholic social thought can be discerned:

1. Some form of nuanced endorsement of the right of private property
2. Rejection of the idea or necessity of class struggle
3. A critical appraisal of capitalism as a system opposed to the medieval organic model of society, but with no formal condemnation of it
4. An emphasis on workers' rights
5. Strong support for unionization and workers' associations
6. A "just wage" sufficient for a laborer's family.[18]

Leo's encyclical addressed the troubled conditions of the workers in terms of the problems of a fair wage, loosely defined as sufficient for the "thrifty and upright" (drawing on the threefold medieval notion of a just wage, just profit, and just price), the unassailability of private property, the legitimate scope of state action, and the right of workers to form coalitions and associations, although these preferably should have hierarchical sanction, be organized to promote moral improvement, and be composed of both workers and employers (significantly referred to as "masters"). Later interpreters saw it leaving open the possibility of all-labor unions. These reforms were presented as possible within the given capitalist economy. In the typical tones of a grand seigneur, Leo emphasized the harm to public welfare posed by strikes, the obligation of governments to eliminate the causes of such strife, and the need for employees to fulfill absolutely the contracts signed voluntarily (*libere et cum aequitate*) in an era when laborers rarely faced voluntary or fair terms of employment.[19]

Rerum Novarum surveys the motives and principles behind contemporary revolutionary change in the realms of political order, economics, and social conditions in response to the misery and destitution of the masses. In one passage remarkable for its bite, Leo lays blame at the feet of the capitalists:

> After the old trade guilds had been destroyed in the last century, and no protection was substituted in their place, and when public institutions and legislation had cast off traditional religious teaching, it gradually came about that the present age handed over the workers, each alone and defenseless, to the inhumanity of employers and the unbridled greed of competitors. A devouring usury, although often condemned by the Church, but practiced nevertheless under another form by avaricious and grasping men, has increased the evil; and in addition the whole process of production as well as trade in every kind of goods has been brought almost entirely under the power of a few, so that a very few rich and exceedingly rich men have laid a yoke almost of slavery on the unnumbered masses of nonowning workers.[20]

In language that echoes the gospel account of the betrayal of Christ, the workers are described as being "handed over" to the greed and competition of the liberal economic system, termed by others as the "ruling spirit" of the time. Conservative commentators have noted that this view that industry and industrialists created the suffering of the working class by making them wage slaves was generally in error, however much it reflected some specific contemporary examples. Instead, the poor in European countries, especially Italy, were oppressed, they argue, because their societies were not capitalistic enough; Catholic social theory concentrated legitimately but excessively on questions of equitable wealth distribution, rather than on the benefits gained in the creation of new wealth, new middle classes, and more stable and lucrative employment.[21] Later critics of liberation theology argue this same position. The encyclical does in fact focus more on finding ways to draw from the store of the common good to benefit the workers to live without hardship, since as it radically claims "it is incontestable that the wealth of nations originates from no other source than from the labor of workers."[22] Sharing with the workers only restores what they have themselves created.

Despite the socialist ring of this sentiment, the socialists are rigorously denounced, putting in place a leitmotiv of condemnations of collectivists, overly centralized economies, and political bureaucracies that is repeated in papal writings down to the 1960s. Socialism is seen as a cure worse than the illness.

> To cure this evil, the Socialists, exciting the envy of the poor toward the rich, contend that it is necessary to do away with private possession of goods and in its place to make goods of individuals common to all, and that the men who preside over a municipality or who direct the entire state should act as administrators of these goods.[23]

What is condemned is the rhetoric of class warfare, an idea "abhorrent to reason and truth,"[24] according to Leo. The socialists also give more latitude to the state than is legitimate. Such intervention by the public authority may come only when "any injury has been done to or threatens either the common good or the interests of individual groups, which injury cannot in any other way be repaired or prevented," and only so far as "the remedy of evils or the removal of danger requires."[25]

Equally significant for this tradition of papal social teaching is the grounding Leo gives to the right of private property in the officially sanctioned scholastic theology of Thomas Aquinas. The encyclical draws on the work on natural law of Leo's own teacher, the Jesuit theorist Luigi Taparelli, S.J. (1793–1862), the neo-scholastic Matteo Liberatore, S.J. (1810–1892), who taught the natural right to personal property, and Cardinal Tommaso Zigliara, O.P., a Thomist, who with Liberatore and others worked on writing and revising the various drafts.[26] The encyclical contained an abbreviated and at times contradictory presentation of Aquinas's position on property, which later was interpreted to endorse liberal economic theory.[27] The basic position of Aquinas, as well as the consistent view of the Scriptures and the Fathers of the Church, was that "the goods of nature and the gifts of Divine Grace belong in common and without distinction to all human kind."[28]

> For God is said to have given the earth to mankind in common, not because he intended indiscriminate ownership of it by all, but because he assigned no part to anyone in ownership, leaving the limits of private possessions to be fixed by the industry of men and the institutions of peoples.[29]

But Leo introduced ideas about property that either nullify or contradict this, perhaps by stressing too strongly what he takes to be a more Aristotelian emphasis in Aquinas that "nature confers on man the right to possess things privately as his own."[30] From this revised perspective, then, each man holds the right of private ownership which must be preserved inviolate and "no one in any way should be permitted to violate his right,"[31] despite what was said about the "institutions of people" legitimately fixing limits. Leo uses, but does not develop, only eight direct citations from the works of Aquinas, some from the *Summa Theologiae* on the right to property, but mostly on the general question of order in society. This truncated Thomism is passed down as a thesaurus of proof texts, reproduced as notes in subsequent papal letters with few variations until the 1960s when references to Aquinas largely drop out and are replaced by more citations from the ancient and medieval Church Fathers and the Bible, both Old and New Testaments. When John Paul II, a significant student of Thomistic theology and not just neo-Thomist imitations, writes his encyclical on labor, Aquinas is cited again, but this time not only the sections on the right to property, but also those that treat the social function of property as the justification for "the socialization, in suitable conditions, of certain means of production."[32]

Politically conservative neo-Thomists have customarily interpreted Aquinas and *Rerum Novarum* as more supportive of the absolute right of private property, a questionable view challenged even by some conservative theologians, who hear instead the unequivocal voice of the tradition asserting the coincidence of the Fall with the loss of common ownership.[33]

Largely unnoticed has been the encyclical's insistence that the issue of the right of private property is fundamentally a safeguard for the needy ("in seeking help for the masses this principle before all is to be considered as basic"[34]), whose meager possessions must not be expropriated by the state and who deserve from employers the basic material possessions needed to support family life. Leo's claim is that the church has primary jurisdiction in this socioeconomic area as a God-given mandate, since "the favor of God himself seems to incline more toward the unfortunate as a class; for Jesus Christ calls the poor blessed . . . embracing with special love the lowly and those harassed by injustice."[35] This is not the developed theology of a "preferential option for the poor" found in statements after Vatican II, but it is entirely consistent with it.

Other conservative and liberal critics, trying to reconcile the historic antiliberalism of the popes with their own allegiance to the classically liberal economic and political institutions of modern Western society, have suggested that Leo XIII was himself a proponent of liberal values: opening the Vatican library for critical scholars, raising the doctrinally liberal John Henry Newman to the rank of cardinal, endorsing the rallying (*ralliement*) of French Catholics from their backward-looking allegiance to the legitimist monarchy to support for the new republican government. He could be considered, then, the liberal swing between the reactionary pontificates of Pius IX (1846–1878) and St. Pius X (1903–1914). Somewhat more cautiously, Michael Novak points out that, while it is misplaced to label the aristocratic Leo a liberal, *Rerum Novarum* nowhere explicitly mentions the word *liberalism,* refers to any specific liberal thinkers, or condemns it. This is, in any case, far from a papal endorsement of liberalism. His encyclical *Libertas* (1888), which argued without the anathemas of his predecessor what was admissible regarding liberal ideas concerning the freedoms of conscience, religion, and a free press, still maintained a stance toward what he called "intolerant" liberalism rooted in Pius IX's "Syllabus of Errors" and Pius X's condemnations of "Modernism."[36]

While the rejection of ideological liberalism did not preclude a doctrine of property apparently consistent with the liberal idea of individual rights, *Rerum Novarum* advanced a natural-law argument which fundamentally undercut the basis of natural rights in the formation of the state or a solemn contract of the people. As the encyclical insists: "There is no reason to interpose provision by the state, for man is older than the state. Wherefore he had to possess by nature his own right to protect his life and body before any polity had been formed."[37] Just as the church endured (*patientia*), but not indifferently (*tolerantia*), certain contemporary practices hithertofore condemned, such as "devouring usury," on the basis of both biblical warrant and the natural law, so now the unrestrained free-market system of liberal rationalists, based on the idea of natural rights, was to be endured until corrected, but never approved.

Perhaps more important in establishing Leo's claim as Pope of the Workers than the unsystematic ideas and social analysis of the encyclical were two practical actions which slightly predated the letter: Leo's support for Cardinal Edward Manning's intervention for the workers in the explosive London dock strike (1889), preventing a civil disaster, and support for Cardinal James Gibbons, Archbishop of Baltimore, who intervened (1887–1888) before the Knights of Labor were condemned by the Vatican as an anarchistic secret society.[38] Interpreted widely as an overall papal sanction of the workers' right to organize, these actions, even more than the encyclical, indicated the direction of Catholic involvement in the social question. While much later *Rerum Novarum* was hailed and subjected to extensive scholarly comment, largely because it was resuscitated by Pius XI as the basis for his own social encyclical, friends and foes of the papacy during Leo's lifetime ignored or minimized it.[39] The document continued to be discussed in reading clubs and such small groups as the Catholic Social Guild, founded by Vincent McNabb, O.P., and Charles Plater, S.J., in 1909 in England, and the Catholic Workers' College (Oxford), founded by Leo O'Hea, S.J., in 1921 to train Catholic trade unionists in organization skills, public speaking, and parliamentary procedure.[40] Otherwise it remained a dead letter until forty years after.

PIUS XI (1922–1939): LIBERAL HERESIES

It was at the height of the world economic collapse during the Great Depression that Pius XI, the son of a silk factory manager, issued his encyclical on the social question: "Forty Years After" (*Quadragesimo Anno*—May 15, 1931) commemorating *Rerum Novarum*[41] and responding to the social crisis resulting from the breakdown of liberal economies. Drafted and revised by Oswald von Nell-Breuning, S.J., a professor of social thought and economics, the letter echoes the work of several other Jesuits: Victor Cathrein (1845–1931), a natural-law theorist and anti-Marxian; Heinrich Pesch (1854–1926), whose theory of "solidarism," the middle path between capitalist individualism and socialist collectivism, is at the center of the encyclical; and Gustav Grundlach (1892–1963), a student of Pesch and later mentor to Pius XII.[42] Pesch's views in particular correspond with Pius XI's approach, since the latter saw himself as continuing in his "social philosophy" the critical stance of Leo XIII, "boldly breaking through the confines imposed by Liberalism" in regards to the proper role of civil authority in insuring a fair distribution of goods for the protection of workers and owners alike. Against the radical individualism of capitalism, the collectivism of communism, and the "totalitarian" centralization of the fascist state, Pesch's "solidarism" is based on the solidarity of humanity in achieving economic justice. It is built on a "social system of labor" and "vocational groups" to determine the proper measure of private property for realization of the common good and the right order of the state.[43]

> To each, therefore, must be given his own share of goods, and the distribution of created goods, which, as every discerning person knows, is laboring today under the gravest evils due to the huge disparity between the few exceedingly rich and the unnumbered propertyless, must be effectively called back to and brought into conformity with the norms of the common good, that is, social justice.[44]

For Pius XI, then, the differences in his society from that addressed by Leo XIII are the even greater concentration of wealth in the hands of a few, "hardly leaving to the worker enough to restore and renew his strength," and the "despotic economic dictatorship" resulting from an extreme disparity of wealth that had abrogated political power on the national and international levels.

> The ultimate consequences of the individualist spirit in economic life are those which you yourselves . . . see and deplore: Free competition has destroyed itself; economic dictatorship has supplanted the free market; unbridled ambition for power has likewise succeeded greed for gain; all economic life has become tragically hard, inexorable, and cruel . . . And as to international relations, two different streams have issued from the one fountainhead: On the one hand, economic nationalism or even economic imperialism; on the other, a no less deadly and accursed internationalism of finance or international imperialism whose country is where profit is.[45]

There is some question about how Pius XI regarded liberal capitalism in general. He certainly decried the teachings of what he loosely calls the "Manchesterian Liberals," especially on the issues of wages, economic control, and general laissez-faire policy, a mélange of theories associated with Richard Cobden, John Bright, and David Ricardo, that was later criticized by Catholic proponents of German *Sozialpolitik*.[46] What seems to be at work is a distinction between *capitalism,* a code word for economic individualism and the idea of profit as an ultimate end in itself, thus irreconcilable with the natural moral law, and *free enterprise,* the system of exchange of wages and work, supported by legitimate ownership of the means of production so as to be mutually beneficial for the "solidarity" of workers and owners. In Pius's view, history shows that ownership itself, like other forms of social life, had changed significantly from one age to the next. The pope quotes approvingly what he takes to be the heart of *Rerum Novarum*: "Each needs the other completely: neither capital can do without labor, nor labor without capital."[47] Conservative critics have argued that in the end, while justly decrying abuses, *Quadragesimo Anno* concludes in reference to capitalism that "this system is not to be condemned in itself. And surely it is not of its own nature vicious." But that citation goes on to say that:

> It does violate right order when capital hires workers, that is, the non-owning working class, with a view to and under such terms that it directs business and even the whole economic system according to its own will and advantage, scorning the human dignity of the workers, the social character of economic activity and social justice itself, and the common good.[48]

Others have seen this as a critique directed more at the heart of capitalism, and not just at extreme abuses, since the essence of liberal capitalism is to hold the market as the final determinant of the economic order, regulating prices, profits, and wages, and assigning the judgment of success or failure (one could say life or death).[49] Novak and others argue in turn that the market itself and the liberal political institutions which create and support it are self-corrective, and that flagrant abuses to the personal dignity of workers and imbalances of equity in achieving the common good will eventually work themselves out. Liberalism has faults, as does the model of "solidarism"; they are both trying to achieve the common good by different methods. For Pius XI, the moral bottom line is that the market forces of "free competition . . . clearly cannot direct economic life." One can understand his reference to Leo XIII's bold overturning of the "idols of Liberalism" as a sign of his own view that the liberal ideology of the market had reified economic, political, and social powers which were then regarded as the "result of inevitable economic laws" that determined all aspects of social life, and thus were treated as almost religious fetishes, idols that robbed working people (and eventually the owners) of human dignity, freedom, and moral choice.[50]

On the other hand, Pius XI includes direct and unambiguous denunciation of the various socialist models of economic and political life. He distinguishes communism, which preaches: "Unrelenting class warfare and absolute extermination of private ownership," from moderate socialism which "inclines towards and in a certain measure approaches the truths which Christian tradition has always held sacred."[51] Significantly, while distinguishing and dismissing more nuanced positions held by moderate socialists, Pius himself gives approval for a particular kind of state ownership of capital: "For certain kinds of property, it is rightly contended, ought to be reserved to the state since they carry with them a dominating power so great that it cannot without danger to the general welfare be entrusted to private individuals."[52] It would not be until John Paul II's *Laborem Exercens* (1981) that such "socialization" of capital was comfortably and unambiguously referred to.[53]

But *Quadragesimo Anno* allows no middle ground of reconciliation between the Catholic Church and socialism, whether as a doctrine, historical fact, or a movement, since the latter in the pope's view substitutes a thoroughgoing materialism for the religious doctrine of the nature and destiny of human life. It substitutes economic efficiency and productivity for the Christian teaching of human well-being in the temporal and eternal realms through the faithful fulfilling by each individual of the "craft or other calling" received from God. It substitutes "the abundance of socially produced goods" for the higher value of human dignity, and fosters "a liberty no less false" in place of the right order of social authority.[54] While it contains some truth ("like all errors") , it cannot be reconciled with true Christianity: "Religious socialism, Christian socialism, are contradictory terms; no one can be at the same time a good Catholic and a true socialist."[55] The pope does not in balance say that one cannot be a true capitalist and a true Christian. But he does point out that the problem with socialism is that it is a mutation of classic liberal ideology: ". . . let all remember that Liberalism is the father of the Socialism that is pervading morality and culture and that Bolshevism will be its heir."[56] Nell-Breuning, the encyclical's ghostwriter, in a 1970 article admitted that there were, in fact, forms of socialism in 1931 which did not manifest the condemned characteristics — for example, the British Labor Party and perhaps Scandinavian socialism — yet no explanation is given why socialism is charged with such a blanket condemnation and capitalism, which had evidently deformed social justice and the common good, is not.[57]

While examining the socioeconomic order, the encyclical advances some remedies based on both commutative justice (the just relations of capital and labor), a concept not used by Leo XIII, and the more familiar distributive justice. More importantly, it raises the political question of how change in the status quo is to be effected and thus different forms of justice assured. No specific form of government is sanctioned, although the "solidarist" model, in which local political units and professional corporations (made up of both employers and employed), each enjoying in its own hierarchical sphere a large measure of autonomy, would direct and limit the possession of capital and the powers of the state.[58] As Nell-Breuning later commented:

> The encyclical wants to establish no specific form of state; the state should merely be relieved of tasks that are not its business. What should be curbed is capitalistic class society, centered on the labor market; it should be converted into a class free society (a pity that this apt phrase had not yet then been coined!). The structures of this society are regulated by the services of the various social groups, contributing to the common good of the whole.[59]

But this "corporatist" model, for which Pius XI sometimes used the early examples of developments in Portugal and Italy, has in hindsight been seen to contribute possible support for fascist regimes in reaction to their caricatures of liberal ideology and institutions, the socialist resistance to fascism also having been undermined by papal edict with disastrous effect between the two world wars. Yet in other encyclicals, Pius XI indicated the dangers implicit in these social forces. *Nova impendet* (October 20, 1931) linked the current economic crisis to the growing European arms race. *Mit brennender Sorge* (March 14, 1937) was a strong attack on National Socialism and the Third Reich's violations of the 1933 Concordat with the Vatican, which had attempted to stabilize church/state relations and protect religious property and activities. In *Divini Redemptoris* (March 19, 1937), issued on the feast of St. Joseph "the carpenter," Pius attacked atheistic communism and the idea that religion is only an ideology of mystification from a particular social class generated to protect its economic and political status. A recurrent theme in the encyclical, however, was "the lamentable ruin into which amoral liberalism has plunged us."[60] National Socialism and communism are seen then as shoots from the same ideological roots of liberalism or as false solutions to the moral and social morass caused by liberalism. They are, then, liberal heresies.

The contributions of *Quadragesimo Anno* can be seen in its insistence on a more direct, aggressive stance by the church in the sociopolitical realm; in this regard it has divested some of the otherworldly rhetoric of *Rerum Novarum*. Christian charity alone is not a sufficient solution: "as if it were for charity to veil the violation of justice which lawmakers not only tolerated but at times sanctioned."[61] For these remedies to be truly effective, then, there must be established "a juridical and social order which will, as it were, give form and shape to all economic life."[62] Reform alone is insufficient; there must be real structural change, if the church, as Pesch also said, is to cease looking like merely an extension of the capitalistic order.

It is also on the question of "subsidiarity"—the Catholic principle that a just order must insure that the functions capable of being carried out by smaller communities and voluntary associations are not absorbed by larger political bodies or a centralized state bureaucracy—that Pius XI gave a classic formulation.[63] As Byers points out, some later interpreters have stressed the idea contained in it of guarantees for full participation by all in decision making, whatever degree of government involvement happens, such being the apparent direction of Paul VI's *Populorum Progressio*. Conservative interpreters see it as an endorsement of the idea that "government governs best which governs least," especially in the realm of economic capitalism, and still others see it as a heuristic description of cooperation between government and private sectors.[64]

In an often-overlooked encyclical, *Firmissimum* (1938), Pius develops an argument that belies the comments that Catholicism in principle is subservient and vulnerable to political tyranny; the pope takes the uncharacteristic stance that questions of justice must have precedence over even order and social harmony. Developing an element of natural-law theology, the absolute right of self-protection of one's life, the Christian is viewed as not bound by loyalty to an unjust regime, and the actions of resistance and rebellion in such instances are morally exonerated. This question of active resistance to an unjust social order gets raised again later in much more muted and moderated tones in the social encyclical and apostolic letter of Paul VI. It should be remembered of Pius XI that it was during his pontificate that those twin martyrs to excessive state power, Thomas More and John Fisher, were canonized as saints (1935). Sometimes the church's "social philosophy" is seen as vividly in its symbolic acts as in its texts. The text of *Quadragesimo Anno*, however, had enough impact to prompt Franklin Delano Roosevelt to declare in 1932 that it was "as radical as I am . . . one of the greatest documents of modern times."[65]

PIUS XII (1939–1958)-JOHN XXIII (1958–1963):
MODERNIZING THE TRADITION

The pontificate of Pius XII, marked by the catastrophe of World War II and then the start of European reconstruction and the Cold War, did not produce any social encyclical with the impact of his papal predecessors, but did contribute to the definition of "social doctrine" on the questions of ownership and distribution of property.[66] He showed a clear preference for the political democracy of "the West," over against the communist and fascist-tolerant corporatist state. His endorsement for "free-enterprise," the economic dimension of political democracy, recognized that capitalism had survived the Depression by the state employing a visible Keynesian hand to construct a new deal for the market economy. But it had survived and even prospered. Despite the general reticence to criticize such a progressive system, Pius wrote in 1947 that "while the Church condemns existing Marxist regimes, she can neither ignore nor refuse to recognize that the worker, in his efforts to improve his lot, confronts a social system which, far from being in conformity with nature, conflicts with the order established by God and with the purposes He ordained for the fruits of the earth."[67] In his radio broadcast on Pentecost 1941, to commemorate the fiftieth anniversary of *Rerum Novarum,* he insisted that economic prosperity must be measured in terms of the opportunity all the people enjoy to share equitably in the wealth produced, not just by the standard of GNP statistics. While the right of private property is a basic value, the individual's right cannot negate the more fundamental and general right of all to the use of material goods.[68] Pius XII made explicit what was unclear in the earlier encyclicals: Private property must be treated in terms of social responsibilities, not just individual rights, and he chose the Feast of Pentecost, during which the ancient hymn "Veni, Creator Spiritus" is sung and the Holy Spirit is invoked as "Father of the Poor," to do it. In summary, Pius appeared to settle for what would at best be, in place of a restructuring of the social order, only the practical expedient of a less bureaucratic free-enterprise system with state authority as an overseer of the common good to guard against capitalistic wealth concentration and socialistic nationalization. His successor was seen in a very different light, although following much the same direction laid out by Papa Pacelli (as Pius XII was popularly known).[69]

When Angelo Roncalli, the Cardinal-Patriarch of Venice, was elected pope in 1958 and took the name John XXIII, many thought this elderly and portly man, who affected the name and regalia of Renaissance pontiffs, would be only an interim occupant of the papal throne. But his calling of the twenty-third general council of the universal church, Vatican II, whose work he would not live to see completed, marked a significant turning point in the relations of the Catholic Church and the modern world.[70] In the spirit of what he called *aggiornamento,* updating the church's response to secular society, John's encyclical on the church as "Mother and Teacher" (*Mater et Magistra* — May 15, 1961) set out to translate traditional issues for the changed circumstances of the modern world and to define the spirit of cooperation needed in facing the common crises of that world, especially the nuclear threat, but also the changing geopolitical map. That kind of cooperation had been tried tentatively before in the social reconstruction of Europe around the turn of the century when, as a young priest, he had worked in his own diocese of Bergamo with the social-action programs of *Opera dei Congressi*, a movement eventually banned by Pius X in his edicts against "Modernism," since the groups were not sufficiently under ecclesiastical control and brought together people of varying philosophical ideologies. John XXIII's term *aggiornamento* may be interpreted as just that form of "modernization" in the church's noncontrolling role in dealing with the shared concern for economic and political matters that his pious predecessor had rejected.

Novak and more conservative critics stress the encyclical's evident embrace of modern liberal institutions and its repetition of the position that the right of private property is sacrosanct, since it is the guarantee of individual freedom.[71]

> The right of private ownership of goods, including productive goods, has permanent validity. . . . Further, history and experience testify that in those political regimes which do not recognize the rights of private ownership of goods, productive included, the exercise of freedom in almost every other direction is suppressed or stifled.[72]

In this regard, Novak links the right of private ownership with the principle of human dignity and cites the following as an indication of papal thinking, moving from the single-issue morality of justice as distributive to one that also includes "productive justice":

> If the whole structure and organization of an economic system is such as to compromise human dignity, to lessen a man's sense of responsibility or rob him of opportunity for exercising personal initiative, then such a system, we maintain, is altogether unjust — no matter how much wealth it produces, or how justly and equitably such wealth is distributed.[73]

Novak has stressed the pope's affirmation of the rights to work, private property, and free association as defining the "true liberal understanding." But one should note that the quotation above is not merely a paean to the protection of human dignity through private ownership to stimulate economic initiative. It comes after a discussion of the measures necessary to maintain the common good, even "when assessing the rate of return due as compensation to the company's management, and as interest or dividends to investors" so that a proper balance may be maintained "through the activity of public authorities."

John XXIII advocates co-partnerships and co-ownership of productive capital by the workers in their companies, and a direct role for their professional associations in setting the economic policies of their countries. Summarizing Pius XI's teaching, Pope John first emphasized that the norm in economic matters could not be special interests, unregulated competition, economic despotism, or nationalism; and secondly the aim must be to achieve in social justice "a national and international juridical order, with its network of public and private institutions," in order to conduct economic activity for the common good.[74] The danger was not only the aggrandizement of state power and ownership, for which the remedy was a reiteration of the "principle of subsidiarity function," but also the fact that public authority had become "the tool of plutocracy."[75]

The rather striking word, "plutocracy" is taken from Pius XII's 1944 broadcast and refers to political control by wealth; in its root it calls to mind the classical deity Pluto, god of the infernal realm. The implicit and explicit validation of an interventionist role for the state has led some to see the encyclical as an endorsement of socialism and the collectivist state, while others see its stress on a more positive role of the state as only raising questions about the traditional outlook. More radical critics ask whether the stress on the inviolability of private property and personal initiative was merely an ideological cover for resistance to social justice.[76] The positive presentation of the interventionist role of the state led some rightwing Catholics, who saw this as a radical change in papal teaching, to retort: "Mater si, Magister no!"[77]

Besides insisting that wages not be determined merely by market forces, but by justice and equity, this was the first encyclical to link aid to underdeveloped nations to the traditional social questions, demanding that here too justice and equity insure that in development no "new form of colonialism—cleverly disguised" be allowed. In order to bring these social principles into action, the pope suggested the technique of small community organization using the method of "See, Judge, Act" to analyze the causes of misery and formulate a social praxis to press community reconstruction.[78] The technique, later useful in the ecclesial base communities of Latin America, was created by the Belgian priest Joseph Cardijn (1882–1967), the founder of the Young Christian Workers movement (YCW) and the one to whom Pius XI said that the scandal of the nineteenth century was the church's abandonment of the workers. John XXIII wanted to insure that the church would not retreat behind a purely otherworldly definition of her vocation or just pronounce on the internal questions of faith and morals, despite the fact that he also suggested as a remedy of the disparity of wealth that at the gospel invitation, the rich could transform matter into spirit by the charitable act of transferring their worldly goods to the poor.[79] The church is not just the guardian of religious principles; she can declare authoritatively how they should be implemented and in that claims a critical role in the economic and political arenas. Opponents of that position ask whether that means the church is seizing privilege and jurisdiction in areas which modern society denies it and whether its exalted position as "Mother and Teacher" is sacrificed at the street level of political discourse.

It was in his other great social encyclical, "Peace on Earth" (*Pacem in Terris* — April 11, 1963), issued just a few months before his death, that John XXIII demonstrated his determination to have the church engage the world and not remain on a pedestal. As he told its drafter, Father Pietro Pavan: "I want this to be a document which both Kennedy and Khrushchev will want to read."[80]

The letter notes major characteristics bringing change in the modern age: improvement in the socioeconomic condition of labor, so that workers are treated as persons of intelligence and freedom; a greater role for women in every area of modern social and economic life; and the increasing establishment of newly independent states, and the need to stamp out the vestiges of racism, unjust political domination in the name of development, and the calamitous arms race. On the national and international levels, special attention must be paid to the "weaker members of society, since they are at a disadvantage when it comes to defending their own rights and asserting their legitimate interests."[81] The powerless have an "option" on the church's help.

The encyclical includes more controversial stances. One is to hold out the prospect of some form of accommodation with communism or mutual cooperation for the purposes of insuring international harmony. Previous papal letters had encouraged the formation of an array of Christian organizations and activities to improve cultural and material living standards: labor unions, mutual insurance societies, cooperatives, agricultural credit banks, and such groups as *Misereor, Adveniat,* the later *Campaign for Human Development, Developpement et Civilisation,* and in the wake of Vatican II, the Pontifical Commission *Justicia et Pax,* with its local diocesan cells.[82] The encyclical endorses the new attitude toward cooperative endeavors with secular groups by distinguishing between what may be "a false philosophy of the nature, origin and purpose of men and the world" and the "economic, social, cultural, and political undertakings" in which one may morally discern "the possible existence of good and commendable elements" that conform to right reason and are lawful aspirations of the human spirit.[83] Rather than seeing the world in clear-cut Manichaean dualisms of good versus evil empires, John's more Augustinian eye views the complex mix of good and evil in every earthly act, idea, and institution.

Also controversial was his broad endorsement of the U.N. Declaration of Human Rights, which Catholic social thinker and Thomist Jacques Maritain helped author.[84] Despite disapproval from conservative quarters, based on a revulsion at papal endorsement of this modern secular (that is, atheistic) body that also dogged Paul VI after his tradition-breaking speech against war at the United Nations, John XXIII gives unqualified praise to the Universal Declaration of Human Rights passed by the U.N. General Assembly on December 10, 1948, an endorsement reiterated in 1971 by the Synod of Bishops in *Justice in the World* and in 1979 in John Paul II's *Redemptor Hominis*.[85]

The declaration lists not only political rights and freedoms (for example, freedom of thought, conscience, religion, expression, peaceful assembly, and so forth), but also, in Article 25, the right to food, clothing, health care, and other forms of social security. It gives an extensive list of the economic, social, and cultural rights indispensable for human dignity and the free development of the individual's personality. In some early sections of the encyclical, the pope lists an extensive number of human rights in the context of the natural law, which has caused some commentators to view this letter as too theoretical and "not quite as innovative" as earlier papal pronouncements.[86] What John XXIII has done, however, is extremely significant. He has identified the U.N. Declaration with the natural-law teaching of the church in the fundamental concept of rights and set it as the basis for dialogue and action with common agencies in modern society.

Novak is one of only a few conservative critics who have praised John XXIII for this endorsement of the U.N. Declaration. He says that *Pacem in Terris*, by affirming those rights, many of which are "borrowed almost directly from the U.S. Bill of Rights," brings them "into the universal patrimony of the church."[87] He neglects, however, to tell the reader that, alone of all the great industrialized nations of the earth, the United States has never endorsed the U.N. Declaration of Human Rights because its roster of economic rights was thought to infringe upon the free market and unrestrained private initiative.

PAUL VI (1963–1978): THIRD-WORLD STRUGGLE

In 1963 John XXIII broke with tradition and did not address his encyclical *Pacem in Terris* only to the venerable prelates of the world church or bishops of a particular country, as was customary, but "to all men of good will," a salutation later employed by Paul VI and broadened by John Paul II "to all men and women of good will." Pope John's expansive greeting was characteristic of the man and also of the general council he called, which continued its work under Paul VI. In the council document on the church's place in the modern world, *Gaudium et Spes* ("Joy and Hope"), approved December 7, 1965, the 3,000 or so council fathers committed the church to cooperate in efforts to resolve social inequalities in the face of mounting disparities:

> While an immense number of people still lack the absolute necessities
> of life, some, even in less advanced areas, live in luxury or squander

wealth. Extravagance and wretchedness exist side by side. While a few enjoy very great power of choice, the majority are deprived of almost all possibility of acting on their own initiative and responsibility, and often subsist in living and working conditions unworthy of the human person.[88]

This is said against the backdrop of what the council calls the "revolution of rising expectations" in the economic sphere, as well as the political explosion of newly independent countries; the fear expressed is that social upheaval will result if the dream for a better life is deferred.

It is this unease that Paul VI echoed in "The Development of Peoples" (*Populorum Progressio* — March 26, 1967) when he said, "Human society is sorely ill," and noted that the cause lay in the lessening sense of human solidarity and Christian charity. For him, "development" is the new name for peace. Novak and other critics reject this negative assessment by the pope and his forecast that poor nations may rise to take economic and political control; it is a rhetorical incitement to riot, blaming the developed world for the underdevelopment of poorer nations and calling for new, intrusive forms of world government to regulate the international economic sphere. The messenger himself is the cause of social misery. The pope's basic mistake, according to Novak, is in a paradoxical view of modern liberalism as solely identified with radical individualism, materialism, and Darwinian struggle.[89] In analyzing the rise of industrialization, a technological process morally neutral in itself and even conducive to the task of development in the area of labor systemization, the pope observes that:

> Certain concepts have somehow arisen out of these new conditions and insinuated themselves into the fabric of human society. These concepts present profit as the chief spur to economic progress, free competition as the guiding norm of economics, and private ownership of the means of production as an absolute right, having no limits nor concomitant social obligations. This unbridled liberalism paves the way for a particular type of tyranny . . . for it results in "the international imperialism of money."[90]

This type of capitalism has "given rise to hardships, unjust practices, and fratricidal conflicts." In the first papal expression of concern for ecology, the pope mentions the care to be taken in the use and preservation of nature and natural resources. The goods of the earth are for the use of all, and "when 'private gain and basic community needs conflict with one another,' it is for the public authorities 'to seek a solution to these questions, with the active involvement of individual citizens and social groups' "; the rights of property and free trade are subordinated to the principle that created goods should "flow fairly to all," as declared by Vatican II.[91] Having traveled extensively, to Latin America, Africa, Palestine, and India, Paul

VI says he can report as an eyewitness to the pressing needs of developing nations and the resulting duties of the rich nations to whom he applies the gospel parable of the greedy rich man whose life is forfeited, despite his wealth (Luke 12:16–21). The principle of free trade does not in fact work in fairly regulating international agreements, since basic economic inequalities in most cases put poorer nations at a disadvantage, so that the market prices "freely" agreed upon are in essence unfair, with the richer nations practicing "economic dictatorship."[92] The encyclical calls for the development of a new understanding of *humanism*, a sense of human solidarity in guaranteeing authentic development in each person, to replace the avarice and *materialism* which can infect rich and poor alike.[93] But it is in decrying the violent means some take to redress real injustice that Paul VI opens the possibility that certain extreme circumstances may make direct action morally acceptable:

> Everyone knows, however, that revolutionary uprisings — *except where there is manifest, long-standing tyranny which would do great damage to fundamental personal rights and dangerous harm to the common good of the country* — engender new injustices, introduce new inequities and bring new disasters. The evil situation that exists, and it surely is evil, may not be dealt with in such a way that an even worse situation results. (Italics added).[94]

The Christian, in attempting to find remedies, can cooperate with various groups, but must not settle for Marxist ideology: atheistic materialism, a dialectic of violence, collectivism, and a denial of transcendence, or for liberal ideology: unlimited individual freedom, undirected accumulation of material goods and power, and the demeaning of social solidarity.[95]

P. T. Bauer, the noted proponent of development theory, has labeled both *Populorum Progressio* and the apostolic letter *Octogesima Adveniens* (May 14, 1971), issued on the eightieth anniversary of *Rerum Novarum*, as "political statements based on bogus arguments."[96] Novak, on the other hand, although more appreciative of *Octogesima Adveniens*, traces the problem, as he sees it, to the pope's underappreciation of liberalism and the realistic need for profit, competition, and property rights to spur economic prosperity, especially for the developing nations. Competition is better than state monopoly, and the liberal theorists — Locke, Smith, and J. S. Mill — all justified property in terms of its service to promote the common good, the same goal sought by the papal teachings. Finally, liberal institutions provide a constant check to keep the economic system free, critical, and non-despotic, as do the other moral-cultural institutions, such as organized religion, which prosper under modern liberal democracy. Novak's book *Freedom with Justice* stresses in its title his basic assumption that political and market freedom, the former guaranteed by the latter, will eventually insure justice. Paul VI's encyclicals have made the cautious observation that freedom can sometimes mask an ideology of radical autonomy "opposing the freedom of others," and that in the social and political spheres, a more just sharing in decisions and goods is a better basis for the exercise of human freedom and authentic development. Paul VI's version of the title would have been *Justice with Freedom*.

JOHN PAUL II (1978–): TOWARD THE MILLENNIUM

"No one is authorized to reserve for his exclusive use that which surpasses his needs when others lack the necessities" (John Paul I).[97]

After the tragically brief pontificate of John Paul I, the Catholic world was somewhat startled to find that the Polish Cardinal of Krakow, Karol Wojtyla, had been elected pope as John Paul II, encapsulating in his regnal name that of his smiling predecessor and the twin papal patrons of Vatican II. It was the choice of a remarkable figure who had worked during the Nazi occupation as a young man in a chemical factory, part of a slave labor camp, and grown to intellectual maturity in a communist state. Linguistically gifted, he pursued in one of two doctorates the subtle notion of the "acting person" in the phenomenological philosophy of material existence constructed by the socialist Max Scheler.[98] A son of the Second World in alliance with the First World seemed especially suited to address the crises of the Third and Fourth Worlds (a term he coined to depict the absolute destitution found in the other three realms). To others he seemed the incarnation of those revolutionary nineteenth-century messianic prophecies of a Slavic pope who would liberate the oppressed, and his own recurrent reference to the "Advent" of Christ and the Third Millennium has underscored his apparent sense of his personal role in the destiny of the world at a turning point, whether eschatological or not.[99]

Like his papal predecessors, John Paul II sees the current economic problems as originating in a moral crisis in which the resulting social conflict rages out of control. The social character and responsibility of religion have been eclipsed and banished to a purely private, interior, and otherworldly arena; piety has been eviscerated and depoliticized, cut off from public discourse. An otherwise praiseworthy self-interest has reinforced this loss of the social dimension, in many cases leaving it to the state or individual interests to encourage principled reflection and action. John Paul's general approaches, outlined in his four social encyclicals addressed inclusively to Christians, Jews, and Muslims—"Redeemer of the Human" (*Redemptor Hominis*—March 4, 1979), "On Human Work" (*Laborem Exercens*—September 14, 1981), "On Social Concern" (*Sollicitudo Rei Socialis*—December 30, 1987), and "The Hundredth Year" (*Centesimus Annus*—May 2, 1991)—are characterized by principles that are personalist (the dignity of the person over what is falsely assumed as the natural order), antideterminist (where relations are not taken as given but as the changeable products of human history), communitarian (against egoism, possessiveness, and class antagonism), decentralist in power (against monopoly capitalism and collectivist socialism), and evolutionist in attaining justice (in which "ideals" are only approximations spurring continued human decision and acting).[100]

In *Laborem Exercens*, whose militant Latin title underscores the priority of labor, John Paul constructs his most detailed analysis of the material and spiritual dimensions of work, based on critiques of communism, liberalism, and a defense of what can only be termed modified socialism.

The critique of communism is a familiar element in papal teaching, but this one begins by attacking the inadequate concept of work found in this ideology. Communism's stress on a nonhumanistic notion—based on the priority of material production of goods over the individual—has resulted in the loss of a sense of the moral value of work. "Work is a good thing for man—a good thing for his humanity—because through work man not only transforms nature, adapting it to his own needs, but he also achieves fulfillment as a human being and indeed in a sense becomes 'more a human being.' "[101]

Labor, whether physical, intellectual, or artistic, in itself is not a curse, but liberating and ethical, a necessity in the full realization of one's humanity, not just to provide material support for life. There is a need for labor not to be mean, degrading, or mindless (characteristics of what he calls "work"), but even boring, repetitive work can be morally rewarding. Also dismissed are:

1. The concepts of the bureaucratic state and state ownership, which in the name of the "dictatorship of the proletariat" create managerial elites that monopolize power

2. Class consciousness, which reduces the individual to a stereotypical role in a class or category, so that whether in the "ruling class" or "work force," the person becomes a faceless, nameless entity of exploitation or production

3. Dialectical materialism (scientific socialism and positivism), which stresses the mechanical and productive understanding of history and the loss of the self-conscious dimension of the subject as actor in historical change (concepts also rejected by humanistic Marxists)[102]

4. The inevitability of class warfare and social revolution (although the pope accepts the idea that unions are part of a struggle *for* the just rights of working people and not *against* others) or struggle for the sake of struggle[103]

5. The determination of practical action purely by economic laws, which is a form of determinism also criticized as it occurs in capitalist societies

6. The idea that morality and spirituality are simply epiphenomena, that consciousness is simply a behavioral aspect of the economic system and not autonomous to set its own future.

In this extensive critique, John Paul II treats Marxism and communism without demonizing either the ideas or the ideologues who hold them. He presents rational analyses and not anathemas as to why someone should reject these philosophical and economic positions.

People in the West, especially in the religious communities, are less prepared to deal with his critiques of liberalism, since he is rejecting not merely its misuses, but rather its underlying principles. His critique begins with the question of what it means to be a truly human individual. In the social distortion of liberalism that places capital before labor, there has been a tragic loss of subjectivity, which robs humans of the resources for creativity and self-development, self-realization, or actualization (depending if the word chosen emphasizes more the concept's approximation to Marxian or Existential philosophy).

For Locke and other theorists of possessive individualism, the individual is only a concept in an argument about private property or as the subject of ownership. The subject in liberal thought has been made subordinate to the inviolable market; freedom is reduced to the freedom to acquire property, not actualize one's own potential (as would be the position of Marx, Hegel, and the "socialist" J. S. Mill). This loss or narrowing of real freedom is grounded in a reified sense of market forces; it is this system that defines and controls the human. In Old Testament terms, this is idolatry. The pope's critique of the natural-rights tradition intends to widen the definition of rights beyond the familiar trinity of Locke's — life, liberty, and property — to include dignity, meaningful labor, health protection, and so on, perhaps for the same reasons that Jefferson creatively misquoted Locke to stress instead life, liberty, and the pursuit of happiness.[104]

The encyclical rejects what it takes to be central elements of economic liberalism: materialism and consumerism. In the former the emphasis is on the material side of human existence; in the latter the belief is imbedded that human life is best measured by consumption. The concept of freedom, then, is identified primarily as the unrestrained opportunity to accumulate wealth and property. This is what John Paul refers to as the "error of economism." It is brought about when labor and capital are separated and set in opposition, a division which does not in practice "spring from the structure of the production process or from the structure of the economic process."[105] Instead, the division is an ideological artifact rooted in a reduction of the concept of labor solely to its economic purpose and the subordination of "the spiritual and the personal" to the material.

> This is still not theoretical materialism in the full sense of the term, but it is certainly practical materialism, a materialism judged capable of satisfying man's needs not so much on the grounds of a particular way of evaluating things and so on the grounds of a certain hierarchy of goods based on the greater immediate attractiveness of what is material.[106]

To call "economism" (the marketplace mentality) an "error" does not mean it is a superficial mistake. In the code of Catholic parlance, *error* is a grave disorder according to the natural law and biblical revelation. As in Pius IX's "Syllabus of Errors," the term means economism is to be regarded as a philosophical and political heresy to be condemned. It is a mortal sin. Under economism, workers are reduced to machines and factors of production. It objectifies and reifies the worker and the work as a material object (a fetish) for the consumer's own acquisitive gratification; one could say it is a form of economic fornication.

The encyclical is the most forceful and direct papal critique of the absolute inviolability of private property that is central to the natural-rights tradition; in its place the emphasis is on the "common good," a core element in the natural-law tradition.[107] The right of private property is maintained, but not "the exclusive right to private ownership of the means of production." Under "suitable conditions," socialization of the latter is justified. This distinction is based on a dual notion of property: intrinsically private property (one's home, car, farm, tools) and capital (factories, laboratories, technology, natural resources). The latter is the product of work, invention, and cumulative thought of generations and, like the earth itself, is the common inheritance of humans. It has a "social mortgage" on it. Socialization may occur because, in reality, every factory has two proprietors: the direct employer (the title owner) and the indirect employer (society or the state) which bears a higher obligation to see property and resources used for the common good.

Excessive bureaucratic centralization in whatever system is best prevented when there is "joint ownership of the means of work": cooperatives, stock/profit sharing, municipal utilities, co-planning. The capitalist has a lawful need for a just profit and incentive for entrepreneurial risk taking, but profit taking should not sacrifice stable jobs or erase the community's long-term investment in a company when it may appear more profitable to relocate to take advantage of a cheaper work force. Generations of workers are the anonymous and nonvoting investors in any company; their interests have moral standing, since their work created the wealth in the first place. Any other conception of private ownership "could constitute grounds for social conflict," since:

> Property is acquired first of all through work in order that it may serve work. This concerns in a special way ownership of the means of production. Isolating these means as a separate property in order to set it up in the form of capital in opposition to labor — and even to practice exploitation of labor — is contrary to the very nature of these means and their possession. They cannot be possessed against labor, they cannot even be possessed for possession's sake, because the only legitimate title to their possession — whether in the form of private ownership or in the form of public or collective ownership — is that they should serve labor and thus by serving labor that they should make possible the achievement of the first principle of this order,

namely the universal destination of goods and the right to common use of them.[108]

The typical understanding of property can only promote egoism and lead to alienation and a loss of community, whether in capitalist individualism or communist collectivism.

The letter also picks up the theme of ecology, introduced earlier by Paul VI, and is developed from John Paul II's theological reading of the creation stories in the first and second chapters of Genesis. The human, although part of the created order according to the Hebraic myth, is divinely commanded to dominate all other life-forms. But liberal materialism and consumerism have eliminated the spiritual component and thus profoundly distorted the integral relationship to nature, substituting an attitude of unrestricted use that has resulted in staggering pollution, depletion of resources, eradication of species, and scarcity. While not a fully articulated "creation theology," the pope's environmental and ecological concerns are rooted generally in his doctrine of human nature (man as responsible steward) and are echoed in a growing body of philosophical and theological works in this area.[109]

The encyclical goes a long way in articulating John Paul's own vision of a just social order that is best described as a modified form of socialism, built on a new view of human rights, political and economic democracy, and a demand for moral self-consciousness and realization, grounded in political/economic rights. He asks directly why reform capitalism, the welfare state, and the so-called workers' states have been unable to bring well-being, even of the purely material sort, to the majority of people in the world. Why? First, there is a need for a new view of basic human rights, which must include the right to work, unionize, strike, good wages, pensions, health care, work safety, social security, and unemployment compensation. The pope reiterates the affirmation given earlier by John XXIII to the concept of economic and social rights articulated in the United Nations Declaration of Human Rights.

The list he gives are deemed basic supports to ensure labor's ability to live in a dignified, humane way. It contrasts with the false needs for merely material accumulation spawned by consumerism. Advertising and other cultural agencies help create the unconscious demand for consumer goods and promote distorted human values. The individual shrinks to his or her identity as a consumer. Second, there is a need to fashion greater access for more people to economic and political power. The pope calls for workers' ownership of the workplace (by profit sharing and stock options, for example) and participation in decision making at every level. This is an attempt to democratize the workplace, and through it the community at large, decentralizing economic/political power. He calls for more community control, which is also an aspect of his critique of the centralized bureaucratic state but it applies equally to situations controlled by big business and multinational corporations. Small businesses, including family farms, increasingly fall victim to capital-intensive enterprises. The big entities lose contact with workers and their local communities, limit decision making by employees, and respond only to "forces of the marketplace." In calling for more political and civil freedoms, the encyclical continues to support the legacy of liberalism that guarantees individual liberties, but it seriously questions the privacy of private ownership, property, and profits when these limit democratic participation for all. And John Paul has endorsed many times the calls for political and economic democracy in the formation of the European Economic Community (EEC) and Parliament (symbolized by the flag of twelve stars) as providing the material and social base for a renewal of European "Christendom."

Thirdly, the letter calls for moral socialism, a collective moral self-consciousness needed to defend distributory and participatory justice. It calls for a reform in thinking, displacing the current, entrenched attitudes: the "all-consuming desire for profit" and "the thirst for power" used to impose one's will on another. The pope relies explicitly and implicitly on a different intellectual and moral tradition, one found in Aristotle, Hegel, and the humanist Marx. The emphasis is on work, creativity, development of human dignity and self-consciousness, and the realization of human potential and full freedom. However, this is to be accomplished in reaction to the modern industrial life engineered by both communism and capitalism. As he wrote in his letter "On Social Concern" (*Sollicitudo Rei Socialis*):

> The Church's social doctrine is *not* a "third way" between *liberal capitalism* and *Marxist collectivism*, nor even a possible alternative to other solutions less radically opposed to one another: rather, it constitutes a *category of its own*. Nor is it an *ideology*, but rather the *accurate formulation* of the results of a careful reflection on the complex realities of human existence, in society and in the international order, in the light of faith and of the Church's tradition. Its main aim is to *interpret* these realities, determining their conformity with or divergence from the lines of the Gospel teaching on man and his vocation, a vocation which is at once earthly and transcendent; its aim is thus to *guide* Christian behavior.[110]

The church does not sanction any particular system, no matter how much that system may claim a divine privilege and demonize its opponent, since no temporal achievement is a full or adequate embodiment of the Kingdom of God. Even in the recent collapse of the Eastern Bloc, the pope has warned against a superficial sense of satisfaction for liberal capitalism, which had produced such negative effects in the Third World.[111] The ideological war and the arms race between East and West have themselves helped produce the misery and poverty of the South and the Third World and generated even more endemic destitution, what he calls "The Fourth World."

Laborem Exercens entails a critique of the concept of "negative freedom" (liberty defined in the natural-rights tradition) — "freedom from" the external coercion of the state. This restricted view of liberty has no sense of ultimate social goals: the general will, the good society, the Kingdom of God on earth. That is, it has no *positive* sense of ultimate social goals, in contrast to the traditions arguing for "freedom towards." The natural-rights tradition currently voiced by conservatives does not comprehend the nature of external coercion as a product of both the state and the economy. Therefore, it does not see that private property; the control of wealth by a few; the existence of extreme poverty and material deprivation; a class system, whether overt or covert; the control of capital over the manner in which work is socially organized; and other such factors, seriously limit the possibilities of individual freedom and the real possibility that each member of society will have the opportunity to realize their full human potential. Why is freedom viewed in political categories only? Why not in economic ones also, unless for an ideological purpose? Are they both not areas of power, authority, and control over others and, therefore, both legitimate areas of concern for those who wish to limit external, arbitrary power and authority over the individual? The pope is preaching redemption from these hidden structures of economic bondage.

The category of "sin" is not customarily applied in the modern world. But the papal letters emphasize that the widespread poverty and misery brought about by the "different forms of imperialism" are the result of structural sin. It is in *Sollicitudo Rei Socialis* ("On Social Concern") that John Paul articulates most fully the concept of "structures of sin," a term frequently used by liberation theologians while applying critical Marxist analysis to Third World society. These structural sins are always rooted in concrete acts and are thus personal; the human always has a choice and cannot claim exoneration because of impersonal forces or some material or psychological determinism. The pope describes his analysis of this condition as theological and biblical and not just sociopolitical. The doctrine of the Trinity, which declares that solidarity and community are at the heart of deity, and the biblical image of the "second tablet" of the Ten Commandments (Exodus 20:12–17; Deuteronomy 5:16–21) require certain actions toward others, while omission of the same is a special offense against both God and one's neighbor: "hidden behind certain decisions, apparently inspired only by economics or politics, are real forms of idolatry: of money, ideology, class, technology."[112]

Laborem Exercens may on consideration be said to contain several markedly conservative elements. For instance, labor and differing kinds of labor, especially in the description of family life and the rearing of children, by being placed in the context of biblical interpretations of the creation myths implies that these structures have been divinely ordained and thus are unchangeable forms of social organization. Also, in the discussion of Genesis, the emphasis is placed on the "priestly" ode of creation in chapter one, which typifies the relation of the human to the rest of nature as one of *domination* and subduing, whereas in chapter two, the earlier Yahwist myth stresses more the human's identity with the soil (humus) and the interaction of the role of tiller, responsible as a steward of resources. The encyclical, more in the tradition of Genesis 1 and the Decalogue, which does not even mention any human responsibility to nature, sees man imposing human will on nature to sustain life. The pope is aware of the dangers of human domination over other humans, but here he does not underscore the dangers of culture's domination of nature. Nevertheless, other statements on the nature mysticism of the thirteenth-century Francis of Assisi and the regulated stewardship of Benedictine work with nature suggest that John Paul is more attuned to the ecological dimension of human realization in and solidarity with the cosmos than this one encyclical suggests.

Laborem Exercens and *Sollicitudo Rei Socialis* are remarkable additions to the tradition of modern papal teachings on social justice. In particular, John Paul has done much to add depth to the earlier statements based on the natural-law tradition and the Bible concerning the common good, the social context of private property, the creative and transcendent nature of human life. He has harmonized with this a recognition of the value of the liberal agenda of civil liberties and political emancipation. But, continuing the direction taken by John XXIII and Vatican II in the endorsement of the U.N. Declaration of Human Rights, he has insisted that economic, social, and cultural rights are also equally normative. Lastly, in his definition of labor, the physical and intellectual activity that creates capital and, more importantly, the soulful, subjective, moral, and ethical substance of humanity, he has contributed some of his most original thinking and embraced intellectually the humanist side of Marx, while rejecting crude communism. The result is a boldly new synthesis of dormant or forgotten classical and critical traditions.

Since 1991 marks the centenary of *Rerum Novarum,* the world public can expect further additions to this library of church statements on the social question. *Centesimus Annus,* issued in the wake of rapid changes in Eastern Europe, is the most recent reaffirmation of papal statements on communism and capitalism. It stresses the need for widespread access to more advanced technological training to protect all persons from a new type of enslavement, beyond mere material deprivation. For the pope the threat of alienation is as real as in 1891. Either because of the dramatic personal history of this charismatic leader or his close identity with the Solidarity workers and the political struggles of Poland, John Paul II has been regarded as particularly suited to epitomize the long, papal legacy of social teachings. When this pope speaks, using many languages and traditions, the world seems ready to listen.

QUESTIONS OF AUTHORITY

The hundred-year heritage of papal encyclicals on social justice carries with it an explicit authority within the Catholic community and at times with the wider society. Whether as "Universal Pastor and Teacher" of the Catholic Church—as Vatican I declared the popes to be in its careful definition of papal infallibility—or as titular head of 800 million worldwide followers, a force in real political terms, the modern popes have exercised singular authority and control in a wide range of matters, and certainly in describing the changing outlines of the "social question."

It is important to note that these encyclicals can also be seen to bear or claim an implicit authority, related but not limited to the peculiar spiritual office of the popes in the Catholic hierarchy. Several factors make these encyclicals, as an historical body of "social doctrine," intellectually stimulating and the basis of ongoing analysis:

1. The insistence on the moral dimension of political economy
2. The arguments for structural change
3. The historical development of a religious institution's position on social problems
4. The reanimation and reintegration of biblical, ecclesiastical, and natural-law traditions in response to modern social crises
5. The blending of conservative morality and progressive ethics.

At the same time, these intellectual strengths also contain intellectual weaknesses that may or may not be consciously addressed by the popes and those using the encyclicals to promote social justice.

From the time of *Rerum Novarum*, the popes and other church leaders have insisted upon the importance of considering the moral dimension in political economy. There is a necessary and appropriate role for theological reflection that does not presume the popes' competency over the technical economic or political ingredients. But they reject the disguised neo-Platonic idea that religion and piety are otherworldly, purely individual, and exclusively interior states, characteristically irrational. What they insist on is a person-centered definition of any system: social, economic, or political. The human has priority. Thus the religious teachings concerning the nature and destiny of human life and human relations are an essential, not tangential, element in every aspect of society.

The popes reject a purely materialist, extreme rationalist, technologist definition of human affairs, and point out that these characteristics of modern intellectual life are profoundly ideological, basic "religious" statements about reality and human purpose. One need not automatically agree with the popes' claims to moral authority or the claim that there is an inherent moral dimension to political economy, but one needs to see that the claims of modern science, political thought, and economic modeling are themselves profoundly rooted in implicit assumptions about human nature and purpose. And these, while not religion in the traditional sense, are held "religiously" as an unquestionable worldview. By analyzing the several political variations of liberal ideology, capitalism or communism, the papal letters have kept this intellectual debate open and explicit, pointing out the hidden preconceptions of the opposing groups.

Whatever facets of the social crisis have been pinpointed by the modern popes, the bottom line consistently has been a call for structural change. They are not satisfied with minor tinkering to fix misuses of the system; more basic change is demanded, whether in the call for associations along the lines of the medieval guilds, the "corporatist" model of Pius XI, or the new definition of economic rights reflecting the U.N. Declaration of Human Rights, which, for example, would require basic structural changes in the United States to be fully realized. Reform is a preliminary aspect, a step toward more fundamental reconstruction. It was only Pius XII who pessimistically abandoned hope for major changes in light of the apparent postwar triumph of the West—a victory marked by egoism, materialism, and domination, politically and technologically. This is the exception that proves the rule. One weakness, perhaps, is that despite the consistent call of the popes, no apparatus has existed to implement their programs of social reconstruction or even to win support from the Catholic laity and, in many instances, the hierarchy also. Popes may teach a social doctrine, but bishops can ignore or minimize it. In terms of the demand for structural change, the encyclicals have often proved more progressive than the letters and actions of national conferences of bishops that they predated or prompted. This seems generally true when the American Catholic Bishops' Conference is considered, both in its more recent statements and its practical actions. Reform has won over reconstruction, despite the papal teaching.

Thirdly, the encyclicals provide a rare window into the process by which a religious institution develops a cumulative tradition, focusing here on social justice. Some other modern church bodies have developed an ongoing internal dialogue about such questions, but none with the richness, durability, and complexity of these papal encyclicals. Also, the special sense of papal authority developed since Vatican I has imbued these institutional statements with a doctrinal aura not reproduced in the polities of other churches. The practice of popes since Leo XIII in reaffirming and reinterpreting the church's social teaching is an important critical device. It is a form of ritual recall, geared to the regular observation of anniversaries of encyclicals which echo the echoes of previous statements, sometimes omitting elements (such as the "corporatist" idea) and sometimes advancing in new directions (such as John Paul's "christening" of the Marxist ideas of alienation and commodity fetishism). The process has evolved in structure to include the opportunity for renewed attention to current social conditions and an intellectual yardstick by which to measure new developments.

In a practical sense, the papal pronouncements can take an initiative not always open to the local churches because of state control or popular indifference which might make the bishops unwilling to be critical of their national forms of political economy and commitment to distributive justice. It is problematic, however, that because the popes are constantly referring reverentially to their pious predecessors, the necessary element of self-criticism in any proposal of social reconstruction is not embraced. In those instances when popes have, for instance, implicitly held to a basic dualism of world and spirit, thus undercutting any real role for religion in social change, the later papal letters ignore rather than reject those politically retrograde and theologically inadequate views.

Fourthly, the recovery of the largely lost traditions of the Scriptures (especially the ancient Hebrew texts), the Church Fathers (the ancient and medieval writers), and the natural-law tradition (especially from Augustine to Aquinas) and their use by the popes to ground the church's theological response to modern social questions is a richly compelling intellectual display. The Bible is seen afresh as a text that applies to this world ("thy will be done on earth") as much as to the "life of the world to come." The Jewish antecedents of Christian concepts of wealth, poverty, liberation, and redemption are recovered, as well as the applied biblical theology regarding usury, debt, social responsibility, ownership, and the state—concepts which had been lost or compromised by the time of the nineteenth-century ascendancy of liberalism.[113] By rearticulating the natural-law tradition, the papal writers renewed an important intellectual school of thought and provided a basis for discussions of political economy apart from, if alongside, the natural-rights school. The natural-law position can be traced in the social thinking of the ancient Hebrew "people of God," the Greek "polis" of Aristotle, and the medieval "communitas" of Aquinas, and thus provides historic alternatives to the models of society and human nature advanced by modern consumer capitalism or communist collectivism. The church has never agreed with either Locke or Lenin about the nature and purpose of human community. And the natural-law concept, rooted in the idea of "right reason" (reason properly exercised within its own limits and not denying other dimensions of human experience and existence), was open to and engaged all humans, providing a universal moral basis (such as that encapsulated in the Golden Rule). Humanistic morality did not totally depend, then, on specifically Christian religious revelation, although it was confirmed by it. In Aquinas's terms: Grace perfects nature; it does not destroy it. While some modern critics inside and outside religious traditions have rejected the idea of natural-law as an ethical ground, its reappropriation shows the motive of the papal writers to construct a social ethic that will be inclusive, if not pluralistic, and not just limited to a specific faith community which adheres to a doctrine of the authority of biblical revelation.

On the negative side, one can see that the papal use of passages from the Bible and Fathers has been little more than proof texting, without any thorough or consistent use of the sources. It is not until Paul VI and even more so with John Paul II that the ideas from the biblical and patristic sources are put into some context and developed as part of an overall theological reading. But even with them, the rich assortment of writers and schools of thought is limited. For example, the complex positions developed in the scholastic tradition of the Middle Ages are reduced substantially to those of Thomas Aquinas alone, as if his was the only valid summary of theology. The scholastic debates on wealth, poverty, and power are not adequately reproduced by referring only to the "Angelic Doctor." The Franciscan theorists, for example, generated a sophisticated body of work on the questions of the use and possession of wealth, the relation of charity and justice, and the church's relation to the state in terms of a fair distribution of goods. They developed a deeply reflective, at times mystical theology of voluntary poverty about the Christian's vocation as one who is "naked following the naked Christ."[114] The more radical calls for life with "Dame Poverty" and for stripping away worldly treasure — a constant ascetic tradition in the history of the church — have been muted in the papal letters.

The encyclicals, even the current ones, omit references to notable laity who have written on and worked for social justice, including the noble laymen who inspired Leo XIII. And while footnoting the Fathers of the Church, no mention has ever been made of the Mothers of the Church who have also contributed significantly to the church's thinking on charity and justice. Some, like Teresa of Calcutta, have sought only by personal service to relieve the daily misery of the destitute; others have called for social reconstruction as a matter of justice. For example, Catherine of Siena, the fourteenth-century Italian visionary who was declared a Doctor of the Church by Paul VI, has much to say about the relations of rich and poor in the church and society, and the way the church used its own material wealth.[115] She wrote and preached at a time when the city-states and communes were experiencing rapid economic growth in industry, trade, monetary exchange, and mercantile expansion.

Long before the Reformation of the sixteenth century, there had already developed an aggressive spirit of capitalism. Yet there was also an uneasy spirit, perhaps aggravated by the tension between newer entrepreneurial values and the traditional religious and cultural values. Life was marked by an obsession with luck at the unpredictable wheel of fortune in the economic, political, and social life of Europe. This tension deeply affected the practice of religion; religious institutions in turn were transformed to serve this new world of traders and merchants. Innovative and radical forms of piety and ecclesial relationship mirrored the changing patterns of social and economic power amidst the declining feudal arrangements. Confraternities of laity, based in the new economic order, were joined with the Third Orders (Tertians), founded by the thirteenth-century mendicants, to integrate spiritually motivated men and women who continued to live and work in the world with the more contemplative communities. Labor and capital were joined in these experiments to provide a new spirituality that did not renounce the world and its wealth, but channeled this energy and enterprise for the common good: in poor relief, education, hospitals, and even burial services. These community-based models for Christian life in the world with possessions while not being possessed by them need once again to be recalled and reinterpreted as possible alternatives for the contemporary institutional life of the church. The Basic Ecclesial Communities (CEBs) found today in the Third World have often been guided by members of the modern-day mendicant orders reinterpreting their tradition of service to the poor and reshaping popular spirituality in the process.

Lastly, any observer of this aspect of church history can note with these popes the not infrequent blending of conservative morality in sexual matters with progressive ethics in social matters. It was Paul VI who issued the controversial encyclical *Humanae Vitae* (1968) that rejected the majority conclusion of the papal commission discussing artificial birth control and continued the traditional ban. This came at the same time that his social teaching called for a greater participation by the laity in political life and economic planning to alter fundamentally the structures of political economy maintaining dependency and degradation in the Third World. John Paul II's comments on such issues as birth control and Vatican documents on abortion, homosexuality, and the role of women continue to maintain the church's traditional stance. Yet *Laborem Exercens* and *Sollicitudo Rei Socialis* deny the legitimacy of the established economic order of East and West in ways that are politically and philosophically revolutionary.

A curious issue is raised by the way that the authority of these varied encyclicals is applied. In the Catholic tradition, an encyclical has been the ordinary teaching device of popes (along with apostolic letters, allocutions, sermons, addresses, in a descending ranking of importance and authority), addressed usually to the faithful (and now to a wider audience) in order to circulate the pope's own theological position on an important and/or controversial matter affecting the whole church. It is not an infallible teaching, but may contain reference to the dogmatic content of the Bible, Canon Law, doctrines, and council decrees. Meant originally as a way for the consensus of the faithful to confirm the orthodoxy of the incumbent Bishop of Rome, encyclicals now function as an authoritative guide for the formation of consciences for the faithful and as the basis for dialogue with the wider community.

A curious dynamic, however, has happened in the reception and teaching of these encyclicals. Those dealing with sexuality are taken to be normative for one's identity as a Catholic Christian, and disagreement is taken as a rupture in one's relationship with the church. To be a Catholic is defined by some as to be in total agreement with *Humanae Vitae* and similar teachings on abortion, sex, and reproduction. These are considered by more conservative elements in the church to be hedged about by the implicit infallibility of the papal authors defining the church's position on questions of "faith and morals."

On the other hand, no such normative status is applied to the encyclicals on social ethics. Someone's aggressive stance as an ideological capitalist is not regarded as a de facto rejection of one's Catholicism. The effect is to convince at least widespread popular opinion that what the Catholic Church has to say about morality only regards sex. The constant tradition of the church from the time of Jesus regarding social justice is lost. No priest or theologian has been silenced by the Congregation for the Doctrine of the Faith for supporting liberal capitalism by speech or life style. No bishop has been removed or limited in episcopal office because he failed to object to, let alone condemn, a government's economic and social policies when these have eliminated basic supports for pregnant women, children, and families in poverty. In the United States, only people such as theologians Charles Curran and John McNeill, or the American nuns forced to leave their religious order—people who in the past raised questions about the interpretation of the church's position on sexuality and reproduction—have been banned from their official positions, expelled, or censured. Whatever the papal teaching about social justice may be, the actual practice of it by the papal office has at times left important questions to be answered.

6

LIBERATION OF THE BIBLE: ADVOCATES AND CRITICS

INTRODUCTION

The Bible has been one formative element in the creation of American self-identity; Americans historically have considered themselves, Jews and Christians alike, as "people of the book," using story, image, and a theology derived from the Bible to shape and explain the saga of national life.[1] The different Bibles and commentaries of diverse American religious groups have in the past provided a normative defense of the status quo in social, political, and economic questions, a sacred charter of culturally established relationships in matters of race, class, income, gender, sexual identity, and so forth. Chattel slavery, a permanent underclass, and female subservience are just some of the institutions and attitudes over which biblical texts have exercised a conservative influence.

But the Bible has also been the basis for revolutionary and transformative thought and action. The ancient accounts of the Exodus and Passover, for instance, still represent a reservoir of meaning in which justice and freedom prevail. In this way Scripture brings ethical guidance to modern situations without blurring the awareness of the text's distance from the contemporary situation.[2] Historically, as well as today, these stories of liberation have constituted a common heritage, a vision of society transformed, whether in the American Revolution, the successive religious "Awakenings" and utopian experiments, the expansion West, abolitionism, the social gospel, or the civil rights movement, all centered on the hope to create a better world.

At the same time, these forces of reform and change have claimed continuity with traditional values and with scriptural foundations. One may note that the Liberty Bell, an icon of national political life, has inscribed on its lip the biblical verse ". . . proclaim liberty throughout the land to all its inhabitants" (Leviticus 25:10). The full passage is an egalitarian proclamation of the Jubilee, with its call for the redistribution of wealth within the community. This symbol and numerous other theological references in American political life—the Pledge of Allegiance's phrase "One nation under God" and "In God we trust" on our currency—are just some of the visible examples of a national religious consciousness extolling political and religious freedom, our local variety of a theology of liberation. The evidence of different ways of reading the Bible has usually been taken to be a positive sign of healthy religious pluralism in America. Particular communities, supporting notions of the authority of biblical or special revelation, have used their own reading of their experience in light of the Bible to guide their theological interpretation of the sacred texts. The problem possible in this mode of biblical interpretation is that, without some self-critical element, the texts can be applied in a self-interested, self-congratulatory way that merely confirms the powerful in their political and economic control. Thus, early English settlers studying the epic entrance of the "chosen people" into Canaan heard themselves uncritically addressed and described as they settled into New Canaan and slaughtered the "heathens" occupying their promised land. At the root of such identifications are implicit assumptions about the nature of God and one's own group in relation to divine power and providence. The American use of the Bible has sometimes stressed order, harmony, and a "peaceable kingdom"; but it has also justified violence, domination, and "holy war."

Norman Gottwald has pointed out two divergent biblical heritages that refer to God and economies: the older Israelite notion of a God of justice as protagonist of the poor and the later monarchical version of God encouraging only charity from the rich, an idea dominant in mainline Jewish and Christian theologies. By ignoring the older notion, the oracles of promise and power made to the poor have been applied to the rich leaders of America instead.[3] This has largely been accomplished by a programmatic redefinition of basic terms such as "the poor" and "poverty"—either spiritualized in an ahistorical way and applied to include today's rich, who are then seen as recipients of the favor and consolation given the "poor in spirit," or negatively applied to the actual poor, whose condition is blamed on laziness, vice, or racial inferiority. Gottwald has noticed the telling absence in standard biblical scholarship of comments on the predominant cause of poverty put forth by the Bible: oppression, the terms for which are now usually translated in a muted or ambiguous way as "affliction," "suffering," and "tribulation."[4] The concept has been depoliticized and the causes of oppression removed from public consciousness and debate. It is this revised version of the Bible that is then used to demonstrate the absolute congruence of the biblical perspective on human nature and the moral foundations of society and the nationalistic and individualistic piety of free-market capitalism, obliterating any sense of criticism or judgment upon the use of American wealth and power.[5]

As we saw in chapter one, *Economic Justice for All* presents its principles and policies as inherently compatible with fundamental American values. One has to ask if it is more consistent with a reformist or revolutionary application of the biblical perspectives it lists, and whether its very "Americanism" tilts it irrevocably toward the kind of sanctioning of underlying political and economic uses of the Bible about which Gottwald warns. The pastoral letter does include a larger component of biblical citation than any previous episcopal statement on social issues. This wider biblical use reflects church documents from Vatican II and the writings of more recent popes. Except for a few tangential notations later in the 188-page letter, however, the biblical material is compartmentalized in a 17-page subsection early on. The passages used are more in the nature of proof texts, employing key words or images for purposes of illustration rather than part of a developed biblical theology, although the basis for such a theology is pregnant in the prominence the document gives to the ideas of "creation," "image of God," and "covenant."

Indeed, the letter states that its biblical perspective is grounded in an understanding that "creation, covenant, and community" are the bases of Israel's faith and thus the bases of the faithful church. The subsection headlines express this tripartite emphasis:

1. "Created in God's Image"
2. "A People of the Covenant"
3. "The Reign of God and Justice"
4. "Called To Be Disciples in Community"
5. "Poverty, Riches, and the Challenge of Discipleship"
6. "A Community of Hope"
7. "A Living Tradition."

The aspects of these doctrines and texts emphasized in the letter largely reflect the current theological agenda of North America and Europe, without reference to the constant biblical themes of oppression, subjection, and struggle. There is also not present a rhetorically passionate and subjective clarion against injustice; this is, instead, a factual, unemotional, objectified, academic use of the Bible. This may reflect more of the American character of the bishops' theology, or the "canon within the canon" that they use in drawing texts from the Bible. The focus is on texts that illustrate the covenant kept in the Israelite and early Christian communities, and the bonds of love and service that are ideally present; this is a traditional appropriation of the Bible for use in an American vernacular theology centered on ideas of "compact" and "commonwealth." While the prophets are mentioned, their use is highly selective; the "canon" of this letter does not include many — really few, in fact — of the more outspoken prophetic denunciations of social and economic injustice.

Amos, the first of the written prophecies and a fiery "social charter" vilifying Israel's contempt for its covenant vow to the poor, is mentioned just twice in one block of references. The exclusion of this forceful oracle of national judgment reflects the omission of this text from most of the lectionaries and preaching of both mainline churches and born-again evangelicals in America. The prophet is silenced. However, a line from Amos: "let justice roll down like waters, and righteousness like an ever-flowing stream" (Amos 5:24) is a familiar quotation associated with the civil-rights movement. What is often forgotten is that the phrase comes at the close of a passage in which God denounces Israel's feasts, solemn assemblies, offerings, and "the melody of your harps." What God despises, strikingly, is the religious life of Israel, the public worship and sacred songs, because the righteous people "trample the head of the poor into the dust of the earth, and turn aside the way of the afflicted" (Amos 2:7). Justice is not done in the courts or marketplace, so how can it be celebrated at the holy places? They turn the true God into an idol for pious reverence by failing to observe the covenant of care for all members in the social and economic life of the community.

It is this element of prophetic critique of the religious structure itself that is significantly lacking in the Bishops' Letter. They need to ask where church policies and actions themselves have been obstacles to justice. A covenant theology, if that is what they wish to develop, needs the prophetic monitor to repeat the call to conversion, as the late-medieval Catholic concern with the need for constant church reform (*ecclesia semper reformanda*) shows. The Bishops' Letter does not include Peter's warning that judgment starts with the household of God, the Christian church itself (1 Peter 4:17).[6]

DEPOLITICIZING SCRIPTURE

As the Catholic bishops worked on the final version of their pastoral letter, they were accused of having misused their claims to authority in ecclesiastical affairs and biblical interpretation in order to "politicize" their ethical teaching, "baptizing" public policies that conservatives found suspiciously similar to the platform of liberal Democrats. Michael Novak indicated central concepts in the bishops' first draft he found flawed: (1) reifying and depersonalizing the economy by inclusion of notions such as "social sin" instead of the customary Catholic doctrines of individual responsibility, virtue, sin, the cooperative nature of economic exchange as the basis of social justice, and the need to preach the moral obligation of self-reliance to the poor; (2) a problematic use of the Bible in questions pertaining to political economy (to which we return below); and (3) the imposition of false, divisive, and unnecessary "economic rights" that would turn citizens into privileged clients of a dangerously powerful state.[7]

He suggests five corrections to the biblical perspectives put forward by the bishops:

1. The evangelical notion of poverty ("poverty of spirit," even for the wealthy) includes and goes beyond material want, since the elimination of poverty is not the culmination of social justice (". . . poverty is a non-exclusive concept")

2. The draft's identification of salvation with "doing justice" undermines the doctrine of faith and grace, substituting a notion of "works righteousness"

3. Unbalanced emphases on community and solidarity overshadow individual responsibility

4. Differences in the meaning of words, such as "poverty," in the ancient world and today are ignored

5. The stress on "creation, covenant, and community" paints a false picture that perfect justice can be actualized in this contingent world, whereas the notion of sin is overlooked, as well as the anti-utopian discipline of prudence.[8]

The bishops, while certainly surprised by criticism about not only their suggestions on public policy but also on their use and interpretation of the Bible, seem to have come to terms with several of these conservative points. They reiterate the special option of the poor and explain why Jesus called them "blessed" because of their openness to God, and why there is constant danger in wealth; but they then state that the early church only proposed "the proper use of possessions to alleviate need and suffering, rather than universal dispossession."[9] They do not explain how to interpret the biblical phrases, ". . . no one said that any of the things which he possessed was his own, but they had everything in common" or ". . . for as many as were possessors of lands or houses sold them . . . and distribution was made to each as any had need" (Acts 4:32–35). "From each according to possession, to each according to need" seems to them too much like proto-Marxism to be enjoined from the biblical model for the contemporary American church. They do not include in their citation about the Jerusalem community in the Acts of the Apostles the story of Ananias and Sapphira, who held back their private property from common use and were severely judged, whether one sees their deaths as literal or metaphorical (Acts 5:1–11).

In response to the conservative emphasis on personal sin, the bishops insist upon the reality of structures of sin, especially in the idolatry of wealth and power. Without being carried off by utopian perfectionism, the bishops underscore the awareness of the victory begun now by God over sin and evil in the life and teaching of Jesus.[10] That is the good news they bring to the conservative pessimists. Otherwise, the conservative position on sinful systems or structures changes in the treatment of the Doomsday judgment depicted in a familiar social-gospel text (in Matthew 25, the judge will say: ". . . as you did it to one of the least of these my brethren, you did it to me"). Conservatives say the story demands a system that actually does assist the poor, and this is clearly the free-market system and economic entrepreneurship.[11] Likewise, the parables in the same chapter, the Wise and Foolish Virgins (Matthew 25:1-13) and The Talents (Matthew 25:14-30), are adduced to show God favors practicality, watchfulness, and prudent stewardship for the creation of new capital, all virtues of the Christian entrepreneur.[12] The assumption is that these parables are literal instructions about the proper use of money; this reading, instead, restricts their meaning and significance for a wider vision of discipleship. The bishops do not cite these same parables, substituting the more formal type of "example stories": the Rich Fool (Luke 12:13-21) and the Dives (Rich Man) and Lazarus story (Luke 16:19-31), dealing with the proper use of material goods. These texts, along with Matthew 25, were especially popular with Paul VI and John Paul II, who applied them to the rich nations, which like Dives do not see the hungry and suffering at their gate.[13]

The bishops' implicit claim is that these texts give a deeper vision of God, personhood, and life in community, whereas the lay report frames a particular sense of business practices which it identifies as a "creation theology," the creativity of free enterprise forming new wealth and jobs. Conservatives have paradoxically called the Bishops' Letter and its biblical perspective, at various times, both subversive and "statist." It can be noted, however, as Leon Wieseltier points out, that one of the chief critics of the bishops' biblical theology, Michael Novak, himself had explained the suffering servant passage in the prophecy of Isaiah ("He is despised and rejected of men . . .") as a parable of "the modern business corporation," that is now regarded as "a much despised incarnation of God's presence in the world."[14]

The bishops, as was said earlier, give special prominence to the idea of the covenant with God and its expression in laws and codes to protect vulnerable human life, thus making life in community possible.[15] This theme is first and most extensively presented in terms of the Old Testament: the Torah and the Prophets. This in itself shows the shift in Catholic biblical theology since Vatican II. The more classic form of Catholic citation for questions of social arrangement and relationship were the New Testament texts and their "love ethic"; the mainline Reformation churches, in turn, customarily used the Old Testament texts, especially those from the period of the monarchy, to stress godly rule, discipline, and covenant. The pastoral letter quotes from Exodus, Deuteronomy, and Leviticus to show the main outlines of the Sinai covenant and the elaboration of that code of law. Even a cursory reading of Exodus shows the key concerns of that society: liberation from oppression, idolatry, questions of land and family, protective regulations, laws about property, theft, carelessness, neglect, trusteeship, the poor, usury (defined as any interest charge), loan pledges, the protection due strangers, and so forth. The prohibition of usury became the traditional stance of Christianity. The first instance, found in the decree (chapter 20) of the Council of Elvira (c. 300-303) excommunicating clergy or laity who charge or receive interest on loans, has never been revoked.

Exodus is clearly not some otherworldly text, but a set of practical discussions about public policies.[16]

This raises in turn the implicit question about the need to reread the New Testament, itself shaped by the Hebraic worldview, although written in Greek. It is also about political issues, not just private, spiritual ones. Whatever salvation, redemption (an economic term, it should be recognized), or even inner enlightenment and personal conversion may be sought in and through these Old Testament texts, the believer is not pointed beyond, but within history, not to a heavenly paradise or afterlife of souls, concepts without central importance in the tradition of ancient Israel. In that tradition, inherited by early Christians, the "kingdom" of God has a social, communal, and political meaning, and the reign of God is prayed for "on earth as it is in heaven." This kingdom, the early church believed, is come even here and now in the life and teaching of Jesus. And the belief in the Resurrection shows that the expectation was that the promise to Israel of new life would be fulfilled in the *body* when a "new heaven and a new *earth*" come (italics added). The covenant, therefore, is best understood in terms of the land, given by God to all, and to which the people are called as responsible stewards.[17]

This theme connects to the accounts of creation in Genesis, the source of important citations concerning the formation of male and female persons in the "image and likeness of God" (Genesis 1:26–27); the human given this dignity was set by God to till the land as its steward (Genesis 2:15). As a reminder of the covenant and the cohesiveness of the community, the practice of the sabbatical year, by analogy from the sabbath rest in Genesis 2:1–3, was instituted (Deuteronomy 15:1f.). Every creditor will release his neighbor's debt every seven years to give a structural guarantee that there will be "no poor among you" (15:4); some of the harvest must be left in the field for the poor to glean (24:19–22); and slaves will be emancipated after six years, since Israel is pointedly reminded that "you were all slaves once in Egypt." These measures, as well as the prohibition on usury (not an exorbitant interest charge, but *any* charge), were meant as legal protection for the poor, widows, orphans, and strangers. The codes reflect and protect the values of community. The economy must serve people first. In Leviticus 17–26, the center of the Holiness Code of Israel, along with proscriptions for ritual sacrifice and sexual prohibitions, the Jubilee year is defined. All property, including land, is to be returned to the original owners every twenty-five years, and the provisions of the sabbatical are to be kept: no sowing/reaping of fields, release of slaves, debts are remitted, and ancestral property must be returned.[18] The debate continues about whether it was strictly observed and, even if it were practiced, whether it would now be a viable social proposal. (Thomas Hanks, for instance, suggested its application in the return of the Panama Canal property to the people of Panama.)

Jesus used the classic Jubilee vocabulary to refer to himself and his ministry as the start of the messianic age (Luke 4:16–21). The concept of Jubilee has appeared before in a Bishops' Letter (*Present Crisis*, 1933) and Paul VI's encyclical *Evangelii Nuntiandi*, but only as a rhetorical reference to the church's Holy Year pilgrimages to Rome; and, as in the American pastoral, no call for basic social restructuring is announced.[19] As in other matters, the Bible is more radical than the bishops or popes. Sabbatical and Jubilee are not just minor adjustments or reforms. The vision they legally structure is to insure that poverty must be eliminated and economic and social equality established, since these are necessary for stable family life, a harmonious community, and justice. The treatment of the poor and marginal are the standard by which a society is deemed just or unjust.

In ancient Israel, the prophets functioned as the self-consciousness of God's will speaking to the people, revealing deity as a "God of Justice" (Isaiah 30:18) who demands justice from all (Deuteronomy 16:20), delights in it (Jeremiah 9:24), and enacts it for the needy (Psalms 140:12).[20] Justice is the foundation of the community in the covenant the prophets remind, recall, and remember for Israel when present prosperity or ease leads to the neglect of the poor. Poverty, wealth, and inequality are social sins; they are also forms of idolatry, since God is not truly God if the family, community, and justice are undermined. God, in those circumstances, is merely a fetish. This is why the prophets denounce economic maldistribution as idolatry; mammon has replaced God.[21]

The bishops observe that the Law (Torah), Prophets, and Wisdom literature of the Old Testament "all show deep concern for the proper treatment" of the poor, vulnerable, and powerless.[22] But the dynamic of warning, judgment, and retribution present in the ancient texts is erased by the bishops in the abbreviated form of the passages they select and in the domesticated interpretation they give to the prophetic denunciations. They present justice without judgment. Examples of this can be found in the following citations included in the pastoral.[23] Skipping over a reference to oppression by iniquitous rulers, the letter uses a passage from the early part of Isaiah, in which the wicked are seen:

> To turn aside the needy from justice
>   and to rob the poor of my people, of their right,
> that widows may be their spoil,
>   and that they may make the fatherless their prey!
>   (Isaiah 10:2)

The pastoral does not highlight or explain the concept of "their right" in reference to the poor. The passage in Isaiah, however, goes on to depict the dread aftermath of this injustice, when God will use Assyria to vent the divine fury:

> What will you do on the day of punishment,
>   in the storm which will come from afar?

> To whom will you flee for help,
>   and where will you leave your wealth?
> Nothing remains but to crouch among the prisoners
>   or fall among the slain.
> For all this his anger is not turned away
>   and his hand is stretched out still.
>   (Isaiah 10:3–4)

The hand of God is no longer stretched out to assist stricken Israel, but to strike it down. The bishops also quote the laudatory description of Josiah, king of Judah, given in Jeremiah:

> He judged the cause of the poor and needy;
>   then it was well.
> Is not this to know me?
>   says the LORD. (Jeremiah 22:16)

They do not, however, include the condemnation of Josiah's son, Jehoiakim, who had extravagantly enlarged his palatial house, using luxurious Egyptian styles. This sumptuary excess is described as "dishonest gain" and "oppression and violence," such that the ruler will die and receive "the burial of an ass." (Jeremiah 22:17, 19). This disparity of the wealth and conspicuous life-style of the ruler over against the "poor and needy" is the basis of inexorable punishment.

From Zechariah the norms for a just community are again listed:

> Thus says the LORD of hosts, Render true judgments, show kindness and mercy each to his brother, do not oppress the widow, the fatherless, the sojourner, or the poor; and let none of you devise evil against his brother in your heart (Zechariah 7:9–10).

This is the standard outline of the covenant, but the stress seems to be on individual responsibility (". . . none of you devise evil . . . in your heart") for its fulfillment. The full passage goes on, however, to state that these are social sins and retribution will come to the whole society, which has spurned the messengers of God:

> But they refused to hearken, and turned a stubborn shoulder, and stopped their ears that they might not hear. They made their hearts like adamant lest they should hear the law and the words which the LORD of hosts had sent by his Spirit through the former prophets. Therefore great wrath came from the Lord of hosts . . . Thus the land they left was desolate, so that no one went to and fro, and the pleasant land was made desolate (Zechariah 7:11–12, 14).

Sometimes, rather than just truncating the judgment part of the pro-phetic oracles, the Bishops' Letter cites a sharp rebuke, but does not men-tion or exposit it in the main text; it is left buried in the footnotes. For example, Proverbs 14:31 is listed in a footnote, but not treated: "He who oppresses a poor man insults his [the poor man's] Maker, but he who is kind to the needy honors him." Oppression of the poor is a crime against the sovereignty of God—perhaps one of the most striking statements about justice in all the Wisdom literature. In a similar act of passing over radical implications, the bishops state several times that since the poor have no advocate, it is "God who hears their cries" (Psalms 109:21; 113:7; Proverbs 22:22–23).[24] The letter does not refer to the extensive theological tradition that designated four major crimes of injustice, listed in the Bible, that "cry to heaven for vengeance," a reference also found in Leo XIII's *Rerum Novarum* and John Paul II's *Laborem Exercens*[25]: oppression of the poor, defrauding laborers of their just wages, willful homicide, and the "sin of Sodom and Gomorrah," which, as both Jesus and the prophecy of Ezekiel define it, is the sin committed when the well-fed and prosperous "did not aid the poor and needy" (Matthew 11:23–24; Ezekiel 16:48–52).[26]

Similarly, in the use of New Testament material, one finds an omission of direct denunciations or a verbal mitigation of those included. The Ser-mon on the Mount from Matthew's gospel is quoted in part: "Blessed are the poor in spirit . . . blessed are the meek . . . Blessed are they who hunger and thirst for righteousness . . . You are the salt of the earth . . . You are the light of the world" (Matthew 5:1–6, 13–14). The Hebrew word for justice (*sedaqah*) is here, and at times in other contexts, translated as "right-eousness," which along with the phrase "poor in spirit" seems to privatize, individualize, and spiritualize this social sermon, ending with what could be taken as a form of congratulation instead of a challenge of responsibility: "You are the light of the world." In other words: Remember who you are and what vocation you have. Later the equivalent Sermon on the Plain in Luke's gospel is cited: "Woe to you who are rich, for you have received your consolation" (Luke 6:24). The bishops term this "a warning," rather than a condemnation, and they go on to say Jesus is just cautioning his followers against greed and reliance on abundant possessions, merely mis-uses of goods. The essential danger of wealth—which leads, as they also say, to arrogance, apostasy, and idolatry—is missed.[27]

They include Luke's familiar tale of the Good Samaritan as an illustra-tion of "the basis of all Christian morality" (Luke 10:29–37). By failing to identify the Samaritan as one of those hated and despised as an heretical outsider by the Israelites and truncating the story to leave out the priest and Levite who merely passed by, the effect is to make it a story of indi-vidual moral choice. There is, however, a wider social dimension, since the heretic and outsider (the word "Samaritan" having lost its original political meaning for us) keeps the covenant of neighbor to neighbor more faithfully than Israel, represented by the established authority figures of the religious institutions. The bishops' use of the story has turned social ethics into private morality. Emphasizing the relevance the gospel of Luke has for the pattern of Christian life today, the bishops present the *Magnificat*, the prophetic victory song ecstatically uttered by Mary, mother of Jesus, as she rejoices in God "who scatters the proud, brings down the mighty, and raises up the poor and lowly."[28] They do not reflect on the "low degree" of this handmaiden, that God has put down the mighty "from their thrones," or that, when God filled the hungry with good things, "the rich he has sent empty away," which constitute the substance of the divine promises made to Abraham's posterity (Luke 1:46–55). It is a battle song on the lines of Hannah's older prayer (1 Samuel 2:1–10) celebrating the downfall of God's enemies, here announced by the female prophet, Mary. It is not a poem of personal piety, but prophecy for the whole community. This section of the Bishops' Letter treating discipleship, the call "to experience the liberating power" of God's spirit, ends with the following point: "Finally, and most radically, it calls for an emptying of self, both individually and corporately, that allows the Church to experience the power of God in the midst of poverty and powerlessness."[29]

But what is meant by this "emptying" (*kenosis*) is never explained, although it seems at the heart of the church's early understanding of the nature and function of Jesus, who "emptied himself, taking the form of a servant, being born in the likeness of men" (Philippians 2:7). How this might be applied in a "radical" way to social, political, or economic affairs is left at the level of a rhetorical hint that something ought to be done, but not what might be done. It certainly is not connected, as it could be, to the notion of justice, which is defined as a "proper relation" to God and neighbor, rather than as "a strict definition of rights and duties." The passage where this treatment of justice appears builds on an impressive array of words and phrases to convey the inner sense of the term: harmony, right, peace, calm, security, proper relations, conversion when they stray, kindness, gratitude, wholehearted love.[30] There is no treatment of the roles that overcoming oppression, conflict, judgment, struggle, and godly force might play in procuring justice.

Throughout the section on the biblical perspective, texts seem to be omitted or truncated to minimize the roles of power and conflict in bringing social justice and change. Instead, organic metaphors of harmony and peace are preferred. These latter images, however, do not give adequate guidance when entrenched power, privilege, and property are confronted. What if some will not share power, control of decision making, or goods? Coming out of a national social experience which has muted or erased its own history of the struggle of labor to attain civil and economic rights, the bishops may just be applying an American mind-set to their reading of a Bible which is not radical to them, but, like their own society's political economy, merely the product of "reform and adjustment."[31]

THE PRAXIS OF PIETY VS. VOODOO THEOLOGY

One of the recurring questions facing the Latin American church is how to fix the proper role that folk religion plays in the devotional life of the Christian community. This religiosity encompasses a wide array of practices and attitudes, including syncretic hybrids of European Christianity, African, and American-Indian elements, distorting some Catholic teachings in the process and attributing magical powers to persons, places, and objects in acts of devotion, effectively displacing Jesus as Savior. Liberation theologian Juan Luis Segundo has noted the basic similarity of this indigenous "voodoo theology" to the way some traditional priests dispense Christian rites. Instead of a prophetic challenge to the powers and structures of this world, the priest is seen "dispensing security, just as the shaman or witch doctor of a primitive tribe does."[32] And yet both progressive and conservative elements of the church concluded in the documents published after the Puebla conference that there were positive elements to be found in popular religion when it is linked more closely to the biblical and doctrinal heritage of the church. This heritage acts as a safeguard against idiosyncratic tendencies in the folk ways, and they, in turn, invigorate and adapt the formal theology to the local situation and ongoing life of a particular people. The point can be made that popular practices can devolve into highly individualistic, privately motivated manipulations of religious power, but the Bible and doctrines of the faith can, perhaps less visibly, also become objects of what can be called occult, nonsocial rites of power that differ in essence from the liturgy (literally "public work") of the whole people. When the Bible and doctrines are isolated or turned inward, away from the community's whole life – social, cultural, political, and economic – then they become empty fetishes.

The U.S. bishops have not, until recently, faced the question of the place of popular religion in shaping authentic Catholic piety. The emergence of African-American styles of worship and Native-American traditions has forced a consciousness of this issue that was ignored when only European forms of devotion were practiced or tolerated by the American church. There is a need, however, to link the rich panoply and variety of these folk religions to doctrinal foundations. *Economic Justice for All* contains, at least in embryo, connections between a number of central symbols, expressions of classic doctrines of the Catholic faith, and the political, economic, and social aspects of the contemporary religious community. We will look at how these moral values suggested by the bishops in their vision of society – community, participation, and empowerment – can be linked to the doctrines of the Trinity, Christ, and Mary included in the letter. This section will also explore how the celebration of the Eucharist, the central praxis of Catholic communal worship, is a summation of these values. The bishops touch on these interrelated doctrines; with a little more cohesion, these could be the basis of a theology of social justice.

The traditional Christian doctrine of the divine nature is that God is one, while also three: Father, Son, and Spirit. This is the early baptismal formula (Matthew 28:19) affirmed in later creeds. It is also the basis of the Catholic concept of life in community, since the internal and external nature of God is proclaimed as relationship, and humans are created in the "image and likeness" of this God. The pastoral letter spends a brief time on this in the course of showing the connection of Christian belief to classical "human wisdom" that defined the human person as a "social animal," whose purpose is "friendship, community, and public life."

"Indeed Christian theological reflection on the very reality of God as a trinitarian unity of persons — Father, Son, and Holy Spirit — shows that being a person means being united to other persons in mutual love."[33]

More could be done to relate this trinitarian symbol to questions of human rights and economics, and some recent writers have seen this doctrine as an important foundation for a theology of social liberation.[34] If the community of the Trinity is the underlying "reality" of human nature and society, then it is "subversive" in challenging systems based on competition, individualism, and inequality of persons. John Paul II has said in *Laborem Exercens* that labor is itself the reflection of the image of God, since it is the way human dignity, freedom, and brotherhood (or friendship) is achieved. In the past the tradition of ecclesiastical interpretation of the Bible saw reflected in the Old Testament texts veiled references to the Trinity, for instance: the creation of the human (Genesis 1:26) in *"Our* image and likeness"; the appearance of three strangers to Abraham and Sarah at Mamre to assure them progeny (Genesis 18:1–15); and the visitation of the angels to Lot in Sodom (Genesis 18:16–19:28). This older, symbolic interpretation did emphasize the central role of the personal and social identity of the human in relation to God. We can also see them as metaphorical attempts to convey the experiences of creativity shared, sterility overcome, and hospitality protected. At times the Trinity has, in effect, been dissolved, as Christians separated the divine persons, as if they dealt with divisible entities. Some reverenced the distant creator or principle of being (the philosophical monad); others sentimentally and individualistically exhibited a "Jesus and me" theology (evangelical pietism); or others emphasized the Spirit as the primary and sufficient evidence of their own salvation or healing (spiritualists, pentecostals, and charismatics). In this kind of separation, however well-intentioned, the dynamic social element of God's essence is lost. It is little wonder that the groups identified with such theologies often unconsciously do not see the value of social reform or their obligation to work toward it. They insist that is God's work alone. Thus the "image and likeness" doctrine is internalized and spiritualized, apart from the public arena of the creation.

The concept of participation is at the core of Christology, the doctrines of the nature and function of Christ, who is the God-Man, "true God and true man," and the Second Person of the Trinity. The bishops give a characteristic reading of the gospel story of Jesus as the divine teacher of the "love ethic," whose self-sacrificing death won redemption for humankind. They do not explore the ways in which this doctrinal symbol of essential and social participation might be related to economic or political issues. Actually they never refer to the roles political, economic, or class relationships have played in the formation, content, and interpretation of the biblical and later texts concerning Jesus Christ, or the myriad ways Jesus has been imaged in American Christianity. Those American images, textual, artistic, and hymnic, have portrayed Jesus as the following: Good Shepherd, healer, "bard of the Holy Ghost" (Emerson), philosopher, teacher of ethical wisdom, judge, Prince of Peace, personal Savior, King of kings, deity.

Each of these has responded to and shaped wider cultural events, and often eclipsed the image of Jesus as prophet and liberator that Tolstoy, Gandhi, Martin Luther King, Jr., and liberation theology have deemed so central.[35] The American vernacular piety has tended to emphasize unthreatening pictures of the Good Shepherd or personal Savior, a prettified, bourgeois Christ; whereas *Laborem Exercens* reminds its readers that Jesus was a craftsman and that Paul earned a livelihood in trade.

Such emphases can be found in current Latin American renditions of the crucifixion: Rather than the beautiful body portrayed by European artists such as Guido Reni, one sees Christ with the coarse features, stunted frame, and rough hands and feet of the *campesino*. Or one can see, in the Chiesa di S. Maria degli Angeli (Barrio Riguero) in Managua, Nicaragua, Serigio Michelini's rendition of the Resurrection as part of the "History of Nicaragua." A young Christ of the Revolution broods over a scene of struggling Sandinista peasants, some bearing the cross and others icons of the martyred and "disappeared." In Brazil, a convulsed figure of Christ screams from the agony of the cross; his broken, naked body is that of a student executed by the military dictators who used in his torture electrical shocks applied to the genitals. Graphic and heartrending depictions of the suffering and death of Jesus are not unusual in Latin American iconography; bloody statues, penitential forms of mortification, and dramatic reenactments of the "Man of Sorrows" were visual and physical ways for suffering peasants to connect themselves to the passion of Christ and gain consolation. The newer images merely make those connections more visible and show the political and economic context in which the suffering occurs, instead of the traditional sense of a timeless, inner drama of spiritual travail. Finally, these are images of a Christ who can liberate the oppressed from such deadly powers in this life, here and now.[36]

Perhaps it is significant that no "national" icon of Christ has evolved in the American Catholic Church. The closest image is the Pantocrator ("All-Ruling"), the Byzantine-style Christ as judge in the mosaic-decorated apse of the National Shrine in Washington, D.C.; against a gold backdrop, a stern, bearded magistrate in classical garb raises a hand in blessing or judgment. It is more like the Olympian image of the American Zeus, George Washington, than the more human companion in the struggle found in the Third World. With one, the Messiah is meant to be adored and worshipped; with the other, divinity is incarnate in the human struggle for liberation. Such different forms of theology, imagery, and piety produce very different forms of praxis and approaches to social change.

At the close of the pastoral letter, the bishops again invoke a reference to Mary as a model of self-sacrificing service and discipleship: "Like Mary in proclaiming her *Magnificat*, we marvel at the wonders God has done for us, how God has raised up the poor and the lowly and promised great things for them in the Kingdom."[37] It is only the positive action toward the poor that is remembered, not the judgment on the proud, powerful, and rich. There is also no sense in which the poor, such as Mary, may claim their rights in a covenant community; because of the letter's phrasing, it is not clear what the "great things" promised might entail and when they will be enjoyed "in the Kingdom."

In John Paul II's *Sollicitudo Rei Socialis* (1987), the pope closes his social encyclical with reference to the devotional practices of that Marian Year and Mary's familiar role of maternal intercession. He includes as petitions social as well as personal problems for which Mary is asked to intercede with Christ: "... we present ... difficult individual situations ... But we also present to her *social situations* and *the international crisis* itself, in their worrying aspects of poverty, unemployment, shortage of food, the arms race, contempt for human rights, and situations or dangers of conflict, partial or total."[38]

He goes on to quote from the *Magnificat* to illustrate that Mary praises God for the very reason that he pulled the mighty down, raised the lowly, filled the hungry, and sent the rich away empty: "Her maternal concern extends to the *personal* and *social* aspects of people's life on earth." His source here is a homily he had voiced, using Luke's gospel, at a mass for Mexican peasants gathered at the Shrine of Our Lady of Zapopan, Mexico (January 30, 1979).[39]

Much closer to this papal reading of the story of Mary as a prophet empowered by the Spirit and now empowered as a model and helper (handmaid) in social change, is a Bible-study dialogue from Solentiname. This village of fisher folk and others in Nicaragua, during the reign of Somoza, met with their priest, Ernesto Cardenal, one-time Trappist monk, revolutionary poet, and later the Sandinista Minister of Culture, to discuss their understanding of Bible readings and to apply them to the analysis of their own social situation. In October 1977, the Nicaraguan National Guard destroyed the community, and several of the surviving members joined the guerrillas in hiding. Cardenal opens one of the discussions that earned Solentiname its revolutionary reputation, since the dictatorship regarded Bible study as a political act.

[*Cardenal:*] I asked what they thought Herod [whom they had likened to Somoza] would have said if he had known that a woman of the people had sung that God had pulled down the mighty and raised up the humble, filled the hungry with good things and left the rich with nothing.

Natalia laughed and said: "He'd say she was crazy."

Rosita: "That she was a communist."

Laureano: "The point isn't that they would just *say* the Virgin was a communist. She *was* a communist."

[*Cardenal:*] "And what would they say in Nicaragua if they heard what we're saying here in Solentiname?"

Several voices: "That we're communists."

Someone asked: "That part about filling the hungry with good things?"

A young man answered: "The hungry are going to eat."

And another: "The Revolution."

Andrea, Oscar's wife, asked: "That promise that the poor would have those good things, was it for their, for Mary's time, or would it happen in our time? I ask because I don't know."

One of the young people answered: "She spoke for the future, it seems to me, because we are just barely beginning to see the liberation she announces."[40]

The standard fashion of Marian devotions in the United States—rosaries, statues, May crownings, hymns, sodalities—has not usually incorporated such prophetic or liberationist elements. As with images of Christ, the American Catholic piety has not coalesced around one image. While a variety of important Marian shrines exist in the United States, such as the Franciscan shrine of Our Lady of Consolation in Carey, Ohio, with its Belgian image of the Virgin, or the Redemptorist Mother of Perpetual Help, a Byzantine-style painting housed in a minor basilica on Mission Hill, in Roxbury, Massachusetts, these are largely pilgrimage shrines for individual spiritual and physical healings.

But there is also the widely venerated image of the Virgin of Guadalupe ("the one who crushed the serpent"). It recalls an apparition in 1531 on Tepeyac Hill, near Mexico City. A dark-complexioned girl, aged fourteen, spoke in the local native dialect to the impoverished Indian convert Juan Diego and revealed herself as the Virgin Mary. This non-Spanish madonna and her image on Juan Diego's native *tilma* "Indianized" the cult of the Virgin for the indigenous and oppressed classes in the New World.[41] It was an image often invoked by the underclass in subsequent social upheavals in Mexico. More recently it has been seen on the *Huelga* ("Strike!") banners borne by Hispanic migrant protestors in Caesar Chavez's United Farm Workers movement. Some may object to the "politicized" use of such a sacred icon. It should be remembered that Pope John Paul II and the Polish church have done this more explicitly by invoking the dark Virgin of Cze-stochowa, enshrined at Jasna Gora, under the title of "Queen of Poland," thus insisting that the prior Soviet-backed regime did not exercise legitimate political sovereignty in that predominantly Catholic nation. As Pablo Neruda, the Chilean poet and social activist has noted, the symbols of the poor and oppressed are powerful; this appears to be true in the political understanding of the Virgin's song that, acting through the lowly, God has brought down the mighty.

It is in the regular liturgical action of the Catholic Mass, the Eucharist, that the values of community, participation, and empowerment can be most dramatically experienced and linked to social change for the benefit of the poor and oppressed.[42] At times the Eucharist has been separated from the liturgical action of the people and "the Host" adored as an object of divine power; this has led to an attitude on the part of some that the consecrated bread and wine are produced by hocus-pocus, magic and mystification replacing the ancient sense of "mystery" in this symbol of the Lord's death and rising again.

It should be remembered, and the eucharistic rite is an act of solemn remembering (*anamnesis*), that the Eucharist is regarded by Catholics as a living symbol and sacrament of grace; it is a symbolic act that takes part essentially in the reality to which it points. Communion and community mutually create each other: Together the people are fed, equalized in status, share their love and suffering, and have the sacred gifts equitably distributed. That is why early Christians were especially agitated when worldly designations of power, privilege, or private property affected the communal celebration (*see* James 2:1–7).

In the Eucharist the "communion of saints" is recalled and experienced; and through the familiar words and actions, believers celebrate their incor-poration into Christ's body. The symbolic elements are reminders that Jesus fed his followers, echoing the sacred meal of liberation and the divine feeding of Israel in the politically charged events of Passover and Exodus. The symbols also point toward the fulfillment of the kingdom in the eschat-ological banquet at the end of the ages, in Paul's words: "For as often as you eat this bread and drink the cup, you proclaim the Lord's death until he comes" (1 Corinthians 11:26). At this table everyone is invited to share, and the poor receive an equal share, not just the crumbs. Whatever the theological changes that are rung on the concept of the Eucharist, it is important to keep clear the basic material nature of the elements used. Bread and wine, "fruit of the earth and work of human hands," are simple and ordinary supports for physical life, before any spiritual interpretation is confected. They become especially powerful symbols of sharing, suffering, new life, and divine presence. How much more of an impact must they have as symbols to those who themselves cultivate wheat and grapes, invest-ing their lives and the lives of their families as stewards of the earth that bears these elements. It is that living meaning of the symbol, rooted in social reality and the historic experience of Israel's liberation, that Jesus and his later followers powerfully elicited "in the breaking of the bread."

THE AUTHORITY OF THE WORD

The subject of how to read the Bible, recognizing the prior cultural and sociopolitical assumptions that are brought to such a reading, and how to apply what is learned from the Bible to contemporary issues, are questions that have created a growing body of literature with special significance for the Christian approach to political economy.[43] Interreligious dialogue between Christians and Jews about the historic context and traditions reflected in the gospels has opened a new contact between these groups.[44] It has also meant that, besides holding the biblical texts up for new theological and hermeneutical examination to explore their meaning within a given religious worldview, these symbolic texts have been subjected to analysis using other languages of intellectual discourse: anthropological, sociological, psychological, and economic. Some of these new languages applied to the ancient texts have been employed in order to fashion constructive ways in which the traditional material might be used for contemporary social analysis and social change, by bringing structures back into touch with their founding traditions.[45]

For various reasons, some contemporary critics have rejected the feasibility of the use of the biblical texts or social reconstructions to guide or critique today's political economy. Paul Heyne, a conservative critic, has observed that one important moral criticism that can legitimately be raised is the depersonalization of social relations in current economic systems. But he rejects as ill-advised any use that might be made of the model of the early church in Jerusalem immediately after Pentecost, presented glowingly in the Acts of the Apostles and used historically in utopian Christian communities as the basis for social and economic relations.[46] He reads this story as a response to the proclamation of Jesus in the synoptic gospels: Take no heed for tomorrow and trust in God rather than possessions. This attitude of spirit-filled spontaneity excludes any programmatic approach to social reform; it is also unworkable in terms of the modern economy, which he defines as "the whole set of impersonal, price-coordinated transactions in which the members of a society engage."[47] There is, therefore, a total disregard in the New Testament for the realities with which contemporary economists must deal. To attempt to resurrect such a community ethos, ignorant of modern economics, or to revive Aristotle's *polis* would crush those healthy, wealth-producing systems which ensure the material basis of modern life. The radical community (*koinonia*) of Jerusalem or Athens cannot be used as a model of the modern state.[48] His assumption is that the "economic realities" are unchanging facts of existence which the values of community, either classical or Christian, could only obstruct or destroy.

On the other hand, some critics have called into question the bishops' use of the early Christian community as a model, because the model of public policy they suggest, in trying to be "realistic" and "anti-utopian," looks too much to the state to supply, regulate, and distribute goods. Michael Goldberg has observed what he takes to be a certain similarity between the bishops' pastoral and the lay report: The early Christian model is too utopian. Whereas the bishops lean toward government for support, the lay report looks to a work ethic of personal merit and the abundance produced by the market. Goldberg concludes: "The bishops, looking to the government for succor, lapse into a new version of Constantinianism, while the lay people, calling for entrepreneurial self-reliance, fall into a kind of neo-Pelagianism."[49]

BEYOND THE ECLIPSE: LIBERATION THEOLOGY AND MORAL RESTRUCTURING

Economic Justice for All does not treat liberation theology or refer to any of the large number of works on the subject available in English, despite the presence at a number of U.S. seminaries and conferences of prominent liberation theologians: Sobrino, Segundo, and Gutiérrez, among others. The letter does refer to the documents of the second and third General Conference of the Latin American Bishops (CELAM) and addresses made by Pope John Paul II during recent visits. Without explaining the context or the controversial issues involved, the pastoral letter gives eight citations from the two Vatican documents on liberation theology, with six of the citations from the more positive instruction.[50] The documents are used to back up a number of general statements: economic choices involve questions of value and human purpose and are not purely technical in nature; the church has a growing body of social teachings; full participation in society demands an adequate standard of living; the option for the poor insures that all will share in the common good; the present distribution of goods clearly shows a "scandal of inequality"; there are specific forms of "social sin"; and parents have a right to choose a school for their children and educate them in their faith.

As can be seen from this list, none of the central issues raised in the Vatican critiques of liberation theology concerning use of the Bible, Marxism, and criticism of the church, is mentioned by the U.S. bishops. Once again, the approach of the letter, downplaying or ignoring controversy, is evident. The bishops have not composed a collective response to the issues raised by liberation theology and what its role might be in a North American context. They have not yet fully explored the relation of the church to the current liberation movements in this country: African, Native, and Hispanic-American, feminists, and the gay/lesbian movements, except for isolated, haphazard, and at times totally negative responses.[51] The construction of a theology of liberation for the American Catholic Church may only come about if the commitment to the "option for the poor," the young, and the marginalized is fully accepted and a program of social reconstruction, aimed at changing dominant attitudes and structures, is undertaken. Until then there will be little dialogue between the richer but smaller and peripheral Catholicism of the North and the Catholic heartland in the South.

In many ways, the language of moral restructuring has been supplied through successive papal encyclicals and speeches and through the statements from the Episcopal Council of Latin America (CELAM), especially the meeting at Medellín (1968) presided over by Paul VI, and Puebla (1979), visited by John Paul II.[52] It was at Medellín that the initial and strongest episcopal support came for the ideas and activities of liberation theologians. The three basic points of this multifaceted movement were laid out at Medellín to answer the calls for emancipation, liberation from all servitude (a key phrase), and personal maturity:

1. Establish an "option for the poor"
2. Express solidarity with the poor and marginalized, including the establishment of new forms of ecclesial communion and revision of the human structures of the church
3. Institute a program not only of evangelization, but also "conscientization," organizing the poor and powerless and educating them to analyze the basic causes of their situation in order to overcome injustice, recognizing that structures of thought as well as political and economic forces can also hamper true liberation.[53]

It was later recognized that this prophetic struggle would open up tensions in the interior structure of the church itself, between proponents of a "spiritual mission" and those in the "work of social promotion" for merely "human betterment." What is remarkable, perhaps, is that bishops at Puebla looked at such diversity and pastoral conflict as *positive,* as evidence of a healthy pluralism within the unity of the church. Others, however, saw this as negative, a threat to unity.

The documents officially translated from Puebla include the sermon delivered by Pope John Paul II at the Basilica of Guadalupe, in which he repeats before the bishops the earlier call for an "option for the poor" and adds a significant modifier:

> With its option for the Latin American human being seen whole, its preferential *but not exclusive* love for the poor, and its encouragement of full, integral liberation for human beings and peoples, Medellín — the Church present there — was a hope-filled call to more Christian and more human goals [italics added].[54]

This second general conference of CELAM seemed the appropriate forum in which to voice papal concerns about divisiveness in the regional church;

it was characteristic of Puebla to include elements apparently radical or conservative, depending on which faction was quoting the document.

The text acknowledges the pressing needs of the region after one-half a millennium of evangelization. It refers to the "muted cry" for justice, freedom, and respect for basic human rights that was heard at Medellín a decade before; but now "a cry is rising to heaven, growing louder and more alarming all the time" (#87). It is to this clamor for justice that the bishops feel called to respond. The letter does not go on to identify the biblical reference of the "cry of the poor," which is one of the four capital sins that "cry out to heaven for vengeance." This call, they state, comes in the context of a rigid ideological contest between communism and capitalism: "Fear of Marxism keeps many from facing up to the oppressive reality of liberal capitalism ... some people, faced with the danger of one clearly sinful system, forget to denounce and combat the established reality of another equally sinful system" (#92). These powers, in turn, control and manipulate the region's economy. In this situation, the bishops see "the growing gap between rich and poor as a scandal and a contradiction to Christian existence. The luxury of a few becomes an insult to the wretched poverty of the vast masses" (#28). Today "the rich get richer at the expense of the poor, who get ever poorer. Hence this reality calls for personal conversion and profound structural changes ... for authentic social justice" (#30).

"There are many causes for this situation of injustice; but at the root of them all we find sin, both on the personal level and in structures themselves" (#1258). The church must denounce such sin in ways that are objective, courageous, and evangelical. "Rather than condemning, it attempts to save both the guilty party and the victim" (#1269). They apparently claim that capitalism can be reformed, since the "significant economic progress that has been experienced by our continent proves that it would be possible to root out extreme poverty and improve our people's quality of life" (#21). On the other hand, "poverty presents a challenge to materialism, and it opens the way for alternative solutions to a consumer society" (#1152).

In a more radical assessment, they observe that the free-market economy still predominates: "legitimated by liberal ideologies, it has increased the gap between the rich and the poor by giving priority to capital over labor, economics over the social realm. Small groups ... often tied in with foreign interests ... profit for themselves while the interests of the vast majority of the people suffer" (#47). Marxist ideologies that offer surcease from these capitalist-induced crimes sacrifice Christian and human values for "utopian forms of unrealism" (#48). The ideology of the national security state, a reaction to alleged threats from the left, has helped to establish totalitarianism or authoritarian regimes, "leading to the abuse of power and the violation of human rights. In some instances they presume to justify their positions with a subjective profession of Christian faith" (#49). Multinationals in control of economic development and modernization have cost much in human terms, "when a cold-hearted technocracy applies developmental models that extort a truly inhuman price from those who are poorest" (#50). The inalienable rights of all humans as children of God include such basic rights as life, health, education, housing, work, legal protection, religious freedom, political freedoms, access to ownership, association, development, good government, and social justice (#1271–1272). Since the fulfillment of persons comes about only through exercise of their fundamental rights, the church, which has not always been sufficiently committed, must be the voice of the voiceless to recognize, protect, and promote those rights (#1268).

Some critics from the left, as well as the right, have rejected or reinterpreted the findings at Puebla.[55] Those, such as conservative Michael Novak, have seen the statement as an unrealistic, utopian vision that misunderstands the economic situation and inadvertently rejects the only real mechanism that can produce the material base needed to alleviate misery: capitalism. It is the church's dogmatic anticapitalism which is itself the cause of underdevelopment and the failure to achieve Western-style success.

On the other side, Enrique Dussel sees the statement reaffirming the institutional church's traditional image as "ally of the rich," especially in its position that misuses of capitalism can be reformed. He calls for a people's church, grounded in Christian praxis, living out its option for the poor and prophetically challenging the macroeconomic systems in place. This church is an "ethical light" to the continent, enshrining such popular saints of the struggle as Oscar Arnulfo Romero, the martyred archbishop of El Salvador.[56] While Puebla defends the economic rights of the oppressed, it chooses to refer to the "anxieties" forced on many people by "systematic or selective repression," accusations, torture, and exile (#42). Dussel sees this as an unauthentic description at a vague psychological level; these human horrors come about, he asserts, because of the poverty, hunger, and political repression that caused people to fight for their liberation against the security forces and elites of the region.[57]

MacEoin and Riley, in turn, criticize what they take to be Puebla's inadequate understanding of the real dangers to Christian faith in erroneously seeing the danger as modern secularist materialism and not the peoples' experience of oppression. Puebla's error from this perspective is to treat Latin American *campesinos* as if they were latter-day Europeans, following the same path of modernization and becoming the new cultured-despisers of religion.[58] The criticisms continue from both left and right, but the legacy of Puebla is still a dynamic one in the emerging Latin American church, in the affirmation of the role of ecclesial base communities, the overall theology of liberation as orthodox, the concept of structural sin, and the ongoing ecumenical responses to its challenge.

CONSERVATIVE CRITICS: CATHOLICISM IN CRISIS

During Pope John Paul II's recent visit to Mexico, he took time, while reaffirming the preferential option for the poor "without being exclusive," to remark on the rapidly unfolding events in Eastern Europe and the signal being sent to Marxist regimes and intellectuals in this hemisphere:

> Hence when the world is beginning to take note of the unmistakable failures of certain ideologies and systems, it is even more incomprehensible that some children of the church in these lands—sometimes moved by the desire to find quick solutions—continue to hold up certain models whose failure is obvious elsewhere in the world.[59]

The Christian, he insisted, cannot support any ideology that advocates class hatred and violence, even if it disguises itself with theological labels. This papal critique of Marxism, clearly a "god that failed," and the warning to well-intentioned liberation theologians, continues to set the tone, if it does not always provide the content, of more critical conservative views in North American Catholic circles.

Juan Luis Segundo, the noted liberation theologian, has remarked on the special role played by this pope in the formulation of the Ratzinger documents on liberation.[60] Joseph Ratzinger and John Paul appear of like mind in regarding elements of liberation theology as a reduction of the Christian gospel of salvation to a purely earthly sense in its uncritical appropriation of Marxist categories. As such, it partakes of a broader intellectual movement in the West, what Ratzinger has characterized as "the new 'tertiary bourgeoisie' with its liberal-radical ideology which is individualistic, rationalistic, and hedonistic."[61] Modernity is now seen as a marriage of East-bloc collectivism and West-bloc individualism. Segundo categorizes Ratzinger's theological program as an attempt to reassert the "transcendence of the person," but one which results in an unselfish, but nonetheless individualistic spirituality capable of only uniting "with a certain limited option for the poor and for justice."[62] In this light, the mitigating words of the 1986 Instruction from Cardinal Ratzinger's office and John Paul's letter to the Brazilian bishops, which said liberation theology is "not only useful, but necessary," are not parts of a blanket approval. It is the practical opinion of the pontiff that criticism had proceeded too far and could not be unanimously supported by the collegial endorsement of all the bishops of the region.[63] His was a reversion to the older prudential distinction between patiently enduring (*patientia*) a controverted position until it can be rectified or the bishops can agree, and tolerant indifference (*tolerantia*) that passively accepts an erroneous position. It is only inopportune for more repressive measures to be enacted at the moment.

Again taking their cue from papal or Vatican statements, North American conservatives have largely deleted or explained away statements that appear to support the liberation project. Instead, liberation theology is criticized on theological points that the Vatican has provided as prep notes: problematic use of the Bible, Marxism, and criticism of the church. Conservatives accuse the liberationists of reducing faith to politics, giving a one-sided political reading of the Bible, overstressing human revolutionary action as redemptive, and using theology to identify God's will with Marxist socialism.[64] McGovern cites Archbishop Alfonso López Trujillo's *Liberation or Revolution?* (1977) as an example of those who see in liberationist theological statements Marxist-Leninism writ large. It is, for the critics, an incitement to violent revolution that distorts the biblical figure of Jesus. As Trujillo asks: "Is Christ a Zealot who seeks radical change by means of violence ... Does He impatiently seek the 'Kingdom,' and does He want to speed his mission by means of violence?"[65] The former archbishop of Medellín is often quoted by North American conservative critics of liberation theology, but not his equally biting affirmation: "We are convinced that capitalism is a human failure."[66] The news media in North America have done little to bring such sentiments to the fore in their sporadic coverage of the Third World; the anti-Americanism that is shown is reputed to be political ideology or religious fanaticism.

Two other critics, James V. Schall, S.J., and Michael Novak have periodically sought theological grounds on which to repudiate liberation theology as a dangerous misappropriation of religion or as a convoluted charade, masquerading Marxists as anonymous Christians.[67] Both critics share some issues in common. They insist that liberation theologians are universally silent about economic failures and human rights abuses in Marxist regimes. However, they do not comment on a similar silence from fellow conservatives about abuses in South Africa, Chile, Guatemala, South Korea, and so on. Both mention the similarities between liberation theology and the historic chiliastic (millennial) and apocalyptic revolutionaries in Western Christianity.[68] After listing numerous heretics in the early and medieval church, including Albigensians, Spiritual Franciscans ("not unlike the modern communists"), Diggers, Levellers, and the like, Schall observes: "Thus, it should come as no ultimate shock that today there are Christian Marxists, Christian Maoists, Christian Trotskyites, Christian Socialists, and Christian Castroites."[69]

One factor in this multiplication of hybrids is the break made by liberation theology with the political realism of the tradition of Augustine and Aquinas. Liberationist thought, for Schall, is the triumph of blind Utopianism over rational realism. Both Novak and Schall see a dangerous mixture of religion and politics in this theology. For Schall it seems a hopeless, last-ditch effort to re-Catholicize Latin America led by theologians grasping for political power and behaving like the legendary revolutionary priest from Mexico, Miguel Hidalgo Y Costillo (d. 1811), more of an Enlightenment dilettante than priest, beheaded for treason but still romanticized by the peasantry. Thus, one may note, if Schall is correct and liberation theology is only a concoction of discontented clerics, then no major analysis of this movement is needed; he has effectively depoliticized the argument. Novak, on the other hand, cites Marxist critics themselves, who see contemporary Marxism as "dogmatic, sterile, helpless, out of touch both with modern economics and with cultural life."[70] But it is just such a barren doctrine that Novak says has attracted the overly enthusiastic and underinformed clerical types; in a rare *ad hominem* jab, Novak refers to the generally respected liberationist Bishop Helder Camara of Brazil as someone who was "in his youth a Fascist as in his maturity a Marxist," to demonstrate the antidemocratic, totalitarian propensity of this type of religious leader. Other liberationists are likened to the "Grand Inquisitor" in Dostoievski's nineteenth-century novel *The Brothers Karamazov* (1886). This fanatical cleric arrests Christ, returned to the world and silently confronting the Inquisitor who has fallen prey to the Tempter and who now offers the hungry people bread in exchange for liberty. For Novak, Pope John Paul II has maintained the integrity of the gospel and the church by refusing a similar temptation held out by the liberationists.[71] It has been commented upon by others that Novak, who once denounced the militarization of life, the appalling mediocrity of the national imagination, and the heedlessness of purely technological progress, the products of a consumerist materialism, now provides a theological rationale for corporate power and the "natural inequalities" of wealth.[72]

The materialist reading of the Christian scriptures, especially applied to the Synoptic gospels and Book of Acts, has resulted in, if nothing else, an awareness of the assumptions brought to any reading of these foundational texts. This approach has also reopened a dialogue between Jewish and Christian liberationists who wish to reaffirm the roots of Jesus' message of the kingdom in the ancient Judaic ideas and structures of justice. Those lost traditions are now seen to have particular relevance for liberation theology in Latin America, the subject of the last chapter of this study.

7

LIBERATION THEOLOGY
AND DEPENDENCY THEORY
IN LATIN AMERICA

INTRODUCTION

This chapter examines the American Catholic bishops' response in their pastoral letter to the problems of development and underdevelopment in the Third World. Thus we view Latin America from a North American perspective, recognizing the problems and inadequacies implicit in this. The church's moral values will be compared to the issues and problems associated with Third World modernization. The strengths and deficiencies of the Bishops' Letter will be measured against the criticisms of conservative theologians and social theorists, as well as the views expressed by the theologians of liberation. How can social ethics be applied to the Third World; what are some of the problems associated with modernization; and how are the issues of human dignity and social justice connected to the actions of multinational corporations, international banking institutions, and U.S. foreign investment policy?

We will begin with a summary statement of the Bishops' Letter and some initial criticisms of it. According to their critics, the bishops recapitulate the same type of mistakes they made in the sections of their letter on ethics and domestic political economy. A further and more developed criticism will come indirectly from conservative theorists who have dealt with the issues of modernization in the Third World: Walt Rostow, Michael Novak, and P. T. Bauer. These three social theorists argue that the underlying reason for the failure of the Third World to develop into healthy industrial and competitive economies lies in its lagging development along the model of Western capitalist societies. Thus they see a different set of political, economic, and cultural causes for the failure of the Third World to evolve along the appropriate stages of economic development for which the First World supplies the historical model. Many of the bishops' recommenda-

213

tions would only exacerbate the problems of an undeveloped economy and not help them. This group of modernization theorists will then be compared to Latin American dependency and underdevelopment theorists, such as André Gunder Frank and Fernando Henrique Cardoso. The latter argue that modernization theory is a political and economic ideology built on abstract, ahistorical models, which consciously fails to examine the dependent and exploitative connections between developed and underdeveloped countries. Finally, the indebtedness of liberation theology to dependency theory is discussed by examining the works of Gustavo Gutiérrez, Leonardo Boff, Hugo Assmann, and Rubem Alves.

BISHOPS' STATEMENT ON THE THIRD WORLD AND ITS CONSERVATIVE CRITICS

The final economic policy issue discussed in *Economic Justice for All*, after employment, poverty, and agriculture in the United States, deals with the problems of development and modernization in the Third World. The moral themes developed in the first part of this work are now connected to the issue of modernization in underdeveloped countries. The emphasis remains on Catholic social teachings about social justice, the common good, the unity of the family, and the preferential option for the poor. The same concerns discussed in the earlier sections of this work are repeated here, but now on the international level: the loss of human solidarity and the community, the infringements on human dignity and individual rights, growing poverty and inequality, and an industrialization which has not led to modernization of Third World economies. The bishops recognize that there are no specific policy recommendations or solutions found within church teachings that would guide them in their policy determinations. They call for creating the social conditions necessary for satisfying basic material needs and social equity.

However, the bishops appear to face a similar problem to the one discussed in chapter four. They begin with a repetition of their fundamental moral principles, proceed to a phenomenological description of the social problems faced by underdeveloped countries, and then finally conclude with some specific economic policy recommendations. As in the case with their analysis of American society, the bishops do not offer a theory of development and underdevelopment in the Third World. There is no analysis of the historical and structural mechanism by which capitalism has developed from the First to the Third World, no examination of how this social system was instituted and rationalized, and no analysis of its effects on the people who live under its direction. There is no analysis or statement of the differences between modernization and dependency theory. This jumping from moral principles to policy recommendations, from universal normative claims to particular practical action, remains unmediated by an understanding of historical movements and structural transformations either in the

West or in the Third World. There is no developed theory of international political economy.

There is thus a wide gap between a political ethics which stresses love and human dignity and the reality of 800 million people living in absolute poverty and starvation. Half the world's population lives in countries whose per capita income is below $400 a year. What types of institutional arrangements in the Third World best provide for the protection of the bishops' ethical principles and the people themselves? Though the bishops state that the key social institutions influencing the development potential of Third World countries are the nation, multinational corporations, and large multilateral institutions, there is no theory which would connect them into a comprehensive picture of what goes on in the international economy and underdeveloped countries. What role do these institutions actually perform in the development toward modernization or toward underdevelopment and dependency? Without an attempt at an explanation of events, any specific recommendations will simply presuppose the validity of the already existing international economy and thus politically bias the types of policy alternatives available.

The bishops begin with a summary of their guiding moral principles: Christian love and human solidarity, basic justice that demands freedom and dignity, respect for political and economic human rights, and a preferential treatment of the poor. It is important that at this point the bishops reiterate their view of ethics as going beyond the issues of simple morality and individual conscience. It also entails a social ethics, which includes an examination of "the political, legal, and economic structures through which policy is determined and issues are adjudicated."[1]

The bishops do call for a "fundamental reform in the international economic order."[2] They break down the components of the international policies of the United States which directly affect the Third World into the specific areas of international aid, trade, finance, and foreign investment. These areas, in turn, are understood within the context of the relationships among the nations, multilateral institutions, multinational corporations, and international banking organizations. "Each relationship offers us the possibility of substantial, positive movement toward increasing social justice in the developing world."[3] Though the bishops recognize the serious and deteriorating nature of the situation in the Third World, their analysis of the problems and their solutions lie within the general structure of these international forms of domination. They call for more social responsibility, more concern for the common good, and more commitment on the part of the United States to aid in development and modernization. The underlying social and economic structures are to be reformed, but not radically altered. In a world characterized by serious conditions of real poverty, material deprivation, and starvation, the bishops call for a more enlightened approach to economic development and modernization.

The bishops are aware of some of the real problems associated with modernizing Third World economies according to the logic of capital and market rationality. There is always a danger of extreme economic and technological dependency. However, a serious problem with their positions on development in the Third World is that these appear to be internally inconsistent, not just conceptually inadequate. In the areas of international finance and private foreign investment, the bishops recognize the damage created by the logic of capitalism, but in the same breath recommend that the system reorient its priorities and structures to accommodate the needs of Third World development. There is neither an analysis of the logic or structure of development theory nor of the possibility of accommodating church principles to historical reality. The problem is much more glaring in these sections than in the first part of their analysis and policy recommendations. The first question which must be asked is: Are the needs and priorities of bureaucratic states, multinational corporations, international banks, and international public financial institutions compatible with the development needs of the Third World? Until this is resolved, the specific content of their recommendations remains problematic.

The bishops state that there is about $60 billion of multinational corporate investment in "developing countries." They then argue that further investment by these corporations should be "consistent with the host countries development goals and with benefits equitably distributed."[4] The technology offered by these corporations should also be appropriate to the economic and social needs of these countries and the biblical claims for social justice. That is, they should follow the social and cultural patterns of the developing countries and should complement their labor-intensive economies. Goods should be produced which help to feed the people and not simply subsidize the urban middle class in the large cities or increase the volume of more profitable cash crops for international trade. Agricultural development should be spread across the economy as a whole, according to the principle of the preferential option for the poor, and should not lead to a further intensification of the class system of domination.

> Such inequitable results, however, are not necessary consequences of transnational corporate activity. Corporations can contribute to development by attracting and training high-caliber managers and other personnel, by helping organize effective marketing systems, by generating additional capital, by introducing or reinforcing financial accountability, and by sharing the knowledge gained from their own research and development activities.[5]

Because of the inadequacy of their general theory, the quotation above remains abstruse and confusing. According to the bishops, the multinational corporations are not necessarily the cause of growing inequality and economic disparity in the developing countries. What status do the ideas in this quotation have? Are they historical and descriptive or ethical and utopian statements? Are the bishops saying that multinational corporations have historically not been the cause of inequality; that they have not been the primary cause of inequality; or that transformed corporations acting within the "structures of accountability," subsidiarity, and democratic participation in the New American Experiment would have a different set of economic and political priorities? Is the ambiguity the result of political compromise, inadequate theory, pragmatic considerations, or simple confusion on the part of the bishops? They say that "the Christian ethic is incompatible with a primary or exclusive focus on maximization of profit," but they do not develop this insight when examining this particular issue.

The reconciliation between ethics and reality is to be brought about by a reorientation of fundamental attitudes and awarenesses, rather than by a serious consideration of structural reforms. These soulful corporations should be more cognizant of their social roles and public nature and, if necessary, be required to adopt an ethical code of conduct which recognizes these facts. Since there is no international agency with the power to implement these policies, the bishops call upon the United States to take a more active and responsible role in international development by enforcing these ethical codes, designing more adequate and generous trade-assistance programs, forcing the market to conform to the ethical standards of human rights and social justice, responding more responsibly to the debt crisis, restructuring international banking loans and rescheduling interest payments, calling for a moratorium or cancellation of some foreign debt, an amelioration of the negative social impact of the International Monetary Fund's austerity policies, and encouraging nonmilitary loans and technical assistance. The priority of the bishops is on providing aid, relief, and equitable distribution within a general critique of the imperatives set by the market.

The most glaring contradiction is to be seen in their call for the alleviation and prevention of hunger and starvation. They contend that the two key reasons for world hunger lie in inadequate market incentives to small farmers and a "lack of access to productive agricultural inputs." The market has not provided the right signals or incentives to provide food for domestic consumption for the growing population. In fact, the market incentives have been directing farmers to produce for the more lucrative international economy and the agricultural needs of the First World. On the other hand, it is the market economy which has produced the inequality of private ownership of the means of production, the dispossession of increasingly large numbers of small farmers, and the growing concentration of land in the hands of small domestic elites. What is the real problem for the bishops? Is it that there is not enough market or that there is too much? Is growing Third World hunger really a question of market incentives or private property, the distribution of consumer goods or the distribution of land, inadequate market rationality or class domination based on the market? That the problem could be related to the class structure, to the inequitable distribution of farm land, and to the maintenance of this system of domination by the state is never mentioned by the bishops. In fact, this section of their letter concludes with a recommendation for population strategies by which the number of poor can be kept under control by means of the "exercise of responsible parenthood." Either the bishops have not read the first half of their own letter on social justice in the economy or they have decided that the problem is too large and complex and therefore only open to immediate remedial stopgap measures. If this is the case, it should have been more clearly stated.

The conservative response to the bishops on the issue of Third World development in *Toward the Future* is limited to a few pages, since their emphasis is clearly on responding to the bishops' domestic policy recommendations. In terms of the Third World, Novak and Simon reinforce the belief that multinational corporations are extremely beneficial to modernization and development. They provide the necessary investment capital, technology, economic infrastructure, education and training, wages, taxes, and economic contracts for the expansion of domestic development.[6] These corporations provide the economic foundations for peace and prosperity, because they promote creativity, competition, employment opportunities, and international peace.

As in their criticism of the domestic policy recommendations of the bishops, the lay commission argues against a redistribution of the social wealth at an international level. Just as redistribution through the welfare state does not lead to creativity or productivity, the simple transfer of funds from the richest to the poorest nations will not help the development process. Before funds can be helpful, the social priorities and attitudes of these countries must be altered, since it is the habits, skills, liberties, and ambitions of a country which ultimately create public and private wealth. The social institutions which inhibit the development of these necessary capitalist characteristics are the state bound to tradition, certain historical forms of Catholicism, and wasteful national prestige. The state should encourage the development of a market economy, recognition of the laws of supply and demand, private property, and the development of individual entrepreneurial skills. "We reject as empirically unfounded the proposition that the wealth of some *causes* the poverty of others. We reject as false the proposition that the poverty of poor nations is caused by the wealth of rich nations."[7] Inequality between nations is the same as inequality between individuals: It is an expression of individual differences in talents, abilities, and drives.

Walter Block is critical of the Bishops' Letter because it deviates from the accepted neoclassical economic theory and its doctrine of comparative advantage in a competitive market economy. He condemns, however, agrarian dualism (domestic production for export based on cash crops), the international division of labor that leaves the underdeveloped countries poorer each year, the debt trap, and the deteriorating terms of trade and foreign exchange difficulties. He argues that economic specialization, trading, and division of labor have made the West so economically successful. Agricultural specialization and free trade, when applied to the Third World, will only improve the productivity, efficiency, and the balance of payments deficits, since everyone gains in international trade.[8] Block views the Bishops' Letter as encouraging foreign investment in the Third World, while being very suspicious of the role of multinational corporations. "If taken at their words literally multinational investment would have to cease, forthwith."[9] He contends that dependency is created by foreign aid between governments and not by the private investment of multinational corporations, which will only help Third World development. Issues of equity and social justice are simply disguised forms of international theft from the more productive to the less efficient countries. The paucity of evidence and analysis on the part of the bishops and the lay commission forces us to continue the discussion of these issues of modernization and underdevelopment in the Third World by further examining the debate between conservative and radical perspectives within the broader community.

MODERNIZATION THEORY AND THE STAGES OF ECONOMIC DEVELOPMENT

A more comprehensive development of these ideas is contained in the conservative criticisms of liberation theology and its theories of social dependency, economic exploitation, and underdevelopment. Michael Novak has a more developed critique of liberation theology in his *The Spirit of Democratic Capitalism* and *Will It Liberate?* Conservatives present different variations of modernization theory, but some of the common themes running throughout their writings include the idea that the failure to modernize is the result of a combination of some of the following:

1. Deficiencies in cultural values compatible with capitalism
2. National religious orientation
3. Individual attitudes (culture of poverty)
4. A centralized state interfering with the economy (the politicization of social life)
5. Lack of market incentives
6. The existence of foreign aid and the resulting technological and economic dependency (the welfare syndrome)
7. The lag in the stages of economic development
8. Too much emphasis on social justice, economic redistribution, and equality and not enough on economic efficiency and productivity.

At the political, economic, and cultural levels, there are structures and values which contradict and undermine the social preconditions necessary for democratic capitalism: a market, political pluralism, and a culture of competition and consumption built around individual creativity, innovations, and production.

Following in the footsteps of the classical liberal model of economic development, which we have already seen in chapter four, conservatives have argued that the international economy is a harmonious mechanism which adjusts to the self-interests of the participating units. Competition, self-interest, and free trade can only foster international economic development, innovation, and the maximization of utility of all parties involved.[10] Under ideal market conditions, all parties benefit from the exchange as developed countries receive cheap labor and raw materials, whereas developing countries, in turn, receive scarce capital, modern science and technology, and technical and organizational skills. Any disparity of economic power that exists between the two trading partners will not lead to uneven developments or exploitative relationships, since in this type of economic arrangement, there is a comparative advantage to every party.

In the end, the closer connection between the Third and First Worlds will help the transition of the former toward higher levels of economic development and modernization. Economic growth in both areas results as both countries benefit equally from the process. Monopolies, exploitation, and imperialism are the product of noneconomic factors, such as political intervention and the residual effects of noncapitalist systems (feudalism) that distort the perfection of market rationality. Efficiency, productivity, and rationality are the key categories that describe the workings of the economic system, since it produces a harmonious integrated world economy, peaceful development, efficient use of natural and human resources, accumulated savings for further growth and development, and the institutionalization of political liberties.

Walt Rostow has expanded this line of thinking into a theory of economic change and modernization in his work *The Stages of Economic Growth*. He argues that all societies developed according to an internal teleological mechanism. All societies on the track to modernization and development must pass through the following stages of economic maturity: traditional society, preconditions for take-off, take-off, drive to maturity, and age of mass consumption. As the subtitle of his work ("A Non-Communist Manifesto") indicates, this theory is to be understood as an alternative to the materialist theory of history articulated by Marx. Traditional societies are characterized by a *Weltanschauung* limited by a pre-Newtonian universe in terms of science and technology. Because of the limits of culture and economy, they have limited access to the possibilities of increased production and efficiency. Traditional societies are forced to remain agricultural and undeveloped, with limited social surplus and little social mobility. They are also characterized by a cultural fatalism, a centralized political system based on the interests of the landowning class, and a small self-sufficient economy based on relatively static production within local communities.

The second stage in Western development occurred at the end of the

seventeenth century, "when science began to be translated into new production functions in both agriculture and industry."[11] The preconditions for
the take-off of a modern economy are found in the building of a centralized
nation state, which in turn supplies the necessary preconditions and economic infrastructure for economic growth, that is, the "social overhead
capital" such as transportation, communication, and educational facilities.
The state is crucial for this stage of development, since there is not enough
private capital to create the necessary social conditions for economic take-
off. Economic progress and the belief in the open possibilities of the future
are reflective of the new changes in this form of society, with its development of technological and entrepreneurial skills. Rostow contends that the
real difference between traditional and modern societies is their different
rates of investment. A modern society must have a rate of investment of at
least 10 percent of the national income, which outstrips population growth
and becomes the basis for new investment and production.

The third stage is that of the take-off period, when the old vestiges of
the traditional society are replaced by a modern industrial system based on
heavy industry and factory production. It is a period of sustained economic
growth, industrial output, and high rates of investment in a widened market.
This stage was characteristic of Britain between 1815 and 1850 and the
post-Civil War United States from 1868–1893. For the take-off to occur,
three conditions have to be met.

1. A rise in the rate of productive investment from, say, 5 percent or
less to over 10 percent of national income (or net national product [NNP])
2. The development of one or more substantial manufacturing sectors,
with a high rate of growth
3. The existence or quick emergence of a political, social and institutional
framework which exploits the impulses to expansion in the modern sector
and the potential external economy effects of the take-off and gives to
growth an on-going character.[12]

The take-off requires economic prerequisites that include capital investment, a broadened market, the development of entrepreneurial skills,
industrial development (coal, iron, and engineering industries), and population and real-income growth. Central, too, is the creation of an entrepreneurial elite class, which carries with it the cultural values of the
Protestant ethic. It is important to note that Rostow maintains that the
investment funds for this stage come from two major sources: income flow
into capital investments through state-engineered income redistribution
(confiscation and taxation) or capital imports of banking institutions and
foreign loans, and the reinvestment of secured profits by private institutions.
The fourth stage further expands this development into new areas, especially into chemical, electrical, steel, and machine-tool industries. The economic rationalization and technical maturity of the take-off period is

expanded into new industries as science and technology move into broader sectors of the economy.

For Rostow, this historical development of modern societies from the take-off to technological maturity takes about sixty years to occur. The fifth stage is an age of high consumption, with an emphasis on the development of consumer and service industries. This period is characterized by the shift in the workforce away from old production-line industries, toward skilled jobs and service occupations; increased urbanization; the creation of the welfare state; and a consumer-oriented economy. Other conservative theorists have called this stage of development the postindustrial society. These are the stages, they assert, through which all societies must evolve in their quest for modernization. "Nevertheless, the economic history of growing societies takes a part of its rude shape from the effort of societies to approximate the optimum sectoral paths."[13] It represents a one-dimensional philosophy of history; there is no development except along the model of Western modernization.

The Third World countries float somewhere between traditional and modern society and thus have much in common with those countries which have already progressed along this linear path of historical evolution. Like their predecessors, they face problems of building the "social overhead capital," supplying investment capital, moving the country from agriculture and trade to industrial development, changing the cultural attitudes of people, and creating a fiscally responsible state. New problems of overpopulation, unemployment, and the diversions of the Cold War must be dealt with. However, according to Rostow, these countries also have advantages which did not exist for the developing Western countries in the nineteenth century. There is a great deal of available agricultural, industrial, and medical technology that can lessen the growing pains and ease the transition from one stage of development to another. To further ease this process of modernization, there is now more economic aid available from developed nations and international financial organizations. In the last instance, it is up to the individual countries themselves and their respective elites, who must make the appropriate decisions toward advancement and modernization along the lines of the Western model. At each stage of development, there are real choices that each society must make to advance to the next level of development.

Though he does not refer to Rostow in particular, Novak continues this line of thought within his development model by examining the particular historical reasons why Latin America did not develop along the path taken by North America. He revives the tripartite analysis of his theory of political economy and states that the problems of underdevelopment lie in the political, economic, and cultural choices made. To blame the underdevelopment of Latin America on the United States is to fail to look closely both at the history of Latin America and at the importance that Latin America has for U.S. corporations.[14] Novak believes that the small sums of corporate capital invested in Latin America—$11 billion by 1965—are too insignificant to explain the poverty and backwardness of the continent. Investment decisions in the Third World and profit remittance to the United States are the result of decisions made by relatively few firms which could not have the dramatic impact claimed by dependency theorists and liberation theologians. One must look instead for the real causes in the economic history of the region.

Like Rostow, Novak sees the historical and cultural inadequacies of Weber's thesis of the relationship between the Protestant work ethic and the cultural values of capitalist accumulation. Instead of placing an overemphasis on the cultural differences between Catholicism and Protestantism, he instead looks to the structural dynamic between the Catholic Church and the Catholic state. The religious and political policies of the Counter-Reformation state undermined the already blossoming capitalist spirit in Portugal, Belgium, Germany, and Italy in the first part of the sixteenth century. Following the analysis of Trevor-Roper, Novak concludes that it was the Spanish model of Catholicism and state mercantilism, economic monopolies, patronage, feudalism, and the disdain for private enterprise that destroyed the capitalist drive of the Hapsburg Empire.[15] This same combination of antidevelopment values and strategies are again making a claim to primacy in the hands of liberation theology and will have the same deleterious effects.

This is the "tragedy of the sixteenth century" being recreated as the "tragedy of the nineteenth century." Religion was a crucial variable to the extent that it rationalized the existence of mercantilism and the state's infringement on private market and individual liberties. Weber's thesis is inadequate because it does not take into consideration the political and economic structures of Catholic Spain. The cultural contempt for capitalism has continued to this day and is explicit in the writings of the Latin American theologians. It is thus Catholicism itself which has led to a continuation of backwardness in this area, because Latin American theology places minimal importance on individualism, competition, and the other values of classical liberalism.

> The widespread Latin American antipathy toward commerce—antipathy rooted both in an aristocratic culture and in traditional Latin Catholicism—is married in Latin America to a widespread desire for an integral, holistic, unitary system. Such a unity is not afforded by the pluralism of democratic society. The latter seems too anarchic, too individualistic, too materialistic to win much loyalty from the clergy, from the aristocracy, and from the rural peasantry ... The absence of a compelling indigenous theory on the part of those in favor of a free private business sector and democracy creates a vacuum, into which liberation theology rushes.[16]

One school of dependency theory has as its major thesis the center-periphery paradigm. The theory contends that, because of their technological superiority, their economic and political might, the advanced industrial nations are capable of exploiting the rich raw materials and cheap labor of the Third World, directing its agricultural modernization in ways most beneficial to the needs of the developed nations and inhibiting the industrialization of underdeveloped countries. That is, underdevelopment is a necessary by-product of this very process of modernization and, along with the further economic advancement of developed countries, there is a corresponding distortion of modernization in the Third World. The structures of political economy result in what Gregory Baum has called "sinful structures."

Novak rejects this thesis as just another continuation of the idea that poverty and exploitation are the product of the creation of wealth. "The theory of the 'center' and the 'periphery' is merely a clever restatement of the proposition that the poverty of the poor is explained by the wealth of the wealthy."[17] Neither in its domestic political economy nor in its relations to foreign countries does democratic capitalism so negatively affect the economic and cultural life of society. Just as the American economy is so vibrant and expansive when one compares the conditions of today to the turn of the century, so too does the Third World appear advanced when compared to its position a hundred years ago. The contact between Western and non-Western societies has only benefited the latter. The introduction of the new values of liberty, freedom, innovation, dynamic exchange of ideas, and so forth has only enhanced the possibilities of these societies. Since private production, a market economy, and the separation of church and state have resulted in material production far greater than alternative social systems, especially those characterized by state planning and collectivization, any contact between developed and underdeveloped societies would be to the advantage of the latter.

Novak, relying on the work of the economist Joseph Ramos, develops a six-point thesis to critique liberation theology and dependency theory. The thesis states that:

1. Only 5 percent of U.S. investment and 7 percent of its production goes to foreign countries
2. Of this small amount, only 20 percent goes to Latin America
3. The after-tax return of U.S. capital in Latin America is about 10 percent, which is lower than it can get in Europe, Australia, Asia, and Africa
4. Profit remittance is part of economic growth and future investment
5. Corporate profits do not depend on investment in the Third World, since only a small number of firms are involved, and almost all invest in developed countries outside the U.S.

6. The U.S. has been facing a trading deficit for the past few years and thus imports more than it exports.

These six points lead Novak to reject dependency theory and with it the idea that it is wealth that creates poverty. The wealth of great countries is due to other influences than exploitation. The problems of Latin America are more connected to the existence of concentrated economic wealth in the hands of small elites and its lack of diffusion to the larger population. What is required is creation of a relatively more equal society, which respects the diffusion of private property; what is missing is a middle class. This diffusion of private property is the key to the expansion of individual liberty and the limitation of state power and authority. However, Novak fails to consider that just because other factors may be involved, such as economic concentration, lack of property diffusion, and the existence of oligarchies, does not exclude the possibility that exploitation remains an important element in explaining a very complex historical phenomenon. These explanations are not incompatible.

Though there are differences between agricultural and industrial sectors of societies, according to Novak, these differences do not correspond to the developed center and underdeveloped periphery claimed by liberation theologians. The critics have lost sight of the fact that, in a "natural system of liberty," the cultural and moral values propel a society beyond its traditional boundaries and structures, even behind the backs of its participants, and give it impetus to engage in creative and innovative economic activity. *"The moral-cultural system is the chief dynamic force behind the rise both of a democratic political system and of a liberal economic system."*[18]

For Novak, it is an undeniable fact that Latin American countries have not produced the inventions and creative technology that have been the hallmark of modernity. The answer lies in the religious and cultural system that has stressed a "private devotion with a strong supernaturalist flavor." This also explains the acceptance of liberation theology and its mystical, utopian, and otherworldly outlook. Novak clearly sees some of the more glaring weaknesses of liberation theology in its utopianism, its vague theorizing, its inability to articulate a broad picture of the future, and its unwillingness to criticize East European socialism. He, in turn, has failed to consider in any depth its ideals of socialism beyond the picture of a political cliché.

He does not really question the political economy of developed societies, the role of the modern state in both developed and underdeveloped countries, and the inconsistencies in the traditions which have stressed liberty vs. freedom, self-realization vs. consumer choice, and creativity vs. entrepreneurial success. One cannot reduce the discussion in social theory and liberation theology to simply questions of liberty vs. collectivism, individual choice vs. state interference, and a market economy vs. a command economy. As we have seen in the previous chapters, differences of traditions, inconsistencies of theories, and contradictory premises are simply ignored in the desire to explain democratic capitalism as capable of integrating equality and liberty, individuality and community, self-interest and the common good, and materialism and idealism.

Although Novak draws upon Ramos's work for his specific analysis of Latin America, he also relies heavily on the writings of P. T. Bauer to provide the overall framework for his modernization theory and critique of dependency theory. Bauer contends that economic backwardness is not the result of an international social stratification caused by technological and economic dependence, since those countries which are the least advanced are also those with the least amount of contact with the First World. Surplus is not expropriated, profits are not remitted, nor are goods exported from these areas. There is really no contact between the First and Third World here. This is true for many parts of Africa. The continent is too poor to be the base of colonial or neocolonial expansion. Thus the opposite is true. "Far from the West having caused poverty in the Third World, contact with the West has been the principal agent of material progress there."[19] The growth of large cities and ports, transportation and communication networks, the introduction of modern science, technology, and education, the eradication of infectious diseases, and the development of cash crop agricultural areas and mineral extraction industries have resulted in economic development to the Third World. Bauer lists the "positive contributions" made by the West to the developing nations, but there is no theory of political economy, no theory of agricultural and industrial change, no historical analysis of the effects of modernization, and no structural analysis of society as a whole.

The poorest of the Third World peoples are those with no contact with the West, such as aborigines, pygmies, and desert people. Countries such as Afghanistan, Tibet, Nepal, and Liberia were, according to Bauer, never colonies and thus their backwardness cannot be explained by colonialism and exploitation. On the other hand, places such as Singapore, Hong Kong, and South Korea are examples of countries that have successfully developed into modern societies. He continues this line of reasoning throughout his work. But the logic is dangerously faulty. To argue that poverty is a universal concept applicable without regard to historical and social contexts becomes the basis for the most questionable manipulation of history. To say that premodern, technologically primitive societies are more poor than developing and underdeveloped societies that are closely dependent on First World technology, skills, organizational methods, and capital is really to miss the point of the differences in the nature of poverty and consequently in the nature of its underlying historical and structural causes.

Since this is, in fact, the basis of his argument, it is important to see that any immediate comparison of underdeveloped societies which does not seriously take into consideration the historical and economic context of poverty is faulty from the start. The poverty of pygmy society in Africa and that of the barrios in urban centers of Latin America may be expressed in the same biological and physiological terms, have the same medical symptoms, and in the end have the same results: suffering, starvation, and death. But despite this, the historical and sociological reality of poverty is certainly not the same. One is caused by a society characterized by "primitive technology," environmental changes, and natural catastrophes. The other form of poverty is the result of social and economic relationships which spring from the very foundations of capitalist society. That is, the former is the result of a technical undevelopment and precarious environment, while the latter results from economic underdeveloping tied to exploitative social relationships. The former is unfortunate, but the latter is unjust and immoral. The concept of poverty is an historically specific category and must be carefully treated as such. Just because poverty is characteristic of a certain level of economic evolution does not mean that the modern phenomena in the Third World are the same or have the same causes. It appears that Bauer's analysis is designed simply to break the connection between Western guilt and Third World poverty, economic exploitation, and underdevelopment.

Bauer asks the question: Since colonialism did not cause economic backwardness, then could it be the result of neocolonialism and the complex arrangements among investment, multinational corporations, and Third World countries? He analyzes various aspects of the international economy and systematically attempts to undermine the dependency theory criticisms. He at first raises, then dismisses, the following claims made to explain the economic backwardness of the Third World: the deterioration of the terms of trade between developed and backward countries; the deleterious effects of increasing foreign debt, foreign investment, and multinational corporations; the manipulation of international prices, industrial power, and competitive advantage of the First World; the brain drain and immigration to the West of highly educated and skilled individuals; ethnic discrimination; increasing external trade and the influx of consumer imports; rising consumption and declining investment; cultural dependence and foreign manipulation of social values and consumer tastes; and finally, the "social cannibalism" of Western industrial and consumer needs.

However, these are not the causes of poverty for Bauer. Increasing economic contact has only helped the Third World in a variety of ways. Foreign investment and multinational corporations have raised incomes and government revenues. International trade has expanded opportunities. In a competitive market, there is no manipulation of the terms of trade or commodity prices. Debts are not exploitative. Competition increases the consumer choices and economic opportunities of the population. The real brain drain results from the inability or unwillingness of Third World governments to use educated minorities. Ethnic discrimination is found in the Third World and in the West, but has not hindered many ethnic minorities from advancement. External trade is the result of the free individual choices made by the people, and it is "disguised condescension" to say otherwise. Foreign trade is healthy and helpful to domestic economies, since it requires new savings and investment, as well as increased work and higher production, to pay for the imported goods. Western patterns of consumptions and goods have been intelligently chosen by the Third World "where they have been of massive benefit to millions of people." And finally, famine and starvation are the result of lack of contact with the West as indicated by the fact that they occur in regions without commercial contact with the West.

If one really wants to uncover the real causes for Third World poverty, for Bauer, they must look in other areas: the politicization of the economy (state interventionism) and rising population resulting from improved medical technology. The patterning of newly independent countries on the models of previous colonial power relations has given rise to the excessive intrusion of the state into the market economy. "These controls have wasted resources, restricted social and economic mobility, and also external contacts. They have also provoked fierce political and social strife. These consequences in turn have brought about poverty and even large-scale suffering."[20] Increasing population in economies which have been stagnating has also contributed to increasing poverty.

Bauer's analysis of modernization, like that of Rostow and Novak, assumes the existence of stages of development through which countries must pass. He even argues that the Third World actually is in a better position for development than was Western Europe at the same stage of development, for it can utilize the already existing technology, available capital, and external markets. What is clearly missing in his analysis is a theory of Western modernization. There is no mention of how economic surplus was accumulated for the take-off period; no mention is made of the historical process of primitive accumulation: the enclosure movement, colonization, militarism, the rise of a centralized state, the new factory system, class discontent, and so forth. It is assumed that Western technology is both appropriate and necessary in order for development to take place. What is lacking, for him, are simply the cultural preconditions for modernization.

> Economic achievement depends on people's attributes, attitudes, motivations, mores, and political arrangements. In many countries the prevailing personal, social and political determinants are uncongenial to material progress: witness the preference for a contemplative life, opposition to paid work by women and widespread torpor and fatalism in certain countries. Moreover, politics of many Third World governments are plainly damaging to economic achievement.[21]

Bauer states that without these cultural prerequisites, the structural transformation of political economy may not be effective enough to produce the desired results. He is especially critical of foreign aid because of this very point. It is only another example of "misplaced condescension" to argue that the Third World requires financial aid, when development in the West did not. Bauer argues that aid has not been used productively, as evidenced by the increasing backwardness, low standards of living, famine, and economic crises. Underdevelopment is the result of not having followed the Western model of development.

On the other hand, dependency theory holds that this discrepancy between loans, subsidies, grants, and capital investment by the West and the continuing underdevelopment of the Third World raises questions about the real purposes for which Western money has been supplied. It claims that Western aims were far from being altruistic. But there does appear to be some agreement between the conservatives and radicals that aid has not been an effective mechanism for economic modernization. Bauer states that this is the result of the burden of the costs of the loans, the wasteful projects for which capital has been used, the coercive measures of international taxation and redistribution, and the resulting increase in centralized state power.

Foreign aid distorts development because it politicizes social life and redirects energy and public focus away from the innovative private sphere into government. Where the goal is to use the state as a mechanism for egalitarianism and social justice, the results are confiscation of property, undermining of creative incentives and capitalist cultural values, and totalitarianism. "Economic differences are largely the result of people's capacities and motivations."[22] Thus the egalitarian ideology results in economic inefficiency, loss of production, and greater inequality, because it undermines the productive foundations of developing societies. It coercively levels those differences that make progress possible. This line of argument corresponds closely with what we have already seen in chapter two when analyzing Murray's argument that it is welfare spending by the state that is responsible for our present problems of poverty and should be eliminated or curtailed.

> In a subtle way, aid tends to perpetuate ideas and modes of conduct adverse to material progress. For instance, advocacy and inflow of aid lends support to the idea that improvement of one's fortunes depends on other people, the government, the rich, one's superiors, or foreigners. Here again aid pauperizes the recipients.[23]

The problem with Bauer's position is that there is no historical or structural analysis of Third World political economy. With his statements about the "dilemma of egalitarianism" and fear of leveling, his criticism of a centralized welfare state and the politicization of social life, with his faith in the metaphysics and rationality of the market, with his avoidance of class analysis and the history of economic crises and dependency relations, with the culture of poverty argument applied to the Third World, with his placing primacy on the ideals of possessive individualism and market choices, with his defense of the ideology of classical liberalism, and finally, with his emphasis on the poverty of noncapitalist cultures, Bauer—under the guise of rational economic analysis and model creation—has constructed a comprehensive theology of economics and metaphysics of liberalism.[24] Cultural differences, histories, and institutional structures are obscured and eliminated as the real analysis occurs at the level of political discourse and metaphysics, that is, at the level of ideology.

TYPES OF UNDERDEVELOPMENT AND DEPENDENCY THEORY

An alternative perspective to modernization theory, with its theory of economic growth, stages of development, and the need for Western technology, is that of dependency theory. This theory originally developed from the works of Latin American theorists in the 1950s and 1960s, but is now being applied worldwide. While the conservatives stressed the positive contributions of multinational corporations in providing skilled expertise, capital, technology, and social organization to less developed countries, dependency theorists charged that modernization was a disguised form of underdevelopment and dependency on the economic priorities and structures of the advanced industrial countries. Dos Santos has succinctly defined this form of modernization as dependency.

> By dependency we mean a situation in which the economy of certain countries is conditioned by the development and expansion of another economy to which the former is subjected. The relation of interdependence between two or more economies, and between these and world trade, assumes the form of dependence, when some countries (the dominant ones) can expand and can be self-sustaining, while other countries (the dependent ones) can do this only as a reflection of that expansion, which can have either a positive or a negative effect on their immediate development.[25]

Rather than bringing technical modernization and economic development, according to André Frank, the West had brought stagnation and underdevelopment. That is, economic underdevelopment is the result of close contact with the West, not isolation from it. Underdevelopment is not simply a stage toward higher development and economic maturation, as Rostow's model would indicate, but a stage caused by a dependent, subservient relationship with advanced industrial nations, multinational corporations, and international banking institutions. It is these groups that determine the economic priorities, goals, methods, and policies that direct the form in which economic expansion takes place. There are other theorists who argue that, even within these dependent relationships, there has been some limited development and industrialization in Latin America.

There are quite a few variations and much debate within dependency theory and little space in this chapter to outline them all. "Dependency theory is actually a very broad, eclectic school of thought whose only common ground is the assumption that underdevelopment has causes external to the underdeveloped nations."[26] This certainly makes it all the more difficult to present it in the form of distinct analytical schools of thought. Relying on the typologies of Ronald Chilcote and others, we have distinguished five distinct theories of dependency: underdevelopment theory, new dependency theory, dependent development theory, surplus extraction theory (monopoly capital theory of imperialism and theory of unequal exchange), and neoclassical Marxism.[27]

Underdevelopment theory is represented by Frank's theory of external underdevelopment and metropolis-satellite dependency, which results from colonial expansion and international commerce. New dependency theory is based on Dos Santos's theory of internal underdevelopment, with its law of the internal development of post-World War II advanced industrial capitalism and the impact of industrialization and the technological penetration of multinational corporations on Third World development. Dependent development theory is a theory of structural dependency represented by Cardoso, who stresses the modernization and industrialization in Latin America, internal political structures, international economic organizations, class relationships, and uneven economic development. Cardoso is critical of Frank's abstract theorizing and his view of a stagnating economy resulting from dependency; he also recognizes the importance of industrial expansion in the Third World, if only within a dependent framework.

The surplus extraction theory is represented by the *Monthly Review* School of Baran, Sweezy, Mandel, Magdoff, and Amin (monopoly capital theory of imperialism), who attempt to show a connection between internal and external dependency caused by monopoly capitalism and the world market in an expansion of Lenin's theory of imperialism. Weaver and Berger have argued that there is another variant of this surplus extraction thesis developed by Emmanuel and Amin (theory of unequal exchange). The latter group maintains that underdevelopment results from the extraction of scarce resources and capital through an unequal exchange in international trade, while the former group stresses the power of multinational corporations and foreign control over industry to repatriate profits back to developed countries.

To this list one should add a fifth variation of dependency theory, which is critical of dependency theory's traditional emphasis on the circulation of commodities, commerce, and market exchange. This fifth variation (neoclassical Marxist theory) turns to an analysis of the modes of production, the historical structures of capital accumulation (primitive accumulation), and class analysis. The theorists in this group contend that an analysis of surplus extraction and repatriated profits through the power of monopoly capital or unequal exchange does not get at the underlying social relations of production in capitalist society. Authors espousing this fifth theory include Marini, Laclau, and Quijano, Shaikh, Brenner, and Warren. There are Marxist, non-Marxist, socialist, nationalist, and reformist approaches to the problem of dependency and economic exploitation. There are those who stress different forms of dependency from foreign commerce and surplus transference, the role of multinational corporations, the internal unequal development between industry and agriculture and between the urban core and periphery, and the distortions created by unequal trade relations, to those who attempt to integrate external imperialism and distorted internal industrial development.

> Clearly, no unified theory has emerged as the emphasis on dependency has permeated both mainstream and radical thought. Weaknesses in the formulation about dependency also are obvious: They fail to take into account class struggle and tend to obscure attention to imperialism; they tend to emphasize relations of exchange (trade and market) instead of class relations based on how goods are produced while exaggerating questions of nationalism and development; and finally, they tend not to offer strategies for achieving development, especially socialist development.[28]

The actual mechanism of dependency varies with each theory and its structural and historical components. Some theorists have emphasized the dependency created by colonialism and the extraction of cheap minerals and scarce resources. Others have stressed the dependency of neocolonialism created in foreign trade, technological exchange, and the huge Third World debt structure resulting from unequal exchange relations. Still others argue that this only concentrates on the mechanism of dependency created in commerce and does not examine the modes of production specific to dependent relations in the Third World.

A comprehensive theory of dependency would have to include all these elements: the historical foundations of colonial dependency and the development of underdevelopment, the unequal trade relations created in its wake, the introduction of Western technology and economic models of development, the penetration of foreign investment and repatriated profits, the debt bondage formed as a result of distorted modernization and an international banking establishment, and the distorted commercialization of agriculture and industry resulting from this whole structure of dependency. These different models of dependency should be understood as less analytically distinct schools of thought and more as expressions of stages in the historical and structural evolution of Third World dependency. Our goal in this work has not been to provide a synthesis of these different perspectives, but to underline our argument that the bishops have in their analysis too summarily discarded the dependent status of many of the Third World economies.

UNDERDEVELOPMENT IN SPITE OF INDUSTRIALIZATION

An integration of the various aspects of dependency would include an historical, structural, developmental, and conflict-based perspective of underdevelopment. In this context, industrialization does not result in autonomous development, broad economic expansion, and a movement to a higher stage of economic maturity and industrialization. Partial development affects only certain groups within the society, further divides the society along class lines, and results in a development whose priorities are determined by foreign investment, banking, and industrial institutions. In their present form, these foreign institutions do help in development, but it is not the type of modernization outlined in Rostow's theory of the take-off stage. Dependency theory locates the origins of exploitation, poverty, economic stagnation, distorted development, and underdevelopment in the close contact with Western institutions and values. This is certainly at odds with the theory of modernization proposed by Rostow, Novak, and Bauer. In his famous essay, "The Sociology of Underdevelopment and the Underdevelopment of Sociology," Frank argues:

It is impossible, without closing one's eyes, to find in the world today any country or society which has the characteristics of Rostow's first, the traditional, stage. This is not surprising since the construction of Rostow's stages takes account neither of the history of the now underdeveloped countries, nor of their crucial relations with the now developed ones over several centuries past. Rostow's approach obliterates the fact that through these relations, the now developed countries have totally destroyed the preexisting fabric of these societies (be it "traditional" or not).[29]

By ignoring the analysis of history and the structures of political economy, Rostow's theory is itself underdeveloped. Frank contends that Rostow's first two stages in his linear model are "fictional" and the two last stages are "utopian." There are no historical examples of countries that have moved along the path from underdevelopment to modernization. Frank also argues that today's advanced industrial countries were never underdeveloped. Underdevelopment is not a static stage in the evolution of world capitalism, but part of an historical process connected to development itself. That is, there is a "development of underdevelopment." They are two sides of the same coin.

In this same essay, Frank states that between 1950 and 1965, the United States invested $9 billion in mainly poor countries, but repatriated $25.6 billion in profits. James Petras, also interested in this issue, calculated that between 1966 and 1976 the difference between the net capital outflow of funds to the United States from Latin America and the net capital inflow of funds was $2.5 billion. In this figure, Latin American payments in the form of royalties and fees accounted for increasingly more of the total amount remitted; between 1972 and 1976 this amounted to 38 percent.[30] These figures do not include money lost to development as a result of declining terms of trade, brain drain, foreign balance of payment deficits, and servicing its enormous debt.[31] Between 1975 and 1984, the total foreign debt of Latin America increased from $89.4 billion to $360.2 billion, while its interest payments went from $5.6 billion to $37.3 billion.[32] This represents a dramatic increase, which only further retarded the capacity for economic growth and industrial expansion. Also this net outflow of funds represents only part of the problem. Much of capital investment in Latin America is financed with local capital, thereby facilitating the outflow of capital to the United States by means of their own money.

Novak had argued that American corporations' investments in the Third World represented such a small portion of their total overseas capital investment and profits that it was a relatively minor operation. Profit exploitation could not be the major reason for investment in this geographical area. But a closer look at some crucial facts relating to overseas investment opportunities provides a different picture.[33]

There are more than 200,000 corporations in the USA today, but 100 companies control more than half the nation's industrial assets. Fifty of the largest banks and insurance companies own half of all financial assets. Ten firms make 22 percent of all the profits.

Of special interest to us is the international scope of this capital concentration. Some 400 corporations control about 80 percent of the capital assets of the entire nonsocialist world. One-third of the assets of US industrial corporations are located outside the United States ... American and other Western corporations have acquired control of more than 75 percent of known major mineral resources in Asia, Africa, and Latin America.

Given the low wages, low taxes, nonexistent worker benefits, and nonexistent occupational and environmental protections, *US multinational profit rates in the Third World are 50 percent greater than in developed countries*. Hence, giant companies like Exxon, Cargill, Coca-Cola, IBM, Honeywell, Woolworth, Upjohn, Mobil, ITT, Gillette, and Reynolds make more than half their total profits abroad.[34]

Though most of U.S. investment lies in developed countries, the Third World represents a crucial investment opportunity for some of America's key and powerful multinational corporations. Investment is also important in order to secure markets in geographical areas which offer unique opportunities for future growth and development. Because of their concentration and economic power, multinational corporations have the ability to over-price imports and underprice exports: a technique called transfer pricing. By this method they can overcharge their consumers in the Third World, reap enormous profits for themselves, and transfer scarce surplus back to their parent countries.

Drawing upon the study of foreign-owned drug companies in Latin America by Constantine Vaitsos, Richard Barnet and Ronald Müller have documented the extent of the dramatic profits in this area. Studying 15 U.S. and European multinationals in the 1960s, Vaitsos concluded that their profits ranged from 38.2 percent to 962.1 percent, with the average being 79.1 percent. The overall profit rate of manufactured goods in Latin America was about 40 percent, which is substantially higher than found in the developed countries.[35] Between 1946 and 1967, nearly $5.5 billion of U.S. investment came into Latin America, while more than $14.7 billion returned in the form of repatriated profits.

However, as late as 1984, Rhys Jenkins had stated that "it is paradoxical that the dependency analysis of the impact of TNCs [transnational corporations] has on the whole been somewhat superficial."[36] Perhaps this could be explained by the evolution of dependency theory itself. Jenkins recognizes this, if only implicitly, since his own study of dependency emphasized the changing internal dynamics of the Latin American economy after World War II. His analysis examined the new form of industrialization in under-developed countries called "dependent development." The larger Latin American countries such as Brazil, Argentina, and Mexico began to indus-trialize in the late 1950s and early 1960s with the help of a new outbreak of international competition between the multinational corporations and greater participation by their governments in the process of industrializa-tion. A result for these countries was the formation of a new form of oligopoly within the major manufacturing industries controlled by United States and European firms.[37] On the average, economic concentration of firms in Latin America is higher than in the United States. In 1970 foreign corporations controlled 70 percent of profits in Brazil's and 45 percent of profits in Mexico's key industries. In 1976 foreign multinational corpora-tions in Brazil controlled 33 percent of the electrical machinery, 44 percent of rubber, 51 percent of nonelectrical machinery, 61 percent of iron and steel, and 100 percent of automobile production.[38]

However, with the transformation of the domestic modes of production, with the commercialization and mechanization of farming, the increasing oligopolistic form of the economy, the internationalization of capital, chang-ing patterns of consumption along Western standards, and the domestic concentration and centralization of industrial power in the hands of oli-gopolistic industry, the Third World is experiencing new forms of depend-ency relations. This has resulted in greater industrialization and de-velopment, but at the cost of the denationalization of industry (control by foreign corporations over domestic manufacturing) and increasing dependency on imported machinery, technology, parts, and services (freight, legal and insurance payments, royalties, licensing and patent fees, trademarks, information, and so forth). This in turn results in a greater imbalance between exports and imports, that is, a balance-of-payments deficit increasing the foreign debt and further dependency on international banking institutions such as the World Bank and the International Monetary Fund.[39]

The financial dependency and high foreign debt leads to loss of control over national sovereignty: monetary and fiscal policy, import and foreign exchange controls, and domestic spending priorities.[40] These policies have dire consequences for social programs, welfare, the national distribution of income and land, and the growing poverty and inequality in Latin America, which requires more spending on military weapons and the national security state in order to stabilize and maintain this form of social system. This, in turn, only deepens the foreign debt and creates further dependency and class inequality.[41] The simple days of colonialism and surplus extraction in mining and commerce have now been replaced by more complicated forms of industrial and financial exploitation.

Other myths associated with these corporations are that they bring into the underdeveloped areas new jobs, tax monies, modern technology, and scarce capital investment, thereby helping to alleviate poverty, provide employment opportunities, and foster regional economic integration and development. However, the truth of the matter is that these corporations are often provided enormous tax breaks and incentives to invest in certain areas through the creation of tax-fee shelters. They are also capable of bypassing the tax laws through their economic power and technique of transfer price payments. They repatriate profits back to their mother country, increasing the foreign debt and fiscal problems of the underdeveloped countries. They introduce capital-intensive technology requiring skilled technicians, which only aggravates unemployment in labor-intensive societies. And finally, they do not necessarily bring scarce investment capital with them, since they obtain their investment money through local banking institutions. Eighty percent of capital financing of U.S. corporations is derived from within Latin America.[42] "There is strong statistical evidence to suggest that corporate industry is financing expansion in the United States from profits of poorer countries."[43] Their expansion into the Third World is precipitated by competition, profit, and their need for vertical and horizontal integration, needs which are part of the structural dynamic of the corporations and the international market system.[44] Thus the underdeveloped countries aid in their own underdevelopment.

Certain writers—Michael Novak, for example—make a Christian apologia for the transnationals. We are told they are the great producers of goods and services, the creators of wealth worldwide, the inventors of technology, and the roaring engines of human progress. ... But the fact is that this gigantic conglomerate operates in the service of capital alone. Its exclusive aim is the augmentation of surplus value and capitalist profit. As a productive, effective cell of capital, the transnational corporation is subject to the limitations of the phenomenon that subsumes it and incorporates it into its logic: capital.[45]

What are the institutional mechanisms used by advanced countries to integrate the Third World into a dependent international political economy? We have already mentioned some. They include the structural changes in Latin America in both agriculture (the use of the development model of modernization, cash crops, and agricultural export industry, the Green Revolution, increasing poverty, and capitalist land-tenure system) and manufacturing industry (science, technology, and social organization of capitalist production, international loans and stabilization policies of the International Monetary Fund, and profit repatriation).

Social scientists usually refer to Brazil as an example of a country that has moved along the linear path of economic development and material prosperity. In terms of the general statistics, there is some basis for this belief. Between 1956 and 1962 the Gross National Product (GNP) increased at an annual rate of 8 percent, while in the late 1960s and early 1970s it grew at a 10 percent annual increase. By 1971 it had the fastest-growing economy in the world, even outstripping West Germany and Japan. This economic expansion was visible not only in the traditional export areas of coffee, sugar, and soy beans, but the leading sectors of the economy were involved in the export of manufactured and industrial goods (automobiles, machinery, and textile goods).

This "economic miracle" has been attributed to Brazil because it followed the Western economic model. This was halted by the recessions, inflation, and oil crisis of the 1970s; the GNP declined by 50 percent in the 1970s. A closer, more detailed look at Brazil's economic growth indicates that, though the growth was real, it was limited to certain groups and areas of the country. It was also based on the faulty premise that foreign investment and borrowing would not hurt the country in the long run.[46] Between 1960 and 1979 the top 20 percent shared in this "miracle," while the annual income of the lowest 80 percent of the population dropped from a 45 percent to a 37 percent share of the national income. Frank argued that the economic development was based on the buying ability of just 5 percent of the Brazilian population. In 1972 the richest 20 percent of the population received 62.2 percent of the national income.

Because of its policies of import substitution, industrialization, and of encouraging self-sustaining economic growth, Brazil found itself in a dependent relationship with Western multinational corporations. Driven by the logic of its own dependent development, it was required to import the technologies, patents, and capital necessary to build and maintain its industrial organization. The result has been an increase in its foreign debt and serious problems with its balance of payments deficit. By the late 1980s the Brazilian foreign debt had reached well over $100 billion, which absorbed an enormous amount of its foreign exchange earnings.[47]

To counter this, the Brazilian government had to accept the stabilization policy recommendations of the International Monetary Fund (IMF). This was a major precondition to satisfy its foreign investors, especially after such high inflation rates tended to destabilize the country. But the stablization policy of the IMF contained in its "Articles of Agreement" requires the liberalization of foreign exchange and import controls, the devaluation of the exchange rate, greater openness to foreign investors, and a variety of domestic anti-inflation programs, such as control of bank credit (higher interest rates), control over government deficit (curbing social welfare spending, abolition of consumer subsidies, and increased taxes), and control over wages.

> To recapitulate: liberalization of exchanges and import controls is the heart of each IMF stablization programme, as required by the Articles of Agreement. All of the other components of the package: exchange rate adjustment, stabilization measures, and foreign aid financing of the deficit are measures which are necessary to counteract the predictable adverse effect of liberalization on the balance of payments.[48]

The result of the introduction of these programs in Brazil during the early 1970s has been a decline of real wages, breaking the unions, increasing class conflict, the overturn of a democratic government by the military, growing economic and social inequality, and a dramatic expansion of export subsidies for manufactured goods. This changed somewhat with the democratic election of President Fernando Collor de Mello in 1990. But now the fledgling democracy is hampered by almost insurmountable economic and financial problems. At the present time, 8 percent of the Gross National Product (GNP) of Brazil, which is the sixth largest industrial country in the world, is being used in the form of net transfer payments in order to repay outstanding loans from U.S. banks. It is interesting to remember that the economic crisis, inflation, unemployment, and social hardships of the Weimar Republic and the subsequent rise of Fascism were partly the result of a 2.5 percent net transfer of the German GNP as war reparations to the Allies after World War I. The net cash outflow in the form "debt reparations" of Brazil are three times this amount. Whether democracy can mature under these conditions of economic liberalism is an open historical question. However, the prognosis under the circumstances seems to be far from positive.[49]

Cheryl Payer, in *The Debt Trap*, argues that this system only results in a "debt slavery on an international scale," with underdevelopment being its inevitable consequence.[50] These programs also tended to aid domestic and international financial institutions, as well as nonproductive capital, at the expense of industrial development. They have resulted in declining industrial expansion in the seventies in both Brazil and Chile, increased bankruptcies, especially among the largest firms, declining labor productivity, higher unemployment, greater underutilization of manufacturing capacity, and finally, increasing dependency on foreign imports. "The result was the emergence of economies which were less developed, less competitive, more dependent on new loans, and suffering from increasingly precarious fiscal and financial status."[51] On top of these difficulties, there was the recession of 1980–1982 in the West, which resulted in a restricting of markets in industrial societies. The end product for all these transformations has been that, for the 1980s, according to Petras, there has been a further concentration of manufacturing among a small number of countries, lack of a depth penetration of industrialization into the Third World, the growth of statism, and the return to the more traditional export of primary goods and raw material. This in turn has led to increasing further reliance on the World Bank and International Monetary Fund for industrial financing and loan repayments, i.e., it has led to further dependency.

THE MISSING THEORY OF POLITICAL ECONOMY

The Bishops' Letter does not spend much time on the issue of Third World development and, as we have already seen, does not deal with the debates surrounding modernization and underdevelopment theories. The result is a very inadequate blending of moral principles and policy recommendations, which shows no historical or structural connections between the two. For Larry Rasmussen, the real weakness of both its domestic and Third World analyses is that it "leaves the concrete workings of economic power unarticulated."[52] The positive aspect of this letter is the clear manner in which the bishops define social ethics and their call to join together ethics and political economy. Ethics that deals only with individualistic moral values and actions without at the same time acknowledging the social context of that action is itself involved in structural sin. It is isolated individual action without real purpose or hope of realizing its moral values.

However, the bishops have failed to develop a comprehensive theory of political economy that would integrate historical and structural analysis of Third World political economy. Having failed to do this, they have fallen back into a moral philosophy that is grounded in a possessive individualism and positivism. They can only recapitulate the given institutions and their values, while radical social change becomes impossible, since the transformation of society and the international economy is always tied to the given institutional arrangements. Summarizing the ideas of Penny Lernoux concerning the bishops' Third World position, the *Religion and Society Report* said:

The draft is not good news for the poor in the Third World, says she. "The solutions suggested, such as aid to the poorest countries, are mere bandaids for the structural problems often originating in the U.S." The bishops should "examine our role as a colonial power" which is "dominated by a small number of giant, interlocking corporations and banks, notwithstanding the rhetoric about free enterprise. In failing to see ourselves as the Third World sees us—as a nation in social sin—the document opts for pie-in-the-sky solutions."[53]

Clodovis and Leonardo Boff are very aware of the political implications of the bishops' use of certain types of concepts in their study. By relying on a functionalist model of society which applies categories such as inequalities, disparities, backwardness, functions, and interdependence, the bishops failed to understand the real nature of economic and social dependence between the First and Third Worlds: class domination, economic exploitation, imperialism, and class conflict.[54] Without a more comprehensive view of social justice and political economy, we can only make society more efficient and possibly more humane, but we can never restructure it to conform to our ethical and political ideals of human dignity, freedom, and social justice.

In spite of its weaknesses, the Bishops' Letter remains an important contribution to contemporary discussions on ethics and political economy because it attempts to break the connection between ethics and Anglo-American analytic philosophy. If, however, the bishops do not go beyond this letter with a more comprehensive and critical theory of political economy, their initial breakthroughs will only result in further lost possibilities.

John Paul II's latest encyclical, *Centesimus Annus* ("The Hundredth Year"), published May 2, 1991, is another commemoration of Leo XIII's *Rerum Novarum*, surveying Catholic social teaching since 1891 and calling for a reform of the free-market system on a global scale in the wake of the collapse of communism. John Paul's particular focus is on the basic human needs of the poor in the Third World and their struggle for training, technology, and a share of today's high-tech market. In April of 1991 Catholic bishops and leading economists from Latin America met in the Dominican Republic to discuss issues raised in the church's social teachings and their impact on economic policy making.[55] Whether in papal letters or in such regional conferences, ideas about the common good and the human costs of economic systems will continue to be discussed and debated. These recent documents join an ever-expanding collection that constitute an important, if sometimes lost, tradition of critical voices that are redefining ethics and social justice.

TITLE ABBREVIATIONS USED IN NOTES

CA	*Centesimus Annus,* John Paul II (1991)
CHD	*Resolution on the Campaign for Human Development*, NCCB, National Conference of Catholic Bishops (1970)
CSO	*Statement on Church and Social Order*, NCWC, National Catholic Welfare Council (1940)
CST	*A Century of Social Teaching,* NCCB (1990)
DR	*Divini Redemptoris*, Pius XI (1937)
ECPC	*Ethical Choices and Political Challenges*, CCCB, Canadian Conference of Catholic Bishops (1983)
EHD	*The Economy: Human Dimensions*, NCCB, National Conference of Catholic Bishops (1975)
EJFA	*Economic Justice For All*, NCCB, National Conference of Catholic Bishops (1986)
GS	*Gaudium et Spes*, Vatican II (1965)
JIW	*Justice in the World*, Synod of Bishops (1971)
LE	*Laborem Exercens*, John Paul II (1981)
MM	*Mater et Magistra*, John XXIII (1961)
OA	*Octogesima Adveniens*, Paul VI (1971)
PC	*Present Crisis*, NCWC, National Catholic Welfare Council (1933)
PP	*Populorum Progressio*, Paul VI (1967)
PR	*Program of Reconstruction*, NCWC, National Catholic War Council (1919)
PT	*Pacem in Terris*, John XXIII (1963)
Puebla	*Third General Conference*, CELAM, General Conference of Latin American Bishops (1979)
QA	*Quadragesimo Anno*, Pius XI (1931)
RH	*Redemptor Hominis*, John Paul II (1979)
RN	*Rerum Novarum*, Leo XIII (1891)
SR	*Program of Social Reconstruction*, NCWC, National Catholic Welfare Council (1930)
SRS	*Sollicitudo Rei Socialis*, John Paul II (1987)
SU	*Statement on Unemployment*, NCWC, National Catholic Welfare Council (1930)

All references to the Bible are found in *The New Oxford Annotated Bible With The Apocrypha*, Revised Standard Version, ed. by Herbert May and Bruce Metzger (New York: Oxford University Press, 1977) unless noted otherwise.

NOTES

INTRODUCTION

1. National Conference of Catholic Bishops, *Economic Justice for All: Pastoral Letter on Catholic Social Teaching and the U.S. Economy* (Washington, D.C.: National Conference of Catholic Bishops, 1986). Abbreviated in Notes as EJFA.

2. Rembert Weakland, *A Conversation with Archbishop Rembert Weakland: Catholic Social Teaching and the U.S. Economy* (Washington, D.C.: American Enterprise Institute, 1985), p. 8.

3. William E. Simon, "The Bishops' Folly," *National Review* (April 5, 1985), p. 28.

4. Liberalism is defined as the philosophical and social system that has developed since the seventeenth century, characterized by possessive individualism, private property, natural rights, and a market economy. For an overview of the development of the political theory of liberalism, *see* C. B. MacPherson, *The Life and Times of Liberal Democracy* (Oxford, England: Oxford University Press, 1977) and Thomas Spragens, *The Irony of Liberal Reason* (Chicago: University of Chicago Press, 1981).

5. Russell Jacoby, *Social Amnesia: A Critique of Contemporary Psychology from Adler to Laing* (Boston: Beacon Press, 1975), p. 4. *See also* Peter Berger, *Invitation to Sociology: A Humanistic Perspective* (Garden City, N.Y.: Doubleday and Company, 1963), pp. 113–114.

6. Though the purpose of this work is to examine the relationships between ethics and political economy, this does not mean that ethics is reducible to economic and political theory. For a more comprehensive treatment of ethical issues, it would be necessary to get involved in social psychology, issues of culture and socialization, forms of legitimation, and the social institutions of everyday life. *See* Jürgen Habermas for the development of some of these issues in *The Theory of Communicative Action*, vol. 2, *Lifeworld and System: A Critique of Functionalist Reason*, trans. Thomas McCarthy (Boston: Beacon Press, 1981).

7. Joachim Ritter, *Metaphysik und Politik: Studien zu Aristoteles und Hegel* (Frankfurt/Main: Suhrkamp Verlag, 1969), p. 145, and his "Moralität und Sittlichkeit. Zu Hegels Auseinandersetzung mit der Kantischen Ethik," in Manfred Riedel, ed., *Materialien zu Hegels Rechtsphilosophie*, vol. 2 (Frankfurt/Main: Suhrkamp Verlag, 1974); Manfred Riedel, *Studien zu Hegels Rechtsphilosophie* (Frankfurt/Main: Suhrkamp Verlag, 1969), pp. 11–41; Herbert Schnädelbach, "Was ist Neoaristotelismus," in *Moralität und Sittlichkeit: Das Problem Hegels und die Diskursethik*, Wolfgang Kuhlmann, ed. (Frankfurt/Main: Suhrkamp Verlag, 1986), pp. 46–57; Otfried Höffe, *Ethik und Politik* (Frankfurt/Main: Suhrkamp Verlag, 1979), pp. 46ff.; Steven Smith, *Hegel's Critique of Liberalism: Rights in Context* (Chicago: University

of Chicago Press, 1989), p. 136; M. I. Finley, "Aristotle and Economic Analysis," in *Articles on Aristotle,* Vol. 2, *Ethics and Politics,* J. Barnes, M. Schofield, and R. Sorabji, eds. (New York: St. Martin's Press, 1977), pp. 146–158; and Martha Nussbaum, "Nature, Function, and Capability: Aristotle on Political Distribution," in *Oxford Studies in Ancient Philosophy,* Julia Annas and Robert Grimm, eds., supplementary volume (1988), pp. 145–184.

8. Joachim Ritter, *Hegel and the French Revolution,* trans. Richard Winfield (Cambridge, Mass.: MIT Press, 1982), p. 70 and pp. 165–168.

9. For an attempt to interpret Marx's economic and political theory in his later writings through his vision of classical antiquity and the Greek polis, *see* George McCarthy, *Marx and the Ancients: Classical Ethics, Social Justice, and Nineteenth-Century Political Economy* (Savage, Md.: Rowman and Littlefield Publishers, 1990), especially chapters one and two.

10. John Rawls, "A Theory of Justice," in *Justice and Economic Distribution,* J. Arthur and W. Shaw, eds. (Englewood Cliffs, N.J.: Prentice-Hall, Inc., 1978), p. 48.

1. SOCIAL JUSTICE AND THE CATHOLIC BISHOPS' LETTER

1. Phillip Berryman, *Our Unfinished Business: The U.S. Catholic Bishops' Letters on Peace and the Economy* (New York: Pantheon Books, 1989), p. 76.

2. The literature is extensive and continues to grow. *See* Nancy S. Barrett, "The Case for Collaboration," *Commonweal* CXII:12 (June 21, 1985), pp. 363–367; J. Brian Benestad, *The Pursuit of a Just Social Order: Policy Statements of the U.S. Catholic Bishops, 1966–80* (Washington, D.C.: Ethics and Public Policy Center, 1982); J. Brian Benestad and Francis J. Butler, eds., *Quest for Justice: A Compendium of the Statements of the United States Catholic Bishops on the Political and Social Order, 1966–1980* (Washington, D.C.: USCC, 1981); Berryman, *Our Unfinished Business,* pp. 75–135; Rebecca Chopp, "Making the Poor the Rich: Rhetoric vs. Strategy in the Pastoral Letter on the Economy," in *Religion and Economic Ethics,* ed. J. F. Gower (Lanham, Md.: University Press of America, 1990), pp. 263–269; John A. Coleman, S.J., "A New Catholic Voice on Social Issues," in *A Cry for Justice: The Churches and Synagogues Speak,* eds. R. M. Brown and S. T. Brown (New York: Paulist Press, 1989), pp. 31–45; R. Bruce Douglass, "At the Heart of the Letter," *Commonweal* CXII:12 (June 21, 1985), pp. 359–363; R. Bruce Douglass, ed., *The Deeper Meaning of Economic Life: Critical Essays on the U.S. Catholic Bishops' Pastoral Letter on the Economy* (Washington, D.C.: Georgetown University Press, 1986); Thomas M. Gannon, S.J., ed., *The Catholic Challenge to the American Economy: Reflections on the U.S. Bishops' Pastoral Letter on Catholic Social Teaching and the U.S. Economy* (New York: Macmillan, 1987); John W. Houck and Oliver F. Williams, eds., *Catholic Social Teaching and the U.S. Economy: Working Papers for a Bishops' Pastoral* (Washington, D.C.: University Press of America, 1984); Eugene Kennedy, *Re-Imagining American Catholicism: The American Bishops and their Pastoral Letters* (New York: Vintage, 1985), pp. 20–110; William E. Murnion, "Early Reactions to *Economic Justice For All*: Catholic Social Teaching and the U.S. Economy," *Horizons* 15:1 (Spring 1988), pp. 141–153; Robert Royal, ed., *Challenge and Responses: Critiques of the Catholic Bishops' Draft Letter on the U.S. Economy* (Washington, D.C.: Ethics and Public Policy Center, 1985); Charles R. Strain, ed., *Prophetic Visions and Economic Realities: Protestants, Jews and Catholics Confront the Bishops' Letter on the Economy* (Grand Rapids, Mich.: Eerdmans, 1989). The text

can be found in the following: Kennedy, *Re-Imagining*, pp. 187–310 (selections from the First Draft); Hugh J. Nolan, *Pastoral Letters of the United States Catholic Bishops, Vol. V: 1983–1988* (Washington, D.C.: USCC, 1989); Douglas Rasmussen and James Sterba, *Catholic Bishops and the Economy* (New Brunswick, N.J.: Transaction Publishers, 1990); Tom Bethell, "Mea Maxima Culpa?" *National Review* (April 15, 1988), pp. 34–36; and *Economic Justice For All: Pastoral Letter on Catholic Social Teaching and the U.S. Economy* (Washington, D.C.: NCCB, 1986). This last work is the text used for this study.

3. It is interesting to note that the bishops seem to be following the formal methodology of Aristotle's *Politics* (chapter seven) in the development of their argument. That is, as Aristotle began with an analysis of the mode of virtuous and ethical living in the *polis* in his *Nicomachean Ethics* and then examined the best political constitution to nurture such a virtuous character in the *Politics*, the bishops begin with a statement about the fundamental moral principle of human dignity (Kant and Rawls) and then argue to the appropriate economic and political structures that would give it life. Aristotle said: "The student who is going to make a suitable investigation of the best form of constitution must necessarily decide first of all what is the most desirable mode of life" (Aristotle, *The Politics*, trans. H. Rackham [London: William Heinemann, 1932], p. 533). This approach of Aristotle is examined further in an article by Martha Nussbaum as she concludes by connecting the Aristotelian method to nineteenth-century German social theory (Martha Nussbaum, "Nature, Function, and Capability: Aristotle on Political Distribution," *Oxford Studies in Ancient Philosophy*, ed. Julia Annas and Robert Grimm [Oxford, England: Clarendon Press, 1988], p. 147). This essay also appears in George McCarthy, ed., *Marx and Aristotle: Nineteenth-Century German Social Theory and Classical Antiquity* (Savage, Md.: Rowman and Littlefield Publishers, 1992).

4. EJFA, #135, p. 68.

5. Coleman, "A New Catholic Voice," p. 38. This section is largely based on Coleman's brief overview.

6. EJFA, #5, p. 3.

7. *Gaudium et Spes*, #43, quoted in EJFA, p. vii.

8. James V. Schall, "Catholicism and the American Experience," *This World*, no. 1 (Winter/Spring 1982), p. 19.

9. *Mater et Magistra*, #219–220, cited in EJFA, #28, p. 15; *see also* ibid., p. ix.

10. Ibid., #65, p. 34.

11. *See* Ibid., # 69–71, pp. 35–37.

12. Pius XI, *Divini Redemptoris* (1937), #49, quoted in EJFA, #120, p. 60; *see also* #72, n. 27, p. 37.

13. Ibid., #123, pp. 61–62.

14. Ibid., #83, p. 43; *see also* the pamphlet "Resolution of the United States Catholic Conference on the Twenty-fifth Anniversary of the Universal Declaration of Human Rights" (November 13, 1973) (Washington, D.C.: USCC, 1973).

15. Ibid., #124, p. 62; *see also* #99, n. 53, p. 51.

16. Ibid., #115, p. 58.

17. John Paul II, "Address to Business Men and Economic Managers," *L'Osservatore Romano*, English ed. (June 20, 1983), 9:1, quoted in ibid., #110, p. 56.

18. Ibid., #3, pp. 2–3.

19. Ibid., #1, p. 11.

20. EJFA, p. 12.

21. Administrative Committee of the National Catholic War Council, *Program of Social Reconstruction* (February 12, 1919). This and other statements by the bishops can be found in Hugh J. Nolan, ed., *Pastoral Letters of the United States Catholic Bishops*, 4 vols. (Washington, D.C.: USCC, 1984), and in David M. Byers, ed., *Justice in the Marketplace: Collected Statements of the Vatican and the United States Catholic Bishops on Economic Policy, 1891–1984* (Washington, D.C.: NCCB/USCC, 1985), pp. 365–475.

22. These can be found in Nolan and Byers; *see also Pastoral Letter on Marxist Communism* (Washington, D.C.: NCCB, 1980). For background, *see* A. I. Abell, *American Catholicism and Social Action, 1865–1950* (Notre Dame, Ind.: University of Notre Dame Press, 1963); Henry J. Browne, *The Catholic Church and the Knights of Labor* (Washington, D.C.: Catholic University of America Press, 1949); John Cronin, *Catholic Social Principles: The Social Teaching of the Catholic Church Applied for American Economic Life* (Milwaukee: Bruce, 1950); Charles E. Curran, *American Catholic Social Ethics: Twentieth-Century Approaches* (Notre Dame, Ind.: University of Notre Dame Press, 1982); James E. Roohan, *American Catholics and the Social Question, 1865–1900* (New York: Arno Press, 1976).

23. SR, #3–6, Byers, pp. 368–369; *see* EHD, Appendix, Byers, p. 475.

24. SR, #9, Byers, p. 370.

25. Robert D. Cross, *The Emergence of Liberal Catholicism in America* (Chicago: Quadrangle Books, 1968), p. 109.

26. SR, #40, Byers, pp. 382–383.

27. Both quoted in Kennedy, *Re-Imagining*, p. 31.

28. J. T. Ellis, quoted in James Hennesey, S.J., *American Catholics: A History of the Roman Catholic Community in the United States* (New York: Oxford Press, 1981), p. 259; the point is also made by George G. Higgins, "Toward a New Society," in *Readings in Moral Theology No. 5: Official Catholic Social Teaching*, Charles E. Curran and Richard A. McCormick, S.J., eds. (New York: Paulist Press, 1986), p. 53. *See* John A. Ryan, *A Better Economic Order* (New York: Harper, 1935); *A Living Wage* (New York: Macmillan, 1906); and *Distributive Justice*, 3d ed. (New York: Macmillan, 1942); the biographical details are supplied in F. L. Broderick, *Right Reverend New Dealer, John A. Ryan* (New York: Macmillan, 1963).

29. SR, #12, 13, Byers, pp. 371–372.

30. SR, #34, Byers, p. 380.

31. SR, #36, Byers, p. 381.

32. Mel Piehl, *Breaking Bread: The Catholic Worker and the Origin of Catholic Radicalism in America* (Philadelphia: Temple University Press, 1982), p. 37; Kennedy, *Re-Imagining*, pp. 30–32.

33. Cardinal Edward Mooney, quoted in Schall, "Catholicism and the American Experience," p. 12.

34. Ibid.

35. SU, #3, Byers, p. 393.

36. Ibid.

37. PC, #18, Byers, p. 402.

38. PC, #19, 20, Byers, pp. 402–403.

39. PC, #22, 21, Byers, p. 403.

40. Aaron Abell, ed., *American Catholic Thought on Social Questions* (Indianapolis: Bobbs-Merrill, 1968), pp. 377–378.

41. Ibid., pp. 392–393.

42. Ibid., p. 433; for the text *see* ibid., pp. 433–447.

43. *See* Byers, pp. 444–445.

44. Karl Marx, quoted in *A Statement on Man's Dignity* (1953), #22, Byers, p. 452.

45. EHD, #17, Byers, p. 473.

46. *See* Byers, p. 446.

47. Benestad, *The Pursuit of a Just Social Order*, p. 103.

48. Ibid., p. 102.

49. Kennedy, *Re-Imagining*, p. 103; *see* ibid., pp. 102–107.

50. Ibid., p. 105.

51. Schall, "Catholicism and the American Experience," pp. 14–15.

52. HED, #19, Byers, pp. 473–474; Schall, ibid., p. 15.

53. *Pastoral Letter on Marxist Communism* (Washington, D.C.: NCCB, 1980), p. 1.

54. Ibid., p. 14; the letter cites John Paul II, "Address to Rural and Peasant People (Oaxaca)," *Origins* VIII, #34 (February 8, 1979); Paul VI, *Populorum Progressio*, #24.

55. Pastoral Letter, pp. 19–20.

56. Ibid., p. 20.

57. Ibid.

58. Berryman, *Our Unfinished Business*, p. 75.

59. Michael Novak, "Polarizing Catholics?," *National Review* (November 15, 1985), p. 46.

60. Works cited include: Martin Anderson, *Welfare: The Political Economy of Welfare Reform in the United States* (Stanford, Calif.: Hoover Institute Press, 1978), Charles Murray, *Losing Ground: American Social Policy 1950–1980* (New York: Basic Books, 1984); Milton Friedman, *Capitalism and Freedom* (Chicago: University of Chicago Press, 1962); Peter L. Berger and Richard J. Neuhaus, *To Empower People: The Role of Mediating Structures in Public Policy* (Washington, D.C.: American Enterprise Institute, 1977); Jack A. Meyer, ed., *Meeting Human Needs: Toward a New Public Philosophy* (Washington, D.C.: American Enterprise Institute, 1982). On the other side works cited include: Gar Alperovitz and Jeff Faux, *Rebuilding America: A Blueprint for the New Economy* (New York: Pantheon, 1984); Robert Kuttner, *The Economic Illusion* (Boston: Houghton Mifflin Co., 1984); S. Danzinger and P. Gottschalk, "The Poverty of Losing Ground," *Challenge* 28:2 (May/June 1985); Martin Carnoy, Derek Shearer, and Russell Rumberger, *A New Social Contract* (New York: Harper and Row, 1983); Charles E. Lindblom, *Politics and Markets* (New York: Basic Books, 1977); Lester Thurow, *The Zero-Sum Society* (New York: Basic Books, 1980); Michael Harrington, *The New American Poverty* (New York: Holt, Rinehart, and Winston, 1984); J. L. Palmer and Isabel V. Sawhill, eds., *The Reagan Record: An Assessment of America's Changing Domestic Priorities* (Cambridge, Mass.: Bollinger, 1984); and M. N. Baily and Arthur M. Okun, eds., *The Battle Against Unemployment and Inflation*, 3d ed. (New York: Norton, 1982).

61. *See* Robert Benne, "Two Cheers for the Bishops," in *God, Goods and the Common Good*, ed. Charles P. Lutz (Minneapolis, Minn.: Augsburg Press, 1987), pp. 57–58, and Kennedy, *Re-Imagining America*, p. 99.

62. E. F. Schumacher, *Small Is Beautiful* (New York: Harper and Row, 1973); see EJFA, n. 116, p. 136; cf. R. F. Sizemore and D. K. Swearer, *Ethics, Wealth and Salvation: A Study in Buddhist Social Ethics* (Charleston, SC: University of South Carolina Press, 1990).

63. *See* Chopp, "Making the Poor the Rich," pp. 263–269.

64. Ibid., pp. 266–267.

65. Stuart M. Speiser, *Ethical Economics and the Faith Community: How We Can Have Work and Ownership for All* (Bloomington, Ind.: Meyer-Stone, 1989), p. 75.

66. EJFA, #298, p. 147; quoted in Berryman, *Our Unfinished Business*, p. 106.

67. Arthur Jones, "Diverse voices add their two cents to economic debate," *NCR* 26:21 (March 16, 1990), p. 16.

68. EJFA, #26, p. 13.

69. The citations from Protestant sources in biblical studies, church history, and religious ethics are noteworthy. Among these are works by Claus Westermann, Martin Hengel, Martin Marty, Richard J. Neuhaus, Thomas Ogletree, Jon Gunnemann, and Charles W. Powers.

70. Benne, "Two Cheers," p. 55; *see The Challenge of Peace* (Washington, D.C.: USCC, 1983); Philip J. Murnion, ed., *Catholics and Nuclear War: A Commentary* (New York: Crossroad, 1983); Berryman, *Our Unfinished Business*, pp. 23–74; George Weigel, *Tranquilitas Ordinis: The Present Failure and Future Promise of American Catholic Thought on War and Peace* (New York: Oxford Press, 1987); Ronald G. Musto, *The Catholic Peace Tradition* (Maryknoll, NY: Orbis Books, 1986); Judith Dwyer, ed., *The Catholic Bishops and Nuclear War* (Washington, D.C.: Georgetown University Press, 1984).

71. Curran, *American Catholic Social Ethics*, p. 284; Cross, *The Emergence of Liberal Catholicism in America*.

72. See Charles A. Fracchia, *Second Spring: The Coming of Age of U.S. Catholicism* (San Francisco: Harper & Row, 1980), p. 55. *See also* John J. Mitchell, *Critical Voices in American Catholic Economic Thought* (New York: Paulist Press, 1989); Neil Betten, *Catholic Activism and the Industrial Worker* (Gainesville, Fla.: University Presses of Florida, 1976); Mary Fox, *Peter E. Dietz, Labor Priest* (Notre Dame, Ind.: University of Notre Dame Press, 1953); Philip Gleason, *The Conservative Reformers: German-American Catholics and the Social Order* (Notre Dame, Ind.: University of Notre Dame Press, 1968); Colman Barry, O.S.B., *The Catholic Church and the German-Americans* (Washington, D.C.: Catholic University of America Press, 1953); Peter Marx, *Virgil Michel* (Collegeville, Penna.: 1957); Dorothy Day, *By Little and By Little: The Selected Writings of Dorothy Day*, ed. Robert Ellsberg (New York: Knopf, 1983); *The Long Loneliness* (New York: Harper & Row, 1963); *Loaves and Fishes* (New York: Harper & Row, 1952); and William Miller, *Dorothy Day* (San Francisco: Harper and Row, 1982); Katharine Temple, "Peter Maurin—Social Realism and Utopian Idealism," *The Catholic Worker* LVII:3 (May 1990); Piehl, *Breaking Bread*; Peter Maurin, *The Green Revolution* (Fresno, Calif.: Academy Guild Press, 1961); Wayne Lobue, "Public Theology and the Catholic Worker," *Cross Currents* 26 (1976).

73. The term *Americanism* is not used in the technical, theological sense, referring to those reputed heresies concerning the grace of the Holy Spirit, obedience to spiritual hierarchy, and modification of Catholic doctrine for pragmatic purposes of evangelization that were condemned as heretical by Pope Leo XIII in the encyclical *Testem Benevolentiae* (1899) and denied as a doctrinal position held by the American church by Archbishop Ireland and most of the hierarchy. *See* R. Aubert, et al., *The Christian Centuries,* vol. 5: *The Church in a Secularized Society* (New York: Paulist Press, 1978), p. 45.

74. Archbishop Ireland, *The Church and Modern Society*, 2 vols. (St. Paul, Minn.:

The Pioneer Press, 1905), 1:76–77, quoted in William Simon and Michael Novak, eds., *Toward the Future: Catholic Social Thought and the U. S. Economy* (New York: Lay Commission on Catholic Social Teaching and the U.S. Economy, 1984), p. 14; it was Ireland who allowed John A. Ryan, whose economic doctrines of reform he did not share, to teach in the St. Paul Seminary; Kennedy, *Re-Imagining*, p. 28; James H. Moynihan, *The Life of Archbishop John Ireland* (New York: Harper & Brothers, 1953); Joseph Nocera, "Making Capitalism Moral," *The Washington Monthly* (September 1985): 39–47.

75. *See* Simon and Novak, *Toward the Future*, pp. 17–24.

76. *See*, for example, E. A. Keller, *Christianity and American Capitalism* (Chicago: Heritage Foundation, 1954); J. P. Fitzpatrick, "The Encyclicals and the United States," *Thought* (Autumn 1954): 391–402; George Weigel, *Catholicism and the Renewal of American Democracy* (New York: Paulist Press, 1989).

77. *See* Ryan, *A Living Wage, Distributive Justice*; John Courtney Murray, S.J., *We Hold These Truths: Catholic Reflections on the American Proposition* (New York: Sheed and Ward, 1960); John A. Coleman, S.J., "Vision and Praxis in American Theology: Orestes Brownson, John A. Ryan and John Courtney Murray," *Theological Studies* 37 (1976): 3–40.

78. David Hollenbach, S.J., *Justice, Peace, & Human Rights: American Catholic Social Ethics in a Pluralistic Context* (New York: Crossroad, 1988), pp. 103, 105–106; Berryman, *Our Unfinished Business*, pp. 132–134; EJFA, #122, pp. 60–61, 61 n.73.

79. EJFA, #7, p. vii.

80. Ibid., #9, p. viii.

81. Ibid., #10, p. viii.

82. Ibid., #6, p. 4.

83. Ibid., #7, p. 4; a condemnation of all forms of racism is found in #182, p. 90.

84. Ibid., #8, pp. 4–5.

85. Ibid., #74, p. 38.

86. Berryman, *Our Unfinished Business*, p. 130–131.

87. Ibid., p. 125.

88. Jaroslav Pelikan, *Jesus Through the Centuries: His Place in the History of Culture* (New Haven, Conn.: Yale University Press, 1985), pp. 218–219.

89. Julia Ward Howe, "The Battle Hymn of the Republic," quoted in ibid., p. 219; the popularity of the hymn in Catholic services after the funeral of Senator Robert Kennedy demonstrates the contemporary ecumenical openness of Catholic liturgy to American Protestant hymns and piety, but also a basis for those who argue for a shared religious vocabulary with which to address social issues. Note also in contemporary usage the text is usually changed to read: "let us *live* to make men free." Apparently the ultimate sacrifice is not needed now to achieve freedom.

90. NCCB, "Eucharistic Prayer for Thanksgiving Day," *The Sacramentary* (New York: Catholic Book Publishing Co., 1985), p. 541. The commemorative prayers of this civic remembrance ordered by President Lincoln do not mention Native Americans, slaves, or the struggle involved in the quest for freedom.

91. *See* Robert Bellah, et al., *Habits of the Heart: Individualism and Commitment in American Life* (Berkeley, Calif. University of California Press, 1985); Donald L. Gelpi, S.J., ed., *Beyond Individualism: Toward a Retrieval of Moral Discourse in America* (Notre Dame, Ind.: University of Notre Dame Press, 1989); Berryman, *Our Unfinished Business*, pp. 20–22.

92. Bellah, *Habits of the Heart*, p. 249; *see* Robert T. Handy, "Walter Rauschen-busch: An Introduction," in *The Social Gospel in America, 1870–1920*, ed. Robert T. Handy (New York: Oxford Press, 1966), pp. 253–263; D. McCann, *Christian Realism and Liberation Theology* (Maryknoll, New York: Orbis Books, 1981); Richard Fox, *Reinhold Niebuhr* (New York: Pantheon, 1985); Alastair MacIntyre, *After Virtue: A Study in Moral Theory* (Notre Dame, Ind.: University of Notre Dame Press, 1981); Rebecca Chopp, "Making the Poor the Rich," pp. 263–269; William McInerny, "Scripture and the Social Order: 'Paradigmatic Construals' of Walter Rauschenbush," ibid., ed. J. F. Gowar, pp. 237–248.

93. Berryman, *Our Unfinished Business*, p. 22.

94. Madonna Kolbenschlag, "The American Economy, Religious Values, and a New Moral Imperative," *Cross Currents* XXXIV:2 (Summer 1984): 168–169, 157; *see* Harry C. Boyte, *Community Is Possible: Repairing America's Roots* (New York: Harper & Row, 1984).

95. *See* Roger G. Betsworth, *Social Ethics: An Examination of American Moral Transitions* (Louisville, Ky: Westminster/John Knox, 1990); Colin Campbell, *The Romantic Ethic and the Spirit of Modern Consumerism* (Oxford: Basil Blackwell, 1990); Lawrence Chenoweth, *The American Dream of Success* (Duxbury, Mass.: Duxbury Press, 1974).

96. *See* Dennis P. McCann, *New Experiment in Democracy: The Challenge for American Catholicism* (Kansas City, Mo.: Sheed & Ward, 1987).

97. EJFA, #27, p. 13, quoted in David Hollenbach, *Justice, Peace, & Human Rights*, p. 83.

2. CONSERVATIVE CRITIQUE OF THE BISHOPS' LETTER

1. William E. Simon and Michael Novak, *Toward the Future: Catholic Social Thought and the U.S. Economy, A Lay Letter* (N.Y.: Lay Commission on Catholic Social Teaching and the U.S. Economy, 1984), p. ix.

2. Ibid., pp. 4–5.

3. EJFA, #14, p. ix.

4. Simon and Novak, *Toward the Future*, p. 8.

5. Ibid., p. 7.

6. Ibid., p. 8.

7. For an attempt to stress the similarities between the Bishops' Letter and the lay commission's report, *see* Peter Flanigan, "The Pastoral and the Letter," *America* (January 5, 1985), and Michael Novak, "Toward Consensus: Suggestions for Revising the First Draft, Part I," *Catholicism in Crisis* (March 1985), p. 7.

8. EJFA, #28, p. 15.

9. Michael Novak in "Four Views of the Bishops' Pastoral, The Lay Letter, and the U.S. Economy," John Langan, et al., *This World*, no. 10 (Winter 1985), p. 113, recognizes that the concepts of dignity used by the bishops and the lay commission are quite different.

10. Ibid.

11. Ibid., pp. 113–114.

12. Anthony Tambasco, "Option for the Poor," in *The Deeper Meaning of Economic Life: Critical Essays on the U.S. Catholic Bishops' Pastoral Letter on the Economy*, ed. R. Bruce Douglass (Washington, D.C.: Georgetown University Press, 1986), p. 50.

13. Irving Kristol, *Two Cheers for Capitalism* (New York: New American Library, 1978), p. 177, and Walter Block, *The U.S. Bishops and Their Critics* (Vancouver, Canada: Fraser Institute, 1986), p. 11.

14. Kristol, *Two Cheers for Capitalism*, p. 177.

15. Simon and Novak, *Toward the Future*, p. 9.

16. EJFA, #69 and 70, pp. 35–36.

17. For an analysis of the political, scientific, epistemological, and psychological frames or unconscious assumptions underlying liberalism that are incompatible with a broader and more comprehensive understanding of democracy, *see* Benjamin Barber, *Strong Democracy: Participatory Politics for a New Age* (Berkeley, Calif.: University of California Press, 1984).

18. Franz J. Hinkelammert, *The Ideological Weapons of Death* (Maryknoll, N.Y.: Orbis Books, 1986), pp. 5–42.

19. Spragens, *The Irony of Liberal Reason*, pp. 115–118.

20. Novak, "Toward Consensus," p. 14.

21. Ibid.

22. For a discussion of the differences between these philosophical traditions, *see* Tom Campbell, *The Left and Rights: A Conceptual Analysis of the Idea of Socialist Rights* (London: Routledge and Kegan Paul, 1983) and Philip Green, *Retrieving Democracy: In Search of Civic Responsibility* (Totowa, N.J.: Rowman and Allanheld, 1985).

23. Simon, "The Bishops' Folly," p. 29.

24. Benne, "Two Cheers For the Bishops," p. 50.

25. Novak, "Four Views of the Bishops' Pastoral," p. 111.

26. Simon and Novak, *Toward the Future*, p. 12. The view that private property is a natural right represents a serious misrepresentation of Catholic social teaching, as we have already seen in chapter two.

27. Ibid., p. 20.

28. John Paul II, "Laborem Exercens," in *The Priority of Labor*, ed. Gregory Baum (New York: Paulist Press, 1982), p. 112.

29. Simon and Novak, *Toward the Future*, p. 26.

30. Ibid., p. 28.

31. Ibid., p. 37.

32. Ibid., p. 58.

33. Ibid., p. 63.

34. Ibid., p. 65.

35. Ibid., p. 77.

36. Murray, *Losing Ground*, p. 9.

37. Anderson, *Welfare*, pp. 23ff.

38. Murray, *Losing Ground*, pp. 64–65.

39. Ibid., pp. 154–155.

40. *See also* Anderson, *Welfare*, pp. 98–127.

41. George Gilder, *Wealth and Poverty* (New York: Basic Books, 1981), p. 115.

42. Ibid., p. 122.

43. Jeanne Kirkpatrick has said that these types of economic and social rights have the form of a "letter to Santa Claus" and have no foundation either in "nature, experience, or probability." Kirkpatrick, "Human Rights and Foreign Policy," in *Human Rights and American Foreign Policy*, ed. F. Baumann (Gambier, Ohio: Public Affairs Conference Center, 1981). *See also* Milton Friedman, "Good Ends, Bad

Means," in Gannon, *The Catholic Challenge to the American Economy*, p. 106.

44. EJFA, #80, p. 42.

45. For an analysis of the theological foundations for the New American Experiment, *see* M. E. Jegaen and C. K. Wilber, *The Earth is the Lord's: Essays in Stewardship* (New York: Paulist Press, 1977); Charles Wilber and Kenneth Jameson, "Toward a New Social Contract," in *An Inquiry into the Poverty of Economics* (Notre Dame, Ind.: University of Notre Dame Press, 1983); McCann, *New Experiment in Democracy*; Dennis McCann, "New Experiment in Democracy: Blueprint for Political Economy?," in *Prophetic Visions and Economic Realities*, ed. C. Strain (Grand Rapids, Mich.: William B. Eerdmans Publishing Company, 1989).

46. For a theoretical overview of the issue of democratic participation and the New American Experiment, *see* chapter ten in the work of the bishops' committee's chief economic adviser, Charles Wilber—Charles Wilber and Kenneth Jameson, *An Inquiry into the Poverty of Economics* (Notre Dame, Ind.: University of Notre Dame Press, 1983).

47. Michael Novak, "Where the Second Draft Errs," *America* (January 18, 1989), p. 24.

48. Simon, "The Bishops' Folly," p. 28.

49. Novak, "Toward Consensus," p. 9.

50. Block, *The U.S. Bishops and Their Critics*, p. 60.

51. This position is best articulated in the "structural-functionalist" perspective on class in Kingsley Davis and Wilbert Moore, "Some Principles of Stratification," *American Sociological Review*, vol. 10 (1945), pp. 242–249.

52. Friedman, *Capitalism and Freedom*, p. 169.

53. Kristol, *Two Cheers for Capitalism*, p. 176.

54. Novak, "Where the Second Draft Errs," p. 24 and "Four Views," p. 114; Block, "The U.S. Bishops' Report," p. 61; Robert Benne, "The Bishops Letter—A Protestant Reading," in Gannon, *The Catholic Challenge to the American Economy*, p. 83.

55. Spragens, *The Irony of Liberal Reason*, pp. 307–308.

56. Benne, "Two Cheers for the Bishops," p. 49. *See also* William Sullivan and Richard Madsen, "The Bishops and their Critics," *Commonweal* (February 26, 1988), p. 119.

57. Novak, "Toward Consensus," p. 11.

58. Friedman, *Capitalism and Freedom*, p. 9.

59. Milton Friedman, "Good Ends, Bad Means," in Gannon, *The Catholic Challenge to the American Economy,* p. 106.

60. Bloch, "The U.S. Bishops' Report," p. 60.

3. THE CREED OF CONSERVATIVE ETHICS

1. Michael Novak, *The American Vision: An Essay on the Future of Democratic Capitalism* (Washington, D.C.: American Enterprise Institute, 1978).

2. Daniel Bell, *Cultural Contradictions of Capitalism* (New York: Basic Books, 1976).

3. Michael Novak, *The Spirit of Democratic Capitalism* (New York: American Enterprise Institute and Simon and Schuster Publication, 1982), pp. 49ff.

4. Peter Bachrach, *The Theory of Democratic Elitism: A Critique* (Boston: Little, Brown and Company, 1967).

5. Novak, *The American Vision*, p. 11.

6. Novak, *The Spirit of Democratic Capitalism*, p. 63.

7. An example of a strong theory of values grounded in neo-Platonism is Allan Bloom, *The Closing of the American Mind* (New York: Simon and Schuster, 1987).

8. Novak, *The Spirit of Democratic Capitalism*, p. 85.

9. Joshua Cohen and Joel Rogers, *On Democracy: Toward a Transformation of American Society* (Harmondsworth, England: Penguin Books, 1983), p. 159.

10. John Clark, quoted in Walter Adams and James Brock, *Dangerous Pursuits: Mergers and Acquisitions in the Age of Wall Street* (New York: Pantheon Books, 1989), p. 148.

11. Michael Best and William Connolly, *The Politicized Economy* (Lexington, Mass.: D.C. Heath and Company, 1982), pp. 59–71.

12. C. B. MacPherson, *The Political Theory of Possessive Individualism: Hobbes to Locke* (London: Oxford University Press, 1962).

13. Novak, *The Spirit of Democratic Capitalism*, p. 106.

14. Ibid.

15. For a critical analysis from a historical perspective *see* Karl Polanyi, *The Great Transformation: The Political and Economic Origins of Our Time* (Boston: Beacon Press, 1944).

16. C. B. MacPherson, *Democratic Theory: Essays in Retrieval* (Oxford, England: Clarendon Press, 1973), pp. 32, 94.

17. Novak, *The Spirit of Democratic Capitalism*, p. 107.

18. Ibid., p. 109.

19. Ibid., p. 112.

20. C. B. MacPherson, *The Life and Times of Liberal Democracy*, p. 61.

21. John Stuart Mill, *The Principles of Political Economy* (Harmondsworth, England: Penguin Books, 1970), p. 133.

22. Novak, *The Spirit of Democratic Capitalism*, p. 115.

23. John Locke, *Second Treatise of Government* (Indianapolis, Ind.: Bobbs-Merrill Company, 1952), p. 15.

24. Rogers Brubacker, *The Limits of Rationality: An Essay on the Social and Moral Thought of Max Weber* (Boston: Allen and Unwin, 1984).

25. William Ophuls, *Ecology and the Politics of Scarcity* (San Francisco: W. H. Freeman and Company, 1977), pp. 146–152.

26. Ibid., p. 146.

27. David Schweickart, *Capitalism or Worker Control?: An Ethical and Economic Appraisal* (New York: Praeger, 1980), p. 108.

28. Ophuls, *Ecology and the Politics of Scarcity*, p. 141.

29. Ibid., p. 151. *See also* Kirkpatrick Sale, *Human Scale* (New York: Perigee Books, 1980); Hazel Henderson, *The Politics of the Solar Age: Alternatives to Economics* (Garden City, N.Y.: Anchor Books, 1981); and Murray Bookchin, *Post-Scarcity Anarchism* (Berkeley, Calif.: The Ramparts Press, 1971).

30. Peter Singer, "Rights and the Market," in *Justice and Economic Distribution*, ed. J. Arthur and W. Shaw (Englewood Cliffs, N.J.: Prentice-Hall, Inc., 1978), p. 211.

31. Ibid., p. 212.

32. For an examination of the underlying assumptions of the natural-rights tradition, the definition of individual rights and capabilities in terms of market competition and possessive individualism, and the nature of rights and equality in

democratic socialism, *see* Green, *Retrieving Democracy,* pp. 8, 36; Campbell, *The Left and Rights,* pp. 103ff.; David Held, *Models of Democracy* (Stanford, Calif: Stanford University Press, 1987), pp. 267ff.; Allen Buchanan, *Ethics, Efficiency, and the Market* (Totowa, N.J.: Rowman and Allanheld Publishers, 1985), pp. 80ff; Ronald Mason, *Participatory and Workplace Democracy: A Theoretical Development in Critique of Liberalism* (Carbondale, Ill.: Southern Illinois University Press, 1982), pp. 3–57; Ernst Block, *Natural Law and Human Dignity,* trans. Dennis Schmidt (Cambridge, Mass.: MIT Press, 1986), p. 63; R. H. Tawney, *Equality* (London: Allen and Unwin, 1964), pp. 164–173; Samuel Bowles and Herbert Gintis, *Democracy and Capitalism: Property, Community, and the Contradictions of Modern Social Thought* (New York: Basic Books, 1986), pp. 3–63; Kuttner, *The Economic Illusion,* pp. 1–49; Kai Nielsen, *Equality and Liberty: A Defense of Radical Egalitarianism* (Totowa, N.J.: Rowman and Allanheld Publishers, 1985), pp. 3–99; William Ryan, *Equality* (New York: Vintage Books, 1981), pp. 3–65, 186–211; Cohen and Rogers, *On Democracy,* pp. 146–183; and the essays by Douglass, Briefs, and Mara in *The Deeper Meaning of Economic Life,* ed. R. Bruce Douglass.

These works provide the foundations for the development of a critical theory of needs which would integrate theories of social justice, human rights, individual capabilities and self-realization, and a critique of political economy. In creating a theory of needs to counteract the narrow theory of natural rights, we would draw upon the Hebrew prophets, Aristotle, Rousseau, Hegel, and Marx. This, however, is a project for another collaborative book.

33. Novak, *The Spirit of Democratic Capitalism,* p. 79.

34. Rawls, *Theory of Justice,* p. 21.

35. Ibid., p. 83.

36. Ibid., p. 62. The first principle protects certain types of liberties such as the right to personal property. In a different essay entitled "A Kantian Conception of Equality," in *Property, Profits, and Economic Justice,* ed. Virginia Held (Belmont, Calif.: Wadsworth Publishing Company, 1980), p. 203, Rawls makes perfectly clear that the basic liberty or right to personal property does not entail a right to private property or the "means of production." It is the failure to develop the class and power implications of this distinction which has produced some very real problems for Rawls's social theory.

37. Norman Daniels, "Equal Liberty and Unequal Worth of Liberty," in *Reading Rawls,* ed. Norman Daniels (Stanford, Calif.: Stanford University Press, 1989), pp. 253–254.

38. Rawls, *Theory of Justice,* p. 78.

39. Daniels, "Equal Liberty and Unequal Worth of Liberty," p. 253. *See also* Carole Pateman's "Introduction" to Mason's *Participatory and Workplace Democracy,* p. xiv, and Buchanan, *Ethics, Efficiency, and the Market,* pp. 81ff.

40. Wilber and Jameson, *An Inquiry into the Poverty of Economics,* p. 235, and J. Philip Wogaman, *Economics and Ethics: A Christian Inquiry* (Philadelphia: Fortress Press, 1986), pp. 20ff.

41. Pateman, "Introduction," p. xiv.

42. Robert Benne, *The Ethic of Democratic Capitalism: A Moral Reassessment* (Philadelphia: Fortress Press, 1981), p. 62.

43. Rawls, *Theory of Justice,* p. 75. Rawls concludes his analysis of the second principle as follows on page 83: "Social and economic inequalities are to be arranged so that they are both (a) to the greatest benefit of the least advantaged

and (b) attached to offices and positions open to all under conditions of fair equality of opportunity."

44. Benne, *The Ethic of Democratic Capitalism*, p. 59.

45. Joseph Schumpeter, *Capitalism, Socialism and Democracy* (New York: Harper and Row, Publishers, 1950), p. 269.

46. Ibid., p. 242.

47. Ibid., p. 263.

48. Samuel Huntington, "The United States," in *The Crisis of Democracy: Report on the Governability of Democracies to the Trilateral Commission*, ed. Michael Crozier, Samuel Huntington, and Joji Watanuki (New York: New York University Press, 1975), p. 114. *See also* Hinkelammert, *The Ideological Weapons of Death*, pp. 98–124; and Jürgen Habermas, *Legitimation Crisis*, trans. Thomas McCarthy (Boston: Beacon Press, 1975), p. 37.

49. Schumpeter, *Capitalism, Socialism and Democracy*, p. 264.

50. Ibid., p. 273.

51. Novak, *The Spirit of Democratic Capitalism*, p. 84.

52. Bachrach, *Theory of Democratic Elitism*, p. 24.

53. Spragens, *The Irony of Liberal Reason*, p. 306.

54. MacPherson, *The Life and Times of Liberal Democracy*, p. 78.

55. Jürgen Habermas, *Toward a Rational Society: Student Protests, Science, and Politics*, trans. J. Shapiro (Boston: Beacon Press, 1970), p. 103. *See also* Habermas, *Legitimation Crisis*, p. 70.

56. Huntington, "The United States," p. 114; *see also* Holly Sklar, ed., *Trilateralism: The Trilateral Commission and Elite Planning for World Management* (Boston, Mass: South End Press, 1980).

57. Hinkelammert, *Ideological Weapons of Death*, p. 123.

58. Habermas, *Toward a Rational Society*, p. 111.

59. For another analysis of the disappearance of democracy using a different analysis of interest-group pluralism, *see* Theodore Lowi, *The End of Liberalism: Ideology, Policy, and the Crisis of Authority* (New York: W.W. Norton and Company, 1969), pp. 27, 86, 96–97.

60. Claus Offe, *Contradictions of the Welfare State*, ed. J. Keane (Cambridge, Mass.: MIT Press, 1984), pp. 51ff.

61. Rawls, *A Theory of Justice*, p. 574.

62. Benne, *The Ethic of Democratic Capitalism*, p. 145.

63. Benjamin Barber, "Justifying Justice: Problems of Psychology, Politics and Measurement in Rawls," in *Reading Rawls*, ed. Norman Daniels, p. 309.

64. This notion that liberalism is logically incoherent is a theme developed by Karl Marx, *Capital: A Critique of Political Economy*, vols. I, II, III (New York: International Publishers, 1967); Tony Smith, *The Role of Ethics in Social Theory: Essays From a Habermasian Perspective* (Albany, N.Y.: State University of New York Press, 1991), chapter 8; Barber, *Strong Democracy;* Cohen and Rogers, *On Democracy*, chapter 6; MacIntyre, *After Virtue*, chapter 5; and Thomas Spragens, *Reason and Democracy* (Durham, N.C.: Duke University Press, 1990), introduction and chapter 1.

4. TOWARD A CRITICAL THEORY OF POLITICAL ECONOMY

1. Joseph Califano, "The Prophets and the Profiteers," *America*, vol. 152 (January 5, 1985), p. 6; Andrew Greeley, "The Bishops and the Economy: A 'Radical'

Dissent," *America*, vol. 152 (January 5, 1985), p. 19; Edward Hennessy, Jr., "A Pastoral for the Poor, Not the Economy," *America*, vol. 152 (January 5, 1985); Patricia Scharber Lefevere, "Economic Pastoral Called Morally Self-Indulgent," *National Catholic Reporter*, vol. 21, no. 25 (January 25, 1985).

2. Alexander Cockburn and Robert Pollin, "Hardheads and Bishops: How to Talk About Economic Strategy," *The Nation* (February 28, 1987), p. 245.

3. EJFA, #12, p. ix.

4. Larry Rasmussen, "The Morality of Power and the Power of Morality," in Strain, *Prophetic Visions and Economic Realities*, p. 136.

5. Ibid., p. 142.

6. According to some social theorists, liberalism undermines its own liberal values for two reasons: its structures of political economy contradict its own stated ideals, and the contemporary political values of liberalism contradict its original values of natural rights as stated during the Enlightenment. *See* Spragens, *The Irony of Liberal Reason*; MacPherson, *The Life and Times of Liberal Democracy*; and Hinkelammert, *The Ideological Weapons of Death*.

7. Clodovis Boff and Leonardo Boff, *The Church and the Economy of the United States: A Look from the Point of View of the Periphery*, unpublished manuscript (Petropolis, Rio de Janeiro, Brazil, April 7, 1987), pp. 17–18. This is the longer and more complete version of an article which appeared in the *National Catholic Reporter* (August 28, 1987).

8. Greeley, "The Bishops and the Economy," pp. 19–25; Norman Birnbaum, "The Bishops in the Iron Cage," in Gannon, *The Catholic Challenge to the American Economy*, pp. 165–170; Thomas Schindler, S.S., "The Bishops' Pastoral: Draft II Disappoints," *The Christian Century* (January 15, 1986), p. 38; Joseph Nocera, "Making Capitalism Moral," *The Washington Monthly* (September 1985), p. 46; Henry Briefs, "The Limits of Scripture: Theological Imperatives and Economic Realities," in Douglass, *The Deeper Meaning of Economic Life*, p. 67; Charles Krauthammer, "Perils of the Prophet Motive," in Royal, *Challenge and Response*, pp. 48–53.

9. Boff and Boff, *The Church and the Economy*, p. 20.

10. Greeley, "The Bishops and the Economy," p. 23.

11. Schindler, "The Bishops' Pastoral," p. 38.

12. Karl Marx, "Critique of the Gotha Program," in *Marx and Engels: Basic Writings on Politics and Philosophy*, ed. Lewis Feuer (Garden City, N.Y.: Doubleday, 1959), p. 120.

13. Birnbaum, "The Bishops in the Iron Cage," p. 176.

14. For a helpful analysis and overview of the programs of the American welfare state and their effects, *see* Harrell Rodgers, *The Cost of Human Neglect: America's Welfare Failure* (Armonk, N.Y.: M. E. Sharpe, 1982); Benjamin Page, *Who Gets What From the Government* (Berkeley, Calif.: University of California Press, 1983); and Harrington, *The New American Poverty*.

15. For the federal government's own response to these conservative criticisms of the poverty statistics of the Census Bureau, *see* U.S. Bureau of the Census, "Conference on the Measurement of Non-Cash Benefits: Proceedings" (Washington, D.C.: U.S. Government Printing Office, 1986) and "Alternative Measures of Poverty," staff study prepared for the Joint Economic Committee (October 18, 1989). The latter document includes new information on poverty statistics adjusted for both shifts in relative prices and consumption patterns in America during the

1980s. Results of these new sets of poverty estimates indicate that poverty is higher than previously thought, running by one standard to nearly one-quarter of the population (p. 2).

16. *See* the publications of the Center on Budget and Policy Priorities: *End Results: The Impact of Federal Policies since 1980 On Low Income Americans* (Washington, D.C.: September 1984); *Smaller Slices of the Pie: The Growing Economic Vulnerability of Poor and Moderate Income Americans* (Washington, D.C.: November 1985); and Isaac Shapiro and Robert Greenstein, *Holes in the Safety Nets: Poverty Programs and Policies in the United States* (Washington, D.C.: April 1988). *See also* John Palmer and Isabel Sawhill, The Institute for Research on Poverty, *Fighting Poverty: What Works and What Doesn't*, ed. S. Danziger and D. Weinberg (Cambridge, Mass.: Harvard University Press, 1986); and Jerry Sazama, *Taxes for the Rich and the Rest* (New York: Union for Radical Political Economics, 1979).

17. Bureau of Labor Statistics, "The Changing Distribution of Income," in *The American Profile Poster: Who Owns What, Who Makes How Much, Who Works Where, and Who Works With Whom* (New York: Pantheon Books, 1986), p. 8.

18. Center on Budget and Policy Priorities, "Analysis of Poverty in 1987" (Washington, D.C.: September 1, 1988), p. 2.

19. Robert Greenstein, "Losing Faith in 'Losing Ground'," *The New Republic* (March 25, 1985), p. 13. *See also* Center for Popular Economics, *Economic Report of the People* (Boston: South End Press, 1986), pp. 66–68; David Ellwood and Lawrence Summers, "Poverty in America: Is Welfare the Answer or the Problem?," *Fighting Poverty*, pp. 78ff; Frank Levy, *Dollars and Dreams: The Changing American Income Distribution* (New York: W.W. Norton and Company, 1988), pp. 186–191; Mary Jo Bane, "Household Composition and Poverty," in *Fighting Poverty*, pp. 209ff.; William Wilson and Kathryn Neckerman, "Poverty and Family Structure: The Widening Gap Between Evidence and Public Policy Issues," in *Fighting Poverty*, pp. 231ff.; Christopher Jencks, "How Poor are the Poor?" in *Taking Sides: Clashing Views on Controversial Issues*, ed. Kurt Finsterbusch and George McKenna (Guilford, Conn.: Dushkin Publishing Group, 1986), pp. 234ff.; Winifred Bell, *Contemporary Social Welfare* (New York: Macmillan Publishing Co., 1987), pp. 127–128.

20. David Ellwood, *Poor Support: Poverty in the American Family* (New York: Basic Books, 1988), pp. 58–60, 77.

21. Center on Budget and Policy Priorities, "Poverty Rate and Household Income Stagnate as Rich-Poor Gap Hits Post-War High" (Washington, D.C.: October 20, 1989), pp. 4–5.

22. Gary Burtless, "Public Spending for the Poor: Trends, Prospects, and Economic Limits," in *Fighting Poverty*, p. 18; Ellwood and Summers, "Poverty in America," p. 94.

23. Center on Budget and Policy Priorities, *Holes in the Safety Nets*, pp. 1–7.

24. Simon and Novak, *Toward the Future*, p. 59.

25. Jencks, "How Poor are the Poor?," p. 235. *See also* Page, *Who Gets What From the Government*, pp. 63–71.

26. Ellwood and Summers, "Poverty in America," p. 84.

27. Burtless, "Public Spending for the Poor," p. 41.

28. Robert Greenstein, "The Bottom Line on Poverty: Cuts in Aid, Food, Health, Housing Hit Families the Worst," *Los Angeles Times* (April 29, 1984).

29. Sheldon Danziger, Robert Haveman, and Robert Plotnick, "Antipoverty Policy: Effects on the Poor and the Nonpoor," in *Fighting Poverty*, p. 65. *See also*

June Axinn and Mark Stern, *Dependency and Poverty: Old Problems in a New World* (Lexington, Mass.: D.C. Heath and Company, 1988), p. 83.

30. Murray, *Losing Ground*, p. 59.

31. Center on Budget and Policy Priorities, "Impact of Government Anti-Poverty Programs Declines; Benefit Cuts Increase Poverty Among Families with Children" (Washington, D.C.: November 25, 1986), p. 2.

32. Center on Budget and Policy Priorities, "One-Third of Proposed Spending Cuts to Come from Programs to the Poor" (Washington, D.C.: January 5, 1987), pp. 1ff.

33. Center on Budget and Policy Priorities, "Analysis of Poverty in 1987," p. 6. For a more detailed analysis of the implications of including noncash benefits in the measurement of poverty, *see* Center on Budget and Policy Priorities, "Analysis of Poverty Using Non-Cash Benefits" (Washington, D.C.: October 1986), pp. 1–7. This report concludes that even with the addition of noncash benefits in the experimental estimates of the Census Bureau released on October 2, 1986, poverty between 1979 and 1985 rose faster than poverty measured using the official estimates. *Also see* William O'Hare and Kathryn Porter, *Real Life Poverty in America*, (Washington, D.C.: Center on Budget and Policy Priorities, July 1990), pp. 3–15, which examines the implications of officially defining poverty as before-tax income excluding capital gains and Patricia Ruggles, *Drawing the Line: Alternative Poverty Measures and Their Implications for Public Policy* (Washington, D.C.: The Urban Institute Press, 1991). Finally, for a general comparison of the numbers of poor and poverty rates using different definitions of poverty, *see* Table E in "Measuring the Effect of Benefits and Taxes on Income and Poverty: 1989," *Current Population Reports*, Series P-90, No. 169-RD (Washington, D.C.: U.S. Government Printing Office, September 1990), p. 10.

34. Center on Budget and Policy Priorities, "Impact of Government Benefit Programs Declines, Adds to Number of Poor Families," p. 2.

35. Rebecca Blank and Alan Blinder, "Macroeconomics, Income Distribution, and Poverty," in *Fighting Poverty*, p. 182.

36. Center on Budget and Policy Priorities, "Economic Recovery Fails to Reduce Poverty Rates to Pre-Recession Levels: Gaps Widen Further Between Rich and Poor" (Washington, D.C.: August 26, 1986), p. 1.

37. Kevin Phillips, *The Politics of Rich and Poor: Wealth and the American Electorate in the Reagan Aftermath* (New York: Random House, 1990), pp. 12–14.

38. Joseph Pechman, *Who Paid the Taxes, 1966–1985?* (Washington, D.C.: The Brookings Institution, 1985), p. 76. *See also* an analysis of the meaning of these numbers in Levy, *Dollars and Dreams*, pp. 12–22. For an update on Pechman's data *see* Robert Greenstein and Scott Barancik, *Drifting Apart: New Findings on Growing Income Disparities Between the Rich, the Poor, and the Middle Class* (Washington, D.C.: Center on Budget and Policy Priorities, July 1990) and Congressional Budget Office, *Overview of Entitlement Programs* (The Green Book) (Washington, D.C.: U.S. Government Printing Office, June 1990), pp. 1159–1206.

39. Joseph Pechman, "Why We Should Stick with the Income Tax," *The Brookings Review*, Spring 1990, p. 11.

40. U.S. Department of Commerce, Bureau of the Census, "Money Income and Poverty Status in the United States: 1989," *Current Population Reports*, Series P-60, No. 168 (Washington, D.C.: U.S. Government Printing Office, September 1990), p. 30.

Census Bureau's Aggregate Income of American Families by Each Fifth

Year	Lowest Fifth	Second Fifth	Third Fifth	Fourth Fifth	Highest Fifth
1968	5.7	12.4	17.7	23.7	40.5
1970	5.5	12.2	17.6	23.8	40.9
1975	5.5	11.8	17.6	24.1	41.1
1980	5.2	11.5	17.5	24.3	41.5
1981	5.1	11.3	17.4	24.4	41.8
1982	4.8	11.2	17.1	24.2	42.7
1983	4.7	11.1	17.1	24.3	42.8
1984	4.7	11.0	17.0	24.3	42.9
1985	4.7	10.9	16.8	24.1	43.5
1986	4.6	10.8	16.8	24.0	43.7
1987	4.6	10.8	16.8	24.0	43.8
1988	4.6	10.7	16.7	24.0	44.0
1989	4.6	10.6	16.5	23.7	44.6

41. Marilyn Moon and Isabel Sawhill, "Family Incomes: Gainers and Losers," in Palmer and Sawhill, *The Reagan Record*, p. 320. *See also* Frank Ackerman and Andrew Zimbalist, "Capitalism and Inequality in the United States," pp. 297–307 and Richard Edwards, "Who Fares Well in the Welfare System," pp. 307–315 in *The Capitalist System*, ed. Richard Edwards, Michael Reich, and Thomas Weisskopf (Englewood Cliffs, N.J.: Prentice-Hall, 1972); Michael Barth, George Carcagno, and John Palmer, "The Coverage of the Transfer System," pp. 321–325, and Gabriel Kolko, "Taxation and Inequality," in *Problems in Political Economy: An Urban Perspective*, ed. David Gordon (Lexington, Mass.: D.C. Heath and Company, 1977); Howard Wachtel and Larry Sawers, "Government Spending and the Distribution of Income," in *The Poverty Establishment*, ed. Pamela Roby (Englewood Cliffs, N.J.: Prentice-Hall, 1974), pp. 63–99; and S. M. Miller and Pamela Roby, *The Future of Inequality* (New York: Basic Books, 1970).

42. Center on Budget and Policy Priorities, *Smaller Slices of the Pie*, pp. 7–8.

43. Ibid., p. 17.

44. Center on Budget and Policy Priorities, "Rich-Poor Income Gap Hits 40-Year High as Poverty Rate Stalls" (Washington, D.C.: October 1990), p. 2.

45. Congressional Budget Office, *Overview of Entitlement Programs* (The Green Book). This 1,500-page report was compiled for the House Committee on Ways and Means.

46. Greenstein and Barancik, *Drifting Apart*, pp. 3, 17. *See also* Congressional Budget Office, "The Changing Distribution of Federal Taxes: 1975–1990" (Washington, D.C.: U.S. Government Printing Office, October 1987), p. xvi.

47. Ibid., p. 7.

48. Center on Budget and Policy Priorities, "Rich-Poor Income Gap," pp. 2–3.

49. Center on Budget and Policy Priorities, *End Results,* p. 14. An alternative description of income distribution in the United States had been provided by another federal government agency: the Bureau of Labor Statistics, that is, until it was discontinued by the Reagan administration in 1983. The bureau distinguished between three standards of living: the "lower," "intermediate," and "upper budget." According to its criteria of measurement, one-half of all Americans during

the seventies were living either in poverty or in a "shabby but respectable standard of comfort" at the intermediate level. Characterizing this level, the BLS said that:

> a family will own a toaster that will last for 33 years; a refrigerator and range that will each last 17 years; a vacuum cleaner that will last 14 years; and a television set that will last ten years. The budget assumes that a family will buy a two-year-old car, and keep it for four years. In that time they will pay for a tune-up once a year, a brake realignment every three years, and a front-end alignment every four years. The budget assumes that the husband will buy one year-round suit every four years and one topcoat every 8½ years. It assumes that the husband will take his wife to the movies once every three months, and that one of them will go alone once a year. The two children are each allowed one movie every four weeks. A total of $2.54 per person per year is allowed for admission to all other events, from football and baseball games to theatre or concerts. Finally, the budget allows nothing whatever for savings. (Andrew Levison, *The Working-Class Majority* [New York: Penguin Books, 1974], pp. 32–33).

For an analysis and update, *see* Ryan, *Equality*, pp. 12–15; Rodgers, *The Cost of Human Neglect*, pp. 19–21; Rose, *The American Profile Poster*, p. 8; and Richard Parker, *The Myth of the Middle Class: Notes on Affluence and Equality* (New York: Harper and Row Publishers, 1972), pp. 14–15 and 99–100.

50. Paul Leonard and Robert Greenstein, *One Step Forward: The Deficit Reduction Package of 1990* (Washington, D.C.: Center on Budget and Policy Priorities, November 1990), p. 11.

51. Chantal Mouffe, "American Liberalism and Its Critics: Rawls, Taylor, Sandel, and Walzer," *Praxis International*, no. 8, pp. 193–206.

52. Joint Economic Committee, *The Concentration of Wealth in America*, pp. 23–29.

53. Democratic Staff of the Joint Economic Committee, *The Concentration of Wealth in the United States: Trends in the Distribution of Wealth Among American Families* (Washington, D.C.: U.S. Government Printing Office, July 1986), p. 24. There was a second revised version of this report in 1986 that was not published, based on the "Survey of Consumer Finances" from the Division of Research and Statistics of the Federal Reserve Board. They are presently in the process of producing another wealth-distribution analysis for 1989–90, which will be completed in 1991. *See also* the classic text in the field—Gabriel Kolko, *Wealth and Power in America: An Analysis of Social Class and Income Distribution* (New York: Praeger Publishers, 1962) and Phillips, *The Politics of Rich and Poor*.

54. Federal Reserve Board, "Survey of Consumer Finances, 1983," *Federal Reserve Bulletin*, Sept. 1984, p. 685.

55. Novak, *The Spirit of Democratic Capitalism*, p. 55.

56. Bellah, *Habits of the Heart*; Christopher Lasch, *The Culture of Narcissism* (New York: Warner Books, 1979); Jacoby, *Social Amnesia*; Stuart Ewen, *Captains of Consciousness: Advertising and the Social Roots of the Consumer Culture* (New York: McGraw-Hill, 1976); Philip Slater, *The Pursuit of Loneliness: American Culture at the Breaking Point* (Boston: Beacon Press, 1970); and Jürgen Habermas's thesis of the "colonization of the lifeworld" in *The Theory of Communicative Action*, pp.

343–373, and his thesis of depoliticization and motivation crisis in *Legitimation Crisis*, pp. 36–40, pp. 75ff.

57. Novak, *The Spirit of Democratic Capitalism*, p. 84.

58. Herbert Marcuse, *One-Dimensional Man* (Boston: Beacon Press, 1964); Lasch, *The Culture of Narcissism*; Spragens, *The Irony of Liberal Reason*; Schumacher, *Small is Beautiful*; Schweickart, *Capitalism or Worker Control?*

59. Royal, *Challenge and Response*, p. 10.

60. Paul Heyne, "The Concept of Economic Justice in Religious Discussion," in *Morality of the Market: Religious and Economic Perspectives*, ed. Walter Block, Geoffrey Brennan, and Kenneth Elzinga (Vancouver, Canada: Fraser Institute, 1985), p. 465.

61. Novak, *The Spirit of Democratic Capitalism*, p. 55.

62. Boff, *The Church and the Economy*, p. 22.

63. Ellwood and Summers, "Poverty in America," p. 83.

64. Samuel Bowles, David Gordon, and Thomas Weisskopf, *Beyond the Waste Land: A Democratic Alternative to Economic Decline* (Garden City, N.Y.: Anchor Press, 1984); Thurow, *The Zero-Sum Society* and *The Zero-Sum Solution: Building a World-Class American Economy* (New York: Simon and Schuster, 1985); Ira Magaziner and Robert Reich, *Minding America's Business: The Decline and Rise of the American Economy* (New York: Vintage Books, 1982); Robert Reich, *The Next American Frontier: A Provocative Program for Economic Renewal* (Harmondsworth, England: Penguin Books, 1984); Barry Bluestone and Bennett Harrison, *The Deindustrialization of America: Plant Closings, Community Abandonment, and the Dismantling of Basic Industry* (New York: Basic Books, 1982) and *The Great U-Turn: Corporate Restructuring and the Polarizing of America* (New York: Basic Books, 1988); Paul Blumberg, *Inequality in An Age of Decline* (Oxford, England: Oxford University Press, 1981); Richard Edwards, *Contested Terrain: The Transformation of the Workplace in the Twentieth Century* (New York: Basic Books, 1979); Steven Rhoades, *Power, Empire Building, and Mergers* (Lexington, Mass.: D.C. Heath, 1983); Seymour Melman, *Pentagon Capitalism: The Political Economy of War* (New York: McGraw Hill, 1970); Sydney Lens, *Permanent War: The Militarization of America* (New York: Schocken Press, 1987); Best and Connolly, *The Politicized Economy*; Center for Popular Economics, *Economic Report of the People*; James O'Connor, *The Fiscal Crisis of the State* (New York: St. Martin's Press, 1973); Harry Braverman, *Labor and Monopoly Capital: The Degradation of Work in the Twentieth Century* (New York: Monthly Review Press, 1974); Paul Baran and Paul Sweezy, *Monopoly Capital* (New York: Monthly Review Press, 1966); Harry Magdoff and Paul Sweezy, *Stagnation and the Financial Explosion* (New York: Monthly Review Press, 1987); John Foster, "What is Stagnation?," *The Imperiled Economy: Macroeconomics from a Left Perspective*, ed. Robert Cherry et al. (New York: Union for Radical Political Economics, 1987); Edward Nell, "Transformational Growth and Stagnation," in Cherry, *The Imperiled Economy*; Victor Perlo, *Superprofits and Crises: Modern U.S. Capitalism* (New York: International Publishers, 1988); Ernst Mandel, *Late Capitalism*, trans. by Joris De Bres (London: New Left Books, 1975); David Laibman, "Technical Change and the Contradictions of Capitalism," in Cherry, *The Imperiled Economy*; Anwar Shaikh, "The Falling Rate of Profit and the Economic Crisis in the U.S.," in Cherry, *The Imperiled Economy*; Manuel Castells, *The Economic Crisis and American Society* (Princeton, N.J.: Princeton University Press, 1980); and Joshua Cohen

and Joel Rogers, *On Democracy: Toward a Transformation of American Society* (New York: Penguin Books, 1983).

65. Seymour Melman, *Profits Without Production* (New York: Alfred Knopf, 1983), p. 161. *See also* Ruth Leger Sivard, *World Military and Social Expenditures 1987–1988* (Washington, D.C.: World Priorities, 1988).

66. Bowles, Gordon, and Weisskopf, *Beyond the Waste Land*, p. 31. *See also* Best and Connolly, *The Politicized Economy*, pp. 183–190; Harrison and Bluestone, *The Great U-Turn*, pp. 7–11; and Mark Glick, "The Current Crisis in Light of the Great Depression," in Cherry, *The Imperiled Economy*, pp. 127–138.

67. Bowles, Gordon, and Weisskopf, *Beyond the Waste Land*, p. 115.

68. Center for Popular Economics, *Economic Report of the People*, p. 125.

69. John Brooks, *The Takeover Game* (New York: E. P. Dutton, 1987), pp. 166–203; Walter Adams and James Brock, *The Bigness Complex: Industry, Labor, and Government in the American Economy* (New York: Pantheon Books, 1986), pp. 152–193; Louis Lowenstein, *What's Wrong With Wall Street: Short-term Gain and the Absentee Shareholder* (Reading, Mass.: Addison-Wesley Publishing Co., 1988), pp. 119–159; David Ravenscraft and F. M. Scherer, *Mergers, Sell-Offs, and Economic Efficiency* (Washington, D.C.: The Brookings Institution, 1987), pp. 20–55; and Jeff Madrick, *Taking America: How We Got From the First Hostile Takeover to Mega-mergers, Corporate Raiding, and Scandal* (Toronto: Bantam Books, 1987).

70. Edwards, *Contested Terrain*, p. 82.

71. Brooks, *The Takeover Game*, p. 171.

72. Adams and Brock, *Dangerous Pursuits*, p. 143.

73. For an analysis and overview of the critics of this view, *see* Brooks, *The Takeover Game*, pp. 223–255. Brooks viewed the acquisitions of large firms as a result of an investment-banking-driven economy.

74. Brooks, *The Takeover Game*, pp. 171–177 and Adams and Brock, *The Bigness Complex*, pp. 109ff.

75. Harvey Segal, *Corporate Makeover: The Reshaping of the American Economy* (Harmondsworth, England: Penguin Books, 1989), pp. 69–119.

76. Madrick, *Taking America*, p. 15. Throughout the 1970s and 1980s, the book value of companies averaged 90 percent above the stock market value, thus making them prime targets for friendly or hostile takeovers. *See also* Segal, *Corporate Makeover*, p. 74.

77. For a summary of this line of argument, *see* Ravenscraft and Scherer, *Mergers, Sell-Offs, and Economic Efficiency*, pp. 211–215; and Brooks, *The Takeover Game*, pp. 237–255.

78. Ravenscraft and Scherer, ibid., pp. 192–194. Ravenscraft and Scherer, after criticizing the efficiency theory and monopoly theory of conglomerate mergers for the period from 1950 to 1976, settled on the empire-building motive of managers and the undervalued assets theory as the best explanations for the merger movements of the 1960s and 1970s. Brooks, who accepted the thesis that investment bankers were behind these mergers, updates the material of Ravenscraft and Scherer for the 1980s in *The Takeover Game*, p. 227. For a summary of the studies indicating the decline in efficiency and productivity, *see* Adams and Brock, *Dangerous Pursuits*, pp. 84–86. "The evidence generated from painstaking statistical analyses strongly suggests that merger-mania *undermines* efficiency in production, that it *obstructs* technological advance, and that it *subverts* international competition" (p. 84). *See also* Adams and Brock, *The Bigness Complex*, pp. 25ff.

79. Harrison and Bluestone, *The Great U-Turn*, pp. 54ff.; Edwards, *Contested Terrain*, pp. 45ff.; Best and Connolly, *The Politicized Economy*, pp. 161–166; Edward Herman, *Corporate Control, Corporate Power* (Cambridge, England: Cambridge University Press, 1981), pp. 188–194; and Robert Pollin, "Structural Change and Increasing Fragility in the U.S. Financial System," in Cherry, *The Imperiled Economy*, p. 152.

80. Samuel Reid, *The New Industrial Order: Concentration, Regulation, and Public Policy* (New York: McGraw-Hill Book Co., 1976), p. 30.

81. Daniel Fusfeld, *Economics: Principles of Political Economy* (Glenview, Ill.: Scott, Foresman and Company, 1982), p. 355.

82. Best and Connolly, *The Politicized Economy*, p. 163.

83. Mark Green, Beverly Moore, Jr., and Bruce Wasserstein, *The Closed Enterprise System: Ralph Nader's Study Group Report on Antitrust Enforcement* (New York: Bantam Books, 1972), p. 11.

84. Michael Parenti, *Democracy for the Few* (New York: St. Martin's Press, 1988), p. 11. *See also* David Kotz, *Bank Control of the Large Corporations in the United States* (Berkeley, Calif.: University of California Press, 1978), pp. 145–149.

85. D. Stanley Eitzen and Maxine Zinn, *Social Problems* (Boston, Mass.: Allyn and Bacon, 1989), p. 28.

86. Reid, *The New Industrial Order*, p. 12.

87. Bluestone and Harrison, *The Deindustrialization of America*, p. 41.

88. Edwards, *Contested Terrain*, pp. 82–85; Best and Connolly, *The Politicized Economy*, pp. 164–165; William Shepherd, *Market Power and Economic Welfare: An Introduction* (New York: Random House, 1970), pp. 28–29, 186–94; John Kenneth Galbraith, *The New Industrial State* (New York: New American Library, 1967), pp. 39–45 and *Economics and the Public Purpose* (New York: New American Library, 1973), pp. 106–117; Blumberg, *Inequality in an Age of Decline*, p. 114, and Herman, *Corporate Control, Corporate Power*, p. 69.

89. Reid, *The New Industrial Order*, pp. 114–115; Bluestone and Harrison, *The Deindustrialization of America*, pp. 40–81; Rhoades, *Power, Empire Building, and Mergers*, p. 110.

90. Rhoades, *Power, Empire Building, and Mergers*, p. 90.

91. Ibid., pp. 115–116.

92. Lowenstein, *What's Wrong With Wall Street*, p. 137, and Ravenscraft and Scherer, *Mergers, Sell-Offs, and Economic Efficiency*, pp. 73–74, 122.

93. Galbraith, *The New Industrial State*, pp. 199–207.

94. Shepherd, *Market Power and Economic Welfare*, p. 197.

95. Reid, *The New Industrial Order*, p. 110.

96. Bowles, Gordon, and Weisskopf, *Beyond the Wasteland*, p. 177; Green, Moore, and Wasserstein, *The Closed Enterprise System*, p. 14.

97. Parenti, *Democracy for the Few*.

98. Simon and Novak, *Toward the Future*, p. 29.

99. Brubacker, *The Limits of Rationality*.

100. David Jenkins, *Job Power: Blue and White Collar Democracy* (New York: Penguin Books, 1974), p. 43.

101. It is not only the workplace that is being technically controlled, but the experiences of everyday life, consumption, play, games, and leisure itself ("colonization of everyday life"). *See* Stanley Aronowitz, *False Promises: The Shaping of American Working Class Consciousness* (New York: McGraw-Hill Book Co., 1973),

pp. 51–134; Robert Holsworth and J. Harry Wray, *American Politics and Everyday Life* (New York: John Wiley and Sons, 1982), pp. 21–40; Ewen, *Captains of Consciousness.*

102. Braverman, *Labor and Monopoly Capital,* p. 180.

103. Edwards, *Contested Terrain,* p. 163. *See also* David Gordon, Richard Edwards, and Michael Reich, *Segmented Work, Divided Workers: The Historical Transformation of Labor in the United States* (Cambridge, England: Cambridge University Press, 1982), pp. 165ff.; Aronowitz, *False Promises;* and Samuel Bowles and Richard Edwards, *Understanding Capitalism: Competition, Command, and Change in the U.S. Economy* (New York: Harper and Row Publishers, 1985), pp. 198–230.

104. Edwards, *Contested Terrain,* p. 178.

105. Howard Wachtel, *Labor and the Economy* (Orlando, Fla.: Academic Press, 1984), pp. 412–450.

106. There are a variety of different schools of thought dealing with a theory of the state, such as the instrumentalism of Miliband and Domhoff (state as an instrument of the capitalist control), the structuralism of Althusser and Poulantzas (state structure as mechanism for class rule), and critical theory of Offe, Habermas, and O'Connor (reintegration of the state and the process of capital accumulation). For an overview of this debate, *see*: Martin Carnoy, *The State and Political Theory* (Princeton, N.J.: Princeton University Press, 1984) and David Gold, C. Lo and Erick Wright, "Recent Developments in Marxist Theories of the State," *Monthly Review,* vol. 27 (1975).

107. Gregory Fossedal, "Corporate Welfare Out of Control," *New Republic* (February 25, 1985), p. 17. *See also* " 'Tax Welfare' for the Corporate Giants," in Philip Stern, *Rape of the Taxpayer* (New York: Vintage Books, 1973), pp. 206–227, and more recently John Carey, "The Myth That America Can Compete," *Business Week,* special issue (1990), pp. 47–48.

108. U.S. Department of Commerce, Bureau of the Census, *Statistical Abstract of the United States 1990,* No. 499, pp. 310–311.

109. Edward Greenberg, *Serving the Few: Corporate Capitalism and the Bias of Government Policy* (New York: John Wiley and Sons, 1974), p. 185; Ackerman and Zimbalist, "Capitalism and Inequality in the United States," in Edwards, Reich, and Weisskopf, *The Capitalist System,* pp. 297ff.

110. O'Connor, *The Fiscal Crisis of the State,* pp. 6–7. For a development of the functionalist perspective in an analysis of the British welfare state, *see* Ian Gough, *The Political Economy of the Welfare State* (London: Macmillan Press, 1979).

111. While O'Connor emphasizes in his works social capital and the accumulation process, it is Offe and Habermas who stress the area of social expenses and legitimation. *See* Offe, *Contradictions of the Welfare State,* and Habermas, *Legitimation Crisis.*

112. Greenberg, *Serving the Few,* p. 31.

113. U.S. Congress, Congressional Budget Office, *Federal Support of U.S. Business* (Washington, D.C.: U.S. Government Printing Office, January 1984), p. ix.

114. Ibid., p. 71.

115. Information for the Direct Expenditure Program and the Credit Program was taken from Congressional Budget Office, *Federal Support of U.S. Business,* p. x. The major spending areas for the Direct Expenditures include direct farm and price subsidies, energy technology development, urban economic development grants,

and research subsidies for agriculture, aeronautics, water transportation, and mining. For details of specific programs *see* pp. 25 and 30.

I. Direct Expenditures Programs   *Projected Outlays for 1984*
(In billions of dollars)

Commodity Credit Corporation	6.1
Energy Supply: Research and Development	1.8
Economic Development	1.4
(Community Development Block Grants, Urban	
Development Action Grants, and Economic	
Development Administration Grants)	
Agricultural Research and Services	1.2
(Dept. of Agriculture Agencies)	
Aeronautical Research and Technology	0.7
(Dept. of Defense and NASA)	
Water Transportation	0.5
(Coast Guard and Maritime Administration)	
Mining	0.5
(Geological Survey and Bureau of Mines)	
Other	1.4
Total	13.7

II. Credit Programs   *Projected Outlays for 1984*
(In billions of dollars)

	Direct Loan Obligations	Primary Loan Guarantee Commitments
Rural Electrification Administration	4.5	0.0
Commodity Credit Corp.	7.4	3.0
Agricultural Credit Insurance Fund	4.6	1.3
Export-Import Bank	2.5	9.0
Small Business Admin. Business Loan and Insurance Fund	1.5	2.9
Other	0.4	1.5
Total Business Credit	20.9	17.7

116. Public Citizen's Congress Watch, *Aid For Dependent Corporations: The Fiscal 1986 Corporate Welfare Budget* (Washington, D.C.: Citizen's Watch, February 1985), p. 13; Doug Bandow, "Corporate America: Uncle Sam's Favorite Welfare Client," *Business and Society Review* (Fall 1985), p. 51; Fossedal, "Corporate Welfare Out of Control," p. 18.

117. The three most important programs in this grouping include the Accelerated Cost Recovery System (ACRS), Preferential Treatment of Capital Gains, and the Investment Tax Credit (ITC). *Federal Support of U.S. Business,* pp. 17–24.

118. Congress Watch, *Aid for Dependent Corporations*, p. 2.

119. Congressional Budget Office, *Federal Support of U.S. Business*. *See also* the discussion within the CBO about U.S. industrial policy in *The Industrial Policy Debate* (Washington, D.C.: U.S. Government Printing Office, December 1983) and its rethinking of the traditional definitions of "public investment" and "federal deficits" in *Trends in Public Investment* (Washington, D.C.: U.S. Government Printing Office, December 1987).

120. Congressional Budget Office, *The Industrial Policy Debate*, pp. 33–42.

121. For an update of these figures, *see* the Executive Office of the President, Office of Management and Budget, *Special Analysis: Budget of the United States, Fiscal Year 1989*, Special Analysis A (Washington, D.C.: U.S. Government Printing Office). *See also* Bandow, "Corporate America," p. 49.

122. Congressional Budget Office, *The Industrial Policy Debate*, pp. 33–42. For a further clarification of the types of investments *see also* Congressional Budget Office, *Trends in Public Investment*.

123. For an analysis and discussion of the proposed elimination or curtailment of the investment tax credit and the accelerated depreciation allowances, *see* U.S. Senate, Hearings Before the Committee on Finance, *Tax Reform Act of 1986*, Part IV (Washington, D.C.: U.S. Government Printing Office, February 5 and 6, 1986). Martin Feldstein (pp. 125–127) argued that these tax code changes would result in a reduction of investment in production and more investment in shopping centers, office buildings, and vacation homes. He also made the case that these tax codes encouraged the substitution of corporate debt for equity, thereby reducing America's international competitiveness. Others argued that the market would be a better allocator of investment capital than the government, with its special privileges and tax exemption provisions in the present code. The deficit reduction package of 1990 includes a new capital gains tax which lowers the rate of the very wealthy in America. *See* Center on Budget and Policy Priorities, *One Step Forward: The Deficit Reduction Package of 1990*, Paul Leonard and Robert Greenstein (Washington, D.C., November 1990), p. 13.

124. Congressional Budget Office, *The Effects of Tax Reform on Tax Expenditures* (Washington, D.C.: U.S. Government Printing Office, March 1988), p. 20.

125. Executive Office of the President, Office of Management and Budget, *Special Analyses: Budget of the United States Government, Fiscal Year 1988* (Washington, D.C.: U.S. Government Printing Office), p. G-2.

126. Ibid., p. F-3.

127. Congress Watch, *Aid For Dependent Corporations*, pp. 21–25.

128. Ibid., pp. 6–7.

129. Ibid., p. 6.

130. Greenberg, *Serving the Few*, p. 215.

131. Rodgers, *The Cost of Human Neglect*, pp. 58–60.

132. O'Connor, *The Fiscal Crisis of the State*, p. 138.

133. James O'Connor, *The Corporations and the State: Essays on the Theory of Capitalism and Imperialism* (New York: Harper and Row, 1974), pp. 40–41; Offe, *Contradictions of the Welfare State*, p. 51; Habermas, *Legitimation Crisis*, pp. 4ff., and "Technology and Science as 'Ideology' " in *Toward a Rational Society*, pp. 81–122; and Castells, *The Economic Crisis and American Society*, pp. 69–72.

134. O'Connor, *The Fiscal Crisis of the State*, p. 113 and Frances Piven and Richard Cloward, *The New Class War: Reagan's Attack on the Welfare State and Its Consequences* (New York: Pantheon, 1982) pp. 29–32.

135. Harrison and Bluestone, *The Great U-Turn*, pp. 91–108. For a further discussion of the effects of Reaganomics on American society, *see* Robert Lekachman, *Greed is Not Enough: Reaganomics* (New York: Pantheon Books, 1982); Stephen Rousseas, *The Political Economy of Reaganomics: A Critique* (Armonk, N.Y.: M. E. Sharpe, 1982); Frank Ackerman, *Reaganomics: Rhetoric or Reality* (Boston: South End Press, 1982); and Emma Rothschild, "The Real Reagan Economy," *The New York Review of Books* (June 30, 1988), pp. 46–53.

136. Best and Connolly, *The Politicized Economy*, p. 221.

137. Frances Piven and Richard Cloward, *Regulating the Poor: The Functions of Public Welfare* (New York: Vintage Books, 1971), p. 7. They readjust their thinking on the issue of the welfare state as simply the tool of capitalist oppression in their *The New Class War*. In the latter work they view the state and the federal budget as the battleground for a displaced economic class conflict.

138. Piven and Cloward, *Regulating the Poor*, p. 165.

139. Michael Novak, "The Rich, the Poor and the Reagan Administration," *Commentary* (August 1983), p. 31.

140. Lowi, *The End of Liberalism*, pp. 244–249.

141. Blumberg, *Inequality in an Age of Decline*, pp. 134ff.

142. Leonard Silk, "Triple Play: The Rich Nations Get Richer. And Then?," *New York Times* (July 1, 1990), section 4, pp. 1–2. The costs for the savings and loan bailout have escalated from $250 billion in May 1990 (Steven Waldman and Rich Thomas, "How Did It Happen?" *Newsweek* [May 21, 1990], p. 27ff.) to $500 billion by July 1990. This occurs on top of a $106 billion balance of payment and trade deficit. While America is facing serious long-term economic problems, Japan in 1989 had a $57.2 billion trade surplus and West Germany a $52.8 billion surplus. On July 16, 1990, the Office of Management and Budget published the latest figures on the estimated federal budget deficit for fiscal year 1991. The deficit is projected to be much higher than originally estimated by the Bush administration—$168.8 billion and over $231 billion when the money for the savings and loan bailout is included. It should be remembered that the actual numbers for the federal deficit are still artificially low because the true deficit is masked in the federal budget by Social Security.

143. Robert Sherrill, "The Looting Decade: S&Ls, Big Banks and Other Triumphs of Capitalism," *The Nation* (November 19, 1990), pp. 589–623.

144. Ibid., p. 589.

145. EJFA, p. 143.

5. THE POPES SPEAK

1. English translations are available in the following: Byers, *Justice in the Marketplace*; Claudia Carlen, ed., *The Papal Encyclicals, 1740–1981*, 5 vol. (Ann Arbor, Mich.: The Pierian Press, 1990); C. Carlen, ed., *Papal Pronouncements, A Guide: 1740–1978*, 2 vol. (Ann Arbor, Mich.: The Pierian Press, 1990); William J. Gibbons, ed., *Seven Great Encyclicals* (New York: Paulist Press, 1963); David J. O'Brien and Thomas A. Shannon, eds., *Renewing the Earth: Catholic Documents on Peace, Justice, and Liberation* (Garden City, N.Y.: Doubleday, 1977); Michael Walsh and Brian Davies, eds., *Proclaiming Justice and Peace: Documents from John XXIII–John Paul II* (Mystic, Conn.: Twenty-Third Publications, 1984).

Studies that include further extensive bibliographies: Jean-Yves Calvez, S.J., and

Jacques Perrin, S.J., *The Church and Social Justice: The Social Teaching of the Popes from Leo XIII to Pius XII (1878–1958)* (Chicago: Henry Regnery Co., 1961); Richard L. Camp, *The Papal Ideology of Social Reform: A Study in Historical Development, 1878–1967* (Leiden: E.J. Brill, 1969); John C. Cort, *Christian Socialism* (Maryknoll, N.Y.: Orbis Books, 1989); Charles E. Curran and Richard A. McCormick, S.J., *Readings in Moral Theology No. 5: Official Catholic Social Teaching* (New York: Paulist Press, 1986); Donald Dorr, *Option for the Poor: A Hundred Years of Vatican Social Teaching* (Maryknoll, N.Y.: Orbis Books, 1983); Gary J. Dorrien, *Reconstructing the Common Good: Theology and the Social Order* (Maryknoll, N.Y.: Orbis Books, 1990); George W. Farell, *Christian Social Teachings: A Reader in Christian Social Ethics from the Bible to the Present* (Minneapolis, Minn.: Augsburg Press, 1971); G. W. Farell, *History of Christian Ethics From the New Testament to Augustine* (Minneapolis, Minn.: Augsburg Press, 1979); Anne Freemantle, ed., *The Social Teachings of the Church* (New York: Mentor-Omega, 1963); Joseph Gremillion, ed., *The Gospel of Peace and Justice: Catholic Social Teaching Since Pope John* (Maryknoll, N.Y.: Orbis Books, 1976); J. N. Moody, ed., *Church and Society: Catholic Social and Political Thought and Movements, 1789–1950* (New York: Arts Inc., 1953); Michael Novak, *Freedom with Justice: Catholic Social Thought and Liberal Institutions* (San Francisco: Harper and Row, 1984); Alec R. Vidler, *A Century of Social Catholicism* (London: SPCK, 1964).

2. John Paul II, *Laborem Exercens* (On Human Work), #3, in Byers, *Justice in the Marketplace*, p. 294.

3. Ibid., #2, p. 293.

4. See Dorr, *Option for the Poor*, pp. 252–275.

5. John Paul II, "On Social Concern" (*Sollicitudo Rei Socialis*) (Washington, D.C.: NCCB, 1987), #1, p. 4.

6. Ibid., #3, p. 6.

7. "The Syllabus of Pius IX" in *Dogmatic Canons and Decrees* (Rockford, Ill.: TAN Books, 1977), p. 209; H. Denzinger, *Enchiridion Symbolorum*, 31st ed. (Freiburg: Herder, 1957), #1700–1780, pp. 482–490; Josef L. Altholz, *The Churches in the Nineteenth Century* (Indianapolis, Ind.: Bobbs-Merrill Co., 1967), pp. 73–89.

8. Novak, *Freedom with Justice*, p. xiii.

9. Sarda y Salvani, quoted in ibid., p. 22.

10. Ibid., p. 33.

11. "Syllabus," #39, *Dogmatic Canons*, p. 197; Denzinger, #1739, p. 487.

12. Quoted in Hubert Jedin and John Dolan, eds., *History of the Church*, vol. IX: *The Church in the Industrial Age* (New York: Crossroad, 1981), p. 229.

13. Aubert, *The Church in a Secularized Society*, *The Christian Centuries*: vol. 5, pp. 144–164. *See also*: Dorr, *Option for the Poor*, pp. 11–51; Edward Cahill, S.J., "The Catholic Social Movement: Historical Aspects," in Curran and McCormick, *Readings in Moral Theology*, no. 5, pp. 3–31; Michael Schuck, *That They Be One: The Social Teaching of Papal Encyclicals* (Washington, D.C.: Georgetown University Press, 1990).

14. See Cort, *Christian Socialism*, pp. 283–288; G. Antonazzi, *L'enciclica Rerum Novarum* (Rome, 1957); Owen Chadwick, *The Popes and European Revolution* (Oxford: Clarendon Press, 1981); Etienne Gilson, ed., *The Church Speaks to the Modern World: The Social Teachings of Leo XIII* (Garden City, N.Y.: Doubleday, 1954); I. Healy, *The Just Wage, 1750–1890* (The Hague, 1966); Peter d'A. Jones, *The Christian Socialist Revival* (Princeton, N.J.: Princeton University Press, 1968);

Oswald von Nell-Breuning, *Reorganization of Social Economy: The Social Encyclical Developed and Explained*, trans. B. W. Dempsey (Milwaukee, Wisc.: Bruce Publishing, 1936); Hermann Scholl, ed., *150 ans de movement ouvrier chrétien en Europe de l'Ouest* (Louvain, 1966), pp. 13–49; L. P. Wallace, *Leo XIII and the Rise of Socialism* (Durham, N.C.: Duke University Press, 1966).

15. Cahill, "The Catholic Social Movement," p. 9; R. J. Ederer, trans., *The Social Teaching of Wilhelm Emmanuel von Ketteler* (Washington, D.C.: University Press of America, 1981), pp. 3–99.

16. Cort, *Christian Socialism*, p. 285; Aubert, *The Church in a Secularized Society*, pp. 144–145.

17. Ibid., pp. 149–150.

18. Byers, *Justice in the Marketplace*, p. 12; Richard L. Camp, "The Rights and Duties of Labor and Capital," in Curran and McCormick, *Readings in Moral Theology*, p. 35.

19. Aubert, *The Church in a Secularized Society*, pp. 224–225.

20. RN, #6, Byers, p. 14.

21. Camp, "The Rights and Duties of Labor and Capital," p. 41.

22. RN, #51, Byers, p. 28. This seems an echo of views in Adam Smith on the role of labor, according to Joseph Schumpeter, *History of Economic Analysis* (New York: Oxford University Press, 1954), p. 558, cited in Novak, *Freedom with Justice*, p. 110.

23. RN, #7, Byers, p. 14. *See also* Francesco Nitti, *Catholic Socialism* (New York: Macmillan, 1895) and Hervé Chaigne, O.F.M., "The Catholic Church and Socialism," *Cross Currents* (Spring 1965).

24. RN, #28, Byers, p. 20.

25. RN, #52, 53, Byers, p. 29.

26. *See* Jedin and Dolan, *History of the Church*, vol. IX, pp. 197, 208 n. 61.

27. Ibid., p. 197. *See* Cort, *Christian Socialism*, p. 285; John Coleman, S.J., "Development of Catholic Social Teaching," *Origins* (Jan. 4, 1981).

28. RN, #38, Byers, p. 24.

29. RN, #14, Byers, p. 16.

30. RN, #10, Byers, p. 15; Denzinger, *Enchiridion Symbolorum*, #1938a, p. 537: "Possidere res privatim ut suas, ius est homini a natura datum ..."

31. RN, #15, 23, Byers, pp. 16, 19.

32. LE, #14, Byers p. 314. The reference, n. 22, is to the *Summa Theologiae*, II–II, q. 134, art. 1, ad 3.

33. *See* Hans Urs von Balthasar, "Natural Law and Private Ownership," *Communio* XVII:1 (Spring 1990), pp. 105–119.

34. RN, #23, Byers, p. 19.

35. RN, #37, Byers, p. 24.

36. Aubert, *The Church in a Secularized Society*, p. 42; Jedin and Dolan, *History of the Church,* vol. IX, p. 195.

37. RN, #13, Byers, p. 16.

38. Aubert, *The Church in a Secularized Society*, p. 150.

39. *See* for example the pious biography by Bernard O'Reilly, *Life of Leo XIII* (New York: C. L. Webster, 1903), or more hostile treatments: Friedrich Nippold, *The Papacy in the 19th Century*, trans. L. H. Schwab (New York: G. P. Putnam's Sons, 1900), and Joseph McCabe, *Crises in the History of the Papacy* (New York: G. P. Putnam's Sons, 1916).

40. Aubert, *The Church in a Secularized Society*, p. 152, n. 6; Cahill, "The Catholic Social Movement: Historical Aspects," pp. 16–17; Charles Plater, S.J., *The Priest and Social Action* (London: Longmans, 1914), pp. 1–150.

41. See bibliographies in Jedin and Dolan, *History of the Church*, vol. IX, pp. 585, 599–600; vol. X, pp. 822–825. *See* the discussions in Cort, *Christian Socialism*, pp. 288–300; Dorr, *Option for the Poor*, pp. 57–75; Cahill, *The Catholic Social Movement*, pp. 3–7; Oswald von Nell-Breuning, S. J., "The Drafting of Quadragesimo Anno," in Curran and McCormick, *Readings in Moral Theology*, pp. 60–68; John F. Cronin, S.S., "Forty Years Later: Reflections and Reminiscences," ibid., pp. 69–76; Novak, *Freedom with Justice*, pp. 110–123.

42. Cort, *Christian Socialism*, pp. 288–89, 300.

43. Ibid., pp. 289–296.

44. QA, #58, Byers, p. 62.

45. QA, #109, Byers, p. 75.

46. Novak, *Freedom with Justice*, pp. 81–87.

47. RN, #28, Byers, p. 28.

48. QA, #101, Byers, p. 74; *see also* Novak, *Freedom with Justice*, p. 77.

49. Dorr, *Option for the Poor*, p. 63; QA, #88, Byers, pp. 70–71.

50. *See* Ibid., #14, Byers, p. 47.

51. Ibid., #112, 113, Byers, pp. 76, 77.

52. Ibid., #114, Byers, p. 77.

53. LE, #14, Byers, p. 314: "From this point of view, therefore, in consideration of human labor and of common access to the goods meant for man, one cannot exclude the socialization, in suitable conditions, of certain means of production."

54. QA, #119, Byers, p. 79.

55. Ibid., #120, Byers, p. 79.

56. Ibid., #122, Byers, p. 80; Cort, *Christian Socialism*, p. 299.

57. Ibid., pp. 298–299.

58. Cahill, "The Catholic Social Movement," p. 7; DR, #54, Gibbons, *Seven Great Encyclicals*, p. 197.

59. Oswald von Nell-Breuning, "The Drafting of Quadragesimo Anno," p. 64.

60. DR, #32, Gibbons, *Seven Great Encyclicals*, p. 188; Cort, *Christian Socialism*, p. 300.

61. QA, #4, Byers, p. 45.

62. Ibid., #88, Byers, p. 71.

63. Byers, p. 42.

64. Ibid., p. 43.

65. Quoted by George Q. Flynn, *American Catholics and the Roosevelt Presidency, 1932–1936* (Lexington, Mass.: 1968), p. 17; cited in Hennessey, *American Catholics*, p. 260.

66. Dorr, *Option for the Poor*, pp. 82–83, 76–86. The comments in this section summarize Dorr's presentation.

67. Aubert, *The Church in a Secularized Society*, p. 582; see Cort, *Christian Socialism*, pp. 302–303.

68. Dorr, *Option for the Poor*, pp. 83–84; *see La sollenità della Pentecoste* (June 1, 1941), *AAS* 33 (1941), 216–27.

69. Dorr, *Option for the Poor*, p. 87.

70. *See* Ibid., pp. 87–116; Jedin and Dolan, *History of the Church*, vol. X, pp. 236–259; Novak, *Freedom with Justice*, pp. 126–133; Jean-Yves Calvez, *The Social*

Thought of John XXIII: Mater et Magistra (London: Burns and Oates, 1964); Gremillion, *The Gospel of Peace and Justice*; Giancarlo Zizola, *The Utopia of Pope John XXIII* (Maryknoll, N.Y.: Orbis Books, 1978). Subsequent encyclical citations are from: Walsh and Davies, *Proclaiming Justice and Peace*; Walter M. Abbott, ed., *The Documents of Vatican II* (New York: American Press, 1966).

71. Novak, *Freedom With Justice*, p. 127f.

72. MM, #109, Walsh and Davies, p. 20. Note should be taken that in this section private ownership is grounded in the natural order and the "individual is prior to society." The traditional grounds for the natural-rights argument are rejected.

73. MM, #83, ibid., p. 17.

74. MM, #38, 40, ibid., p. 9.

75. MM, #117, #36, ibid., pp. 22, 9.

76. Walsh and Davies, p. 1; Dorr, *Option for the Poor*, p. 112.

77. Ibid., p. 107.

78. MM, #236, Walsh and Davies, p. 39.

79. Ibid., #121, Walsh and Davies, pp. 22–23.

80. Quoted in Roland Flamini, *Pope, Premier, President: The Cold War Summit That Never Was* (New York: Macmillan, 1980), p. 85.

81. PT, #56, Walsh and Davies, p. 56.

82. Aubert, *The Church in a Secularized Society*, p. 584.

83. PT, #159, Walsh and Davies, p. 73.

84. Novak, *Freedom with Justice*, p. 238 n. 26; *see* Maritain's *Christianity and Democracy* (New York: Charles Scribner's Sons, 1944), *Man and the State* (Chicago: University of Chicago Press, 1951), and *The Person and the Common Good* (New York: Charles Scribner's Sons, 1941). Paul VI also favored Maritain and cited from his works, including *True Humanism* (New York: Charles Scribner's Sons, 1938), in *Populorum Progressio* (1967).

85. JIW, #64(1), Walsh and Davies, p. 201; RH, #17.3, Walsh and Davies, p. 259. *See* Jedin and Dolan, *History of the Church*, vol. X, p. 259: While Nuncio at Paris, Roncalli had been the first permanent observer of the Vatican to UNESCO.

86. *See* PT, #11–27, Walsh and Davies, pp. 49–51. The negative assessment is by Walsh and Davies themselves.

87. Novak, *Freedom With Justice*, p. 131.

88. GS, #63.2, Walsh and Davies, p. 120. *See* Abbott, *The Documents of Vatican II*, pp. 183–316.

89. Novak, *Freedom With Justice*, pp. 134–135.

90. PP, #26, Walsh and Davies, p. 149.

91. Ibid., #23, 22, Walsh and Davies, p. 148; *see* GS, #69, Walsh and Davies, pp. 123–124.

92. PP, #58, 59, Walsh and Davies, p. 157.

93. Ibid., #20, 18, Walsh and Davies, p. 147.

94. Ibid., #31, Walsh and Davies, p. 150. It is in essence a reiteration of the natural-law principle that one has the right to protect one's life, even from institutions of the state.

95. OA, #26, Walsh and Davies, p. 176.

96. P. T. Bauer, "Ecclesiastical Economics Is Envy Exalted," *This World*, No. 1 (Winter/Spring, 1982), p. 69, cited in Novak, *Freedom With Justice*, p. 138.

97. John Paul I (Albino Luciani), quoted in *U.S. News and World Report* (October 9, 1978), p. 43.

98. *See* George H. Williams, *The Mind of John Paul II: Origins of His Thought and Action* (New York: The Seabury Press, 1981).

99. See RH, #16, Byers, p. 285 (and #1–7); SRS, #4, USCC, p. 7; Williams, *The Mind of John Paul II*, p. 314, in which the third Christian millennium is seen as the advent of a renewed humanity, rather than as a judicial second coming of Christ.

100. *See* Gregory Baum, *The Priority of Labor: A Commentary on Laborem Exercens* (New York: Paulist Press, 1982); G. Baum and R. Ellsberg, eds., *The Logic of Solidarity: Commentaries on Pope John Paul II's Encyclical "On Social Concern"* (Maryknoll, N.Y.: Orbis Books, 1989); Peter Hebblethwaite, "The Popes and Politics: Shifting Patterns in 'Catholic Social Doctrine,'" *Daedalus* (Winter 1982); N. von Hoffman, "Papal Economics," *The New Republic* (November 4, 1981), pp. 18–21; John W. Houck and Oliver F. Williams, eds., *Co-Creation and Capitalism: John Paul II's Laborem Exercens* (Washington, D.C.: University Press of America, 1983); Kenneth A. Myers, ed., *Aspiring to Freedom: Commentaries on John Paul II's Encyclical "The Social Concerns of the Church"* (Grand Rapids, Mich.: William B. Eerdmans Publishing Company, 1988); Quentin L. Quade, ed., *The Pope and Revolution: John Paul II Confronts Liberation Theology* (Washington, D.C.: Ethics and Public Policy Center, 1982).

101. LE, #9.2, Walsh and Davies, p. 285.

102. For radically different interpretations of Marx's theory of knowledge, the methodology used in his later critique of political economy, and his rejection of scientific socialism, positivism, and the British view of science, *see* Patrick Murray, *Marx's Theory of Scientific Knowledge* (Atlantic Highlands, N.J.: Humanities Press International, 1988).

103. LE, #20.2, Walsh and Davies, pp. 301–302.

104. The concept of the "pursuit of happiness" entailed an expansion of the utilitarian notion of liberty and rights by integrating or blurring the distinctions between private rights and public happiness ("participator in the government of affairs"). *See* William Scott, *In Pursuit of Happiness: American Conceptions of Property From the Seventeenth to the Twentieth Century* (Bloomington, Ind.: Indiana University Press, 1977), pp. 41–43; Richard Schlatter, *Private Property: The History of an Idea* (New York: Russell and Russell, 1977), pp. 195–201; Gary Wills, *Inventing America: Jefferson's Declaration of Independence* (Garden City, N.Y.: Doubleday, 1978), chapter 10; Staughton Lynd, *Intellectual Origins of American Radicalism* (New York: Vintage Books, 1968), pp. 67–86; Richard Matthews, *The Radical Politics of Thomas Jefferson: A Revisionist View* (Lawrence, Ks.: University Press of Kansas, 1984), pp. 77–95; Ryan, *Equality*, pp. 8–9; Garrett Ward Sheldon, *The Political Philosophy of Thomas Jefferson* (Baltimore, Md.: The Johns Hopkins University Press, 1991), pp. 11–12; and Hannah Arendt, *On Revolution* (Harmondsworth, England: Penguin Books, 1965), pp. 126–131. Adrienne Koch in *The Philosophy of Thomas Jefferson* (Chicago: Quadrangle Books, 1964), p. 42, even makes a connection between Jefferson's use of the term *pursuit of happiness* and Aristotle's concept of happiness as *eudaimonia* (political deliberation and development of rational capabilities).

105. LE, #13.1, Walsh and Davies, p. 290.

106. LE, #13.2, Walsh and Davies, p. 291.

107. LE, #14.1, Walsh and Davies, pp. 292–293; John Paul has later noted that

after the Fall, the exercise of ownership is "difficult and full of suffering" (cf. Genesis 3:17–19), SRS #30, NCCB, p. 54.

108. LE, #14.2, Walsh and Davies, p. 293. In the encyclical "On Social Concern," John Paul II applies a "hierarchy of values" in the framework of the right to property to the issue of the church's own use of wealth: "Thus, part of the *teaching* and most ancient *practice* of the Church is her conviction that she is obliged by her vocation — she herself, her ministers and each of her members — to relieve the misery of the suffering, both far and near, not only out of her 'abundance' but also out of her 'necessities'. Faced by cases of need, one cannot ignore them in favour of superfluous church ornaments and costly furnishings for divine worship; on the contrary it could be obligatory to sell these goods in order to provide food, drink, clothing and shelter for those who lack these things," SRS, #31, NCCB, pp. 58–59. More recently John Paul has deflected the suggestion that the church sell art treasures for relief services, observing that the church of the present day is only steward of the accumulated offerings of centuries. Such a gesture was imagined for the Slavic pope in Morris West's novel *The Shoes of the Fisherman* (1963) to relieve famine in China.

109. *See*, for example, Matthew Fox, *The Coming of the Cosmic Christ* (San Francisco: Harper & Row, 1988); Carolyn Merchant, *Death of Nature: Women, Ecology, and the Scientific Revolution* (San Francisco: Harper & Row, 1983).

110. SRS, #41, USCC, p. 83.

111. *See* John Paul II, "Is Liberal Capitalism the Only Path?" *Origins* 20:2 (May 24, 1990), #3, p. 19; the speech was delivered in Durango, Mexico, on May 9, 1990.

112. SRS, #37, USCC, p. 71; on the topic of "Structures of Sin," *see* Mark O'Keefe, *What Are They Saying About Social Sin?* (New York: Paulist Press, 1990).

113. *See* the variety of work on this in C. Avila, *Ownership: Early Christian Teaching* (Maryknoll, N.Y.: Orbis Books, 1983); Justo L. González, *Faith and Wealth: A History of Early Christian Ideas on the Origins, Significance, and Use of Money* (San Francisco: Harper & Row, 1990); John C. Haughey, ed., *Faith That Does Justice: Examining the Christian Sources for Social Change* (New York: Paulist Press, 1977); Martin Hengel, *Property and Riches in the Early Church* (Philadelphia: Fortress Press, 1974); St. John Chrysostom, *On Wealth and Poverty*, trans. Catharine P. Roth (Crestwood, N.Y.: St. Vladimir's Seminary Press, 1984); Schlatter, *Private Property*; Peter Spufford, *Money and Its Use in Medieval Europe* (Cambridge: CUP, 1987); Terry Tastard, *The Spark in the Soul: Four Mystics on Justice* (New York: Paulist Press, 1990); R. H. Tawney, *Religion and the Rise of Capitalism: A Historical Study* (Gloucester, Mass.: Peter Smith, 1962); Jacob Viner, *Religious Thought and Economic Society*, ed. Jacques Melitz and Donald Winch (Durham, N.C.: Duke University Press, 1978); and Jan L. Womer, ed., *Morality and Ethics in Early Christianity* (Philadelphia: Fortress Press, 1987).

114. For a brief treatment of the Franciscan attitude to poverty and wealth, *see* Pelikan, *Jesus Through the Centuries*, pp. 133–144; Lester K. Little, *Religious Poverty and the Profit Economy in Medieval Europe* (Ithaca, N.Y.: Cornell University Press, 1978), pp. 146–169; M. D. Lambert, *Franciscan Poverty: The Doctrine of the Absolute Poverty of Christ and the Apostles in the Franciscan Order, 1210–1323* (London: SPCK, 1961); Raymond de Roover, *Business, Banking, and Economic Thought in Late Medieval and Early Modern Europe*, ed. J. Krishner (Chicago, Ill.: University of Chicago Press, 1974).

115. *See* Suzanne Noffles, O.P., trans., *Catherine of Siena, The Dialogue* (New

York: Paulist Press, 1980), and Francis and Clare [of Assisi], *The Complete Works*, trans. R. J. Armstrong, O.F.M., Cap., and I. C. Brady, O.F.M. (New York: Paulist Press, 1982). Clare bases the monastic vow of voluntary poverty in the imitation of the life of Jesus (*The Complete Works*, p. 192):

> O God-centered poverty,
> whom the Lord Jesus Christ
> Who ruled and now rules heaven and Earth,
> Who spoke and things were made,
> condescended to embrace before all else!

6: LIBERATION OF THE BIBLE

1. *See* Ernest R. Sandeen, *The Bible and Social Reform* (Philadelphia: Fortress Press, 1982).

2. *See* Michael Walzer, *Exodus and Revolution* (New York: Basic Books, 1985); Richard Bauckman, *The Bible in Politics: How to Read the Bible Politically* (Louisville, Ky.: Westminster/John Knox, 1990).

3. Norman K. Gottwald, "From Biblical Economics to Modern Economies: A Bridge over Troubled Waters," in William K. Tabb, ed., *Churches in Struggle* (New York: Monthly Review Press, 1986), p. 141.

4. Ibid., p. 144.

5. Ibid., p. 146.

6. *See* Denis Baly and Royal Rhodes, *The Faith of Christians* (Philadelphia: Fortress Press, 1984), pp. 14–15.

7. Novak, "Toward Consensus," pp. 8–10.

8. Ibid., pp. 8–9.

9. EJFA, #51, p. 28.

10. Ibid., #41, p. 23.

11. Dennis Hamm, "Economic Policy and the Uses of Scripture," *America* (May 4, 1985), pp. 368–369.

12. Simon and Novak, *Toward the Future*, pp. ix–x.

13. Hamm, "Economic Policy," p. 370; Paul VI, *Populorum Progressio*, #49, Byers, *Justice in the Marketplace*, p. 213; John Paul II, *Redemptor Hominis*, #16.3, Walsh and Davies, *Proclaiming Justice and Peace*, p. 256; *Sollicitudo Rei Socialis*, p. 63; EJFA, #44, p. 24.

14. Michael Novak, quoted by Leon Wieseltier, "The Poor Perplex," *The New Republic* (January 7 and 14, 1985), p. 11.

15. The bishops give an ecumenical reference to the work of Thomas W. Ogletree, *The Use of the Bible in Christian Ethics* (Philadelphia: Fortress Press, 1983), pp. 47-85.

16. *See* Dan Cohn-Sherbok, *On Earth as It Is in Heaven: Jews, Christians, and Liberation Theology* (Maryknoll, N.Y.: Orbis Books, 1987), pp. 73–91; Walzer, *Exodus and Revolution*; EJFA, #35–36, pp. 19–20.

17. Mary E. Jegen and Bruno Manno, eds., *The Earth Is the Lord's: Essays on Stewardship* (New York: Paulist Press, 1978).

18. The Bishops' Letter refers in a footnote to the debate over whether the Jubilee was actually performed or was only an ideal. *See* Thomas D. Hanks, *God So Loved the Third World: The Bible, the Reformation and Liberation Theologies*, trans.

James C. Dekker (Maryknoll, N.Y.: Orbis Books, 1984), pp. 97–105; R. North, *Sociology of the Biblical Jubilee* (Rome: Pontifical Biblical Institute, 1954); Sharon H. Ringe, *Jesus, Liberation, and the Biblical Jubilee* (Philadelphia: Fortress Press, 1985).

19. EJFA, #36, p. 20; Paul VI, *Evangelii Nuntiandi*, #81.1, Walsh and Davies, p. 242; PC (1933), #100, 101, Byers, pp. 419–20.

20. Cited in EJFA, #38, p. 21.

21. For a further development of the concepts of justice, freedom, community, and the critique of idolatry, *see* Hengel, *Property and Riches in the Early Church,* pp. 12–22; Walter Pilgrim, *Good News to the Poor: Wealth and Poverty in Luke–Acts* (Minneapolis, Minn.: Augsburg Publishing House, 1981), pp. 19–32; Stephan Mott, *Biblical Ethics and Social Change* (New York: Oxford University Press, 1982), pp. 59–81; Gregory Baum, "The Ambiguity of Biblical Religion," *Theology Today* (January 1977), pp. 344-353 – later incorporated into *Religion and Alienation: A Theological Reading of Sociology* (New York: Paulist Press, 1975); John Donahue, S.J., "Biblical Perspectives on Justice," in Haughey, *The Faith That Does Justice,* pp. 68–112; Joseph Comblin, "Freedom and Liberation," in *The Mystical and Political Dimension of the Christian Faith,* ed. Claude Geffré and Gustavo Gutiérrez, trans. J. D. Mitchell (New York: Herder and Herder, 1974), pp. 98–99; Leonardo Boff, "Salvation and Liberation," in *The Mystical and Political Dimension of the Christian Faith,* pp. 85–86; Jose Miranda, *Marx and the Bible: Critique of the Philosophy of Oppression,* trans. Robert Barr (Maryknoll, N.Y.: Orbis Books, 1974), pp. 1–34; Jose Miranda, *Communism and the Bible,* trans. Robert Barr (Maryknoll, N.Y.: Orbis Books, 1982); José Míguez Bonino, *Toward a Christian Political Ethics* (Philadelphia: Fortress Press, 1983), pp. 79–86; Juan Luis Segundo, *The Historical Jesus of the Synoptics,* vol. 2 of *Jesus of Nazareth Yesterday and Today,* trans. John Drury (Maryknoll, N.Y.: Orbis Books, 1985); Phillip Berryman, *Liberation Theology* (New York: Pantheon Books, 1987), pp. 45–62; Michael Clevenot, *Materialist Approaches to the Bible,* trans. William Nottingham (Maryknoll, N.Y.: Orbis Books, 1985); Abraham Heschel, *The Prophets* (New York: Harper and Row, Publishers, 1969); Gerhard von Rad, *Old Testament Theology,* vol. 1 of *The Theology of Israel's Historical Traditions,* trans. D. Stalker (New York: Harper and Row, 1962); Jose Faur, "The Biblical Idea of Idolatry," *Jewish Quarterly Review* (July 1978), pp. 1–15.

22. Cited in EJFA, #38, p. 21.

23. Ibid.; the passages cited below are all from this section.

24. Ibid.; and #49, p. 27.

25. *See* Gen. 4:10; Deut. 24:15; James 5:4; RN, #32; Byers, p. 21; and LE, #8.2; Walsh and Davies, p. 302.

26. *See* Sirach 34:22, "To take away a neighbor's living is to murder him; to deprive an employee of his wages is to shed blood."

27. EJFA, #4, p. vi; #48, p. 26.

28. Ibid., #48, p. 26.

29. Ibid., #52, p. 29.

30. Ibid., #39, p. 22.

31. Ibid., #23, p. xiii.

32. Juan Luis Segundo, quoted in Gary MacEoin and Nivita Riley, *Puebla: A Church Being Born* (New York: Paulist Press, 1980), p. 109.

33. EJFA, #64, p. 34; the text cites GS, #31; Byers, pp. 179–180.

34. *See* Michael J. Himes and Kenneth R. Himes, "Rights, Economics, and the Trinity," *Commonweal* CXIII:5 (March 14, 1986), pp. 137–141; Leonardo Boff,

Trinity and Society, trans. Paul Burns (Maryknoll, N.Y.: Orbis Books, 1988).

35. *See* Pelikan, *Jesus Through the Centuries.*

36. *See* José Míguez Bonino, *Faces of Jesus: Latin American Christologies* (Maryknoll, N.Y.: Orbis Books, 1984); Leonardo Boff, *Jesus Christ Liberator: A Critical Christology for Our Time,* trans. P. Hughes (Maryknoll, N.Y.: Orbis Books, 1978).

37. EJFA, #365, p. 182.

38. SRS, pp. 100–101.

39. Ibid., p. 101 n. 91; *see* Joan Chittister, *Job's Daughters, Women and Power* (Madeleva Lecture) (New York: Paulist Press, 1990).

40. Ernesto Cardenal, *The Gospel in Solentiname,* vol. 1, trans. Donald D. Walsh (Maryknoll, N.Y.: Orbis Books, 1982), pp. 30–31.

41. *See* Michael P. Carroll, *The Cult of the Virgin Mary: Psychological Origins* (Princeton, N.J.: Princeton University Press, 1986), pp. 182–194; Mary O'Connor, "The Virgin of Guadalupe and the Economics of Symbolic Behavior," *Journal for the Scientific Study of Religion* 28:2 (June 1989), pp. 105–119; Ena Campbell, "The Virgin of Guadalupe and the Female Self-Image: A Mexican Case History," in James J. Preston, ed., *Mother Worship: Theme and Variations* (Chapel Hill, N.C.: University of North Carolina Press, 1982), pp. 5–24.

42. *See* Rafael Avila, *Worship and Politics* (Maryknoll, N.Y.: Orbis Books, 1981); Tissa Balasuriya, *The Eucharist and Human Liberation* (Maryknoll, N.Y.: Orbis Books, 1979).

43. *See* J. Severino Croatto, *Biblical Hermeneutics: Toward a Theory of Reading as the Production of Meaning,* trans. Robert Barr (Maryknoll, N.Y.: Orbis Books, 1987); Jacques Ellul, *Jesus and Marx: From Gospel to Ideology* (Grand Rapids, Mich.: Eerdmans, 1988); Robert Morgan with John Barton, *Biblical Interpretation* (New York: Oxford Press, 1988); Richard J. Neuhaus, *Biblical Interpretation in Crisis: The Ratzinger Conference on Bible and Church* (Grand Rapids, Mich.: Eerdmans, 1989); Larry L. Rasmussen and Bruce C. Birch, *Bible and Ethics in the Christian Life,* rev. ed. (Minneapolis, Minn.: Augsburg Press, 1989).

44. *See* Cohn-Sherbok, *On Earth as It Is in Heaven.*

45. *See* Joe Holland and Peter Henriot, S. J., *Social Analysis: Linking Faith and Justice,* rev. ed. (Maryknoll, N.Y.: Orbis Books, 1983); Howard Clark Kee, *Knowing the Truth: A Social Approach to New Testament Interpretation* (Philadelphia: Fortress Press, 1989); Mott, *Biblical Ethics and Social Change,* pp. 133–296; Dermot A. Lane, *Foundations for a Social Theology: Praxis, Process and Salvation* (New York: Paulist Press, 1984), pp. 110–169; M. Douglas Meeks, *God the Economist: The Doctrine of God and Political Economy* (Minneapolis, Minn.: Fortress Press, 1989).

46. Paul Heyne, "Christianity and 'The Economy'," *This World* (Winter 1988), p. 36.

47. Ibid.

48. Ibid., p. 38.

49. Michael Goldberg, "Two Letters on the Economy: Two Sides of the Same Coin?" *The Christian Century* (April 10, 1985), p. 349; "Constantinianism" is the doctrine of state control of the church and doctrinal matters, and "neo-Pelagianism" is the doctrine that human works can gain the spiritual merit necessary for salvation. The Augustinian position, held by Western Christians, is that divine grace alone is necessary, without regard for "works' righteousness." Catholics were often labeled as followers of the two errant doctrines in older Reformation debates.

50. Congregation for the Doctrine of the Faith, *Instruction on Certain Aspects of*

the *"Theology of Liberation"* (Washington, D.C.: USCC, 1984); *Instruction on Christian Freedom and Liberation* (Washington, D.C. USCC, 1986); Joel Kovel, "The Vatican Strikes Back," in Tabb, *Churches in Struggle,* pp. 172–184. For a quick overview of liberation theology, *see* Arthur McGovern, S. J., *Marxism: An American Christian Perspective* (Maryknoll, N.Y.: Orbis Books, 1980), pp. 172–209.

51. The status of Black Americans in the church has been addressed by the NCCB, *Brothers and Sisters to Us: Pastoral Letter on Racism in Our Day* (Washington, D.C.: USCC, 1979). A statement on AIDS badly divided the hierarchy, as did a proposed letter on the role of women in the church and society. The Hispanic community remains the focus of much of the bishops' discussion of evangelism, critical of the proselytizing amongst this traditionally Catholic population by Protestant fundamentalists and evangelicals. The commemoration of the Columbus voyage will undoubtedly elicit a number of pastoral statements on the relationship of the church to the Native-American population and the cultural problems raised by evangelization and conversion. *See also* James A. Griffin, "Horizons of Faith," *The Catholic Times* (Columbus, Ohio: May 9, 1991).

52. The U. S. Catholic bishops have consciously acknowledged their place in a worldwide religious body whose demographic center now has shifted to Latin America, Asia, and Africa, away from Europe and North America. The face of Catholicism at the coming millennium will be largely Hispanic, female, and poor. Those facts will shape the priorities and concerns of the global Catholic Church. After publicly claiming their role in creating a moral vision to encompass *"all* people," it is remarkable that the U. S. hierarchy has failed to take significant notice of the statements on social issues produced by the episcopal conferences of Canada (Canadian Conference of Catholic Bishops – CCCB) and Latin America (Episcopal Council of Latin America – CELAM). *Economic Justice for All* mentions in passing or in its footnotes the important elements of the "option for the poor" voiced at Medellín and Bogota, Columbia (1968), and Puebla de los Angeles, Mexico (1979), but no connection is made to issues or opportunities facing the North American church in relation to Latin America; the emphasis is on what those in the U. S. can do *to* or *for* the Third World, not what they can do *with* or learn *from* the largest Catholic Church in the world. The work of present-day liberation theologians is entirely absent from this pastoral letter, although many common problems are treated by those sources: the meaning of a biblical "option for the poor," the crisis in Third World development and debt, the environmental problems: depletion of the rain forest and natural resources, acid rain and industrial expansion, the need for a stable cash crop as a substitute for drug production.

53. *See: Synthesis of the Puebla Document* (Ottawa: CCCB, 1979), pp. 4–8; texts of the relevant documents are also in Gremillion, *The Gospel of Peace and Justice;* John Eagleson and Philip Scharper, eds., *Puebla and Beyond: Documentation and Commentary* (Maryknoll, N.Y.: Orbis Books, 1979); *The Church in the Present-Day Transformation of Latin America in the Light of the Council,* vol. 2: *Conclusions,* English trans. [Medellín] (Washington, D. C.: USCC, 1970); and the *Third General Conference of Latin American Bishops, Puebla: Conclusions,* English trans. (Washington, D.C.: NCCB, 1979).

54. *Puebla,* p. 19; subsequent references to the many sections quoted will be included in parentheses in the text.

55. *See* Enrique Dussel, "Analysis of the Final Document of Puebla: The Relationship Between Economics and Christian Ethics," *Concilium* 140, ed. D. Mieth

and J. Pohier (New York: Seabury, 1980), pp. 101–110; Karen Lebacqz, *Justice in an Unjust World: Foundations for a Christian Approach to Justice* (Minneapolis, Minn.: Augsburg Press, 1986), pp. 100–115; Gary MacEoin and Nivita Riley, *Puebla: A Church Being Born* (New York: Paulist Press, 1980), pp. 104–119; Novak, *Freedom with Justice*, pp. 183–194; Peter Hebblethwaite, "CELAM Draft Drops Latin Input," NCR 14:26 (April 21, 1978), p. 20.

56. Dussel, "Analysis . . . of Puebla," p. 105.

57. Ibid., p. 109.

58. MacEoin and Riley, *Puebla*, pp. 108–109.

59. John Paul II, "Liberation and Commitment to the Poor" (Mexico City, May 12, 1990), in *Origins* 20:2 (May 24, 1990), p. 31.

60. *See* Juan Luis Segundo, *Theology and the Church: A Response to Cardinal Ratzinger and a Warning to the Whole Church*, rev. ed., trans. John W. Diercksmeier (San Francisco: Harper & Row, 1987).

61. Cardinal Joseph Ratzinger, quoted in *ibid.*, p. 153.

62. Segundo, *Theology and the Church*, p. 153.

63. Ibid., p. 158.

64. McGovern, *Marxism*, pp. 193–196.

65. Alfonso López Trujillo, *Liberation or Revolution?* (Huntington, Ind.: Our Sunday Visitor, 1977), pp. 16–17, quoted in McGovern, *Marxism*, p. 196.

66. Ibid., p. 184.

67. *See* James V. Schall, S.J., *Liberation Theology in Latin America* (San Francisco: Ignatius Press, 1982), pp. 3–126; Michael Novak, "Liberation Theology and the Pope," in Quade, *The Pope and Revolution*, pp. 73–85.

68. Novak, "Liberation Theology," p. 84; Schall, *Liberation Theology*, p. 47.

69. Ibid.

70. Novak, "Liberation Theology," p. 85; Novak does not comment on the fact that such Marxist critiques of Marxism exist, thus contradicting the conservative view that it is a rigid, monolithic, and static ideology.

71. Ibid.

72. *See* Michael Novak, *A Theology for Radical Politics* (New York: Herder and Herder, 1969). Compare to his *The Spirit of Democratic Capitalism*.

7: LIBERATION THEOLOGY AND DEPENDENCY THEORY

1. American Catholic Bishops, EJFA, #259, p. 125.

2. Ibid.

3. Ibid., #264, p. 128.

4. Ibid., #278, p. 135.

5. Ibid., #280, pp. 137–38.

6. Simon and Novak, *Toward the Future*, p. 45.

7. Ibid., p. 50.

8. Block, *The U.S. Bishops and their Critics*, pp. 74ff.

9. Ibid., p. 88.

10. Michael B. Brown, *The Economics of Imperialism* (Harmondsworth, England: Penguin Books, 1974), pp. 38–39.

11. Walt Rostow, *The Stages of Economic Growth: A Non-Communist Manifesto* (Cambridge, England: Cambridge University Press, 1961), p. 6.

12. Ibid., p. 39.

13. Ibid., p. 14.

14. Novak, *The Spirit of Democratic Capitalism*, pp. 276ff.

15. This approach by Novak is too incomplete and relies on a too narrow understanding of historical reality. For a more complete picture of underdevelopment and economic exploitation in Latin America, *see* André Gunder Frank, *Capitalism and Underdevelopment in Latin America* (Harmondsworth, England: Penguin Books, 1969). And for an analysis of the effects of this system of exploitation on the decline of Spain and its failure to achieve agricultural and industrial development, *see* Earl Hamilton, *American Treasure and the Price of Revolution in Spain 1501–1650* (Cambridge, Mass.: Harvard University Press, 1934); and J. H. Elliott, "The Decline of Spain," in *Crises in Europe 1560–1660*, ed. Trevor Aston (New York: Doubleday and Co., 1967), pp. 175–205. A different view, which emphasizes the dependency of Spain on the Hapsburg Empire, is held by Immanuel Wallerstein in his *The Modern World-System*, vols. 1 and 2 (New York: Academic Press, 1980).

16. Novak, *The Spirit of Democratic Capitalism*, p. 289.

17. Ibid., p. 285.

18. Ibid., p. 185.

19. P. T. Bauer, *Equality, The Third World, and Economic Delusion* (Cambridge, Mass.: Harvard University Press, 1981), p. 70.

20. Ibid., p. 83.

21. Ibid., p. 100.

22. Ibid., p. 19.

23. Ibid., p. 107.

24. Joan Robinson, *Economic Philosophy* (Chicago: Aldine Publishing Company, 1962), p. 21. For an analysis of another form of modernization theory, *see* the summary of the Harvard Business School's Multinational Enterprise Project in Thomas Biersteker, *Distortion or Development? Contending Perspectives on the Multinational Corporation* (Cambridge, Mass.: MIT Press, 1978), pp. 27–48.

25. Dos Santos, quoted in Ronald Chilcote and Joel Edelstein, *Latin America: Capitalist and Socialist Perspectives of Development and Underdevelopment* (Boulder, Colo.: Westview Press, 1986), p. 20.

26. Thomas Angotti, "The Political Implications of Dependency Theory," in *Dependency and Marxism: Toward a Resolution of the Debate*, ed. R. Chilcote (Boulder, Colo.: Westview Press, 1982), p. 126.

27. The construction of a schema to organize these different approaches could have taken different forms, depending on whether the analytic distinctions were based on their differences in policy recommendations, structural analysis, methodology, or ideology. These five models of dependency and their representative authors include:

• Underdevelopment Theory: André Gunder Frank, *Capitalism and Underdevelopment in Latin America* (New York: Monthly Review Press, 1969); Walter Rodney, *How Europe Underdeveloped Africa* (London: Bogle-L'Ouverture Publications, 1972); Wallerstein, *The Modern World-Systems*.

• New Dependency Theory: Theotonio Dos Santos, "The Structure of Dependence," *American Economic Review* (May 1970), pp. 231–236.

• Dependent Development Theory: Fernando Cardoso and Enzo Faletto, *Dependency and Development in Latin America*, trans. M. Urquidi (Berkeley, Calif.: University of California Press, 1979).

• Surplus Extraction Theory: a. *Monopoly Capitalism and Imperialism:* Baran and

Sweezy, *Monopoly Capital*; Ernest Mandel, *Late Capitalism*, trans. Joris DeBres (London: Verso, 1975); Harry Magdoff, *The Age of Imperialism: The Economics of U.S. Foreign Policy* (New York: Monthly Review Press, 1968); b. *Theory of Unequal Exchange:* Arghiri Emmanuel, *Unequal Exchange: A Study of Imperialism Of Free Trade* (New York: Monthly Review Press, 1972); Samir Amin, *Accumulation on a World Scale: A Critique of the Theory of Underdevelopment,* 2 vols. (New York: Monthly Review Press, 1974).

• Modes of Production and Primitive Accumulation Theory: Ruy Mauro Marini, "World Capitalist Accumulation and Sub-Imperialism," *Two Thirds* (Fall 1978); Ernesto Laclau, "Feudalism and Capitalism in Latin America," *New Left Review* (May–June 1971); Aníbal Quijano, *Nationalism and Capitalism in Peru: A Study in Neo-Colonialism* (New York: Monthly Review Press, 1971); Anwar Shaikh, "On the Laws of International Exchange," Part II, *Science and Society* (Winter 1979–80); Robert Brenner, "The Origins of Capitalist Development: A Critique of Neo-Smithian Marxism," *New Left Review* (July–August 1977); Bill Warren, "Imperialism and Capitalist Industrialization," *New Left Review* (September–October 1973).

For a comparison of these different schools of dependency, *see* Ronald Chilcote, *Theories of Comparative Politics: The Search for a Paradigm* (Boulder, Colo.: Westview Press, 1981), p. 298. See the chart on page 298 for a comparative analysis of Cardoso, Bacha, O'Brien, and Chilcote and their classifications of the different schools of dependency theory. *Also see* Ronald Chilcote, *Theories of Development and Underdevelopment* (Boulder, Colo.: Westview Press, 1984), pp. 49–107; *see also* articles in *Dependency and Marxism,* no. 1, ed. Ronald Chilcote; James Weaver and Marguerite Berger, "The Marxist Critique of Dependency Theory: An Introduction," in *The Political Economy of Development and Underdevelopment,* ed. Charles Wilbur (New York: Random House, 1984), pp. 45–64; Anthony Brewer, *Marxist Theories of Imperialism* (London: Routledge and Kegan Paul, 1980); and Cristóbal Kay, *Latin American Theories of Development and Underdevelopment* (London: Routledge and Kegan Paul, 1989). There is another model of dependency that began in the mid 1970s, which could be added to the above list. Known as the *theory of postimperialism,* it stresses capitalist domination and class exploitation, the managerial bourgeoisie, a doctrine of domicile (mutual interests and integration of international bourgeoisie and national bourgeoisie), the growing importance of international banks and Third World industrialization, transnational corporations and an integrated world economy, and, finally, a critique of Marxist dependency theory. Its chief representatives include Richard Sklar, David Becker, Jeff Frieden, and Sayre Schatz. David Becker, et al., eds., *Postimperialism: International Capitalism and Development in the Late Twentieth Century* (Boulder, Colo.: Lynne Rienner Publishers, 1987).

28. Chilcote and Edelstein, *Latin America,* p. 86.

29. André Gunder Frank, "Sociology of Development and Underdevelopment of Sociology," in *Dependence and Underdevelopment: Latin America's Political Economy,* ed. J. Cockcroft, A. Frank, and D. Johnson (Garden City, N.Y.: Doubleday and Company, 1972), p. 347. *See also* Paul Baran and Eric Hobsbawm, "The Stages of Economic Growth: A Review," *Kyklos,* vol.14, no.2 (1961).

30. James Petras, *Class, State and Power in the Third World* (Montclair, N.J.: Allanheld, Osmun, and Company, Publishers, 1981), pp. 76–78.

31. Paul Harrison, *Inside the Third World* (New York: Penguin Books, 1984), pp. 363–364; Paul Bairoch, *The Economic Development of the Third World Since 1900,*

trans. Cynthia Postan (Berkeley, Calif.: University of California Press, 1975); UN Commission on Transnational Corporations, *Multinational Corporations in World Development* (New York: United Nations, 1973) and *Transnational Corporations in World Development: A Re-examination* (New York: United Nations, 1978).

32. James Petras, *Latin America: Bankers, Generals, and the Struggle for Social Justice* (Totowa, N.J.: Rowman and Littlefield, 1986), p. 89.

33. For a good overview, *see* Albert Szymanski, *The Logic of Imperialism* (New York: Praeger, 1981), pp. 326ff. For an analysis of the decline of direct investment in the Third World, *see* United Nations Center on Transnational Corporations, *Transnational Corporations in World Development: Trends and Prospects* (New York: United Nations, 1988), pp. 17ff.

34. Michael Parenti, *The Sword and the Dollar: Imperialism, Revolution, and the Arms Race* (New York: St. Martin's Press, 1989), pp. 10–11.

35. Richard Barnet and Ronald Müller, *Global Reach: The Power of the Multinational Corporations* (New York: Simon and Schuster, 1974), p. 160.

36. Rhys Jenkins, *Transnational Corporations and Industrial Formation in Latin America* (New York: St. Martin's Press, 1984), p. 13.

37. For a detailed empirical and historical examination of Brazil, Mexico, and Chile using dependency theory, *see* Peter Evans, *Dependent Development: The Alliance of Multinational, State, and Local Capital in Brazil* (Princeton, N.J.: Princeton University Press, 1979); Douglas Bennett and Kenneth Sharpe, *Transnational Corporations Versus the State: The Political Economy of the Mexican Auto Industry* (Princeton, N.J.: Princeton University Press, 1985); and Theodore Moral, *Multinational Corporations and the Politics of Dependence* (Princeton, N.J.: Princeton University Press, 1974).

38. Harrison, *Inside the Third World*, p. 345, and Richard Newfarmer, ed., *Profits, Progress and Poverty: Case Studies of International Industries in Latin America* (Notre Dame, Ind.: University of Notre Dame Press, 1985), pp. 387–391. The mode of production has also transformed the countryside: economic concentration and centralization is also occurring in agriculture as a result of the Green Revolution, commercialization of agriculture, production of cash crops, mechanization of production, and land concentration in the hands of the wealthy. *See* Frances Lappé and Joseph Collins, *Food First: Beyond the Myth of Scarcity* (New York: Ballantine Books, 1978), pp. 124–180 and Susan George, *How the Other Half Dies: The Real Reason for World Hunger* (Montclair, N.J.: Allanheld, Osmun, and Company, Publishers, 1977), pp. 87–106.

39. Raymond Vernon, *Storm over the Multinationals: The Real Issues* (Cambridge, Mass.: Harvard University Press, 1977), pp. 153–161. For an analysis of the balance-of-payments deficits in Mexico between 1969 and 1976 caused by the imports of auto materials, *see* Bennett and Sharpe, *Transnational Corporations Versus the State*, pp. 180–181. *See also* Tom Barry and Deb Preusch, *The Central American Fact Book* (New York: Grove Press, 1986), pp. 162–168; Tom Barry, Beth Wood, and Deb Preusch, *Dollars and Dictators: A Guide to Central America* (New York: Grove Press, 1983), pp. 58–59; Petras, *Class, State and Power in the Third World*, pp. 76–83; Michael Todaro, *Economic Development in the Third World* (New York: Longman, 1985), pp. 409–411; United Nations, *Transnational Corporations in World Development*, p. 262.

40. Cheryl Payer, *The Debt Trap: The International Monetary Fund and the Third World* (New York: Monthly Review Press, 1974), p. 33, and *The World Bank: A*

Critical Analysis (New York: Monthly Review Press, 1982); Lernoux, *Cry of the People: The Struggle for Human Rights in Latin America—the Catholic Church in Conflict with U.S. Policy* (Harmondsworth, England: Penguin Books, 1982), pp. 227–229; James Petras and Howard Brill, "The International Monetary Fund, Austerity, and the State in Latin America," in Petras, *Latin America*, pp. 21–46; and André Gunder Frank, *Crisis: In the Third World* (New York: Holmes and Meter Publishers, 1981), pp. 132-156.

41. Frank, *Crisis,* p. 260; Penny Lernoux, *Cry of the People*, pp. 174ff.; Jenkins, *Transnational Corporations*, pp. 222–223; and Tom Barry, *Roots of Rebellion: Land and Hunger in Central America* (Boston: South End Press, 1987), pp. 8–19.

42. For a survey of the literature on the questions of growing inequality and poverty in Latin America, *see* Michael Francis, "Dependency: Ideology, Fad, and Fact," in *Latin America: Dependency or Interdependence*, ed. M. Novak and M. Jackson (Washington, D.C.: American Enterprise Institute, 1985).

43. Lernoux, *Cry of the People,* p. 221.

44. George, *How the Other Half Dies,* pp. 117-119, 138ff.

45. Enrique Dussel, *Ethics and Community*, trans. R. Barr (Maryknoll, N.Y.: Orbis Books, 1986), p. 155. *See also* George, *How the Other Half Dies*, p. 70.

46. Payer, *The Debt Trap,* p. 147.

47. Frank, *Crisis,* pp. 7–9.

48. Payer, *The Debt Trap,* p. 40, 48, 641.

49. We would like to thank Professor Richard Jacobs, Department of Political Science, Illinois State University, for this analogy between Weimar Germany and Brazil. For an analysis of President Collor's freezing of prices, wages, and bank accounts over $1,000 in order to stem the tide of the most serious Brazilian recession in a decade, *see* "Brazilian Belt-Tightening," *New York Times* (May 23, 1990), p. 1.

50. This view is shared by Teresa Hayter, *Aid As Imperialism* (Harmondsworth, England: Penguin Books, 1971); Frank, *Crisis,* pp. 148–156; Todaro, *Economic Development in the Third World*, p. 439; and Graham Hancock, *The Lords of Poverty: The Power, Prestige, and Corruption of the International Aid Business* (New York: Atlantic Monthly Press, 1989). *See also, The World Bank: Annual Report 1989* (Washington, D.C.: The World Bank, 1989), pp. 20–35, pp. 129–137.

51. Petras and Brill, "International Monetary Fund," in Petras, *Latin America*, p. 37.

52. Rasmussen, "The Morality of Power and the Power of Morality," in Strain, *Prophetic Visions and Economic Realities,* p. 137.

53. "Catholic Bishops and American Economics: A Survey of Comment, and Some of Our Own," in *The Religion and Society Report*, March 1985, p. B4. Summary from Penny Lernoux, "Pastoral offers 'pie-in-sky' solutions," *National Catholic Reporter*, vol. 21, no. 34, November 23, 1984.

54. Boff and Boff, *The Church and the Economy in the United States*, pp. 27ff., unpublished manuscript from which a shorter version appeared in the *National Catholic Reporter*, August 28, 1987.

55. John Paul II, *Centesimus Annus* ("The Hundredth Year") (Washington D.C.: USCC, 1991); Nancy Sherwood Truitt, "Latin Bishops Look for Liberation in a Market Economy," *The Wall Street Journal* (May 10, 1991), A 11; Editorial, "Pope points toward economic third way for common good," *NCR*, Vol. 27:28 (May 10, 1991), p. 20; Editorial, "Economic debate can now focus on capitalism," *NCR*, Vol. 27:29 (May 17, 1991), p. 28. See also NCCB, *A Century of Social Teaching: A Common Heritage, A Continuing Challenge* (Washington D.C.: USCC, 1990).

INDEX